FRONTSOLDATEN

FRONTSOLDATEN

The German Soldier in World War II

Stephen G. Fritz

THE UNIVERSITY PRESS OF KENTUCKY

Copyright © 1995 by The University Press of Kentucky

Scholarly publisher for the Commonwealth,
serving Bellarmine College, Berea College, Centre
College of Kentucky, Eastern Kentucky University,
The Filson Club, Georgetown College, Kentucky
Historical Society, Kentucky State University,
Morehead State University, Murray State University,
Northern Kentucky University, Transylvania University,
University of Kentucky, University of Louisville,
and Western Kentucky University.

Editorial and Sales Offices: Lexington, Kentucky 40508–4008

Assorted excerpts from *The Forgotten Soldier* by Guy Sajer, copyright © 1967 Editions Robert Laffont. English translation copyright © 1971 by Harper & Row, Publishers, Inc. Reprinted by permission of HarperCollins Publishers, Inc.

Assorted excerpts from *Jahrgang 1916* by Friedrich Grupe, copyright © Universitas in der F.A. Herbig Verlagsbuchhandlung GmbH, Munich.

Library of Congress Cataloging-in-Publication Data

Fritz, Stephen G., 1949–
    Frontsoldaten : the German soldier in World War II /
Stephen G. Fritz.
      p.   cm.
    Includes bibliographical references and index.
    ISBN 0–8131–1920–0 (alk. paper)
    1. Germany. Heer—History—World War, 1939–1945. 2. Germany.
Heer—Military life. 3. Soldiers—Germany—History—20th century.
I. Title.
    D757.1.F75 1995
    940.54′1343—dc20   95–13091

This book is printed on acid-free recycled paper meeting the requirements of the American National Standard for Permanence of Paper for Printed Library Materials.

D
757.1
.F75
1995

CONTENTS

PREFACE

This is not a book about war in the sense that such histories are usually understood; instead, it concerns the nature of men at war. Indeed, war serves as merely the backdrop against which human actions and emotions can be illuminated. As a consequence, I do not take a traditional "top-down" approach, relying on official documents and assessments of events, but rather approach history from the "bottom up," from the perspective of the common fighting man. This approach, of course, has certain limitations, foremost among them the fact that the broad strategic sweep of traditional military history is absent. Nor is there any of the usual conjecture over matters of tactics, leadership, command decisions, or the relative merits of various weapons. Not only have those matters been dealt with elsewhere by other historians, but pursuing them here would negate the entire intent of everyday history. My purpose is to allow average German soldiers to speak, with a minimum of external interference; to hear their words and see the war through their eyes so as to get at the reality of the combat experience as lived by the men in the bunkers and foxholes. It is this sense of immediacy and drama, unfiltered and uncluttered by excessive analysis, that is at the heart of everyday history.

By its very nature, everyday history relies extensively on the comments of average people, which is why I have leaned heavily on quotations from the soldiers themselves. This does not mean, however, that there is no analysis or that the book is simply an edited collection of combat experiences. In reading countless letters and diaries, I analyzed them for personal, social, political, or ideological content, looked for recurring themes, created a systematic framework within each chapter in order to focus the words of the average soldiers, and then commented in a concise, analytical fashion. I could certainly have summarized much of this material in my own words, but then it would have lost the intimacy and impact of the moving stories of "little men" that are the strength of everyday history.

Because I sought to explore the lives of ordinary men by way of their own perceptions as set down in letters and diaries, I purposely avoided a reliance on official documents and memoranda. For the same reason, because I was concentrating on the average soldier, I chose not to include Waffen-SS units in my study. By the latter stages of the war draftees were being used in some of these units, but by definition the SS were employed—and saw themselves—as elite formations apart from the ordinary *Landsers*. Not that my approach to their everyday history is meant in any way to glorify the average German soldier: as I take pains to point out in the chapters on combat and ideology, these ordinary men, to an extent far greater than previously acknowledged, were ideologically motivated and participated in grievous atrocities for racial and ideological reasons. By the same token, however, I attempt to point out the human fears, anxieties, emotions, insights, joys, sorrows, and tribulations that these men, like other soldiers, experienced from the perspective of the foxhole.

The scope of the book is comprehensive; I have included material from North Africa, Italy, France, and the Balkans, although admittedly these selections are overshadowed by those from Russia. There is, of course, a straightforward reason for this: the overwhelming majority of German combat troops, approximately 80 percent of the total, fought on the eastern front. And since I focus on combat, not on occupation duties, the bulk of the relevant letters and diaries concerned events in Russia.

The translations, unless otherwise noted in the bibliography, are entirely my own, although for difficult or ambiguous phrases I consulted Christa Hungate, professor of German at East Tennessee State University and herself a native German speaker. As far as possible I have attempted to follow the original style of the writer, which is why some excerpts seem particularly articulate and others are more rough-hewn. I have tried as well to convey the spirit of various colloquialisms and slang terms, substituting the closest American equivalent if a literal translation proved impossible. From the American perspective, the *Wehrmacht* had a bewildering variety of ranks and titles, so in the interest of comprehensibility I have simplified the German ranks into their nearest American equivalents, using the *Handbook on German Military Forces* of the (then) U.S. War Department as my guide.

In any work of this sort the author incurs a great many obligations, and I am certainly no exception. My curiosity about the everyday history of the *Landser* was prompted originally by discussions with average Germans during many visits to their country, and in conversations with colleagues and others in the United States, all of whom convinced me that there existed extensive interest in an account of the average German soldier. To all of them, I extend my thanks for steering me to a project that has proved to be immensely stimulating and personally fulfilling. As anyone at a regional state university knows all too well, the demands of teaching mean that time is, in most instances, more important than money. For his efforts at securing release time for me to complete this project, and for the many discussions I have had with him relating to the average soldier in World War II, I owe a debt of gratitude to Ronnie Day, chair of the History Department at East Tennessee State University. Countless conversations with Colin Baxter, another colleague, not only stimulated my imagination but helped to sustain me when my energies were flagging. Tim Jones, a graduate research assistant in the Department of History, proved a valuable sounding board for ideas and engaged me in numerous discussions on military history, theory, and practice. I am also grateful to another department colleague, Margaret Ripley Wolfe, whose generous, thoughtful, propitious, and astute advice was of enormous help to me personally and in the completion of this book. I must thank Christa Hungate not only for her assistance with translations but for graciously allowing me to participate in the ETSU Summer in Germany program, which she created and runs so well, and stress the importance of her friendship to me and my family. Thanks also to the Research Development Council at ETSU, which provided a grant to fund the initial stages of this project. Without the efforts of Beth Hogan, director of the Interlibrary Loan Service at the university's Sherrod Library, I could not have conducted this research. She tirelessly tracked down innumerable requests for obscure collections of letters and diaries, all in good humor, even claiming that she enjoyed the challenge! To all these people, I offer my thanks. Their efforts in my behalf have provided me a lesson in the meaning of professionalism and collegiality.

Finally, I owe more than words can express to my wife, Julia, who displayed constant support and encouragement, endured my ill humor at times of discouragement, made insightful comments on various parts of the text, and went beyond the call of duty in explaining the vagaries of computers to me. I can truly say that without her this book could never have been completed. Nor would it have had as much meaning without the birth of my beautiful daughter Kelsey, whose arrival in the midst of my work on this project enriched my life beyond measure. To both of them I can only say (with Shakespeare):

> So are you to my thoughts as
> Food to Life,
> Or as sweet-season'd showers
> Are to the ground.

1. THE VIEW FROM BELOW

Burrowed deep into the snowbound desolation of the late Russian winter, shaken and exhausted by the horrors of the "ghostly weeks of defensive battles" that had just passed, Günter von Scheven in March 1942 nonetheless exalted the German *Landser* (foot soldier or infantryman). "I don't believe that today in Germany any artistic feat can equal the performance of a simple soldier, who holds his position under a heavy barrage in a hopeless situation," he wrote in a heartfelt letter to his father. "This unknown soldier cries again in nameless greatness over the battlefield. . . . Anonymous, seen by only a few comrades, silent, he dies a lonely death, goes over into the inaccessible, his mortal remains absorbed into the abyss of the east as if he had never existed." Scheven expressed well the sense of existential loneliness felt by many of these men, a despair based on the fear that theirs was a silent scream, without echo in the vast wasteland of war. "Generals have since written accounts of these events, locating particular catastrophes, and summarizing in a sentence, or a few lines, the losses," Guy Sajer noted bitterly in his aptly named autobiography, *The Forgotten Soldier*, "but they never, to my knowledge, give sufficient expression to the wretchedness of soldiers abandoned to a fate one would wish to spare even the most miserable cur. They never evoke the hours upon hours of agony. . . . They never mention the common soldier, sometimes covered with glory, sometimes beaten and defeated . . . , confounded by murder and degradation, and later by disillusion, when he realizes that victory will not return him his liberty."[1]

To the south, in the Crimea, Alois Dwenger expressed similar sentiments. "I am often angered by the hollow accounts from incompetent pens," he noted scornfully in May 1942.

> Recently I read a report of an attack where . . . they recounted so many details and in the process forgot the everyday life of the war, the actions of simple soldiers.
>
> These simple infantrymen are, without doubt, heroes. There in his hole . . . lies only a *Landser*, and he may not stick his nose out without getting it cracked and yet he must observe the enemy. Therefore he always peeks carefully out from cover, any moment a bullet can hit him. Shells strike every day . . . shaking and spraying the ground, the dugout trembles, shrapnel whistles overhead. In the nights, where nothing is to be seen but more heard, the eyes tearing from perpetual staring, the imagination working feverishly, he sits wrapped in his shelter half, freezing, hour after hour, listening with strained nerves. In the gray dawn he crawls into the dugout, frozen through and dead tired; it is crowded, damp, loud, half-dark; the lice torment. I believe that true heroism lies in bearing this dreadful everyday life.[2]

Over fifty years later, much of Dwenger's complaint regarding the neglect of the *Landser*, or what the men themselves more vulgarly called the *Schütze Arsch*, remains true. Although the average soldier has been at the center of events in this century of wars, historians have traditionally focused on matters "at the top": the strategy, tactics, decision-making, and organization which, although of undeniable importance, do not constitute the whole of war. From this perspective, the common soldier appeared only as an object, a mere vehicle for receiving and carrying out orders. "Depersonalized, the anonymous crowd that just receives orders performs the events [of this drama]," Claus Hansmann complained in his diary. "A strategic picture far removed from the bloody tragedy. What's that got to do with him who stands at the top? He can't hear the screams, nor the agitated panting. . . . Is he supposed to think about them, the seven that the Dnieper carried off, is he supposed to calculate how far they have now gone, how soggy their uniforms are, how pale their faces? Is he supposed to think about the hearts that are breaking at this moment, the mothers, wives, children?" Little wonder, then, that Hansmann branded "the soldier's existence [as] merely an oath to the death." "The soldier must have so much luck and so often," lamented another *Landser* in hauntingly similar terms. "Soldier's oath, soldier's joy, soldier's tunes, soldier's death, everything is one!"[3]

War, even the most primitive, as Robin Fox points out, has always been a complicated, intricate, highly organized act of human imagination and intelligence, so the fascination with the "larger" dimensions of war is readily understandable. But as Leo Tolstoy suggested, the true reality of war, as well as history, lies in the unconscious, common swarm life of mankind. "I am no general staff officer or military expert who sees the war only through the eyes of a tactician," the German *Landser* Kurt Vogeler commented in December 1941, "but a man, who has experienced the war as a man." Indeed, as Field Marshal Archibald Wavell wrote to the famous military historian B.H. Liddell Hart, "If I had time . . . to study war, I think I should concentrate almost entirely on the 'actualities of war,' the effects of tiredness, hunger, fear, lack of sleep, weather. . . . The principles of strategy and tactics . . . are absurdly simple: it is the actualities that make war so complicated and so difficult, and are usually neglected by historians."[4]

John Keegan has suggested much the same, that there remain areas, largely unexplored by historians, where social history and military history abut. Military history "from below," war from the perspective of the common soldier, constitutes one of those areas. After all, as Wolfram Wette has pointed out, the German armed forces in World War II comprised almost twenty million men, of whom fewer than 1 percent were officers in the narrow sense of the word (that is, holding the rank of major or higher). The great remainder, the 99 percent of the *Wehrmacht* not of the "elite," consisted of enlisted men, noncommissioned officers, and junior officers. These men came from a variety of social, economic, and educational backgrounds yet had one thing in common: they lived the war from below, where the problems of everyday life could be frighteningly concrete. In order to understand the real war, the war from below, then, the historian has to provide a face for the anonymous *Landser* and examine his dual role as both perpetrator and victim. As perpetrators, whether out of conviction or not, these common men existed as part of a great destructive machine, ready and willing to kill and destroy in order to achieve the goals of a murderous regime. In the role of victims, they lived daily with the physical hardships, the psycho-logical burdens, and the often crushing anxieties of death and killing that constitute the everyday life of all combat soldiers. Seen by their political leaders as instruments in the furtherance of Nazi goals (the individual must die even as the *Volk* lives on), perhaps the most ironic fear of the *Landser* was that he would achieve ultimate success and die as a fallen hero. "There is no bitterer death," wrote one *Landser* in his diary, "than a hero's death." Or as he puzzled on another occasion, "Is the hero's death, then, the ideal of this world?"[5]

The past often exudes a legendary quality, and nowhere is this truer than in dealing with the immensity of World War II. The historian cannot hope to recapture wholly the past life of the average *Landser* but can merely strive to depict the drama as accurately as possible in terms of human aspirations and perceptions, to assimilate the experience of others and distill it into an honest and thoughtful perspective. "When today I look at pictures of the war in the illustrated magazines," wrote one anonymous soldier, "I notice immediately: virtually all give anything but the core of the war." "Superficially, as it appears in the weekly newsreels, the soldier's life seems to be beautiful and above all romantic," noted another of these common soldiers to his parents, "but how soon and how quickly these illusions and delusions disappear in the raw reality [of war]."[6]

Claus Hansmann provided a remarkable portrait of "raw reality" for the average soldier.

> In the rain, the tents stare at us stiff and clay-like while we hurry to dig out the marshy field. . . . Before us the . . . gray desolation leaves us so all alone. . . . With upturned collars and heads drawn in, two sentries stamp back and forth at their posts. . . . The area stands breathless under the pressure of the evening fog . . . that penetrates our uniforms, constantly, coldly. Hastily we knock together the contrary tents and cover the bunker. . . . We throw our things down into the hole. . . . In the darkness we bump into and press against each other. Someone lights a tallow candle. . . . Soon we chew on dried-out bread with the eternally same salted canned meat. . . . We are so tired we can't think. . . . The light reveals our rain-blackened coats and our swollen boots misshapen by the mud and stubble. We scrape . . . the mud from our pants and legs with a knife. . . .
>
> The silence weighs on us. Then, with a sigh, someone begins: "Ah, if only this damned swindle would just finally end!" All along our backs, which are leaning against the wall, penetrates the coolness of the earth. Amid the smoke . . . another voice which seems strangely transformed by the darkness: "If we could just once forget everything . . . !"
>
> The words make broad circles in us, like stones that fall into

deep water. . . . "The little people must always pay in war. . . ." The breathing and confused dreams become deeper, we press against one another for a little warmth. So we lie there in our miserable existence.[7]

The historian can achieve this actuality, wretched or otherwise, as Christopher Browning has pointed out, only through an intense depiction of the common experiences of ordinary people. This book is thus not about war but about men: the average, common German soldiers of World War II. War itself forms the background and environment, but as in all great tragedy the theme is human destiny and suffering, as experienced by a group of individuals, a group bound together in a common effort to endure the unendurable. It is about fear and courage, camaraderie and individual pain, the feelings of men under extreme stress, and the unique sensations that war produces; it is about the patient creation and recreation of relationships after one catastrophe and their destruction by another. One doesn't have to empathize with these men in order to depict accurately what they experienced. Nor does trying to understand and recount their perceptions and feelings mean absolving them of responsibility or forgiving them their actions in a brutal war of aggression. The picture that emerges from their personal observations is therefore subtle, complex, and contradictory in its message: ideology, self-interest, and historical perceptions are nuanced by personality traits. War indelibly imprinted the man in the front lines: "You have the feeling," reflected one *Landser*, "that this 'soldierly being' will never end." For the anonymous soldier, the real war was intensely personal, tragic yet ironic, a frightful harvest of emotions, agonizing yet sometimes magnificent, and, above all, deeply stirring. "There was the war," Guy Sajer recalled, "and I married it because there was nothing else when I reached the age of falling in love."[8]

If the everyday approach seems at times impressionistic and nonanalytical, it still touches on our ability to comprehend social and historical reality, in this case to portray and understand the core experience of war at its most basic level. It also says something about whether the theoretical abstractions with which historians of necessity operate are capable of grasping human phenomena made up of countless individual perceptions and actions. After all, there remains no better road to an understanding of human behavior than through the eyes and ears of actual participants. Their observations, feelings, and horrors are original, not watered down by analysis or trite entertainment. Too often, however, historians so hunger after the analytical and explanatory that they lose contact with the mysteries and dynamics of individuals and groups which constitute history. Thus the authentic, personal side of history, the insight into the human soul, spirit, and behavior, is sacrificed for the sake of some nebulous conjecture or, equally repugnant, some effort to mold the historical record to fit one or another ideological doctrine. In either case, the personal is renounced for the impersonal, and in the case of war the actual killing and bloodletting done and suffered by human beings gives way to the sanitized intellectual exercise of evaluating strategy and tactics. Since the average soldier is too often consumed by the great events of history, the approach of everyday history seeks a sensitivity to the human tragedies entwined in these impersonal cataclysms, yet one that is perceptive and accurate without becoming softhearted.

In studying the harsh and terrible circumstances faced by the anonymous soldier, one can learn not only something of the effect of war on the individual spirit but also something of life: the cruelty, horror, and fear that hollow men on the inside, as well as the compassion, courage, spirit of comradeship, and steady endurance with which the spareness of life is overcome. Not the least of the paradoxes of war is the fact that though war brings out the worst in us, it also elicits our best qualities. The story of the *Landser* is thus not merely a chronicle of the human heart in conflict with itself; it contains as well universal elements central to all of us. "Too many people learn about war with no inconvenience to themselves," Guy Sajer complained. "They read about Verdun or Stalingrad without comprehension, sitting in a comfortable armchair, with their feet beside the fire, preparing to go about their business the next day, as usual. One should really read such accounts under compulsion, in discomfort . . . , from a hole in the mud. One should read about war in the worst circumstances, when everything is going badly. . . . One should read about war standing up, late at night, when one is tired." The reality of war will continue to remain largely inaccessible to those who have not experienced it firsthand, but by learning something of the anonymous soldier they can at least glimpse the full dimensions of war, with all its complex and ambivalent range of emotions. "The substance of my task," Sajer maintained in writing his memoirs, was "to reanimate, with all the intensity I can summon, those distant cries from the slaughterhouse."[9] War is vile, but the chronicle of the *Landser* shows that not all who fight wars are vile.

As Peter Knoch has pointed out, however, much has been contested about the concept of everyday history. Basic questions have been posed. Can one properly speak of an "everyday" life in war? Aren't war and everyday life mutually exclusive? In fact, isn't war the precisely opposite phenomenon of any meaningful conception of everyday life? At first glance, it appears difficult to overcome these objections. Still, the very length of German involvement in World War II, almost six years, led many *Landsers* to adapt to a war environment. The average soldier could not simply step out of his human existence but, instead, lived in a world that became routine and "true" to him. In addition, as their letters and diaries illustrate, many of these men were not reduced to a state of unreflective consciousness but sought to understand the essence of the everyday life of war. Moreover, as Detlev Peukert has argued, everyday history has no object of its own but seeks to legitimize the independent experiences of its subjects, to mediate between individual life experiences and impersonal historical analysis, and to provide a perspective on various life-styles and differing areas of social reality. Peter Borscheid, in fact, emphasizes that the everyday life of war does not remain in an isolated world that can be studied in laboratory fashion. Rather, war itself is a catalyst for significant social change, so there exists a complex and dynamic relationship between the life of men at war and the more general everyday life of those in civilian society.[10]

Everyday life in war, of course, does have its distinctive qualities, from bearing the burden of the permanent expectation of maiming or death to the continual assimilation of suffering and destruction. It represents a life with neither security nor rest, neither emotional peace nor stable relations, where uncertainty is the most notable daily characteristic. For the *Landser*, each battle touched off complex emotions and often savage desires. In war, then, there is an inescapable underlying intensity that does not exist in peacetime life. In order to build a picture of the soldiers' everyday life, historians increasingly use letters, diaries, and memoirs—the most reliable human documents available—to discover the common experiences of men at war. Each one who participated fought his own war, but out of the myriad individual perceptions emerge common themes and patterns.

Problems, of course, surround this approach. The typical *Landser*, for example, rarely had the luxury of a writing table, or the time and solitude in which to record all his thoughts and insights concerning the nature of war. In any case, the great bulk of enlisted men were typically unversed in expressing themselves analytically, so that many firsthand accounts remain sunk in the banalities of humdrum everyday existence, or else speak of intimate matters of personal separation rather than of the character and texture of life at the front. Often, the very soldiers with the most direct experience of battle remain least able to reflect on that experience in writing, whether because of the magnitude of the trauma they suffered or because of the inadequacy of language—or of their ability to use it—to express what it was they saw and experienced. One factor that set the *Landser* apart from the average GI or Tommy or Ivan, however, was his generally greater descriptive power and higher degree of literacy. Reading through their letters and diaries, one is struck by their remarkable level of intelligence and lucidity. In part this was a consequence of the rigorous German educational system, but it also owed much to the manner in which the *Wehrmacht* utilized its personnel. Unlike the American army, which until 1944 shunted its most educated men into specialized roles, the *Wehrmacht* deployed a remarkably high percentage of its manpower as combat troops.[11] As a result, even college educated men found themselves in the frontmost ranks. In addition, Nazi doctrine emphasized the notion of a *Volksgemeinschaft* roughly modeled on the legendary trench socialism of World War I, a national community whose social harmony, unity, and political authority rested on the integration of people from all walks of life, thus transcending class conflict. Since the German army had a high proportion of educated men in the forward lines, men who had the inclination and ability to reflect on their experiences and commit them to paper, the result is a remarkably rich record of life at the front as chronicled in letters, diaries, and memoirs.

Caution must nevertheless be exercised especially in using memoirs, since these, if not based on contemporaneously kept journals, can fall prey to faulty memory or the desire to refine or embroider one's experiences and thus lose the ring of authenticity. Moreover, since the average *Landser*'s direct experience was necessarily limited, historians risk assuming a universality where none may exist; to guard against this, they must search as wide a selection of sources as possible while seeking common elements or themes. Then, too, the reality of censorship meant that many *Landsers* constantly felt the necessity of taking the scissors to their thoughts—not only to avoid transmitting military information—such as troop strengths, dispositions, and activities—but to keep political statements and attitudes circumspect, since critical utterances about the government could lead to the death penalty. "The censor obviously might not see everything that is written," confirmed one *Landser*, then admitted, "but believe me, much crap is still written home."[12]

Still, the flood of letters to and from the front (estimated at 40-50 billion total, and in some individual months as many as 500 million) meant that many passed through censorship unopened; and the longer the war continued, the less seriously many *Landsers* regarded the censor. As two of the leading authorities on German *Feldpostbriefe* (letters from the field) concluded after studying thousands of such missives, "the mass of soldiers expressed their opinions and views in a surprisingly open and uninhibited fashion." So despite the problems, much can be gained from a study of letters and diaries, especially if the historian relates these necessarily individual and narrow documents to a wider context. By illustrating the actualities of combat from a personal point of view, the historian can better demonstrate the impact of war in all its dimensions. Such an approach also brings a vivid sense of immediacy and reality to the often impersonal topic of war. Furthermore, it affords insights into the mysteries of individual actions and group dynamics, as well as to psychological and emotional behavior under conditions of extreme stress. Above all, these documents remain personal reminders of the human elements within the gigantic events of World War II.[13]

In emphasizing this individual dimension of war, however, the historian needs to avoid engaging in a trite idealization of the "common man" and instead seek to provide an honest and accurate portrait of everyday life at the front. Taken together and used judiciously, letters and diaries can aid in the quest to see the *Landser* as subject as well as object. Just as important, they provide valuable insight into what remains one of the puzzling ironies of the war: why the average *Landser* fought so furiously in defense of such a seemingly deplorable regime. No one forced the soldiers to make positive comments about the Nazi regime and the war, so that if some letters have the ring of propagandistic mimicry about them, others reflect a genuine sympathy and support for Hitler and Nazism. An army—and the men within it—cannot be completely separated from the value system that produced it. Indeed, an army tends to reflect the society from which it sprang, so that if the men of the *Wehrmacht* fought steadfastly in support of Hitler and Nazism, something within the Hitler state must have struck a responsive chord.

As Hegel long ago pointed out, men will fight to defend ideas much more readily than material interests, an insight given renewed validity by an examination of the behavior of the average *Landser*. From the

German perspective, World War II, especially that part of it fought in Russia, was the ultimate ideological war, since at its core it was understood as a war of ideas, with the enemy idea threatening the validity of the National Socialist concepts that a surprisingly large number of *Landsers* embraced. And the staying power of the average German soldier, his sense of seriousness and purpose—which often went beyond sacrifice, courage, and resolution to fanaticism—depended in large measure on the conviction that National Socialist Germany had redeemed the failures of World War I and had restored, both individually and collectively, a uniquely German sense of identity. The dual tragedy of the *Landser*, then, lay in the fact that in the name of animosity toward a seemingly alien and threatening enemy idea he committed unspeakable acts of aggression and destruction, at the same time being consumed himself, both physically and spiritually, by the machine of war. "So important is the defense of our ideas, our definitions of ourselves and our societies," Robin Fox points out, "that we will willingly strive to destroy their perceived enemies and exhibit the highest forms of human courage in so doing." Ultimately, though, this is the profoundest justification of a study of the common soldier, for as Fox concludes, "It is ideas that make us human after all."[14]

2. SWEAT SAVES BLOOD

"July 18, 1942. I arrive at the Chemnitz barracks, a huge oval building, entirely white. I am much impressed, with a mixture of admiration and fear." So Guy Sajer began his chronicle of life in the *Wehrmacht*, life at war. "We live with an intensity I have never before experienced," he continued. "I have a brand-new uniform . . . [and] am very proud of my appearance. . . . I learn some military songs, which I warble with an atrocious French accent. The other soldiers laugh. They are destined to be my first comrades in this place. . . . The combat course is the most severe physical challenge I have ever experienced. I am exhausted, and several times fall asleep over my food. But I feel marvelous, filled with a sense of joy which I can't understand after so much fear and apprehension. On the 15th of September we leave Chemnitz and march twenty-five miles to Dresden, where we board a train for the east. . . . Russia means the war, of which, as yet, I know nothing."[1]

Sajer's recollections capture well the jumbled feelings of trepidation, exhilaration, and excitement with which many *Landsers* went off to the training centers of the *Wehrmacht*. The average soldier felt anxiety about separation from his family and friends, about being removed from his familiar surroundings, about whether he would measure up, about what was to come. But at the same time there lurked the thrill of a new adventure, of being part of a mighty organization, of forming sturdy bonds of camaraderie, and of stepping into the unknown. For most, this appeared to be a rite of passage, an initiation into a new life. "I felt," remembered Siegfried Knappe of the bus trip to his training center, "as if we were rolling out of my childhood and into a new adult world." In December 1942 a *Landser* echoed that sensation in a letter to his mother from training camp: "The first sharp bullets whistled over our heads and out of boys we became men."[2]

For the nearly twenty million men who passed through the *Wehrmacht* during World War II, the first encounter with a soldier's existence came at the induction center where they were examined, classified, and assigned to duty. Compared to those of the U.S. Army, the German army's methods of classification and assignment seemed unscientific and crude. The great majority of recruits took neither a written nor a mechanical test but underwent only a physical examination. During this examination, however, the review officers carried on conversations with the recruits designed to provide them a picture of each man's general character, and, if necessary, to allow them to weed out any who were obviously mentally deficient. Since the *Wehrmacht* concerned itself more with character—such emotional and temperamental qualities as will power, mental stamina, courage, loyalty, independence, and obedience—than with aptitude, its procedures aimed less at establishing intellectual or mechanical abilities than at discerning a recruit's personality, behavior patterns, demeanor, and ability to cope.[3]

Although Martin Pöppel claimed that "a great show was made of these [psychological tests], but they were actually quite simple," Alfred Wessel, who originally hoped to join a *Luftwaffe* unit, recalled them in much greater detail. "We had to do exercises, we had to do calculations, write essays and take dictation," he remembered. "And then the most interesting was that they took us by bus through [Osnabrück], and then into a house. Then we were led all through the house and into the cellar, from the cellar by elevator up to a loft, and from one room to another. . . . Then we went again by elevator to the cellar. And then we were asked questions. That was in the cellar in a dark room, no windows. . . . 'You are now here, there is the compass. In your opinion in what direction does St. Peter's Church lie? And where have you seen this and that,' and so on." Totally unprepared for this, Wessel and his cohorts had to act, and react, as quickly and as well as they could. That proved to be the point of the exercise, for the review officers were less interested in the answers to these questions than in the attributes displayed by the men when confronted with the need to make quick decisions in a confusing and disorienting atmosphere.[4]

For the *Landser* the process of basic training marked the first step on the journey of being transformed from civilian to soldier. It was a difficult step for most, with many assaulted by pangs of homesickness, loneliness, and bewilderment. It involves a considerable mental and psychological strain to be ripped from one's family and deposited in a situation where one's identity and sense of importance are subject to new conditions. "The clock shows ten," Rudolf Halbey wrote in his diary from a troop training center in November 1942. "Early tomorrow morning at this time mother will leave again. . . . How strange, this last get-together! Sad and dreamlike. I will remain strong. Tears come to mother anew. I take her in my arms, she kisses me and whispers in a tear-choked voice: 'If prayers can help, oh, then everything will be all right.' I take hold of her loving, concerned, workworn hands. . . . No words. A last kiss, and I am outside in the clear, cold November night."[5] The overwrought sentiments of a nineteen-year-old, perhaps, but an honest depiction of the wrenching emotions that many young recruits experienced as they left home for the first time and journeyed into the unknown. For Halbey, as for so many others, the unknown meant death: he lived as a soldier not quite a year before falling in Russia in October 1943.

Basic training, although harsh, was a means to an end. Its purpose was not to punish men but to acquaint them with such things as weapons handling, tactics, and discipline, as well as to instill certain group values, loyalties, and a spirit of camaraderie. It aimed ultimately at control and motivation on the battlefield. Training also served to hone the instincts and skills of the new recruits, to condition reflexes, to provide the security of a learned routine in moments of crisis, and, not least, to inculcate the habit of obedience—a singular virtue when the soldier encountered the numbing shock and paralysis of battle. Ideally, training also promoted group pride as it bound men together into cohesive units, and as it persuaded them that they actually were soldiers, an integral part of a powerful organization. As Richard Holmes has pointed out, a large part of a soldier's behavior on the battlefield, and thus the cohesion and fighting effectiveness of the army to which he belongs, will depend on training. And few armies were more effectively trained than the *Wehrmacht*. The remarkable cohesion and fighting performance of the German army, its ability time and again to cobble units together out of broken fragments and use them effectively, owed much to the extensive, realistic, and continual training given the *Landser*.[6]

All wars are fought by boys, for it is only the young who have the physical stamina and sense of invulnerability necessary to endure the rigors of combat. And here the *Wehrmacht* had a decided advantage, for by the time war broke out, many young Germans had already undergone considerable military-style training in the Hitler Youth (*Hitlerjugend*, or HJ) and the National Labor Service (*Reichsarbeitsdienst*, or RAD). "Shortly after the Nazis came to power," Martin Pöppel remembered, "I transferred from the Catholic boy scouts' organization . . . to the Hitler Youth and was accepted into its *Jungvolk* section [for boys aged ten to fourteen]. . . . A year later I was made a patrol leader. . . . Then whilst I was with the . . . compulsory Labor Service at Donauwörth, I saw an article in an illustrated magazine about the new paratroops. . . . That was for me. . . . A bit of spirit, something out of the ordinary." In similar fashion, Alfons Heck recollected the paramilitary nature of the Hitler Youth, with its camplike atmosphere during important events such as the Nuremberg Rallies, its emphasis on loyalty and obedience, the summer training in military skills, and the stress on eliminating class distinctions and building group loyalty and cohesion.[7]

Friedrich Grupe recalled the sense of excitement in his small town in the Harz Mountains in the months and years after the Nazi rise to power, an enthusiasm aimed particularly at mobilizing the young. "You should serve a community," stressed the HJ appeals, "live a life of comradeship, be harder and ready to fight, carry the will within to greater deeds." Caught in the frenzy of emotions, Grupe ardently followed the path laid down for most young men in Germany: Hitler Youth, Labor Service, *Wehrmacht*. By April 1937 he had graduated from HJ to RAD, an experience that well prepared him for the army: "The work and the life in the [Labor Service] barracks camp are physically and also psychologically harder than we had imagined. Early in the morning at 4:00 A.M. out of our beds to a long cross-country run with early morning exercise, then washing up, breakfast, ceremonial raising of the flag, and already by 5:00 A.M. marching to the labor site in work overalls with spades at our shoulders."[8]

In like fashion, Karl Fuchs underwent the transition from the Hitler Youth to the Labor Service, and in a letter to his parents left a similar picture of a taxing military-style routine.

We have to get up at five o'clock every morning. After reveille we have fifteen minutes of morning calisthenics. In half-an-hour I have to be washed, dressed, and have my area cleaned up. It is very difficult for me to make my straw bed in accordance with military regulations. If the bed is not made properly, the supervising officer simply throws the whole thing on the floor and you have to start all over again. . . .

After the cleanup of our barracks we have a hearty breakfast of rye bread and coffee. At 6:30 we start with drill. This normally lasts until 9. . . . From 9–10 we have classroom instruction. After that comes second breakfast and a cigarette break. From 10:30–1:00 there is more drill. . . . Then comes lunch. From 2–3 we are busy with general cleanup of the area. . . . From 3–4:30 we have physical education (mostly jogging through the forest), and the afternoon activities conclude with more classroom instruction and singing. Dinner is at 7.[9]

As both Grupe and Fuchs illustrated, the daily routine of the Labor Service had a clear paramilitary content whose aims were not only to instill the rudiments of military training and physical stamina but also to foster character, comradeship, and cohesion. Grupe furnished evidence of the idealism created among many young Germans by this intense process of socialization, noting in his diary in 1937:

This community of working men is something unique. From all sections of society we come here together and wrest higher yields out of the soil through hard work. . . .

Despite everything, probably just because of our burdens borne in common, the feeling of comradely identity grows rapidly. . . . We're experiencing here what we understand to be "*Volksgemein-schaft* [national community]." And we're putting our conception of National Socialism into action: We are all the same in our service for our people, no one is asked his origins or class, whether he is rich or poor. . . . Snobbery, class consciousness, envy, and idleness are left out on the street. This is the way from "I" to "We."[10]

Not surprisingly, given the degree of hard work, intense physical training, and military drill to which they had already been subjected, when these tens of thousands of graduates of the HJ and RAD flooded into *Wehrmacht* training centers, they were generally better prepared for what lay ahead than were their counterparts in Great Britain and the United States. Still, the training they encountered proved of such intensity and realism that even those with "degrees" from these preparatory institutions were often taken aback. "They went to work on us," noted Siegfried Knappe of his military drill instructors, "assuring us that, Labor Service notwithstanding, we not only did not know how to march, we did not even know how to *walk*. Then they went about teaching us, in their own way. It was beneath them to recognize our Labor Service training."[11]

The earnestness of training also impressed Martin Pöppel, himself a veteran of the *Hitlerjugend* and *Arbeitsdienst*. "The Sarge, *Hauptfeld-webel* Zierach, . . . reigned supreme with his fat punishment book," Pöppel recalled. "Whenever he looked at us poor squirts we started to tremble. . . . Our training was unbelievably hard, but basically fair. It passed quickly even if only because we were drilled so hard from morning till night that we never got a moment to think." Nor did the situation improve when Pöppel left basic training for more advanced instruction:

> Our arduous training continued. For example, we did a 25 kilometer march with full equipment and radio set. . . . This was followed by night exercises including an orientation race using sketches and prismatic compass. . . .
>
> In August we went to Wildflecken troop training grounds. The marches, exercises, night alerts, the shooting and radio practices were all even worse than before. Every day we fell into our beds completely exhausted. In action later on, we realized time and again how valuable this training had been for us. Sweat saves blood, that was a truism that was often confirmed later. We didn't know it yet, though, so we cursed and swore at everything and everyone. . . . However, this tough training eventually began to produce results. . . . After our period at the troop training grounds ended, I never forgot one of our mottos about the damn place: *Lieber den ganzen Arsch voller Zwecken, als vierzehn Tage Wildflecken* (Better an assful of nails than two weeks at Wildflecken.)[12]

Karl Fuchs, another HJ and RAD graduate, wrote to his father: "We have to learn and train until we perfect all of our skills. Infantry training is almost behind us and in eight weeks we have to be fit for combat. . . . The intensity of training is tremendous and there is no rest for anyone." Still, Fuchs claimed, and perhaps here one sees the significance of his earlier indoctrination, "all of us are eager to make progress and no one complains." By contrast, Guy Sajer, an Alsatian and thus a novice in this sort of thing, was stunned upon arriving at a training center in Poland in September 1942. "I have just put my bundle down on the wooden bed I have chosen for myself when we are ordered to return to the courtyard," he related. "It is now about two o'clock in the afternoon, and . . . we haven't had anything to eat since the rye bread, white cheese, and jam we were given the evening before. . . . This new order must be connected with lunch." Sajer discovered to his chagrin, however, that eating was the last priority for their new drill instructor: "A *Feldwebel* (sergeant) wearing a sweater proposes with an ironic air to share his swim with us. . . . He makes us trot at a brisk gymnastic pace for about three-quarters of a mile to a small sandy pool. . . . The *Feldwebel* . . . orders us to strip . . . , [then] plunges into the water first, and waves us after him. . . . The temperature of the air can be no more than forty, and the water . . . is really very cold." Now, surely, Sajer believed, they would be fed. Again, disappointment reigned: "On the double, we catch up with our leader, who is already more than halfway back to our enormous residence. We are all frantically hungry. . . . A young . . . giant accosts one of the noncoms, staring at him as if he wished to devour him. 'Are we going to have anything to eat?' 'Lunch here is at eleven,' the noncom shouts. 'You arrived three hours late. In threes, to my right. It's time for target practice.' "[13]

So, it's on to the firing range, which itself is a few miles distant: "There are at least a thousand men, and the firing is nonstop," Sajer noted. "Night falls. We are all ravenous. We leave the shooting range with guns on our shoulders. . . . We march down a narrow graveled road which does not appear to be the same one we took when we came. In fact, we shall have to tramp four miles in quick-step, singing before we get back. . . . Between songs, I glance at my breathless companions, and notice a look of anxiety on every face. As I plainly don't understand . . . [one] whispers: 'The time.' Good Lord! I catch on. . . . We've missed supper. The whole section seems to react, and our pace accelerates. Perhaps they've saved something for us. We cling to this hope."

Driven by hunger and the tormenting fear that the nightly provisions would have vanished by the time they returned, Sajer's unit spontaneously exerted themselves beyond what they had believed to be their own capacities, which was precisely the outcome aimed for by the training officers. "At the sergeant's order we halt, and wait for his next order to break ranks and fetch our mess tins," Sajer recalled upon his return to camp. "But, alas, that moment has not yet come. This sadist obliges us to put our guns back in the gun rack, in their proper numerical order, which takes another ten minutes. We are frantic. Then, abruptly: 'Go and see if there's anything left . . . !' We surge wildly toward our quarters. Our hobnailed boots throw off sparks as they clatter against the courtyard pavement. We rush up the monumental stone staircase like eighty madmen. . . . Every face wears the same burning look of exhaustion. . . . I open my mess tin. I haven't had a chance to wash it since my last meal. . . . [Still] I bolt my meal with ravenous hunger. . . . As we haven't been given anything to drink, I go over to the horse troughs like everybody else, and swallow down three or four cups of water." Although he had finally been fed, the long, torturous day still refused to end for Sajer: "Evening assembly and roll call take place in a large hall where a corporal addresses us on the subject of the German *Reich*. It is eight o'clock. Lights out is sounded. . . . We go back to our rooms and fall into a dead sleep. I have just spent my first day in Poland." Sajer himself recognized the purpose of all this arduous training, however, when he remarked of his drill sergeant, "He wasn't really a bully, but a man with a clear idea of a job to be done. . . . He made us realize, rightly enough, that if we couldn't stand a little cold and a vague, possible danger, we would never survive at the front."[14]

Given the nature of their task, to prepare men for the hardships of combat, it is hardly surprising that most recruits had a love-hate relationship with their drill instructors. While resenting the harsh and rigorous training the instructors put them through, most *Landsers* nonetheless realized that it aimed at the one thing most important to them: survival in combat. Many men even came to see their drill sergeants in paternalistic terms, as Friedrich Grupe illustrated:

> I will not so soon forget my drill instructor, "big mouth" Schmidt, as he shooed us up the heights of the training area. . . . I had the munitions box for the machine gun, filled to bulging with the heavy ammunition, in both hands. I gasped uphill with it, my knees failing in their duty, my heart hammering in my neck.
>
> But there above stood my sergeant, with his arms crossed, shouting: Come on, get going, don't plead exhaustion as an excuse . . .! Many ran as if they were already drunk, but there was no mercy. [But] in the evenings "big-mouth" Schmidt comes into the barracks room, sits informally with us, and laughs and jokes and sings with us just like a good comrade. . . . You get accustomed to it, especially the companionship with the comrades, which helps you get over much.[15]

This "language of family," as Richard Holmes put it, recurred again and again in the letters and memoirs of *Landsers* and even made its way into their jargon: the slang expression for the senior sergeant in a company was "mother." Nor was this a happenstance occurrence, for training aimed to build a sense of group identity and solidarity out of the shared privations, as well as to weld young men from diverse backgrounds into motivated, cohesive fighting units. "I've become such an integral part of my company," admitted Karl Fuchs in a letter to his father that admirably illustrated this bonding process, "that I couldn't leave it ever again." Similarly, Hans Werner Woltersdorf claimed that "my unit was my home, my family, which I had to protect."[16]

Furthermore, Holmes asserted, "There is a direct link between the harshness of basic training and the cohesiveness of the group which emerges from it." If so, the tough and realistic German training goes a long way to explaining the remarkable performance of the *Wehrmacht* during World War II. Also important, however, was the fact that the Germans conducted continual training even of combat experienced troops just behind the front lines. "We went back to our old precampaign schedule of training," Siegfried Knappe noted after the victory in France. "We had to be prepared for whatever might happen. We planned a full schedule for every day, from 5:00 A.M. until 8:00 P.M. Even though these were the same troops we marched into France with, . . . we kept them active and practicing. We wanted to keep their skills sharp and to train them in other functions so that if someone was wounded, we would have someone else who could do that job."[17]

"They may well have cursed me every time I made them dig holes in the hard ground in the burning heat in order to cram themselves into the protective covering of the earth," recalled Hans Werner Woltersdorf, a lieutenant, of the training exercises he conducted in occupied France, "every time they had to bring their antitank guns, mortars, or infantry guns into position so that all the movements became second nature to them; and when, stop watch in hand, I demanded that it take not twenty but only ten seconds to be ready to fire. They had to realize that 'Take cover, charge, forward march!' is no punishment drill or sadistic form of harassment but life insurance." Life insurance, indeed; as Woltersdorf himself acknowledged:

> How often did I have to go without sleep in Russia while we continuously pushed forward against the enemy lines, or later, while the Russians stormed our positions . . . day and night without a respite, when we used Pervitin to keep awake and I had hardly more than twenty-four hours sleep in ten days. That is why I did night drills. . . .
>
> The normal daily routine was followed by the first night drill. . . . It was miserable. Just as the men were thinking they would

make up the lost sleep the next day, I announced that they had only forty-five minutes in which to wash and eat breakfast before resuming their normal daily schedule. After this, they thought, they would sleep that much better the following night. I will never forget their despairing expressions when I announced that evening that they had to assemble in one hour in full marching order with all weapons, light and heavy, in order to repeat the night drill.

At sunrise they stood there again, covered in dust, filthy, and wanting nothing more eagerly than to be able to hit the hay now. But it wasn't to be! Two hours later, weapon and gun roll call, because weapon care and constant readiness for action are essential![18]

Such intense, rigorous training paid dividends when these men experienced the extreme conditions of the Russian front. "When, seven months later, the Russians had us surrounded in Zhitomir," Woltersdorf recalled, "I predicted that we wouldn't get much sleep over the next few days. 'We're used to that . . . ,' said Alfons. 'You know: Bordeaux!' " As Woltersdorf concluded, "Nothing is more burdensome than having to suffer harassment and injustice, but nothing increases self-confidence more than having withstood hardships." Hard training, he added, also "had a useful side effect, in that the men regarded their respective commanders as the common enemy, and nothing unites people more than shared rage against someone or something."[19]

Martin Pöppel, too, emphasized the continual operational training he experienced in the paratroops. "The Regiment with all its units, is established in its field positions, which we have worked tirelessly to complete," he noted in his diary of preparations before the Allied Normandy invasion. "Alarm exercises by day and by night increase our combat readiness." Like Woltersdorf, Pöppel however, soon had reason to appreciate this exhaustive training. Writing on D-Day, June 6, 1944, he noted of a German counterattack: "06.30 hours. From Rougeville *Oberleutnant* (First Lieutenant) Prive makes an attack through the open countryside, pushing towards us. We use light signals to show the direction of the enemy. He pushes closer and closer. In copybook fashion, again showing the value of our tough training, his groups advance, one covering and shooting whilst the other moves forwards firing with sub-machine guns from the hip. . . . Arms are raised aloft in the thick bushes as the enemy surrenders. A real triumph for Prive, who takes more than sixty American prisoners."[20]

Guy Sajer, despite his rigorous basic training, first realized how

relentless such instruction could be when he joined an elite combat
division. "One sweated blood," he remarked. "One was either hospital-
ized after a week of almost insane effort or incorporated into the division
and marched off to the war, which was even worse." Nor was this mere
hyperbole. As Sajer recalled, he had an inkling of how difficult things
were going to be when "our noncoms . . . advised us to sleep, although
it was still early, as we would need all our strength tomorrow. We knew
that in the German army words of that sort often had a significance far
greater than their literal meaning. The word 'exhaustion,' for instance,
had nothing to do with the 'exhaustion' I've encountered since the war.
At that time and place, it meant a power which could strip a strong man
of fifteen pounds of weight in a few days."[21]

Indeed, Sajer's foreboding was more than realized the next day and
in the agonizing days that followed. "The sun had barely touched the tops
of the trees with pink light when the door flew back against the dormitory
wall as if the Soviets themselves were bursting in," Sajer remembered.
"A *Feldwebel* produced some piercing blasts on a whistle and made us
jump. 'Thirty seconds to get to the troughs,' he shouted. Then everybody
stripped and outside in front of the barracks for P.T. One hundred and
fifty of us, stripped to the skin, ran for the troughs on the other side of the
buildings. . . . In no time, we had washed and were lined up in front of our
barracks . . . , then [were] put . . . through a gymnastic routine . . . [that
left] our heads . . . spinning." But as Sajer soon realized, the morning
exercises proved only a mild irritant compared to what was to come:

> It was then we made the acquaintance of *Herr Hauptmann*
> (Captain) Fink and his formidable training methods. He arrived
> wearing riding breeches, and carrying a whip under his arm.
>
> "The task which you will all have to assume sooner or later
> will certainly require more of you than you supposed. Simply
> maintaining a decent level of morale and knowing how to handle a
> weapon will no longer be enough. You will also require a very great
> deal of courage, of perseverance and endurance, and of resistance
> in every situation. . . . I must warn you that everything here is hard,
> nothing is forgiven, and that everyone in consequence must have
> quick reflexes. . . ."
>
> "Attention!" he shouted. "Down on the ground, and full length!"
>
> Without a moment's hesitation, we were all stretched out on
> the sandy soil. Then Captain Fink stepped forward and, like some-
> one strolling down a beach, walked across the human ground,

continuing his speech as his boots, loaded with at least two hundred pounds, trampled the paralyzed bodies of our section. His heels calmly crushed down on a back, a hip, a head, or a hand, but no one moved.[22]

A rude awakening, certainly, but Captain Fink had still more elaborate tortures by which to toughen the men. One involved the simulation of carrying wounded comrades from the battlefield: "Hals and I made a seat of our hands for a wincing fellow who must have weighed at least 170 pounds. Then Captain Fink led us to the camp exit. We walked as far as a low hill which seemed to be about three-quarters of a mile away. Our arms felt as though they would break under the weight. . . . Every so often an exhausted man let his grip slip . . . and the supposed victim slid to the ground. Whenever this occurred, Fink . . . would . . . assign them an even heavier load. . . . This torture went on for nearly an hour, until we were all on the point of losing consciousness and at the extreme limit of our capabilities. . . . Finally, he decided to shift us to a new exercise." The new drill, however, proved just as difficult and far more dangerous:

> "Picture to yourselves that over there behind that hill there is a nest of Bolshevik resistance." He gestured toward a hillock about a half mile away. "Furthermore," he went on in a jovial tone, "imagine that you have the best of reasons for taking that hill. . . . Therefore, you will . . . proceed toward your objective on your bellies. I shall precede you, and shall fire on anyone I see. Understood?"
>
> We gaped at him, astounded. . . . We threw ourselves down on our stomachs, and began to squirm forward. . . . He began firing almost at once. . . .
>
> His bullets whistled down among us until we had reached our objective. . . . During our three weeks of training, we buried four companions to the strains of "Ich hat ein Kamerad," victims of so-called "training accidents." There were also some twenty wounded.[23]

For all their difficulty, exercises such as these might be considered common to all the armies of World War II. Certainly new recruits had to be toughened and given physical stamina, and the only sure way to prepare men for the rigor of combat was under realistic conditions of live ammunition. So physical training, instruction in weapons use, throwing grenades, bayonet practices, tests of endurance—all these in some way entered into the training of all soldiers, although in the U.S. Army the limits of realistic training were quickly reached when live ammunition exercises produced noticeable casualties.[24]

The *Wehrmacht*, however, went beyond these measures of instruction. "In addition there was the famous *Härteübung* (hardness training)," Sajer noted,

> which was almost continuous. We were put on thirty-six hour shifts, which were broken by only three half-hour periods, during which we devoured the contents of our mess tins, before returning to the ranks in an obligatory clean and orderly condition. At the end of these thirty-six hours, we were allowed eight hours of rest. Then there was another thirty-six hour period. . . . There were also false alarms, which tore us from our leaden sleep and forced us into the courtyard fully dressed and equipped. . . . Sometimes a fellow would drop from exhaustion . . . obliging [his comrades] to get the fellow onto his feet again, slapping him and spraying him with water. . . . Nothing ever affected the routine. . . . Captain Fink simply carried on, in total disregard of our bleeding gums and pinched faces, until the stabbing pains in our heads made us forget the bleeding blisters on our feet.

This seemingly gratuitous exercise in cruelty actually aimed at preparing the men for the severity of the Russian front, as did another exacting bit of rehearsal.

> One day we were given anti-tank exercises. We were ordered into the trench in close ranks, and forbidden to leave it, no matter what happened. Then four or five Mark-3 [tanks] rolled forward at right angles to us, and crossed the trench at different speeds. The weight of these machines alone made them sink four or five inches into the crumbling ground. When their monstrous treads plowed into the rim of the trench only a few inches from our heads, cries of terror broke from almost all of us. . . . We were also taught how to handle the dangerous *Panzerfaust* [anti-tank gun], and how to attack tanks with magnetic mines. One had to hide in a hole and wait until the tank came close enough. Then one ran, and dropped an explosive device . . . between the body and the turret of the machine. We weren't allowed to leave our holes until the tank was within five yards of us. Then . . . we had to run straight at the terrifying monster, grab the tow hook and pull ourselves onto the hood, place the mine at the joint of the body and turret, and drop off the tank.

Amazingly, after all this tribulation and ill treatment, Sajer could say, echoing Woltersdorf: "Despite all the hardship we had been through, my vanity was flattered by my acceptance as a German among Germans, and as a warrior worthy of bearing arms. . . . It seems scarcely credible that by the time we left we all nourished a certain admiration for the *Herr Hauptmann.* Everyone, in fact, dreamed of someday becoming an officer of the same stripe."[25]

For all its difficulty, most *Landsers* recognized the value of their harsh training. "In the war," remembered Fritz-Erich Diemke, "we survived . . . because of this hard training." Noted Gustav Knickrehm after the war, "The advantage of our armed forces lay in this monstrous training. . . . You carried out all orders automatically. . . . You thought about home, about your loved ones, you thought about it all. But you stood erect and shot. . . . You acted automatically as a soldier. And the thing is, that helped to preserve your life. Any who deny that today are idiots." Siegfried Knappe concluded of his drill officers that they attempted "to put us under stress similar to a combat situation." And later, before the French campaign, Knappe pointed to another goal of this constant activity: "We immediately began a vigorous training program . . . to get the men accustomed to working together. We practiced all day, every day, to try to achieve the cohesiveness necessary to fight."[26]

The link between the harshness of basic training and the group cohesiveness that emerged from it was precisely what allowed the German army to excel. According to one scholar, "The Germans consistently outfought the far more numerous Allied armies that eventually defeated them. . . . On a man for man basis the German ground soldiers consistently inflicted casualties at about a 50 percent higher rate than they incurred from the opposing British and American troops *under all circumstances.* This was true when they were attacking and when they were defending, when they had a local numerical superiority and when, as was usually the case, they were outnumbered."[27]

As Martin van Creveld maintained, this superiority was the result neither of Allied inexperience ("Not the least astonishing aspect of the matter is that the *Wehrmacht* fought equally well in victory and in defeat") nor of some supposed innate German militarism or character defect: "What comparative studies exist . . . do not allow the conclusion that Germans [inherently] make better soldiers than Americans." Indeed, he insisted, "our inference from all this [research] is that Americans, by upbringing, education, and personality make first-class soldier material. . . . Paradoxically, the same cannot be proven of Germans. . . . From the available evidence, there is no reason to believe the German national character to be more or less suitable to war than the American one."[28] The differing levels of cohesion and fighting effectiveness, van Creveld sought to demonstrate, lay in such things as organization, doctrine, and—not least—arduous, realistic, and continuous training.

Still, as in any army, there existed a fine line between the hard, necessary training so essential for survival in combat and that harassment, whether petty or sadistic, which Paul Fussell has termed "chickenshit." To Fussell, chickenshit meant the "petty harassment of the weak by the strong; open scrimmage for power and authority and prestige; sadism thinly disguised as necessary discipline; a constant 'paying off of old scores'; and insistence on the letter rather than the spirit of ordinances."[29] On the basis of admittedly impressionistic evidence, it would seem there was less petty, personal harassment of troops in the German army than in the Anglo-American armies. The *Wehrmacht* made a concerted effort to promote a strong spirit of comradeship between junior officers and their men. Hans Werner Woltersdorf, queried after the war in a prisoner-of-war camp about German performance, "referred to the special leadership principle, which appeared to be completely new to them. The necessary qualification for an officer's career was not the high school diploma but exemplary ability, the true authority. Everyone who led a unit had to be the best man in his unit as well; not the uniform, not being in command, but example made the leader."[30] Moreover, in a time and place where the total life of the individual was to belong to the party and state, the process of stripping a recruit of individual identity predated his experiences at a training camp, so the process of basic training might have seemed less of a shock.

Even many of the claims of harassment that were made by men in later oral histories could equally be considered evidence of the rugged instruction that better prepared the average German soldier for combat. Johann Eisfeld, for example, remembered as harassment the fact that his company "had to scramble over a scaling wall every morning, with the combat pack on: . . . helmet, gas mask, . . . [and] rifle." Eisfeld also complained that they were given no time to dry their wet clothing and often had to wear the damp uniforms the next day. Similarly, Erich Albertsen griped that during basic training his unit had to "march every day . . . with a full pack [weighing] twenty-five kilos," and like Eisfeld, his company also had to clamber over the barracks wall encumbered by these packs. Max Landowski still resented the fact that on Christmas Day 1940 he and other recruits had to tend the horses and clean the stalls; this to him, at a distance of four decades, represented harassment. And finally, Fritz-Erich Diemke, prompted by his interviewer, remembered that his unit of recruits had to march eleven kilometers in a snowstorm, bivouac and pitch tents in the open, spend the night there, and suffer the indignity of cold food.[31] All of these cases of alleged *Schikane* (harassment), however, can equally be seen as examples of the rugged training that prepared the average German soldier well for the rigors of combat. Certainly, enemy attacks hardly came only at the convenience of German soldiers, nor were the Allies necessarily going to allow their adversaries time to warm and dry their uniforms. Night fighting and long, grueling marches were also a common feature of combat. And whether it was Christmas or any other holiday, certain essential duties had to be performed.

Indeed, a number of men recalled their time in the barracks with great equanimity. What stood out to Fritz Harenberg, in retrospect, was not any particular harassment, but something else. "I liked the military period in the barracks better than the Labor Service," he recalled. And why? "We received very good food. Cutlets . . . as big as a toilet lid, . . . salad, potatoes, gravy and everything. And not once a week, many times in a week." Heinz Rieckmann recalled tough discipline, but "I cannot say it was slave-driving. . . . I was in an old barracks that had no running water. We had to run down to get it, and it was December . . . and already cold. . . . We had to bathe in the wash basin with bare upper bodies in the winter. And we had to go and pick up coffee . . . and whoever had barracks room duty had to clean and keep the room polished the whole day. . . . It was a lot of discipline. But I cannot say that it was inhumane."[32]

"Harassment," puzzled Hermann Blohm. "The training was hard, especially in the infantry. But this influence also . . . allowed me a certain calm. . . . I don't want to say that you were inwardly free. You were still a soldier, a bearer of weapons. But other than that nothing further was demanded of you. How you yourself led your life interested nobody further." "We were driven hard," remembered Georg Timm, but "for me the exercises were sport." And Werner Karstens, forced to do three days of punishment exercises that included marching in full gear while carrying a thirty-pound sandbag, did not recollect even this as harassment. After all, he had earned this penalty by pretending to be a drill sergeant and ordering a group of reservists—all doctors, lawyers, and professors—through a series of drills. In recalling the tale, Karstens beamed with pleasure at the joke he had played on the learned reservists, poking fun at the pretensions and ingrained obedience to authority of these men in a sort of updated version of the *Hauptmann von Köpenick*, (a popular play of the late 1920s that ridiculed the German mania for obedience to those in authority) while fully admitting that "they *had* to punish me." Finally, both Franz Ehlers and Albert Gädtke recalled training officers who had been punished—one by being sent to the front and the other by the cancellation of a furlough—for ordering overstrenuous exercise and mistreating their men.[33]

Nevertheless, there were clear cases of harassment and sadistic discipline during training. Eisfeld, Albertsen, Landowski, and others spoke of drill sergeants singling out particular recruits for special punishments, finding dirt in completely clean barracks rooms, forcing the men to clean the barracks with toothbrushes, tossing bedding and locker contents onto the floor or out a window, dumping full garbage bins in a freshly cleaned room so that it had to be cleaned again, and denying leave at the last moment for inconsequential reasons. "I could still remember all too well the four hours of punishment handed out to me," Guy Sajer noted of his personal experience with chickenshit. "I had to put on the 'punishment pack,' a knapsack filled with sand, which weighed nearly eighty pounds. I weighed one hundred and thirty. After two hours my helmet was burning hot from the sun, and by the end I needed all my will power to keep my knees from buckling. I had nearly fainted several times. That is how I learned that a good soldier does not cross the barracks yard with his hands in his pockets."[34]

Clearly apparent here is a major characteristic of harassment: the disparity between the transgression and the punishment. Assigned to Christmas Eve stable duty, Siegfried Knappe and his mate were dutifully removing all the soiled straw when a commotion erupted. "[We] stopped our work," he recalled, "and looked around to see what was happening. The moment we stood up, Weizsacker pounced on us. 'Ah ha! The intellectuals are loafing,' he shouted gleefully. . . . 'Well, if you have so much free time, I have a perfect solution, especially designed for intellectuals and smartmouths. . . .' Weizsacker motioned for Vogel to get into the stall with Weinreich and me. 'Now, let's see you guys clean this place out with your hands! . . . That's right. . . . Hang up your pitchforks.' " These actions amounted to harassment as an instrument of arbitrary, subjective will, as a means to intimidate men through the exercise of petty authority, to make a man seem, in the words of Günter Dettmann, "like a piece of crap."[35]

If these examples illustrate the existence of mean, cheap chicken-shit, others point to a more sadistic, and dangerous, variety of "instruction." Werner Karstens recalled a friend and comrade who fell afoul of regulations while they were in training in Stettin. Having met a young woman, his buddy failed to make it back to camp before lights out. In a not atypical example of collective punishment, his entire barracks room unit then suffered the consequences of his misbehavior. His "comrades" exacted revenge, however—what the *Landsers* called *Heiliger Geist* (Holy Spirit) or comrades' justice: the next night they assaulted and viciously beat him with the leg of a stool. Injured so badly that he had to be sent to the hospital, the nineteen-year-old youth eventually suffered amputation of his arm and then died following the onset of infection. A moment's indiscretion thus caused a young man to be victimized in a cruel act of "self-justice" by his erstwhile comrades.[36]

Nor were such occurrences necessarily isolated or limited to the men themselves. Karstens once saw a drill sergeant slam a recruit with all his force into a door. The unfortunate victim, rendered senseless as a result, was quickly mustered out of the army. And finally, in a further example of cruelty, this time psychological, Karstens remembered that when a man in their training unit, sent as a courier to Berlin, died in a traffic accident, the subsequent actions of their captain bordered on pathological insensitivity. The victim's buddies, while forbidden to attend the funeral, were forced to listen to their captain lament not their comrade's death but the loss of the vehicle! This heartless example of callous dehumanization left a bitterness in Karstens that the years could not erase.[37]

Similarly, Hans Werner Woltersdorf had "no time for the subservient muscle-men who acted authoritarian because they weren't authoritative. . . . There would always be those who would rely on a pose, or some injustice, intrigue, or demonstration of power to attempt to compensate for what they lacked." Woltersdorf particularly recalled "an intelligent lad with character" who had been exposed unmercifully to such harassment. Yet the young man had not only endured, but later, in combat, "had torn up his convalescent leave permit so he could get to the front." Entrusted by his commander with "a daredevil raid, . . . he led his raiding party through a mine field that went through the Russian lines, noiselessly took care of the Russian sentries, blew up an ammunition dump, and created a state of hopeless chaos so that he and his men could make their way back through the Russian lines. Going out he went first, coming back he came last; he brought all his men back in one piece, but then, just as he thought he'd made it, he stepped on a mine. . . . There was very little," concluded Woltersdorf sadly, "that got me down the way [this] tale did."[38]

Guy Sajer noted that what kept him and his comrades going in the midst of the exhausting training process was not only a desire for success but the pervasive dread of the "punishment battalion." Sajer remembered with uneasiness "a hut in the courtyard, a roof supported by four stakes, for those who retained some trace of individualism or disobedience."

> This structure was familiarly known as *Die Hundehütte* (dog house). . . . Soldiers being disciplined spent their thirty-six hours of active training like everyone else. However, at the end of this period they were led to the *Hundehütte* and chained, with their wrists behind their backs, to a heavy horizontal beam. Their eight-hour rest period would be spent in this position. . . . Soup was brought to them in one of the big tureens for eight, from which they had to lap like dogs. . . . After two or three sessions in this chalet, the wretched victim . . . lapsed into a coma, which would put a merciful end to his sufferings. . . . There was a horrible story about a fellow named Knutke, who had been to the hut six times but who still refused . . . to follow the section out for training. One day, they took the dying man to the foot of a tree and shot him. "That's what the hut leads to," everyone said. "You've got to avoid it." So, despite groans of pain, everyone marched.[39]

Here, clearly, was an illustration of murderous discipline, perpetrated by training officers who acted in a ruthless, homicidal manner. Confronted with harassment of this magnitude, a *Landser* could only hope to endure, defend himself as well as possible, and maintain his self-control.

If for some *Landsers* training marked a rite of passage to manhood, for others it was simply a bewildering time, even without the harsh exercises and petty harassment. "I have a request of you," wrote a sixteen-year-old, who had been plunged into overwhelming circumstances by the war, to his parents in late 1944. "I got my pocket knife stolen, perhaps you could get ahold of one somewhere. My suspenders are also shot, they will have to make do, but I don't know how I'm going to do it. Perhaps Uncle P. still has some. Then could you send me some writing paper, I still had some in my pack, but now it is gone. Perhaps

I'll find it again, but I hardly think so. . . . P.S.: I lost my watch." On this level, war was not ironic but concrete, full of pathos and human confusion, concern and consternation. And, as all recruits knew, combat was still to come. Some professed to be eager for action: "I would be ashamed of myself then," claimed a *Landser* from the relative comfort and safety of a *Kaserne* (barracks) in Erfurt, "if I come home and the others are all telling stories of their action." But for most, actual combat signified a giant step into an unknown world. As Guy Sajer recalled, "I didn't know what to think. What really happened on a battlefield? I felt torn by curiosity and fear."[40] Soon enough, he and millions of others would know the reality all too well.

3. Living on Borrowed Time

T oday, as I went over unprotected slopes and came under the fire of a . . . Russian heavy machine gun," wrote Harry Mielert to his wife in April 1943, "I involuntarily had to think about your observation that in war shots are fired in order to kill people. . . . Then I also had to think: the man over there . . . was after my blood and without doubt would have been happy if he had bumped me off." This amazing observation from a *Landser* who had been at the front for almost two years illustrates that combat is the goal toward which all the activities of an army are directed, yet actual battles often take place less frequently than supposed, and the number of troops on "the sharp end of war" may be only a relatively small proportion of the soldiers in an army.[1] As incredible as it seems, then, a soldier might occasionally forget the purposes for which he was trained.

For the *Landser*, combat consisted of a thousand small battles, a daily struggle for existence amid terrible confusion, fear, and suffering. Combat meant fighting in small groups, in sinister blackness or in cold, lonely bunkers, in crowded houses from room to room, on windswept steppes against steel monsters, with each unit and each man—confused men with a need for one another—fighting for their lives, longing to escape their fate, leaving a trail of torn, mutilated, and dead flesh in their wake. At the front, the *Landser* lived in a complex world, one both physically unstable and emotionally chaotic. He might spend much time in the front line as little more than an apprehensive spectator, then suddenly be thrust into the vortex of raging events. His horizon necessarily limited to the small area immediately opposite him, he rarely knew much of the larger events of the war. His daily life consisted of alternate bouts of boredom, panic, anger, fear, exultation, bewilderment, sorrow, and perhaps even courage.[2] Dreading isolation, he desperately sought community with his fellow soldiers. Above all, he saw himself not as a cog in a grand military machine but as an individual who very much wanted to survive. The *Landser* thus had a personal, if ironic, relationship to combat. He wanted to avoid death yet felt a blow to his pride if kept out of battle. Life seemed fleeting as fate, that elusive and fickle creature, teased the *Landser* by juggling events just out of his control.

"The time appears to have come. . . . We lie in front of our tents, write letters and worry a bit," Friedrich Grupe recorded in his diary of the last days before the German attack on the Soviet Union:

> The last quiet night, the night of 21 June. The noise of the motors has subsided. . . . In a wide square the battalion stands before its commander. . . . Then he reads the Führer's appeal. . . . "Soldiers of the eastern front, you are about to embark on a difficult and portentous struggle. . . ." The soldiers stand quiet and serious. For many tomorrow will be the baptism of fire; for some, the last passage . . . No one is inclined to talk.
>
> Night comes. . . . We dig in and lie in the foxholes. . . . It's almost 2:00 A.M. In little more than an hour hell will break loose.
>
> 3:00 A.M. Helmets are put on, hand grenades in the belt, rifles loaded. Everyone stares ahead, nerves outwardly strained. Then the first barrage cracks out behind us!
>
> Now the earth rumbles and shakes, before us flashes the glow of fires. . . . The time of the infantryman is here. We race forward.[3]

Although Grupe's account resonated with suppressed tension even as he tried to maintain a certain matter-of-factness about the whole business, other *Landsers* betrayed different emotions on the eve of battle: they noticed that their initial enthusiasm for the great test waned and a sickening sort of apprehension increased. Before the attack on France, Siegfried Knappe observed that among his comrades "spirits [were] quite high . . . although [we] were tired of waiting and eager to move out. If they were afraid of the prospect of combat, I could not detect it. They were joking and playing around." Still, Knappe admitted, "all the reserve officers we talked to who had experienced trench warfare during the World War were very concerned about what was going to happen."

Similarly, Wilhelm Prüller recorded in his diary just before the assault on Poland, "We're sitting on our lorries and telling dirty jokes." But as the time for actual combat neared, the tenor of his diary entries changed: "If only this waiting were over," he noted just fifteen minutes before the attack was to commence. "If only something would happen. . . . One's thoughts go in a circle, as if they wanted to turn a huge mill-stone. Everything on edge." To Wolfgang Döring the twenty-four hours before his first attack "belonged to the most unforgettable and really most stirring and beautiful of my life." Helmut Pabst, on the other hand, wrote that he had seen men before their first attack "white in the face . . . [and] trembling." The eve of initiation into battle could indeed be stifling. "The air was thick to the point of suffocation," recalled Alfred Opitz just before the assault on Russia. "It smelled of something enormous."[4]

As battle approached, many *Landsers* began to realize that something immense—a "monster that is crushing the world," as one put it—had been loosed. Apprehensive, anxious, restless, silent, withdrawn, they waited uneasily for their baptism of fire, the stress increased by the uncertainty of what was to come and the fear of their reaction to it. Once in combat, they experienced a wide range of emotions, from surprise to shock to a sense of transformation. His first encounter with the death and destruction of battle caused Harry Mielert to reflect in a letter to his wife, "We live such a strange life, so removed from all time . . . , so without law, so concerned of necessity only with our bare lives that one cannot say anything of the details." Similarly, Ernst Kleist remembered the confusion of his first battle more than anything else; he called it "ghastly" but found it "almost impossible to create a true picture of the situation. You actually understood only that it moved inexorably forward in a tempo not seen until now. . . . What can you compare it to? . . . This war is just a crazy inferno, . . . a drama of destruction." "Battle now has a property to it," Kleist decided two weeks later. "One can only just act, one can no longer think." To Kurt Reuber, war seemed "a chaos in which everything goes except customary laws," while Meinhart Freiherr von Guttenberg concluded bleakly that "war is a hemorrhage." Rudolf Halbey likewise could see in combat nothing but "chaos and screams . . . , bullets whistling . . . , orders, shots, . . . hand grenades." Even for those who escaped that swirling confusion, impressions were often limited. "Already on the second day I got my baptism of fire," wrote an anonymous soldier. "I must say, though, that I did not behave notably. [I] was pretty much totally moving around in dust and had my head stuck in that crap." This sense of bewildered detachment struck Hans-Friedrich Stäcker as well: he admitted to a certain dizziness in battle as "a hot wave of blood shot through the heart and pulled me forward."[5] For many, combat produced just such a sense of unreality, of events shrouded in a dream.

Others, however, would have agreed with Harald Henry that combat proved only too real. His first encounter with battle led him to observe that it made a "shattering impression . . . of enormous destruction." For Henry, combat produced no grand exhilaration, merely "tears of helpless rage, . . . [of] despair and pain." If Henry's baptism of fire resulted in a general sense of desolation, some recalled the gruesome face of war in more detail. "We were familiar with the dust and the smells of burned powder and gasoline from maneuvers," noted Siegfried Knappe,

> but this was our first exposure to the smell of death. . . . I learned that the smell of rotting flesh, dust, burned powder, smoke, and gasoline was the smell of combat. . . .
>
> My first sight of a dead soldier was an unexpected shock. . . . The word "killed" still had a clinical connotation about it compared to its meaning when you saw lying on the ground before you a bloodied, mutilated, foul-smelling corpse that had previously been a vital, living human being.
>
> The first dead soldiers I saw . . . lay where they had fallen, their limbs in grotesque positions, their eyes and mouths open. . . . It was devastating to realize that this was what we had to look forward to every day.[6]

The sight of the insomniac dead, lying with open, imploring eyes, staggered other men as well. "What shook me the most," agreed a *Landser* of his first days in battle, "were the first dead! They were . . . lying motionless and quiet in a roadside grave like a bunch of dead cattle. . . . We knew that now a transformation had taken place in us, that out of us soldiers men were made"—but at what cost? "What has the war made of us men!?" he agonized to his parents a few days later. "I have had to reorder myself totally . . ., and I can tell you that this transformation has been damned difficult for me. I still remember with horror and dismay how the first dead frightened me and how shattered I stood before the first graves of fallen comrades. Today after five weeks of battle . . ., you view the most terrible wounds or mutilations without batting an eyelid. . . . It certainly is true, war kills all feelings." Acknowledged another soldier, after his first encounters with death, "We are all so deadened that we are totally indifferent to everything. . . . Man is just a creature of habit," he insisted, "and gets used to everything." A callous attitude, perhaps, although one shared by other *Landsers*. "Fearfully torn bodies of Russian soldiers often lie next to [their shattered tanks]," noted Friedrich Grupe in his diary. "At first I was disturbed by this sight, then I looked away, and finally my eyes and feelings have become accustomed to this gruesome sight." "I can remember very distinctly the first deaths I encountered in the war," agreed Guy Sajer. "The thousands upon thousands which followed are blurred and faceless: a vast cumulative nightmare."[7]

A nightmare, indeed, but one often strangely veiled by the numbness that followed the initial shock of battle. Following the frenzied activity of combat, Siegfried Knappe felt "almost in a daze, from exhaustion, from excitement, and from the sudden silence following the incredible roar of combat." Since any battle comprised a swirling chaos of confusing and disconnected events, the *Landser* found himself confronted with a host of images and sensations, many of which made little or no sense. "I myself retained nothing," admitted Sajer after a battle, "but a chaotic impression of flashing lights and thunderous noises over a sense of such total disorientation that I [was] no longer capable of distinguishing east from west or up from down." As a result of this confusion, the tendency of the soldier on the front lines was to shut down and to concentrate only on those things necessary for his survival. It often proved difficult, as Sajer insisted, "even to try to remember moments during which nothing is considered, foreseen or understood, when there is nothing under a steel helmet but an astonishingly empty head and a pair of eyes which translate nothing more than would the eyes of an animal facing mortal danger." Indeed, he concluded, "It's strange how much a helmet interferes with thought."[8]

Along the same lines, Harry Mielert considered one of the worst aspects of the front to be "the mean indifference into which the immediacy of war . . . easily drags us." Mielert declared that he felt "totally removed from all immediate personal concerns; my concerns are impersonal: building positions, munitions, equipment, war material, weapons, overall the technical aspects of war. . . . That now and again comrades lie there wounded or dead belongs to everyday life just like many things at home." Neither good nor bad, death became merely a part of the ebb and flow of life at the front. "You have to go through a lot during a war, but you get hard and immune to everything," Wilhelm Prüller acknowledged. "But the front is the front. . . . There's no going soft here."[9] The horrible, the unimaginable, was absorbed into the daily routine, to which, just as at home, the average soldier accustomed himself.

Despite the novelistic and cinematic images of great hordes of men directly confronting one another, the actual battlefield often proved surprisingly inanimate, empty, and lonely. "My field of vision extends only about a hundred yards," remarked one *Landser*, "and covers approximately a hundred men." Agreed Corporal F.B., "We soldiers . . . see only a small section of the front and don't know the [larger] intentions." This limited horizon contributed to the feeling of bewilderment and abandonment that seized many *Landsers*. "The old experience of every soldier out here is again growing in me," noted Harry Mielert, "how totally alone . . . a man is placed here directly at the front." Reflecting on the savage fighting in Stalingrad in February 1943, Mielert remarked, "They are defending themselves with entrenching spades and rifle butts. When a soldier has no more ammunition he is lonely. Ammunition . . . gives him confidence and security; it also has a metaphysical impact on his heart. The other is like the struggle between wild animals." After a tough battle, Guy Sajer also expressed this sense of loneliness: "I was sick of the whole thing. My stomach was turning over and I felt cold. I looked for Hals or some other friend, but couldn't see any familiar faces. . . . Their absence weighed on me. I felt very much alone . . . trying to find some excuse for hope and encouragement."[10]

His outfit battered by a series of frightful Russian night attacks, and fearing his imminent death, Leopold von Thadden-Trieglaff composed a sorrowful letter—his last—in which he vented his feeling of being "now totally bereft, lonely, and abandoned." The bleakness he glimpsed proved prophetic: he was killed the next day. Similarly, Friedrich Andreas von Koch, not yet nineteen and destined to fall in battle within a few months, noted in April 1943, "Combat and battles are for me no special experience. It is all so profane, so impersonal." Meinhart Freiherr von Guttenberg also expressed this sense of unease, remarking after a battle, "I am unable to collect my thoughts. Everything is so desolate around me and I also feel as if it is constantly becoming desolate and empty within myself." This forlorn feeling of isolation was not uncommon, and Ernst Kleist thought he knew why. "Anxiety grips me often," he reflected, "not anxiety in the face of battle or death. But events grow so gigantic that I feel myself to be smaller than a nothing." Kleist's insight was seconded by Harry Mielert: "There are no longer any individual events anymore."[11]

Overwhelmed by the enormity of the war, plagued by a fear of being inconsequential, facing a solitary death—all these emotions intensified the feeling of existential loneliness felt by the *Landser*. Life at the front meant living on the edge of unimaginable horror and suffering. "I have lived through hell," Harald Henry remarked of an experience in October 1941 which he termed "inconceivable"; in another letter he spoke of combat as "agony without end." "Hell is seething in all its cauldrons," he opened a letter a few days later, referring to "we tormented humans" who cannot bear the suffering much longer. "Yet the last hell," he concluded, quoting Bertholt Brecht, "is never the very last."[12]

Given the agonizing nature of combat, some *Landsers* not surprisingly proved unequal to the task of describing the monstrous actualities they experienced. Helmut von Harnack attempted in a letter to his father to express the reality, but words failed him. "The picture will only really be completed," he maintained, "when the simple front fighters of this campaign come home on leave and again find the power of speech." Another soldier admitted that he would like to unburden himself, "would really like to tell you all the experiences I've participated in. But we cannot and may not write everything." Rembrand Elert tried to portray the savagery of the German retreat from Russia during the winter of 1944, faltered and then concluded, "One who was not a participant can have no conception [of what it was like]." Likewise, Wilhelm Prüller confided to his diary, "Those who haven't fought on the front don't know what war is." Whether from lack of language skills, fear of the censor, or simply because they despaired that people at home could not understand, many *Landsers* found it impossible to convey the reality of their world—even though, as Walther Weber conceded while on convalescent leave in March 1942, "these two months of the Russian winter war are an experience whose severity has been stamped into me and which stays with me."[13]

Still, despite the horrors to which they were subjected and the limited horizons of the front fighter, many soldiers provided an amazingly urgent and concrete picture of combat. For some, it seemed almost a living organism and the battlefield a startlingly personal place where danger and death prowled, always seeking more victims. As Harry Mielert remarked, "One has the impression that a wild animal is menacing us," a sensation doubly shared by Kurt Reuber, caught as he was in the Stalingrad vise: "Can you imagine an animal stalked by death," he wrote to his wife in late December 1942, "that after running for its life, thrashing about wildly, then finds itself placed in a life and death struggle." It was a struggle against stacked odds, since, as Friedrich Grupe noted of one especially menacing area of the front, "Death lurked everywhere."[14]

To be sure, a grim fate constantly threatened any front soldier. "The worst was four days ago," Mielert confessed to his wife in October 1943 of the savage fighting around Gomel,

> when I had to defend a place with four men against five . . . tanks with Russian infantry aboard, and then was ordered not to leave this position until receiving an arranged signal. It was awful. . . . I lay with the. . . . men in a forlorn post. . . . At close range we fought the infantry . . . , but the threatening steel colossi roared on past us, shooting from all barrels. . . . Amid the dust and dirt and din I saw the green star-cluster signal flare, the arranged signal that I should now withdraw. Now began a race for our lives. The tanks pursued us over two kilometers, constantly firing and blocking the way. With a rifleman I succeeded as the only ones to make it back to our own lines. The others were overrun, trampled, or shot to pieces. These minutes have extracted the last reserves from me.

Nor did that sense of being stalked, of being under personal siege, leave Mielert. "They were horrible days," he wrote two months later, just two weeks before his death. "None but the participants can understand what happened here. . . . I have been hunted as one would only hunt a wounded animal, have sat five hours in a swamp, in ice cold water up to my stomach, under continuous fire from a tank."[15]

Little wonder, then, that Mielert professed bitterly that the world had always been a cruel place. "Only now," he noted, "the wolf howls and drinks blood openly." Nor did he leave any doubt as to who the wolves were. "We have bitten our way through," he observed. "In the process we have acquired hard teeth." Hard indeed; in dispassionate tones, Mielert said of street fighting in Russia, "The city is burning. In the market square stand a pair of tanks that are shooting wildly in all directions. We wait until they have no ammunition left, then 'crack' them. We threw the penetrating Russian infantry back into the cold river. Only a few saved themselves. We are pitiless. Now it is just as comfortable, as romantic, as it is dangerous here." Pitilessly, dangerously romantic, men stalking other men in a perilous contest of chance where only death proved triumphant. As Mielert and most other *Landsers* knew, "the luck of war swung daily . . . [as] every second determined our being."[16]

In this game of chance perhaps nothing seemed so terrifying or personally dangerous as having to go on night patrol behind enemy lines. After one of the seemingly endless night skirmishes with the Russians, Claus Hansmann and his comrades sat in their foxholes, regrouping, taking notice of who had been killed and wounded, when the dreaded happened. "Above on the embankment appeared a shadow. It is Karl. 'You Claus,' he whispered furiously. '[We] have to go forward to fetch the Lieutenant [who had been killed]. . . . Three Pioneers are also going out to look for a flame thrower that's lying out there. The commander also thinks it's nonsense, but it's orders from battalion.' "[17] In the sardonic jargon of the *Landser*, Hansmann had just been ordered on a *Himmelfahrtskommando* (trip to heaven) or suicide mission in order to engage in a little *Knochensammlung* (bone gathering) of dead comrades.

Weary, fearful, and staggering under the burden of lonely despair, Hansmann nonetheless stole out into the sinister night:

> I creep forward. Lightly veiled moon. . . . The others wait in the shadow of the houses. A last cigarette, hasty puffs, we speak to each other softly. . . . "Nah, it makes no sense, but let's go . . . !"
>
> Slowly we slip through the grass fresh with dew. . . . Singly, we creep past a bare spot, then we reach the clover field. . . . The heavy silence is suspicious, oppressive. Finally some bursts of fire in the distance. . . . Dear God, all of this for a dead lieutenant and a shot-up flamethrower. The moon suddenly peeks out of the edge of a cloud. We lie petrified with pounding hearts. . . . In front of us, perhaps forty meters . . . , we hear voices. A couple of Russians are conversing, . . . , then two Russians come hunched out of a trench towards us. They must discover us! In a split second the hopelessness of this undertaking dawns on us: If we actually find the corpse, how are we supposed to bring it back through the enemy lines? Crawling, we could hardly hold onto the dead guy, and finally, he is in fact dead . . . ! Therefore, the only salvation: hand grenades! The first, then others: explosions, crashes, screams. . . .
>
> We quickly throw what we have and take to our heels, simultaneously shooting in short bursts. . . . We race along, whistling bullet bursts overtake us, behind us their impact. Then finally our bunkers. Everyone unhurt? The last one slides into the trench. Nothing happened. O.K., good night.[18]

Nothing happened—not physically, at least—but patrols such as these appeared to the *Landser* a taunt directed at good fortune and his personal well-being, as each feared the vulnerability, isolation, and helplessness of being exposed in no-man's-land, the psychological torture of being suspended between security and danger, with only the blackness of the night as a comfort.

Leopold von Thadden-Trieglaff illustrated well that sense of having, during combat, an intimate relationship with death. "I am standing before the door of heaven and wait outside to see Ernst-Dietrich [his fallen brother]," he wrote in March 1943. "The most terrible night and the hardest battle of my life lay behind me. . . . During the night the enemy attacked us in a width of six kilometers with overwhelming strength . . . [and] broke through on my right flank. . . . I myself dashed forward in order to direct the firefight. . . . I knew that must mean death for me, but God stood next to me. They were terrible, indescribable minutes until I was able to gather thirteen men and place them in a hole in the ground that was supposed to be a bunker." But Thadden-Trieglaff's personal torture had barely begun. "Deep darkness," he noted of the sinister night.

> The cries of "Hurrah" from almost all sides by the attacking Russians; shouts, screams, . . . withering fire. . . . We dished it out to the mass of Russians who had penetrated the position on my right . . . [and] answered their cries of "Hurrah" with mocking shouts. . . . We stood like oaks with the consciousness of impending death.
>
> Finally at 2:30 A.M. the enemy broke through on my left. . . . We knew that . . . we were now completely destitute, isolated, and deserted. . . .
>
> We held out through the night. I knew that Captain M. would get tanks through to me and haul me out. . . . In the meantime, I had the first wounded in the small band. The first-aid packets were soon used up. I felt so sorry for the poor fellows. . . . With morning the situation became even more frightening.[19]

Frightening indeed, for with the first light the Russian assault would inevitably resume. "As the morning dawned . . . a hail of fire rained on us, from right, from left," confirmed Thadden-Trieglaff. "In a few minutes our bunker was full of wounded and I struggled to quiet the poor fellows. . . . Screams and groans, and singing. I had to strain every nerve in order to remain as calm as before. . . . In this moment of deepest despair . . . I discovered that the neighboring company . . . had withdrawn. . . . I myself sat about six hundred meters behind the present Russian lines. . . . Had they given up on us?" In a moment of anguish and despair Thadden-Trieglaff feared that he and his men had been abandoned to a harsh fate. But no: "About 6:00 A.M. . . . finally German 'Hurrahs' were to be heard. German tank motors roared; German machine gun fire and flak guns resounded. . . . We were rescued . . . ! As I returned to my command post in the village I gaped at the dead comrades. I was so shaken that I almost cried. . . . When might this hideous defensive struggle come to an end? When will spring finally come? Deep snow, daily radiant sunshine. . . . At night it is icy cold in this wretched region. We struggle to get into the ground."[20] For the twenty-year-old Thadden-Trieglaff the appalling fighting and his ironic struggle to get into the ground came to an end all too soon. He was killed the next day.

Combat could be an amazingly personal and lonely experience. In the latter stages of the war, German recruits were taught to destroy a Russian tank by letting it roll over their foxholes and attaching a magnetic mine as it passed, or by emerging and firing a shot into the tank's rear with a *Panzerfaust*. In theory, most efficient; in practice, potentially agonizing. "The first group of T-34's crashed through the undergrowth," recalled one *Landser* of such an incident:

> I heard my officer shout to me to take the right hand machine. . . .
> All that I had learned in the training school suddenly came flooding back and gave me confidence. . . . It had been planned that we should allow the first group of T-34's to roll over us. . . . The grenade had a safety cap which had to be unscrewed to reach the rip-cord. My fingers were trembling as I unscrewed the cap . . . [and] climbed out of the trench. . . . Crouching low I started towards the monster, pulled the detonating cord, and prepared to fix the charge. I had now nine seconds before the grenade exploded and then I noticed, to my horror, that the outside of the tank was covered in concrete. . . . My bomb could not stick on such a surface. . . . The tank suddenly spun on its right track, turned so that it pointed straight at me and moved forward as if to run over me.
>
> I flung myself backwards and fell straight into a partly dug slit trench and so shallow that I was only just below the surface of the ground. Luckily I had fallen face upwards and was still holding tight in my hand the sizzling hand grenade. As the tank rolled over me there was a sudden and total blackness. . . . The shallow earth walls of the trench began to collapse. As the belly of the monster passed over me I reached up instinctively as if to push it away and . . . stuck the charge on the smooth, unpasted metal. . . . Barely

had the tank passed over me than there was a loud explosion. . . . I was alive and the Russians were dead. I was trembling in every limb.[21]

For Guy Sajer, too, the intimate nature of battle resonated vividly, with soldiers shouting personal oaths at each other in the heat of the moment. "The Russians pressed their attack, bringing on their tanks, " he remembered. "Our cries of distress were mingled with the screams of the two machine gunners and then the shouts of revenge from the Russian tank crew as it drove over the hole, grinding the remains of the two gunners into that hateful soil. . . . The treads worked over the hole for a long time, and . . . the Russian crew kept shouting, 'Kaputt, Soldat Germanski! Kaputt!' " Surveying a battlefield, Claus Hansmann noted not only the familiar scenes of carnage, "the horse corpses smothered in a flood of blood, the broken wheels, shattered shafts, . . . widely strewn mountains of munitions of all calibers, weapons," but also something more hauntingly personal: "the laundry and the pitiful personal effects of the dead thrown into the swamp. Yellowed prints of family photos and the faded ink trails of letters once written with warm hearts, primitive shaving gear and the tragic still-life of mementos become impersonal spill out of the packs and pockets of unknown men. In a muddy tide the water laps over wetly glistening carcasses and washes blood from the corpses."[22]

If Sajer and Hansmann depicted the personal horror of combat, Wilhelm Prüller recorded an episode that conveyed the presense of the absurd in battle. "The C.O.'s jeep . . . got stuck again," he noted. "As the driver was trying to decide how to get the jeep going, he saw that the car was sitting over a hole out of which the barrel of an enemy trench mortar was protruding. He had to leave the jeep and saved himself only by galloping like a wild boar over the numerous Russian holes, each one full of Russians and well camouflaged. It is," Prüller concluded with some understatement, "a nice story." Fighting his way into Kursk in November 1941, Prüller found a more personal danger, now far from funny: "Every second a bullet wings past us. You never know where it comes from. Pressed flat against the house walls, bent down, your gun ready to shoot, your grenade in the other hand, you creep along." But a month later Prüller chronicled an incident in which a Russian tank "play[ed] hide and seek around the house corners with our men."[23]

Bernhard Beckering too noted the often ludicrous nature of personal experiences of combat. "The villages in which we were located were attacked. During the rescue of the American wounded we were attacked in an open field from the air by four [American] machines. This opaque muddle is almost comical." Absurd, yet for others, like Prüller, there were also daily reminders of the very dangerous small war within the larger struggle. "Once we took fire from all sides," recalled Werner Paulsen of an intensely personal moment. "In front of us. Behind us. It rang out everywhere. . . . We absolutely didn't know where the firing came from. . . . Where was it best to run . . . ? I ran into a cornfield and there I remained lying. . . . I heard only Russian [voices]. . . . When it was dark I . . . crawled back. . . . toward the road. . . . I was totally alone there. The next day Germans came. Tanks came driving down the road. And then I hopped aboard these tanks." It was an intimate and ominous brush with death: from Paulsen's platoon of fifty men, only four returned.[24]

Hans Werner Woltersdorf had a similar experience of being the prey in a deadly game of cat and mouse. Cut off with five other men by a Russian attack near Zhitomir on the day before Christmas 1943, Woltersdorf's squad groped its way through dense woods searching desperately for a way back to German lines. Emerging from the woods, Woltersdorf noticed "open terrain, farmland, and after that, a good kilometer away, a village. . . . Who occupied it? Our troops, surely. . . . We had no choice but to go over the open terrain. . . . After fifty meters the first shot was fired. We darted from side to side, and they shot at us as if it were a rabbit hunt. . . . Fifty meters ahead of us . . . was a ditch, a life-saving ditch!" Although his men reached the ditch one had been hit in the ankle by Russian fire. Dragging the wounded man along, Woltersdorf struggled through the thick muck. "Was this to be my end?" he wondered. "I imprinted the date of my death in my mind. . . . I aimed a couple of shots at the group [of Russians] . . . and drove them under cover. . . . Only fifty meters up ahead our ditch led into a cross-ditch, which was wider, deeper, and filled with brown water."

They reached the deeper ditch, but the Russians kept advancing. At the point of giving up, Woltersdorf glimpsed a speck in the distance. "It was neither a tank nor a lorry, it was much too fast. It was a private car, a German one. . . . A hundred meters more. We got ready to jump. Forty meters more. Now we jumped on to the road, holding our submachine guns in front of us. The driver stopped. . . . 'For God's sake, don't do anything stupid,' he cried, 'jump in; they're coming.' " Shaken but alive, Woltersdorf reflected on his luck with the god of war: "In the following days, more than sixty men returned in similarly bizarre fashions; the rest . . . , those who had sat and sung and laughed, sitting on the wall of the Tude bridge—."[25] Left unspoken, Woltersdorf knew what the fate of the remainder had been. The real war was deeply personal, as each *Landser* fighting his own lonely battle understood.

On yet another occasion, Woltersdorf experienced again that sense of battlefield intimacy, of war reduced to isolated combat between individuals. "We had grown used to destroying tanks in close combat," he noted, but on this occasion the destruction proved intensely personal:

> We sneaked up to it through the wood from behind. . . . My heart was pounding. . . . I climbed carefully onto the tank from behind and approached the hatch cover. . . . Damn! How did one get the cover open? I braced myself against the turret with my thighs and tore at the cover until I realized that a bolt was fastened with a padlock.
>
> So the crew was locked in. . . . They were riding in a sealed coffin. . . . I quickly withdrew my thigh from the close-combat opening and held firmly to the disc that closed it. Now what . . . ? My hand grenade was too thick to fit through the hole.
>
> Then I thought of my flare pistol. . . . Carefully I inserted the muzzle of the flare pistol into the hole. . . . Very quickly: muzzle in. They fired immediately, but I had the pistol out again already. . . . They were shouting, loud commands and shrill cries of fear. . . . Then there was a fearful thunderclap. . . . The turret rose a few centimeters, tilted to one side, and came crashing down. . . . I couldn't get the men from the Moscow tank brigade out of my head. What a drama must have been played out in their coffin![26]

That same sense of a private struggle pervaded the thoughts of a German lieutenant fighting in Stalingrad:

> We have fought during fifteen days for a single house, with mortars, grenades, machine-guns and bayonets. Already by the third day fifty-four German corpses are strewn in the cellars, on the landings, and the staircases. The front is a corridor between burnt-out rooms; it is the thin ceiling between two floors. . . . There is a ceaseless struggle from noon to night. From story to story, faces black with sweat, we bombard each other with grenades in the middle of explosions, clouds of dust and smoke . . ., floods of blood, fragments of . . . human beings. Ask any soldier what half an hour

of hand-to-hand struggle means in such a fight. . . . The street is no longer measured by meters but by corpses. . . .

Stalingrad is no longer a town. By day it is an enormous cloud of burning, blinding smoke; it is a vast furnace lit by the reflection of the flames. And when night arrives, one of those scorching, howling, bleeding nights, the dogs plunge into the Volga and swim desperately to gain the other bank. The nights of Stalingrad are a terror for them. Animals flee this hell, . . . only men endure.[27]

Only men persisted; the savagery of combat led twenty-year-old Hans-Heinrich Ludwig to a similar judgment: "Man is so tough," he concluded a letter simply; no elaboration was necessary.[28]

In these accounts one gets a sense of combat as a deeply private experience, as an individual encounter with life, fate, and suffering in the spaces that the larger war failed to fill. Battle could make a *Landser* feel forlorn and abandoned, with little but his weapon and his few comrades to comfort him. Many fought, indeed, with a quiet expectation of death. As Friedrich Leonhard Martius wrote despairingly from the eastern front, "We are still in our wolf's den and some of us go out daily: weapons and iron for a mighty struggle against flesh and hearts." Mused Max Aretin-Eggert, "The individual will always be consumed more and more by the war and the organizational machine. But even in this process of consumption there lies an unimaginable performance by our troops."[29] In a struggle that was personal to the end, some soldiers saw themselves as men with a trade, and in a strange way they were proud of it.

If some men functioned to the rhythm of the deadly machine, remote from anything but the need to feed it, they could not outlast it. For many *Landsers*, therefore, the defining characteristic of combat was its elemental destructiveness. "At 4.00 alarm is sounded," recounted Wilhelm Prüller of one of the many Russian assaults in December 1941:

Supported by artillery, the Russians attack to the north of the railway. . . . I place [my] Platoon between the houses and spread out the carbines. . . . One MG (machine gun) is to shoot continually at the Russians lying in front of us . . . to keep them from advancing. The other MG's and all those with carbines are to go into position. I shall have a white Verey light shot up, and in that moment we shall aim and shoot with all our various weapons. . . . For 9 seconds it's like broad daylight, you can see the whole ground in front of us. . . . My boys are already shooting like mad. . . .

Slowly it gets light and now the enemy is lying in front of us on a silver plate. . . . I yell at the top of my lungs to the Russians: . . . "Hands up! Surrender!" One by one the hands go up. . . .

The prisoners are herded together into a house, but there aren't as many as we'd expected. When we return, we discover the reason: the many enemy dead still there. All shot through the head. . . . Some of the dead are still burning, set on fire by our Verey lights. Then we start counting: . . . 150 dead.[30]

Ferocious slaughter defined combat for a terrified Guy Sajer as well. "We were going to be part of a full-scale attack," he remembered of the German assault at Belgorad in the spring of 1943. "A heavy sense of foreboding settled over us, and the knowledge that soon some of us would be dead was stamped on every face. . . . All of us were haunted by so many thoughts that conversation was impossible. . . . Sleep was [also] impossible . . . because of our anxiety about what lay ahead." Apprehension and uncertainty preceded the battle, yet this was not the first experience of combat for these men. But as Sajer well knew, no one got used to traversing that thin line between life and death. Indeed, when cold steel could crack skulls like eggshells, the consuming passion was to dig deep into the ground—yet out they went into the night. "Our brains emptied, as if we had been anesthetized," he noted. "Everyone grabbed his gun and, . . . sticking close together, followed the trench to the forward positions. . . . We moved out in good order, exactly as we'd been taught. . . . One by one, we left the last German positions, and crawled out onto the warm earth of no man's land. . . . During such moments, even naturally reflective characters suddenly feel their heads emptying, and nothing seems to matter."[31]

Training, the comfort of a learned routine, enabled Sajer and his buddies to stifle their fear and negotiate their way into no-man's-land. Still, no amount of training could adequately prepare a young man for the elemental terror of combat, the awful loneliness of confronting the hidden gun that lay ahead. "Our immediate surroundings . . . were shaken by a series of thunderous explosions," Sajer recalled. "For a minute we thought that the whole mass of creeping soldiers we had seen just the minute before had been blown to pieces. Everywhere. . . . young men were jumping up and trying to rush through the tangles of barbed wire. . . . I could see what was happening only with the greatest difficulty. . . . Through the . . . smoke, we were able to observe the horrible impact of our projectiles on the lost mass of Red soldiers in the trench in front of us."[32]

Despite the chaos and confusion, Sajer had a vivid impression of how delicate even the bodies of tough men were, how they could be torn to raw chunks in a flash:

> A huge tank rolled over the ground . . . which was overflowing with the bodies of Russian soldiers. Then a second and a third tank plunged through the bloody paste, and rolled on, their treads stuck with horrible human remnants. Our noncom gave an involuntary cry of horror at the sight [of] . . . this foul reality. . . .
>
> It is difficult even to try to remember moments . . . when there is nothing under a steel helmet but . . . a pair of eyes which translate nothing more than would the eyes of an animal facing mortal danger. There is nothing but the rhythm of explosions . . . and the cries of madmen. . . . And there are the cries of the wounded, of the agonizingly dying, shrieking as they stare at a part of their body reduced to pulp. . . . There are the tragic, unbelievable visions . . .: guts splattered across the rubble and sprayed from one dying man onto another; tightly riveted machines ripped like the belly of a cow which has just been sliced open, flaming and groaning; trees broken into tiny fragments. . . . And then there are the cries of officers and noncoms, trying to shout across the cataclysm to regroup their sections and companies.
>
> The battle was not yet over, and the extreme tension it generated was almost unbearable. . . . During our advance, we crossed a frightful slaughtering ground. . . . Each step made us realize with fresh horror what could become of our miserable flesh. . . . We [encountered] an open-air hospital . . . from which the shrieks and groans came so thick and fast it sounded like a scalding room for pigs. We were staggered by what we saw. I thought I would faint. . . . We crossed the enclosure with our eyes fixed on the sky, seeing as if in a dream young men howling with pain, with crushed forearms or gaping abdominal wounds, staring with incomprehension at their own guts.[33]

As with many other soldiers (Heinz Küchler claimed, "The pictures that you see border on delusions and nightmares"), the horrible scenes produced in Sajer a sense of unreality, but it was a nightmare that refused to end:

> The Russians began a bombardment of unprecedented ferocity. Everything became opaque, and the sun vanished from our eyes. . . . Screams of fear froze in our constricted throats. . . .

Suddenly a human figure crashed into our hole . . . [and] shouted to us . . . : "My whole company was wiped out. . . .!" He carefully lifted his head just over the edge of the embankment as a series of explosions began to rip through the air beside us. His helmet and a piece of his head were sent flying, and he fell backward, with a horrifying cry. His shattered skull crashed into Hals's hands, and we were splattered with blood and fragments of flesh. Hals threw the revolting cadaver as far as he could, and buried his face in the dirt. Nothing remains for those who have survived such an experience but a sense of uncontrollable imbalance, and a sharp, sordid anguish. . . . We felt like lost souls, who had forgotten that men are made for something else.[34]

Sajer and his comrades had been into the realm of death, had smelled death, had witnessed firsthand the promiscuous, wholesale, anonymous death that accompanied combat, and it was an experience forever stamped into their being. Others, too, attested to the extravagant horrors, to what Wilhelm Prüller termed the "revoltingly wonderful" nature of warfare. Following a pitched battle with Russian tanks, Hans Woltersdorf noted, "Now we finally had the opportunity to take a look at the tank that only a shot in the track had stopped. Had the first grenades not pierced it? Indeed, they had. The men looked into the tank, and they were near vomiting, so they didn't look further but instead went away, embarrassed. A headless torso, bloody flesh, and intestines were sticking to the walls. . . . It wasn't good to look into the tank. . . . One always sees oneself sticking to the walls in a thousand pieces like that, without a head."[35] It was not good to look at, or to think too much about such sights, yet the distressing reality of combat intruded constantly. "Next to us barked the shots of another anti-tank gun," Friedrich Grupe recorded in his diary of the abhorrent events all around. "The column divided, Russian soldiers sprang out of the trucks, were caught by the bursts of the machine guns, often remained hanging between the running board and the ground, burning bodies fell out of the vehicles." And after a second skirmish: "In the roadside graves lie mountains of dead. . . . We discover completely charred corpses." Another encounter left Grupe virtually numb as he viewed the tormented postures of the dead, left as a thousand bloody rags. "The remaining [Russians] we saw lying there when it became light," he wrote with an uncomfortable sense of foreboding, "mowed down by our machine guns in long rows on a sled path, a whole company. . . . Man after man they lie mute and rigid. We swallow

silently at this picture of horror." Spring was blooming, Grupe concluded, "but death triumphed here."[36]

Harry Mielert recounted a "strange occurrence" to his wife in a
letter in March 1943, only a small incident but one that well expressed
the malignant atmosphere, the revulsion felt by many at the madness of
battle:

> In the last great mass attack on our position . . . a village in front of
> our main battle line was totally destroyed and all the cellars, which
> the Russians had defended stubbornly, were blown up. . . . Our
> combat outposts are now in the aforementioned village. . . . A cellar
> entrance appeared in the melting snow and a *Landser* . . . went inside
> and found four dead Russians. While he was attempting to turn two
> of them on their sides . . . , two of the dead rose up. . . . [They]
> groaned and with difficulty raised their hands. They were brought
> into the light of day, where they [told us] . . . the following: After
> the attack these four had crept into the cellar. German soldiers threw
> hand grenades inside. . . . Two men were killed by the hand gre-
> nades, these two wounded. They fed themselves on the potatoes
> which lay there by the hundreds. In this way they held out four
> weeks, together with two dead bodies, their own excretion, their
> feet . . . frozen, and yet they still wouldn't venture out.

The anonymous terror, at least for a moment, had again been personal-
ized, but Mielert tried to no avail to gain an insight into the nature of the
abhorrent. "We tried in vain to glean some impressions from them," he
noted. "What they said was: cold and tired." So common, so profane, so
human. With disappointment, Mielert concluded merely, "You can see
from this example what humans can withstand."[37] The deeper malignity
of combat eluded even so reflective a soldier as Mielert. Here suffering
seemed merely banal and sordid, not sweet or heroic. Perhaps the only
real lesson to be learned was that even in the midst of war's cruelties,
life went on.

During the winter battles of 1941–1942 and again in the scorched
earth retreat out of Russia, the *Landser* clung stubbornly to life amid
devastation on a scale difficult to imagine. "It is not possible to give an
impression of these ghostly weeks," wrote Günter von Scheven in the
midst of the bitter fighting of February 1942. "The horrors I have gone
through hammer at me in my sleep." Echoed Werner Pott, less than two
weeks after the Soviet counteroffensive in front of Moscow, "For weeks
we've been in action without let-up or rest, day after day. . . . marching

in snow storms at -25 C, frozen noses and feet that make you want to scream when you have to take your boots off, filth, vermin, and other such unedifying things. . . . Next to all the personal exertions I feel sorry for the civilian population whose houses have been set afire in our retreat and who have been abandoned to famine. The complete cruelty of the war is obvious!"[38]

Everything, even the earth, seemed to be burning. "We ride into the uncertain night that is filled with the droning of motors," noted Helmut Pabst in August 1942 while on the move toward the Volga. "The earth shudders under powerful blows, incendiary bombs glitter . . ., violent flashes in the darkness. . . . The scene is framed with continually changing crescents of trembling flares: 'Here we are comrades, here we are!' That is the mute cry of the outermost limits that has something strangely unreal about it. We ride toward this frontier . . ., amid the ruins of the dead city in which only the fire lives with its insipid, sweet smell." Six months later, retreating back across the Volga, that river of fate, Pabst painted a picture of bleak and still fiery destruction: "In the streets yawn gaping holes. . . . The flames beat red in the hollows of a stone building, powerfully they shoot through the roof. The area has become desolate in these days: houses and spires, the last milestones, stand no more. . . . Flashes twitch behind us and fill the space from horizon to horizon. The muffled detonations roll back to us. It is a drama of horribly beautiful power." In this "landscape of horror and death" the completeness of the destruction stunned even hardened veterans such as Pabst, who admitted that what he witnessed "was only a part of the destruction, a laughably small part." As another *Landser* wrote in March 1943, "Today we had to take all of [the males] from the village that were left behind last time. . . . You can imagine the wailing of the women as even the children were taken from them. . . . Three houses in a village were set on fire by us, and a woman burned to death as a result. So it will be uniformly along the front in all the villages. . . . It was a fantastic sight for the eye to behold, as far as you could see, only burning villages."[39]

It was an example of the wanton cruelty and destruction, added to the horrors of battle, that accompanied the *Wehrmacht* in Russia. Christopher Browning has pointed out that for the average German in Eastern Europe, the mass murder policies of the Nazi regime were hardly exceptional or aberrational but a routine part of everyday life. "A partisan group blew up our vehicles," noted Private H.M., a member of an intelligence unit, "[and] . . . shot the agricultural administrator and a corporal assigned to him in their quarters. . . . Early yesterday morning 40 men were shot on the edge of the city. . . . Naturally there were a number of innocent people who had to give up their lives. . . . One didn't waste a lot of time on this and just shot the ones who happened to be around."[40] Such executions occurred almost daily. Claus Hansmann has left a remarkably vivid image of an execution of Soviet partisans:

"In a gray, war-torn street in Kharkov. Agitated, expectant faces in pale misery. Businesslike, the men of the field police emerge and tie with oft-practiced skill seven nooses on the balcony railing and then disappear behind the door of the dark room. . . . The first human package, tied up, is carried outside. The limbs are tightly bound . . ., a cloth covers his face. The hemp neckband is placed around his neck, hands are tied tight, he is put on the balustrade and the blindfold is removed from his eyes. For an instant you see glaring eyeballs, like those of an escaped horse, then wearily he closes his eyelids, almost relaxed, never to open them again. He now slides slowly downward, his weight pulls the noose tight, his muscles begin their hopeless battle. The body works mightily, twitches, and within the fetters a bit of life struggles to its end. It's quick; one after the other are brought out, put on the railing. . . . Each one bears a placard on his chest proclaiming his crime. . . .: Partisans and just punishment. . . . Sometimes one of them sticks out his tongue as if in unconscious mockery and immoderate amounts of spittle drip down on the street. . . . Then a few laugh, jokes meant to reach those yet above.[41]

And why this seemingly callous reaction? "You are pleased at the death of another," explained Hansmann, certainly aware of a soldier's relief that the gods of war had passed him by this time. "You laugh, an unexpected little play . . . , laugh somehow relieved." And then it is over. What next? "The dead are boring," Hansmann mused. "They accuse the living only in silent reproach. The streets become empty. The people move on, you turn toward the market square, in order to buy onions and garlic. You have shown them the last bit of attention, you are hungry!" A sudden human drama, a bit of diversion, and then off to eat: a commonplace sequence in the everyday life of war. As Hansmann observed elsewhere, "In death all are the same. . . . Equally stiff, equally silent, and the same clods of earth weigh heavily on them."[42]

Not all the men took such occurrences for granted, however. "At the moment I am experiencing horrible days," wrote Lieutenant A.B. of railroad construction company 115 in October 1942. "Every day 30 of my prisoners die, or I must allow them to be shot. It is certainly a picture of cruelty. . . . The prisoners, only partially clothed, partly without coats, could no longer get dry. The food is not sufficient, and so they collapse one after the other. . . . When one sees what a human life really means, then an inner transformation in your own thinking happens. A bullet, a word, and a life is no more. What is a human life?" In the war in Russia, certainly, precious little.[43]

The burden of atrocity weighed even more heavily on other *Landsers* because of an inner recognition of the brutality of their own actions. "The world has seen many great, even violent wars," despaired Kurt Vogeler, "but probably at no time in its existence has there been a war that can be compared with this current one in Eastern Europe. . . . The poor, unhappy Russian people! Its distress is unspeakable and its misery heart-rending. . . . This era . . . knows nothing more of humanity. Brutal power is the characteristic of our century. . . . What an unfortunate war is this human slaughter in Eastern Europe! A crime against humanity!" Similarly, Heinz Küchler shuddered at the brutality of the Russian war, where "all evidence of humanity appears to have disappeared in deed and in heart and in conscience." In response to complaints from home about the destruction of German cities, Johannes Huebner tellingly replied from Russia, "Death is the wages of sin." Harry Mielert shared the sentiment: "The quintessence appears to me to be that there is a punishment for a person . . . who does evil to others." Private L.B. merely issued a stark warning. "None," he wrote, "will remain unpunished by this war, each will get his just desert, in the homeland as at the front."[44]

In the heat of battle, however, at the moment of wild release and furious excitement, some atrocities seemed almost natural acts. In a crisis of battle, the collapse of one side into fear and panic seemed to goad men to commit brutalities; sensing weakness and fear on the other side apparently provoked some into an enraged ruthlessness. Guy Sajer recalled that following a failed Russian attack in which a number of his comrades had been killed and mutilated,

> the sound of firing and the groans of the wounded incited us to massacre the Russians. . . . An attacking army is always more enthusiastic than an army on the defensive. . . .
>
> Much later that night we witnessed a tragedy that froze my blood. . . . A prolonged and penetrating cry rose from the hole on my left. . . . Then there was a cry for help. . . .

We arrived at the edge of a foxhole, where a Russian, who had just thrown down his revolver, was holding his hands in the air. At the bottom of the hole, two men were fighting. One of them, a Russian, was waving a large cutlass, holding a man from our group pinned beneath him. Two of us covered the Russian who had raised his hands, while a young *Obergefreiter* (corporal) jumped into the hole and struck the other Russian a blow on the back of his neck with a trenching tool. . . . The German who had been under him . . . ran up to ground level. He was covered with blood, brandishing the Russian knife with one hand . . . while with the other he tried to stop the flow of blood pouring from his wound.

"Where is he?" he shouted in a fury. "Where's the other one?" In a few bounding steps he reached the . . . prisoner. Before anyone could do anything, he had run his knife into the belly of the petrified Russian.[45]

"It isn't easy to kill a man in cold blood," Sajer concluded on another occasion, after having shot a partisan face to face, "unless one is entirely heartless or, as I was, numb with fear." Indeed, it almost seemed that acts of cruelty performed in the midst of personal fury were necessary for one's own well-being, to purge the constant fear and "refresh" oneself psychologically. Atrocities often took place under conditions of severe physical and psychological strain. After three days of nearly continuous battle during which they had witnessed scenes of unimaginable horror and brutality and had had virtually no sleep, Sajer and his group "were so exhausted that we stood up only when our fire had subdued the isolated and hopeless resistance from some entrenched hole," he recollected.

Sometimes one or two prisoners might emerge from their hideout with their hands in the air, and each time the same tragedy repeated itself. Kraus killed four of them on the lieutenant's orders; the Sudeten two; Group 17, nine. Young Lindberg, who had been in a state of panic ever since the beginning of the offensive, and who had been either weeping in terror or laughing in hope, took Kraus's machine gun and shoved two Bolsheviks into a shell hole. The two wretched victims . . . kept imploring his mercy. . . . But Lindberg, in a paroxysm of uncontrollable rage, kept firing until they were quiet. . . .

We were mad with harassment and exhaustion. . . . We were forbidden to take prisoners. . . . We knew that the Russians didn't

take any, . . . [that] it was either them or us, which is why my friend
Hals and I threw grenades . . . at some Russians who were trying to
wave a white flag.

Extreme exhaustion, the strain of seeing their friends killed, and simple
fear all combined to cause young men to commit actions that under less
trying circumstances would have revolted them. As the battle came to an
end, Sajer admitted,

> we began to grasp what had happened. . . . We tried to blot out the
> memory of the. . . . tanks driving heavily over that moving mass of
> human flesh. . . . We suddenly felt gripped by something horrible,
> which made our skins crawl. . . . For me, these memories produced
> a loss of physical sensation, almost as if my personality had split, . . .
> because I knew that such things don't happen to young men who
> have led normal lives. . . .
> "We really were shits to kill those Popovs . . . ," [Hals said].
> He was clearly desperately troubled by the same things that
> troubled me. . . . "[That's] how it is, and all there is," I answered. . . .
> Something hideous had entered our spirits, to remain and haunt us
> forever.[46]

In this instance, human beings had responded to the overweening
pressure of war with spontaneous acts of violence they later regretted.
Almost certainly, however, the great majority of atrocities resulted from
the ideological nature of the war in Russia, from deliberate action on the
part of German authorities and their executioners, the ordinary men of
the German police forces and army. In an order issued in May 1941, even
before the German attack on the Soviet Union, Field Marshall Wilhelm
Keitel, the titular head of the German armed forces (OKW), stressed that
the upcoming campaign was to be a war against the Jews and Bolsheviks
and that the *Wehrmacht* should move ruthlessly against these alleged
enemies of Germany. To arouse the necessary ardor, he absolved soldiers
from the jurisdiction of military courts if they should engage in atrocities
against Russian civilians, and he approved measures of "collective
reprisal." As Christopher Browning has noted, the order amounted to a
license to kill, a license that was renewed by the infamous *Nacht und
Nebel* (Night and Fog) decree of December 1941, also issued by Keitel.[47]

The average *Landser*, moreover, betrayed little sense of shock or
outrage at such orders. The world was seething with death, and its
proximity evidently stifled many a soldier's compassion. War became a

job, casual labor, common work, and whom or how one killed didn't seem to make a great difference. Furthermore, the rank and file of the *Wehrmacht* were probably more thoroughly Nazified than has heretofore been acknowledged; indeed, average *Landsers* were consistently among Hitler's strongest supporters. As a consequence, their letters and diaries disclose, there existed among the troops in Russia such a striking level of agreement with the Nazi regime's view of the Bolshevik enemy and the sort of treatment that should be dealt them that many soldiers willingly participated in murderous actions.[48]

"As a rule, the Russian prisoners were used to bury the dead," noted Guy Sajer, "but it seemed they had taken to robbing the bodies. . . . In fact, I think the poor fellows . . . were probably going over the bodies for something to eat. The rations we gave them were absurd. . . . On some days, they were given nothing but water. Every prisoner caught robbing a German body was immediately shot. There were no official firing squads for these executions. An officer would simply shoot the offender on the spot." This sort of casual cruelty was repeated endlessly throughout the vast expanse of Russia. "Once in winter," remembered Max Landowski, "a [Russian] deserter came over. He was well clothed. . . . He had felt boots, . . . a Steppe coat, and a good fur hat. And as the deserter stood there, we began to take an interest in his things. Someone took the hat away from him, another pulled his boots off, a third needed his coat. In fact, the fellow finally stood there only in his underwear. Then the lieutenant said he should be taken back for interrogation. . . . A short time later there was a bang, and then the [German] came back. He reported, 'Order carried out.' He had shot him." "We're drawing ever closer to Moscow," wrote Private H. in July 1941. "Everywhere there is the same picture of destruction. . . . All of whatever Commissars etc. [sic] are taken prisoner or grabbed are shot immediately. The Russians don't do it any differently. A cruel war here."[49] Cruel indeed, but the noteworthy aspect was not the savagery of the war, but rather the commonplace attitude displayed by this soldier. "We take some prisoners, we shoot them, all in a day's work": this outlook recurred frequently in the *Landsers'* correspondence, betraying an unspoken agreement with Nazi ideological goals.

"Someone has totally persuaded . . . the Russians that the Germans were slaughtering all prisoners," Captain F.M. of the Seventy-third Infantry Division wrote incredulously, "and they also believed it." But why shouldn't the Russians believe it? After all, as Private A.V. admitted in a letter, "sometimes we also see someone who has been hanged. Those are people who have violated the property of the army or who hung around in the woods as partisans and committed terrorist actions. They remain hanging as a deterrent for two or three days." The war against the partisans proved especially cruel, perhaps because it degenerated into a chaotic affair in which neither side respected the conventions of war. "The *Feldwebel* [sergeant] was staring at something in the ruins of the cabin," Guy Sajer recalled of a nasty incident in the autumn of 1942.

> We could see a man leaning against the wall. His face, half covered by a wild, shaggy beard, was turned toward us. . . . His clothes . . . were not a military uniform. . . . His left hand . . . was soaked with blood. More blood was running from his collar. I felt a twinge of unease for him. The *Feldwebel*'s voice brought me back to reality.
> "Partisan!" he shouted. . . . "You know what you're going to get . . . !" We carried the partisan outside. . . . The lieutenant looked at the bearded man, who was clearly dying. "Who's this?"
> "A Russian, *Mein Leutnant*, a partisan. . . ."
> "Do you think I'm going to saddle myself with one of those bastards. . . ."
> He shouted an order to the two soldiers who were with him. They walked over to the unfortunate man lying on the snow, and two shots rang out.[50]

This kind of casual brutality occurred frequently across occupied Russia. "The partisans make it difficult for us to keep the railroads operating, so that we must act with the strongest methods," Railroad-Inspector K.S. confided almost nonchalantly, as if recounting a trip to the local market. "In case of attacks a number of people are picked out of the local population, especially Jews, and are shot there on the spot and their houses set on fire. . . . Recently you could observe hardly 50 meters away . . . how a group of prisoners of war were simply shot down by the guards." Because of the daily reports of German soldiers found killed, and since the countryside was so unsafe, confessed Private H.T., "anyone found at night wandering around in the woods or on the main roads without identification from the competent authority is—." Perhaps because of fear of the censor this *Landser* left the punishment to his correspondent's imagination. But as Sergeant A.R. conceded, the most brutal measures proved acceptable in the war in Russia. "Above all, here we must reckon with a small war of bandits," he wrote. "Just yesterday in a neighboring place a German officer was shot by Russians in civilian clothing. Because of that, though, the whole village was set afire. This eastern campaign is quite a bit different from the western campaign." Corporal H.G. summed it up:, "This is not exactly a struggle of country against country, but rather one between two fundamentally different ideologies."[51] Again, what made such letters remarkable was the widespread acceptance by average soldiers of these harsh and brutal measures, indeed the almost complete absence of any sense of moral or personal outrage.

In fact, indifference can itself be seen as an expression of support for the ideological goals of the Hitler regime. The testimony of one soldier was perhaps not atypical. "It was near Velikie Luki," Private Landowski remembered. "We were on the march. . . . The road ran through a ravine. . . . We made a noontime rest, and then all of a sudden shooting broke out. The SS there in that ravine had driven together around 300 Russian prisoners and shot all of them. . . . It was barely 500 meters away from us, where we had taken our rest. But I saw the dead. . . . [They lay] all one on top of the other. . . . I assumed that they had somehow been driven together in a small group, because they stood fairly close together. And then they were aimed at from both sides. With machine guns." And how had he reacted to seeing Russian prisoners shot by the SS?

> It was already clear to us that it would have repercussions. That our prisoners [in Russian hands] would be treated in the same way. . . . *Oberst* [Colonel] Blunk was certainly a good officer. He had received high decorations, he was also not so nervous. I had experienced how he himself went forward into the first position and fired a rifle and threw grenades. And this man let a woman be hanged. I saw the woman hanging there. . . . It was a Russian woman, and the *Oberst* had ordered her to bake bread. . . . Now it may be that she had replied, "no flour." . . . But despite her having done nothing else, she was just hanged. She hung on a kind of barn directly next to the street, and then in Russian it was written on a placard why she hung there. A young woman.[52]

But he had not done anything to intervene. After all, a "good officer" had done it, and as Friedrich Grupe noted after the war, "We marched . . . always conscious that as good soldiers we had to fulfill our hard duty."[53] Left unspoken, of course, was the fact that it was hard duty in service of the Nazi regime.

Offhand brutality was no unusual occurrence. Matthias Jung remembered the consequences for Russian civilians after eighteen German soldiers had been killed in a partisan attack: "The whole place, everything [was destroyed]! Totally! The civilians who had done it, all the civilians who were in the place. In each corner stood a machine gun, and then all the houses were set on fire and whoever came out— In my opinion with justice!" The civilians not incinerated had obviously been shot to death, but such was the nature of the war in Russia that this unwarranted violence seemed justified to an average soldier. Fritz Harenberg remembered an incident of gratuitous brutality in Sarajevo: There was a Jewish cemetery close to his quarters, he recalled, and one day "there arrived among us the Waffen-SS . . . and the Gestapo. And then somebody revealed to the Gestapo that buried in the Jewish cemetery were money and valuable things. The Gestapo drove the Jews together, they had to dig it up. Hauled a lot out of there, found a lot."[54] In front of his eyes Jews were gathered together and forced to dig up their own cemetery, certainly a painful form of degradation. And yet Harenberg condoned it, accepted the official explanation that valuables were buried there, recollected it as nothing more than a part of everyday army life, the normal routine.

Herbert Selle remembered that at a public execution of Jews in August 1941 in Zhitomir, soldiers were "sitting on rooftops and platforms watching the show. The execution was arranged as a form of popular entertainment." Another soldier detailed the incident:

> One day a *Wehrmacht* vehicle drove through Zhitomir with a megaphone. Over the loudspeaker we were informed . . . that at a certain time that day Jews would be shot in the market-place. . . . Upon arriving there I saw that fifty to sixty Jews (men, women, and children) had assembled. . . . There were also, of course, members of the *Wehrmacht* among the onlookers. . . . Finally all of the Jews assembled there had to get on to the truck. . . . Then an announcement came over the loudspeaker that we should all follow the lorry to the shooting. . . .
>
> There was a ditch, filled with water. . . . SS men stood at either side of this ditch. One by one the Jews had to jump over the ditch. . . . Those who fell in the ditch were beaten with various types of blunt instruments by the SS men and driven or pulled out of the ditch. . . .

> About thirty meters behind the ditch I saw a stack of logs. . . .
> This wooden wall was used as a bullet butt. . . . There must have
> been five or six people lined up there each time. They then received
> a shot in the neck from the carbines. Row upon row were shot in the
> same way. The dead from each row were dragged away immedi-
> ately. . . . I stood about twenty meters from the ditch and about fifty
> meters from the wood-stack.[55]

Not even beatings and mass murder as public spectacle was unusual. Another *Landser*, also in the vicinity of Zhitomir, recalled that one
afternoon in late July 1941, hearing rifle and pistol fire, he investigated
and found executions being carried out behind an embankment. "In the
earth was a pit about seven to eight meters long and perhaps four meters
wide. . . . The pit itself was filled with innumerable human bodies, . . .
both male and female. . . . Behind the piles of earth dug from it stood a
squad of police. . . . There were traces of blood on their uniforms. In a
wide circle around the pit stood scores of soldiers from the troop
detachments stationed there, some of them in bathing trunks, watching
the proceedings. There were also an equal number of civilians, including
women and children."[56]

Not only did some *Landsers* witness the shootings as grand entertainment, but on occasion they actively assisted the police in the grisly
business. One member of an *Einsatzgruppen* (mobile killing squad)
claimed after the war that "on some occasions members of the
Wehrmacht took the carbines out of our hands and took our place in the
firing-squad." Little wonder, then, that after watching the murder of
four-hundred Jews by execution squads in Lithuania, one *Landser* remarked, "May God grant us victory because if they get their revenge,
we're in for a hard time."[57] So much had the perceptions of many
Landsers been shaped by Nazi ideology and propaganda that the unthinkable became banal. These men did not think of the innocent human beings
who were being killed but worried instead about the consequences to
them personally. Atrocities were being committed, but it was just a job,
after all, so pick the best weapons and get on with it.

Certainly, the depersonalization of the enemy, whether civilian or
soldier, was a common tendency in combat. "As a soldier, you don't think
[of the enemy] as an individual at all," Harry Mielert reflected. "You
shoot at 'profitable targets'; that the guy out there is a man with a family,
perhaps is even happy at the news that he has become a father. . . . and
soon should get a leave . . . , you don't think of that at all." This

dehumanization of the enemy was especially pronounced on the eastern front, where the Russians were portrayed as subhuman foes not only of Germany but of Western civilization. From the outset, the Nazi regime alternately depicted the war as a product of an alleged Jewish-Bolshevik conspiracy to destroy Germany or as a crusade against the subhuman "Asiatic" hordes of Bolshevik Russia, propagandistic lines that intersected at various points. More remarkable, however, was the fervor with which many *Landsers* embraced the twin themes of this ideological crusade. Asiatic hordes, beasts, a universal plague—over and over in their letters many *Landsers* parroted the Nazi line. The process of depersonalizing and dehumanizing the enemy certainly made it easier for the average soldier to break the social and cultural taboo against killing. Observed Corporal L.K., "They are no longer people, but wild hordes and beasts, who have been bred by Bolshevism in the last twenty years. One must not allow any sympathy to grow for these people."[58]

For most *Landsers*, though, the enemy—however depersonalized—came to be not merely an abstract concept but a real and constant presence that had to be taken seriously. Helmut von Harnack, in a letter to his father in January 1942, acknowledged "the extreme modesty of the personal needs of the Russian soldier, who in his mixture of doggedness and toughness possesses an enormous power of resistance." Private M.S. claimed, "I have never yet seen such tough dogs as the Russians." After marveling at the "often superhuman, purposeless resistance of encircled groups" of Russian troops, Private R.L. conceded that "the Russians are really tough," an admission that came only grudgingly, since he also referred to them as "a people that requires long and good schooling in order to become human." Another *Landser* found "something diabolical" in the fanatic Russian resistance. [59]

The furious, often savage Soviet assaults stunned many *Landsers*. In one minor action "the number, duration and fury of those attacks had exhausted and numbed us completely. Not to hide the truth they had frightened us. Our advance had been . . . an ordinary move on a fairly narrow sector, and yet they had contested it day after day and with masses of men. . . . How often, we asked ourselves, would they attack and in what numbers if the objective was really a supremely important one? I think that on that autumn day in 1941 some of us began to realize . . . that the war against the Soviet Union was going to be bigger than we had thought, . . . and a sense of depression . . . settled upon us." "Their attacks are quite desperate and quite hopeless," echoed another soldier of the savage fighting at the Kiev pocket in September 1941. "They are driven back with such losses that one wonders how they can find the courage . . . to keep coming on. Some of the dead have been out there for weeks and are badly decomposed. The sights and smells are bad enough for us, but they have to attack across this carpet of their own dead comrades. Do they have no feeling of fear?"[60]

The *Landser* initially held a contemptuous view of British and American soldiers as well. "We had no respect whatever for the American soldier," claimed Heinz Hickmann. Another *Landser* thought "the Americans. . . . liked a little bit too much comfort." Adolf Hohenstein was puzzled by the American reluctance to exploit their successes. "We felt they always overestimated us," he said. "We could not understand why they did not break through [at Normandy]. The Allied soldier never seemed to be trained as we were, always to try to do more than had been asked of us." Similarly, Martin Pöppel, in his first encounter with the British in Sicily, thought they were "certainly not eager to fight, and their equipment looks fairly pathetic. . . . In my opinion their spirit is none too good. They tend to surrender as soon as they face the slightest resistance." After interrogating a Canadian prisoner taken in Italy in September 1943, Pöppel noted in his diary, "He claims they are by no means hungry for battle and don't know why they are fighting."[61]

This contempt for what he saw as stupidity and poor training gradually changed as Pöppel engaged in fiercer fighting with Allied units. Confronting Americans in Normandy, he initially professed admiration only for their medical equipment and rations, but when an SS battalion deployed next to his unit, Pöppel wrote in his diary: "The SS think they can do it easily [break through American lines], they've arrived with enormous idealism, but they'll get the surprise of their lives against this enemy, which is not short of skill itself." As the western campaign unfolded, Pöppel found himself more and more impressed with Allied skill and especially Allied equipment. Following his capture, he noted with bitterness, "We drove past kilometer after kilometer of Allied artillery positions, thousands of guns. With us it was always 'Sweat Saves Blood,' but with them it was, 'Equipment Saves Men.' Not with us. We didn't need the equipment, did we? After all, we were heroes."[62]

Even for "heroes," the pressures of gruesome atrocities and the daily dehumanization that so characterized the war, especially on the eastern front, added to the dreary aspects of the battlefield; the shattering noise, the sight of charred, smoking bodies, and the odor of rotting corpses all took their emotional and psychological toll on the *Landser*. The feeling of helplessness under artillery attack, for example, could reduce the strongest man to a quivering mass of nerves. "Here and now the Russian artillery fire again pushes me into the deepest corner of my foxhole," acknowledged Harry Mielert in July 1941, "and teaches me the prayer of distress: Lord, have mercy upon us . . . ! The last fatalism, the feeling of being completely in the hands of God and therefore surrendered to His mercy, I still don't have." [63]

Others too were driven to near despair by the strain of being shelled. "We have suffered here greatly under Russian artillery fire," complained Corporal W.F., "and we must live day and night in our foxholes in order to gain protection from shrapnel. The holes are full of water. Lice and other types of vermin have already snuck in." Lamented Corporal M.H., "We . . . are constantly being heavily attacked by the Russian artillery. I don't know how long our nerves can yet stand up." Dieter Georgii, under Russian air attack, wrote, "The ears hurt from the air pressure; it is difficult to keep control over your nerves. Since Friday no sleep and no food. . . . A moment of despair comes over us." As Helmut Wagner put it with self-conscious understatement, "Artillery and fighters 'get on our nerves.' "[64]

Artillery and air attacks could easily trample the nerves, and the will, of the strongest and toughest men. "Russian shells were coming over in profusion," recalled Guy Sajer of a Soviet attack on the Dnieper:

> With a cry of despair and a prayer for mercy, we dived to the bottom of our hole, trembling as the earth shook and the intensity of our fear grew. The shocks . . . were of an extraordinary violence. Torrents of snow and frozen earth poured down on us. A white flash, accompanied by an extraordinary displacement of air, and an intensity of noise which deafened us, lifted the edge of the trench. . . . Then with a roar, the earth poured in and covered us.
>
> In that moment, so close to death, I was seized by a rush of terror so powerful that I felt my mind was cracking. Trapped by the weight of earth, I began to howl like a madman. . . . The sense that one has been buried alive is horrible beyond the powers of ordinary language. . . . At that moment, I suddenly understood the meaning of all the cries and shrieks I had heard on every battlefield.[65]

Confronted with such elemental fright, even a combat veteran like Sajer succumbed to the force of sheer terror.

Not only individuals but whole units could be paralyzed by the savage power of an artillery or aerial bombardment. "The incredibly heavy artillery and mortar fire of the enemy is something new for seasoned veterans," reported the Second Panzer Divsion in Normandy: "The assembly of troops is spotted immediately by enemy reconnaissance aircraft and smashed by bombs and artillery . . . ; and if, nevertheless, the attacking troops go forward, they become involved in such dense artillery and mortar fire that heavy casualties ensue. . . . During the barrage the effect on the inexperienced men is literally soul-shattering. The best results have been obtained by platoon and section commanders leaping forward and uttering a good old-fashioned yell. We have also revived the practice of bugle calls."[66] Against the stress of artillery or air attack and the sense of helplessness and panic, blaring bugles and bellowing commanders served to boost the *Landser*'s spirit, stiffen his courage, and bolster morale—archaic human responses to the frightful destruction of modern battle.

Eventually, of course, many a *Landser*'s luck ran out, and he unwillingly contributed to the otherwise impersonal casualty statistics; the longer a man was in combat, the more assuredly would he fall wounded. In this agonizing moment, as metal tore into one's own flesh and the pain and fear pierced one's soul, the personal nature of the war—which perhaps up to now meant watching comrades die or coping with individual anxieties, reduced itself to the bare essentials. Seeing a friend die, as Siegfried Knappe admitted, "brought the utter destructiveness of war home," but being wounded himself meant that "my own mortality became a part of my mind-set from that moment on." Some *Landsers* however, displayed a curious detachment when hit. Knappe himself remembered that on being wounded for the first time, he thought, rather ridiculously, "The [enemy] machine gunner was obviously a good shot." More than a year later in Russia, hit a second time, Knappe's first reaction was simply, "so I am lucky, . . . glad to be wounded and out of the fighting, and especially to be out of the horrible Russian winter." Similarly, Hans Woltersdorf, wounded for the second time, prayed "that if my leg was hit, it would be the left one, which was not of much use to me anyway"; he added laconically, "My prayer was answered." Wounded and untended, Martin Pöppel reflected, "Left alone like that, you find yourself having stupid thoughts. Should I pray? For Christ's sake no: I never needed the Lord before, so I'm not going to bother Him now." Even as the initial shock began to wear off, to be replaced by agonizing pain, a *Landser* might maintain that sense of disengagement. During his evacuation, listening to the other wounded talk of their experiences, Knappe realized that he was observing them as a scientist might an experiment, that he was hoping "to learn how the human mind tries to cope with the horrors of combat."[67]

Although a *Landser* might realize rationally that the quicker the evacuation, the better his chances of survival, the actual process of being sent to the rear could itself bring excruciating pain and suffering. "The trip to Vyazma was approximately 120 kilometers," remembered Knappe of his second medical evacuation. "Nine of us were in the bed of the truck. . . . Over frozen ground, it was a cold, jolting, painful ride. . . . By the time I was put aboard an ambulance train . . ., I already had lice under my bandage, a terrible experience." A hospital train offered scant improvement. Hans Woltersdorf recalled being among wounded men who were

> crowded together like sardines in the cattle car. . . . There were moans, groans, and whimpers in that car; the smell of pus, urine, stomach and lung wounds, and it was cold. We lay on straw, each of us covered only by a woollen blanket. The train waited for hours on sidings.
>
> After many days a doctor finally came crawling breathlessly into our car. He had long ago given up reacting to the many wishes, pleas, and complaints, indeed listening to them at all, and he concentrated on his task of distinguishing the nearly dead from the still alive, making room for new wounded, and changing dressings only when it was necessary. In my case it was necessary.
>
> "I'm afraid we have no chloroform," he said. "Grit your teeth."
>
> Then he tore the whole septic kit and caboodle from my stump in one go. . . . [I] imagined a leg amputation in the Middle Ages to be something like that.

His left lower leg amputated, Josef Paul endured a variety of modes of torturous transportation in the process of being evacuated back to a hospital in Germany, first being put on an airplane, then loaded onto a medical train that was under constant fighter attack, after which he found himself on a horse-drawn cart, then back on a medical train; all this only to be overtaken, captured by the Russians, and sent to a Soviet prisoner of war camp.[68]

Perhaps the greatest agony for the wounded was the fear of being

left behind during a retreat, of dying unrecognized, unburied, unfound—
or, even if found in time, of the rescue operation being overrun. Claus
Hansmann has left a poignant and vivid description of the human
workings and emotions involved in a frantic effort to evacuate the fallen.
"Where was the cheerful train that we had often imagined, where were
the laughing comrades at the windows, the last jokes about the lost
horrors of Russia, the common delousing at the border?" he puzzled.
"Where was all this? Dark cattle cars in whose straw feverish wounded
groaned . . . . Thoughts gnaw into our innermost being." As the wounded
were literally carried out of harm's way, Hansmann took note of a
"murdered wood: stumps and gnarled roots, cold stalks tower bone pale
and murky in the dampness. . . . As far as the eye can see . . . only this
sinister feeling of oppressiveness. . . . Here the brutal reality of war
seized for the first time a young heart."[69]

Darkness brought no relief from the torment. "Night . . . where the
battle writhes in our blood. It shrieks like a storm in us. . . . Sleep, startled
awake, someone gives us an injection, bandages, tablets, and something
to drink. . . . Full of despair the feelings vacillate in us. . . . Where the
wounds are can be healed, yet these scars will also still desecrate." With
these wounds to his soul fresh and burning, Hansmann continued his
feverish ruminations:

> Are you awake? Are you dreaming? On the ground there is an
> enormous shuddering, and . . . the pain presses in wild waves. . . .
> You want to raise your head. . . . Your head rolls weakly to the side,
> and your mouth opens, your tongue seeking cool drops on your
> bearded lips. . . .
>
> Someone carries you on a stretcher. . . . Slowly distant im-
> pressions sink into your consciousness: the crunching of footsteps,
> voices, the smell of soldier's coats, the room, which had seemed
> infinite, narrows. But what are these men saying? This damned fog!
> If you could only understand these sounds. . . . That must be Russian
> they are speaking above you! . . . You are so cold and clammy, can
> just raise your head over the edge of the stretcher, then your whole
> stomach seems to spring up and you are practically nauseous. . . .
> Finally you hear, "Well, are you doing better?" Yet you still can't
> answer. . . . Then you're already asleep again.

But soon the rumblings of war and the throbbing pain jarred Hansmann
awake again:

An "Are you hungry" you can't understand at all. "Hungry?" Oh no, no, pain. The voice turns away, you are lifted up, get tablets and cool water that you eagerly slurp. Wounded new arrivals come and rest in the straw; they lie silent, as if fallen under a nightmare. Only here and there muffled voices and rustling about. . . . Unrest all through the night hours, then it is morning. Through the buzzing rumors of many men rings clear: "Comrades! The ambulance column can't make it through, we have information that they are waiting for us twenty-five kilometers from here. The time is short, we must withdraw. . . ."

Your thoughts become more agitated, red flaming shapes under your eyelids. The cool raindrops appear to turn to steam on your skin, though slowly you become cooler. The wetness and cold on your body drive the fever from your head. . . . Next to you at the same level you see unkempt faces, filthy bandages, excited unrest. Are the Russians already behind us? . . . Now comes the moment where old, sometimes derided prayers push in. [70]

Amid much suffering and groaning the stretcher-bearers, most of them Russian auxiliaries, took up their loads like beasts of burden and set off into the unknown, threatened by enemy forces, with safety almost an impossibly long distance away for wounded men being carried across swampy terrain. Exhaustion mixed with fear and pain characterized the lonely column. "Night at last," Hansmann recorded:

The same impressions of the smell of straw and damp, sticky uniforms. Again the doctor, also unkempt, becomes steadily more uneasy. Again questions, tablets, something to eat; then sleep, from time to time awakened by groans, screams. . . . The medics can't do any more. One sleeps sitting up. He is called, hears nothing, finally someone crawls behind him, then he starts awake with wild eyes and inarticulate cries, and then laughs wearily, hopelessly. . . . Then quite a few shots reverberate! Is that Ivan already? Anxiety, panic bursts into the open. Everyone's petrified. . . . Many look for a knife, a stick; others quickly crawl with tightly clenched teeth into a corner.

But all the excitement proved to be a false alarm, this time. Everyone looked around embarrassed, each ashamed of his weakness and guilty at his open expression of fear. At first light, still no vehicles had appeared, so

tired, worn out, already strung out at the start, the column presses on like a sluggish caterpillar through rain and woods. Even without having to open your eyes you see what they're suffering. These contorted, pale, blanched faces, these eyes that cling exhausted to the glutinous muddy trail. The complete filth and the old blood encrusted on their uniforms and bandages. Everyone clings to life. . . . All along the valleys roll threatening reverberations. Our haste grows, overwhelms all our exhaustion. Only the bearers are steady, indifferent. . . . Where is there a resting place in this world? The unlucky remain behind. . . . Gone, can't bear to look.[71]

Doggedly the column lurched on in a desperate quest for safety, the journey itself proved almost overwhelmingly agonizing. "How long has this odyssey lasted already?" Hansmann speculated at one point. "Is it days, weeks in the monotony of the pain that mistreats your body? . . . Days in icy, clinging dampness, in the shower of fall storms. . . . Are you lost in this devil's forest, are your exertions, this arduous torment, for nothing?" At the moment of ultimate despair, however, salvation appeared like a bolt from the blue: "Something shoots like an electric current through the group! Ahead under a tree a waving form. At closer glance it is a soldier. Already from a distance he shouts: 'Just five kilometers, Comrades!' Five kilometers, five thousand meters it sings in us, then ambulances, warmth, care, everything! The steps become more assured, the strange silence lifts, already confident conversations, conjectures flicker." Almost before they knew it, the five kilometers and the sufferings of the last few days were past and, most improbably, comfort and safety had been reached. "Ambulances under trees, medics, all so fresh and energetic," Hansmann rejoiced. "Slowly the suffering column leaves the darkness of the forest. All come with the same look of hope, like pilgrims who have seen a Mecca. . . . Finally after the long march through the night the muffled echo of an entrance door. . . . Now it's your turn, again you're carried, along quiet, long corridors full of hospital air. Through a door a bright room, a voice: it is a woman! Everything is all right."[72] Hansmann's tale emphasized something every *Landser* eventually came to understand, that survival on the battlefield often came to depend on the mysteries of chance; all one's personal precautions, superstitions, and cynicism availed little in the face of "Fate."

For some *Landsers*, then, combat ultimately produced tragic human moments of frightening clarity when the fog of battle cleared and they became horribly aware of what was happening around them, not merely of the death and destruction but of the deeply personal essence of war. "Daily I engage in hour-long discussions with my comrades and preach humility," warned Siegbert Stehmann in the heady days of victory in June 1940, then added insightfully: "There are people who are inwardly destroyed by victory!" This was a revelation to which Guy Sajer added, in blunter terms, "Even a victorious army suffers dead and wounded." Indeed, Sajer insisted,

> the front line troops . . . had already made up their minds about the future. . . . Much of the time we felt desperate. Can anyone blame us? We knew that we would almost certainly be killed. . . . If our courage incited us to hours of resignation, the hours and days which followed would find us . . . filled with an immense sadness. Then we would fire in a lunatic frenzy, without mercy. We didn't wish to die, and would kill and massacre as if to avenge ourselves in advance. . . . When we died, it was with fury, because we hadn't been able to exact enough retribution. And, if we survived, it was as madmen, never able to readapt to the peacetime world. Sometimes we tried to run away; but orders, adroitly worded and spaced, soothed us like shots of morphine.[73]

Still, as Sajer knew, this calm soon wore off, to be replaced by "the fear of ultimate success as a dead hero," a death that offered slim solace to those so honored. "It is small comfort to have shared your own destruction with others," lamented an anonymous soldier at Stalingrad, to which another added, "Now it's either die like a dog or off to Siberia." From Stalingrad, indeed, most would have agreed that "there are only two ways left: to heaven or to Siberia." But this forlorn choice revealed the ultimate impotence of men confronting the war machine. "At home . . . in many newspapers you will find beautiful, high-sounding words in big black borders," concluded the same *Landser*, writing from Stalingrad. "They will always pay us due honor. Don't be taken in by this idiotic to-do. I am so furious that I could smash everything in sight, but never in my life have I felt so helpless."[74] Combat, as most discovered, was not a romantic adventure but a continual series of shattering incidents, until many *Landsers* decided that only an ambulance or a grave-digger offered a way out.

4. WITHSTANDING THE STRAIN

A mid the savage fighting and appalling misery of the German retreat from Russia in the autumn of 1943, Harry Mielert was struck by the personal anger he felt, a rage based on fear, the pervasive death and destruction, and a sense of anomie. "All connections are broken," he despaired. "Where is man? Anger roars through all the cracks in the world." Mielert's fury expressed well the complex emotions produced by combat and life at the front. An army's first and most important function is, of course, to fight; but it is individual human beings, not some impersonal machine, who do the actual fighting, suffering, and dying. Every *Landser* thus lived with the likelihood that he would be killed or wounded, and the longer he was at the front, the greater the possibility. Combat therefore produced a study in extremes of behavior with enormous mood shifts: one was alternately frightened or resigned, laughing or crying, screaming or cheering. After a battle a *Landser*'s nerves would take over, but although his knees might shake and his hands tremble, he was happy to be alive. At the moment of killing or being killed, each man discovered a powerful consciousness of self and realized acutely the menace all around him. Each one came to know only too well the thin line between life and death. "I had learned," noted Guy Sajer, "that life and death can be so close that one can pass from one to the other without attracting any attention." "The bullet that you hear," observed Helmut Pabst drily, "is already past."[1] He left unspoken the tormenting knowledge that the bullet that struck home remained unheard.

Every man had a breaking point, a fact the *Landser* understood and, if only grudgingly, accepted. The constant strain and tension of life on the edge of death would eventually snap the resolution of even the toughest soldier. Given such continual terror, a fear to which one could never become accustomed, how did the average *Landser* find the strength to endure? Not surprisingly, the first instinct of many men under fire was to flee, to cope with stress simply by escaping it. Cowardice, after all, may be just a kind of honesty about fear. "Something hung in the air," noted Claus Hansmann of an episode that was certainly repeated hundreds of times during the war:

> We marched hurriedly rearward. . . . As we go along we hear in the ranks that Russians are supposed to have broken through. . . . Staff members roar to the rear, horses and wagons travel past in a gallop, truck drivers: all in a hurry, already it smells almost like a rout. And suddenly a shout from behind: "Go to the right, our tanks are coming! . . ." Everyone breathes a sigh: well, finally, tanks! And then come horrible seconds: [enemy] tanks duck out of the yellow-brown cloud of dust and open fire on vehicles and the column. Then there is no more stopping us. Munitions boxes fly into the ditches, rifles are thrown away, gas masks, gun belts, machine guns. . . . Everyone flees from them, and the men run, becoming a poor, spineless herd of animals. . . . Autos drive into the swamp, wagons overturn, horses run on through, and the men likewise have thrown off all reins and fled. . . . The reason? Yeah, the reason . . . well, is just immaterial.[2]

Hansmann, like virtually all *Landsers*, understood that everyone panicked from time to time; in reaction to a mortal threat a group of men in a very real sense could lose their human qualities and become a herd of animals.

As the *Landser* well knew, there was no such thing as being too seasoned to panic; even seemingly immunized combat veterans occasionally succumbed to the desire to escape danger by running. Overwhelmed by a Russian assault, Guy Sajer and his comrades—hardened veterans all—gave way to this primal terror and the urge to flee. "The human tide continued to roll toward us, making our scalps crawl," he recalled. "'It's useless!' shouted the veteran. . . . 'We haven't got enough ammunition. We can't stop them. . . .' Our frantic eyes moved from the lips of one man to the other." Their sergeant refused to order a retreat, but orders were no longer needed, for the men were acting out of animal terror, instinctively: "The veteran had just jumped from the trench and was galloping toward the woods. . . . We grabbed our guns in frantic haste . . . [and] followed him. For a moment we were almost mad with terror. . . . 'You bastard!' the [sergeant] yelled. 'I'll report you for this!' 'I know,' the veteran said. . . . 'But I'd take one of our firing squads over Ivan's bayonet any day.' "[3]

Nor was this kind of fear an isolated occurrence. "Although our luck had been almost incredible, and had spared us so far," Sajer reflected on another occasion,

> it must almost surely run out. . . . I suddenly felt terribly afraid. . . . It would probably be my turn soon. I would be killed, just like that, and no one would even notice. . . . I would be missed only until the next fellow got it. . . . As my panic rose, my hands began to tremble. I knew how terrible people looked when they were dead. I'd seen plenty of fellows fall face down in a sea of mud. . . . The idea made me cold with horror. . . . I went on crying and muttering incoherently. . . .
>
> "Hals," I said. "We've got to get out of here. I'm afraid. . . ." Suddenly it all seemed unbearable. My trembling hands clutched my head . . . and I sank into total despair.

Although his friend stopped him from running that time, a few days later Sajer again witnessed an elemental scramble to flee the horror: "As we had feared, we heard the roar of war again. The noise . . . in itself was enough to send a wave of terror through the . . . men trapped beside the water. . . . Every man grabbed his things and began to run. . . . Frantic men were abandoning everything on the bank and plunging into the water to try to swim to the opposite shore. . . . Madness seemed to be spreading like wildfire . . . [as] the howling mob . . . pass[ed] us by."[4]

Still, the great majority of *Landsers* came to realize that courage consisted simply of a dogged determination to resist the human tide fleeing rearward. Even if momentarily panicked, most did not give way to the quivering terror that could make men incapable of action but instead managed to cope with the stress of life at the front. Sometimes the courage to go on could be engendered by the most seemingly mundane means, such as the "good old-fashioned yells" of platoon and section commanders and "the practice of bugle calls." Human responses to a human crisis of fear thus proved effective, as did the apparent triviality of playing to the vanity of men by offering them medals. Embarrassed, Harry Mielert wrote to his wife, "For us men these [medals] are . . . very significant. They raise our courage, and we are ready for the craziest things." Indeed, the simplest conceit could persuade the spirit to endure. "How many times . . . had I thought myself invulnerable, filled with the pride we all felt," Sajer mused, "admiring our shoulder straps and helmets and magnificent uniforms, and the sound of our footsteps, which I loved, and love still, despite everything."[5]

Painstakingly observing special holidays also served to connect the men to a wider world and sustain their morale. "The most beautiful night of the year, but for soldiers also the most dangerous night is over," Mielert reflected on Christmas day 1942. "We sang our beautiful Christmas songs in firm spirit, if also with our rifles at hand and our pockets full of hand grenades. In each bunker stood a small green tree with a pair of lights. I [spent time] with each group of my company. They all had photographs with them and hauled them out with pride as well as sheepishly to show me. . . . The toughest, the 'old soldiers,' they are the most affected. . . . They don't quite cry openly, but you see it, how they trembled, and it required the total dryness and coarseness of male humor to get over this softness. We drank a bottle of wine, ate some cookies, smoked a cigarette, then it was over."[6]

"From the army radio resound the familiar Christmas melodies," Friedrich Grupe noted in his diary of a Christmas celebration, also in 1942.

> The 24th of December 1942 is a wonderful winter day. Snow covers the devastation, transforms this wretched copse that has been shot to pieces into a magical forest. In the evening a magnificent full moon rises over the battlefield.
>
> In the bunker stoves crackles a warming fire. About 4:00 P.M. the sergeant from the 1st squad comes and brings us a glittering, decorated Christmas tree. Now begins a lavish exchange of Christmas presents.
>
> We actually feel now that it is Christmas. We . . . don't think about the fact that the Red Army will try to force a breakthrough to the highway. . . . Mail has also come. We sit quietly at the rough table made from birch and with the reading of the mail all our thoughts are at home, while someone plays on the accordion the Christmas songs that we have sung a thousand times. . . .
>
> The *Landsers*, stamped by suffering, sit forward in their bunkers with their companies and probably all become soft in this hour.
>
> The battalion leader goes with me through all the positions in

the main line. We don't leave any bunker out. . . . An urgent closeness reigns. . . . The hard, stubbled faces of the soldiers are relaxed;
they attempt to laugh, shy and embarrassed.

There they are, these men who have just a short time ago
repulsed attack after attack in merciless close combat and have
looked death in the face a hundred times. They sing "Silent Night,
Holy Night," their white-painted helmets in their hands, and at the
same time attempt to sing so softly that Ivan, outside hardly eighty
meters away, cannot hear them.[7]

If only for a moment, the war stopped as the men engaged in the familiar
and comforting celebration of Christmas, complete with a decorated tree
in each bunker.

To forget the war, the death and destruction all around, the anxiety
over his own fate—that remained the goal of every *Landser*. "At many
of the sentry posts I confronted the powerful reek of alcohol," Grupe
confided to his diary. "To be sure the consumption of alcohol while on
duty is punishable, but . . . after weeks of hard, difficult fighting, after
all the blood and death, they have earned such pleasure and rest."
Moreover, this urge to blot out the fear could come at any moment, even
in battle. "Everything rumbled, blazed, trembled," Harry Mielert noted
during one particularly savage Russian artillery bombardment. "Cattle
cried, soldiers searched through all the buildings, barrels of red wine
were taken away in small *panje* wagons (horse carts), here and there men
were drinking and singing, in the meantime explosions again and new
roaring fires." During a frightful retreat through dense woods, in which
he was under constant fire, Prosper Schücking likewise recorded, with
no comment, "In the evening I passed a camp of an infantry battalion in
which the men were drunk." As Grupe commented laconically, "Beer
played an essential role." And vodka, Guy Sajer noted, "is the easiest
way to make heroes. . . . We drank everything we could get hold of, trying
to blot out the memory of a hideous day."[8] Little wonder, then, that the
Landser referred to alcohol as *Wutmilch*, the milk of fury, the means to
summon courage for yet another game of chance with death.

Humor, as well, served to distract the *Landser* from daily reality.
Grupe recorded that in his sector of the eastern front the nightly appearance of an antiquated Soviet biplane—known to the *Landsers* alternately
as the "sewing machine," the "coffee mill," or "iron Gustav"—occa-
sioned many jokes. The wooden plane, would drone overhead and then
suddenly turn off its motor, the sign that the pilot was going to toss a bomb

overboard. The arrival of this nightly ghost gave rise to "many crazy stories told by the *Landser*: One night a paymaster was underway with a full keg of good brandy in his *panje* wagon. Gustav fluttered over. Just as our little paymaster had stooped down over the open spigot of the keg in order to enjoy the aroma, the airplane flew devilishly low over him and to his horror out of it came, while the motor was turned off, a deep, jovial voice: 'Giddap, giddap, pony!'" Another version of the story, according to Grupe, had it that "both occupants of the airplane loudly and clearly scolded the paymaster."[9] Through such a story the *Landser* not only ridiculed, and thus minimized, the irritating nightly "air raid" but also mocked the "hardships" of those in the rear—and to the *Landser* the rear was any area behind the front lines—who didn't live in the land of mice, lice, bugs, and constant danger.

Men sought to maintain a sense of balance and alleviate their common suffering by sharing humor. Some jokes poked fun at the conditions around them: "As we were marching to the front as a relief unit a comrade's helmet slipped off his head. He poked around in the mud with a stick to find the smelly hat again. Suddenly he discovered a human face. Dumfounded, he asked: 'Gee, how did you get there?' At that the face said: 'You'll be even more surprised when you learn that I'm sitting on a horse and riding.'" Other tales spoofed the involuntary situation in which they found themselves, although the humor often betrayed more than a hint of bitterness or jealousy: "A butcher bought a pig from a farmer. The wife, however, made as a condition that first her husband, who was at the front, had to give his consent. Her husband thereupon wrote the following postcard: 'Dear Mr. Butcher!! Am in agreement with the sale of my wife, and you can pick up the sow tomorrow.'" Or, as one *Landser* supposedly wrote to his girlfriend, "Honey! I'm sitting in my bunker and writing to you while all around me here it is continuously creaking; you are probably now already in bed, and hopefully that is not the case with you."[10]

Not surprisingly, many jokes ridiculed those in authority: an alleged inscription on an officer's quarters in the field read, "Entrance for shells, shrapnel, and bombs permitted only with the approval of the commander." One bit of humor managed to make fun of both those in authority and the often limited rations for those in the field: "At an inspection tour of the kitchen by the Captain. Everything is in the best of order. He asked the leader of the group: What is your occupation? 'Cook, Herr Captain!' And you!: 'Butcher!' Finally he asked yet another soldier standing off to the side: 'Smith, Herr Captain!' What do you do then in the kitchen? 'I administer the iron rations [the emergency field rations], Herr Captain!' " And again, with a similar play on word meanings: "The captain held personal instruction today. 'What is a *Kriegsgericht* [court martial]?' was his first question. Our Langer, who otherwise never pushed himself to the front, reported immediately and said: 'Peas with bacon is a *Kriegsgericht* [war dish], Herr Captain.' " And again: "A man was washing his mess tin in a nearby pond which was completely overgrown with so-called duck weed. A general passed by, hesitated, and asked the soldier: 'Tell me, do you not know bacillus?' The soldier answered, standing to attention: 'No, Herr General, he is not on the staff, he probably must be in the first company.' "[11]

Yet other witticisms expressed the all too real wistful yearnings felt by many for the pleasures of nonmilitary life, as did a rhyme titled "Bunker Fantasy":

> How comforting it is, when the silk and satins
> of the world of women surround us again,
> and no longer do we have to listen in the night,
> to dark ghosts in forest and heath;
> when all the stubble, now wild and bearded, has finally disappeared
> and socially acceptable, all the way to our shirt,
> we shall fasten our necktie instead of our gun belt.

And one alleged sign read: "Notice! Those who don't leave fast enough for furlough will in the future be punished with arrest."[12]

In addition to humor, many *Landsers* found music an important form of comfort and escape. Nervous and worried on the eve of Operation Barbarossa, Friedrich Grupe found solace in the "sounds of the accordion coming from the men's quarters and the singing of the familiar soldiers' ballads!" Not even the rigors of combat in Russia negated the need for music. "From the tent of the company commander comes familiar music over the gray *Wehrmacht* radio," Grupe wrote in his diary in the summer of 1941. "I sit there in the evenings before the loudspeaker and through these melodies sink into reminiscences and dreams of the future. The *Landsers* listening outside also have become still and don't let the muffled sounds of the firing in the distance disturb their reverie." On another occasion, Grupe described hearing Lale Andersen sing "Lili Marlene" over the radio as "like a dream." "In the transmitter car next to my tent they've turned on the wireless," recorded Wilhelm Prüller.

"They are just playing 'Hörst du mein heimliches Rufen' [Do you hear my secret call?—a popular song at the time]. My God! How wonderful this Sunday morning at home would be." Noted another soldier from the devastation of the Normandy hedgerows, "Last night we had a little 'soldier's hour' and sang our soldiers' and folk songs into the night. What would a German be without a song?"[13]

Certainly familiar tunes helped remind the *Landser* that another world did exist, one removed from the death and destruction of the battlefield. But even unfamiliar music could prove soothing, at least temporarily. "In this nocturnal silence, suddenly music falls on our ear," Prüller noted of one evening in Russia. "Wonderful music. A balalaika is playing. . . . Ukrainians . . . sit down in the park and play us their songs. We listen to them for hours. . . . because we fancy that they could almost be Viennese songs. . . . But no, the ever quicker tones of the balalaika, often a crazy pace, remind us that we are deep in Russia, that we are hearing Russian songs." Like Grupe, though, Prüller found "one single comfort: we still heard the Belgrade *Wachtposten* ('Lili Marlene'). The song has really won the hearts of us soldiers. Despite the pouring rain, we all stood round the transmitter car and listened to the music. . . . I've got to hear it, otherwise, I'm not wholly myself."[14]

Martin Lindner, from the melodic city of Vienna, noted, "The north German officers especially love the Viennese . . . wine songs. You almost die laughing at the enthusiasm with which they sing along in our dialect. . . . I just heard Bach's D-minor toccata on the radio. In its first tones it mirrors the upheaval and violence of our times. . . . When of an evening you walk along our quarters there is no tent and no house without music." Perhaps the significance of music for the *Landsers* was best revealed, however, by a soldier trapped at Stalingrad. "Kurt Hahnke . . . played the Appassionata a week ago on a grand piano in a little side street close to Red Square," he wrote to his parents in his last letter. "The grand piano was standing right in the middle of the street. . . . A hundred soldiers squatted around in their great-coats with blankets over their heads. Everywhere there were the sounds of explosions, but no one let himself be disturbed. They were listening to Beethoven in Stalingrad."[15] Although they were trapped, with death or captivity the only way out, music nonetheless provided a bit of comfort and solace to at least some *Landsers* in their moment of extreme agony and terror.

The *Wehrmacht* sought to provide musical diversion through such means as the popular radio *Wunschkonzerts* (musical request programs) broadcast to the troops, as well as by organizing stage shows to entertain troops at the front. These efforts sometimes backfired, however, for as Claus Hansmann noted furiously of one such performance,

> we come from "outside," this artificial world is too thin for us! We are angry, we can't forget. . . . Fifteen months bloody handwork in the broad Russian spaces have accustomed us too much to the other side. . . . We can't look at the magazine heroes. . . . We can't listen any longer when they indulge in musical twaddle. . . . Then we see only the endless trail of blood, . . . ruined lives, burned down dwellings. . . . We hear through the music the howling, screaming, shrieking, the roar and bursting, see the hit and wounded. . . . Cheap theatrics disgust us, the jokes are too banal, the voices too sentimental. We can't bear it any more. They should put us at the front, the cool rifle butt on the cheek brings us to reality; in our pouch we feel bullets, hand grenades, the helmet presses comfortingly. Comrades are also there. There we are men, but here . . . ? Not that we have become heroes. . . . We have the same faults as before, but we are conscious of the abyss. We can be pitiless, gruesome, when we must. . . . Only silliness and boring amusements are unbearable to us.[16]

Also unbearable, for many *Landsers*, was the absence of love, either erotic or affectionate. War seemed to enhance sexuality for many men, whether from being deprived of normal female relationships, for sheer physical gratification, out of a desire for affection, or in order to reaffirm that they were alive and that another world still existed. As insulation against cold reality, sex could offer at least temporary comfort and satisfaction. The problem for the average *Landser* was the lack of opportunity. For moral, military, and racial reasons, intimate fraternization with the enemy, especially in Russia, was strongly discouraged. Indeed, a *Landser* who engaged in sexual intercourse with a Russian woman faced the possibility of punishment for race defilement. Still, given the chance, many men willingly broke the rules to seek sexual release with local women. Sprinkled through his account of the wreckage of war, Guy Sajer noted numerous instances of *Landsers* socializing with Ukrainian women and enjoying simple moments of laughter and gaiety, encounters that often turned overtly sexual. "Hals had made the acquaintance of a Russian girl," he noted, "with whom he was able to arrange a mutually profitable relationship. It turned out he was not the only one to enjoy the good woman's favors. One evening he arrived to find himself a part of a troika. The other masculine member was the Catholic chaplain, who had survived hell and was indulging a few sins of the flesh as his consciousness of life returned." Other of his comrades, too, reveled in the physical release of sex, as when "four of them had trapped a Polish woman of about forty in a barn. She had yielded to their ardor, which had lasted the four hours remaining."[17]

Some men expressed their unabated sexual desires in remarkably frank and openly erotic comments. Claus Hansmann revealed both an insistent sensuality and an aching need for affection. "Over the wretched, empty furrows that extend from our miserable hut treads now the deathly pale sheen of the moon," he confided to his diary. "The feeling of apprehension, the many thoughts and burdens desert me, and almost cheerfully the fantasy of life bears a fruit that perhaps will never mature. First there are only the eyes, inscrutable, then hesitantly, tentatively the picture forms for me. . . . Shyly and furtively your image laughs. . . . The taste of your kisses presses on my lips. . . . My arms yearn for you. . . . Never before has your expression had such power over me and your caress such sweetness. . . . The blue dreams of your eyes are so enigmatic, they are the last that remains with me when you disappear in the fog."[18]

If Hansmann's writings retained a certain literary quality, another *Landser* left little to the imagination in his recitation of his erotic fantasy. "Oh, pipsqueak, but of course I at times also like to dream about wonderful things, as you did recently, of when we kissed so marvelously and lay in the green grass in Beibrigg," he wrote to his girlfriend, then spelled out what was really on his mind: "Your boobs peeked out; well, once I would like to know all that happens. But of course I would like not only to dream of it at times, but rather experience it in reality once again. My little cock is already yearning for you again. My 'stovepipe' would like *so* much to heat you up once again."[19]

Despite its physical release, for many *Landsers* sex did not satisfy the deeper thirst for companionship and love. As Sajer noted, when a consciousness of life returned, men revealed an aching need for female affection. For all his sexual activity, Sajer's best friend Hals "had fallen in love once more. . . . With him, falling in love was compulsive. He really couldn't help himself, and lost a piece of his heart every time we stopped in a rest zone." Sajer knew the reason for this compulsion, and had himself come to realize that love was necessary: "I had to learn how to live, because I hadn't been able to die." And indeed, Sajer did fall helplessly in love; he had to "unleash [his] emotions," for "the war had no power over my love for this girl, and holding back my emotion was out of the question." Still, as he came to realize, "My happiness was mixed with too much suffering. I couldn't simply accept it, and forget all the rest. My love for Paula seemed somehow impossible, in this setting of permanent chaos. As long as children were dying . . ., I would never be able to live with my love."[20]

Friedrich Grupe exhibited a yearning for companionship as well, noting in his diary that some "young, attractive French girls came by [the post]. Could a starved *Landser* simply let them pass? What a wonder that some of the young women stopped for more than a half hour." While training in East Prussia in the spring of 1941, Grupe again revealed this yearning not for sex but for affection: "I made friends with a young BDM [*Bund deutscher Mädel*, Association of German Girls] leader and spent many unforgettable hours with her." Doing what? Nothing so tawdry and brusque as sexual indulgence. "In the evenings we sat in a cafe in Allenstein and observed the people dressed in their spring clothes." It was the companionship he sought and received that was important, and that he missed when the time came to leave. "We took leave of Arys with a heavy heart," he confessed. "I carry the picture of an East Prussian girl with me, on this path into uncertainty."[21]

Along with unfulfilled sexual desires and the gnawing yearning for affection, some *Landsers* also had to cope with the specter of jealously and its often ugly consequences. "Thanks a lot for that 'lovely' letter which I received today," complained Karl Fuchs to his wife shortly before his death. "The person who wrote these words is a stranger to me. . . . I'm faced with enough nonsense out here every day that I'd just as soon not receive any from home. . . . Apparently you've grown indifferent to me. I suppose the main thing is, though, that you're leading a dazzling life and are becoming more beautiful from day to day."[22] Here Fuchs voiced the fear of many *Landsers*, that while they languished on the edge of death their wives or sweethearts back home were enjoying the good life. To them, it seemed the ultimate act of betrayal.

"I hope," wrote an anonymous soldier in April 1940 to his fiancée, shortly before he was to be granted wedding leave, "that I will find you happy and cheerful and not in such a state as you were in when you wrote your last letter to me." And what was the reason for the foul state of mind? His fiancée obviously had gone against his wishes and was working despite his injunctions. "If only you were my wife already and we had moved into our home," he continued, "you would naturally be under my care and would have to obey my orders precisely. I can just not understand that despite your promise not to do it, you are still slaving away at the shop. You know that it is not good for you and that I will no longer tolerate it, and should nothing change you will get to know the other side of me. I'm letting you know now for the last time." The authoritarian tone here betrayed a fear that he was losing influence, that his fiancée had grown away from him in some important way. Indeed, some marriages did fail to survive the strains of war. "Now that I know where I stand," a *Landser* wrote bitterly from Stalingrad, "I release you from your vow. . . . I looked for a wife with a generous heart, but it wasn't supposed to be that generous. . . . I advise you to choose good grounds for divorce and," he added perhaps unnecessarily, "speed up the procedure."[23]

Separation from loved ones proved difficult for all involved, for it was not only front soldiers who felt the pangs of loneliness and jealousy. "Now again I have here a letter that a widow of a fallen soldier wrote me," Harry Mielert complained to his wife. "She wants to know precisely the details of his death, be informed about his suffering and last words. . . . These wives cause me terrible pain. They cling with the greatest obsession to everything which remains mortal and earthly." To write letters to grieving widows was an onerous duty, certainly, for it served to heighten fears of one's own mortality. In the massive uprooting caused by war, however, women whose husbands or lovers were at the front suffered equally the desperate longing for love. "It appears to me," Mielert reassured his wife in March 1943, "that you fear that if I fall you also will be quickly forgotten. . . . Should I have to be in life-long imprisonment in Siberia, I would never give you up, never, and I also think that if I lay in a grave and my spiritual being had another existence I would not forget you, so that one day you must also come to me, to an absolute unification. That is the achievement of love. It goes beyond all borders."[24]

Such a pledge of undying love was harmless enough in itself, but emotion could get the best of a *Landser*. As Mielert also noted: "The real contact [with their husbands] that so many wives seek to get through fantasies such as newsreels, radios, and newspapers" failed to satisfy, so that an unresolved yearning remained on both sides. "You are so dear to me!" he confessed. "Have I deserved it? Yet as an impulsive woman you can rage and stamp your feet that I'm not attempting by all means to come to you." This anger, though, often had dire consequences, as Mielert was well aware, for he knew "some men who deserted out of love." Amid all the ironies of the battlefield, perhaps this was the greatest, that some soldiers reached the breaking point not from fear but out of love. As Mielert concluded in September 1943, what "we rough warriors . . . lack is love. That's why we're all so lonely among ourselves."[25]

In his loneliness and fear the *Landser* often sought solace even in the intangible. Ironically, that age-old staple of all armies, spreading rumors (what the *Landsers* called *Latrinenparole*, or latrine talk), evinced a reassuring tone, since the rumors most often concerned an end to the war or at least one's impending removal from the front lines. Despite the bustling commotion in preparation for the attack on the Soviet Union, activity that could have only one purpose, Alfred Opitz recalled that many *Landsers* chose to believe the rumor going round that "a great undertaking in the direction of the east was imminent, however not against the Soviet Union . . . but against England, which would be attacked in the Middle East. For this purpose the Soviet Union agreed to a transit march of seven German divisions through south Russian territory in the direction of the Caucasus-Iran. Meanwhile, the Soviet Union would remain neutral." On the eve of Barbarossa, Wilhelm Prüller too heard that Stalin would "let us march through voluntarily." Friedrich Grupe picked up the same gossip. Despite the fact that "the company had already been given instruction about Russia [and] that the Cyrillic alphabet had been learned," Grupe noted that "the strangest rumors were swirling around the camp: that German troops had supposedly gotten the permission of the Soviet regime . . . to travel through Russia in order to come to grips with the Tommies in India. Then our troops supposedly will link up with Rommel in the Caucasus." In similar fashion, Lieutenant H.H. related, in a letter of late May 1941, "The wildest rumors about Russia are circulating here. The one says that we have leased the Ukraine for 90 years and have received permission for a transit march toward Turkey and Iraq. The other asserts that the danger of war has been averted because of Stalin's attitude. . . . Each latrine races after the other [in rumors]."[26]

Amid the appalling hardships and severe conditions of the winter war of 1941–42, who could be surprised that Prüller day after day in his diary related the latest gossip about being relieved and sent to the south of France, or Rumania, or Turkey, or anywhere warm. In the midst of the bitter fighting of February 1942, Corporal R.M. relayed a hot rumor:

The southern army will break through the Caucasus to the Caspian Sea and divide itself into two parts. The one will move to the mouth of the Volga, the other through the Caucasus in a southerly direction. . . . Turkey will emerge from its heretofore strong neutral position to our favor and with its weapons will help force the victory. . . . In Africa at a suitable point a great offensive will be started with the goal of connecting with the comrades coming out of southern Palestine. An invasion of England will come in the course of the summer of 1942. . . . Between these battles . . . Japan ought in the meantime to have given the death blow to the English and Americans in the Pacific and India.

Martin Lindner, a university student from Vienna, speculated in July 1942 on an advance

over Stalingrad toward Astrakhan and then rolling up the Caucasus. . . . After this isolation of inner Asia, Japan and we will take action against the Anglo-Saxons. . . . The Mediterranean must be totally controlled by us, naval control of the Mediterranean excludes an advance from Africa against Europe. Then Europe will have more peace, raw materials, and time to prepare itself for a clearing action in the East. The East will secure our freedom of foodstuffs and in addition from there comes oil, coal, and iron ore in substantial quantities. You will see how everything is resolved; in any case, somehow we will be finished with our enemies.[27]

Such fantasties corresponded in many cases to Nazi dreams of *Lebensraum*. But in addition, they allowed the common soldier to believe that the war with Russia would not take place or, if it did, that Germany had powerful allies whose help would soon produce a conclusive victory. These rumors gave the *Landser* hope, a commodity often in short supply at the front: hope that the war would soon be over, hope that Germany would be victorious, hope that in the end all would be well.

Still, since hope and courage often proved inconsistent, and *Landsers* suffered under a constant threat of breakdown in combat, the *Wehrmacht* attempted to strengthen the morale and stiffen the resolve of its forces in a number of ways. One was to stress camaraderie and peer pressure by grouping friends together. Returning to the front after a stay in a military hospital, Guy Sajer was returned not only to his old unit but to his old rifle squad. "I'll take you to your friends," his captain said. "I know that being with friends can make up for the lack of a comfortable bed, even for the lack of food. . . . I always try to group my men as friends." And, Sajer recalled, "I suddenly felt the full strength of my attachment to all the friends . . . nearby, an emotion which struck me as . . . profound."[28]

Another way to brace men at the front was through constant action, the almost inevitable attacks and counterattacks for which the *Wehrmacht* was legendary. Nothing could be more demoralizing to a soldier than sitting immobile in the face of danger, nursing a feeling of helplessness. "In the morning enemy trench mortars begin to fire at us," Wilhelm Prüller noted in his diary, "and we suffered some losses. The more passively we react to it, however, the worse our losses are. . . . There's only one answer in this situation, too: attack." This *Flucht nach vorn* (flight to the front) was thus designed to capitalize on a soldier's inclination, while under stress, to take action to escape the situation. "There is only one thing," exclaimed Franz Rainer Hocke in July 1944, "always through, never back. Who slinks away before bombs and shells runs toward death." One *Landser* claimed that constant action was "perhaps the best part of a soldier's life"; another reveled in the "hurried rush forward. That type of war brings joy." Even a retreat could bring with it a strange sense of comfort and satisfaction. "The journey back was an experience," wrote a *Landser* in August 1943. "This war of movement is still more fun than the war of position; it's only a shame that it's backward instead of forward." As a common saying of German soldiers going into Soviet captivity had it, "Heads high, comrades, we're going forward again."[29]

Whether they were advancing or retreating, mail from home proved to be a lifeline for many *Landsers*, helping them cope with the constant harsh reality of death, reminding them that they had survived and still lived, and reassuring them that another world not demarcated by combat did exist. "Days in which no mail comes are not days at all," complained Harry Mielert in January 1943. "A few lines can throw a rosy, invigorating light in this desolate realm. . . . When I still think of October–November 1941, where we occasionally would go a week without receiving mail, how did we hold out?" Indeed, Mielert wrote to his wife later, "You can't imagine what so delighted me today: yesterday evening we withdrew over our latest battlefield, across riddled horses and Russians, horses, cows, and people rolled flat by tank columns. . . . We marched into a village, and in the prepared quarters lay on a table a whole pile of letters for me!" Amazingly, with his nerves strained to the breaking point by savage fighting in the late autumn of 1941, Private H.M. declared that the lack of mail was "his greatest worry."[30]

Through letters the *Landser* sought to preserve a sense of another life, a world not defined by death and destruction. "Your letter from home tore me away from the mean indifference into which the immediacy of war, without connection to home and neighbors, so easily drags us," reflected Mielert, "and I again have great joy in life." Taking a walk on a sunny day in a birch forest with his comrades, Friedrich Grupe noted "horse cadavers, destroyed equipment, dead Red army soldiers lying around." Little wonder that mail, for Grupe, represented "greetings from a no longer existing world," or that he wrote bitterly in his diary: "Some *Landsers* are yet writing a greeting home. What should they write? 'All is going well with me. . . .' But what will become of me tomorrow?" At the front, after all, there were only "the dead or the dead to be." This fear that the war would not be over until you yourself were dead infected other men as well. Still, the great majority of *Landsers* would have agreed with Martin Pöppel, who noted in his diary in January 1942, "another large delivery of post, which cheers everyone up to no end." For Pöppel, as for most soldiers, mail had mystical properties. "Post from home, that magic word, that dream, made reality again by letters. . . . Naturally everyone dives on the post whilst the work, well that can wait until morning. " After all, if only for a brief time, it was "a little bit of home in this miserable existence."[31]

As the war continued, however, even letters from home lost some of their ability to bring cheer. As Pöppel noted in his diary: "My wife wrote to me: 'Today we are worn out after this terrible hail of bombs. To be hearing the howling of these things all the time, waiting for death at any moment, in a dark cellar, unable to see. . . . Everything gone. . . . Is everything going to be destroyed. . . ?' No, here at the front we mustn't think about it either. . . . We understood the feelings of the people at home, suffered with them and feared for our loved ones who had to bear terror bombing."[32]

The Allied aerial bombardment of Germany piled another layer of concern on top of the *Landsers'* almost insurmountable daily struggle just to stay alive. The reason for this transformation was duly noted by many *Landsers*. A feeling of impotence about the destruction of German cities pervaded their letters, for they now worried, as did Prosper Schücking, about "the terrible air attacks at home. A fellow back from leave told me that Hannover is 91 percent destroyed, Herrenhausen is also annihilated, a true shame." "How wonderful to be allowed to sleep in a bed again!" exclaimed Martin Lindner while on his last leave. "Only the people have become so different," he mused, "they are driven by a great unrest. It is as if they are all rushing toward a catastrophe, like a train racing over a precipice."[33]

Because of the heavy volume of mail between home and front, and as a result of the occasional home leaves, the *Landsers* remained fully informed of the horrific events in the homeland. "Before we in our gypsy life again resume our further pull-back, a quick greeting to you on the Berlin 'front,' " wrote Max Aretin-Eggert with self-conscious irony. "In the event, now the dead of the great cities are themselves being dissolved in flames. . . . Does the god of war rule . . . in a blind rage?" Even the hardships of the Russian front seemed to pale in comparison with the difficulties at home. "A third year of the Russian campaign looms," despaired Jürgen Mogk in September 1942, "but that means nothing when one considers the wider future. It is not the insufficient bread that is wearing down the German people, but rather something far more terrible: the bombardment of German cities by the English! Each of us would rather go hungry than lose his house and home, and yes his loved ones."[34]

The home front as a real "front" had an irony to it that some *Landsers* understood more than others. "On Easter Sunday I lay in my swimming trunks with a comrade in the warm spring sun," wrote Sergeant K. in May 1943, "and we talked back and forth about what we would do if we were at home. . . . And a few days ago I found out that just at the same time as we dreamed of home, the rubble was smoking in my home city of Mannheim. What a bitter irony!" But Corporal E.G. failed completely to see the irony of German methods turned against the Reich itself. "I regret extraordinarily that you there have to suffer so from the English aerial terror actions," he raged:

> [My] thoughts are tormented that the beautiful city of Düsseldorf is also fallen victim to a vile British terror attack, [that] immense art, cultural, and material treasures are annihilated with brutal force and the criminal war methods of the Tommies have caused nameless suffering. . . . Even innocent German men, women, and children were killed in the most barbarous manner . . . , accomplished only through the . . . brutal attack methods of a predatory state which once wanted to be the representative of the so-called "civilized world(!) [sic]." Now we actually know only too well what Churchill

and his infamous clique of British . . . war criminals mean by the concept of "civilization"!

Nor did Sergeant H.K. doubt the "criminal" methods used by the British in waging war against the German home front: "It is not decisive for the war if the Cologne Cathedral or the Hans Sachs house are turned into ruins. . . . These pigs . . . think they can soften us up in that way. But that is a mistake, a mistake. Ah, if only the Führer would send a pair of Estonian, East Prussian, Franconian divisions to England. They would deal a death dance that would give the devil himself the creeps. Oh, I have a rage, a wild hatred."[35]

In the earlier days of the war it had been possible for Harry Mielert to write to his wife, "You should know everything, and I cannot revive the eternal lie that I am cheerful and happy. I also regard this belief, that the home front should not know what happens here, as false. If one has no confidence at all in the psychological powers of resistance of the homeland, then it is in a bad way." Now total war had so transformed the face of battle that not only was the civilian population experiencing the reality of war, but letters from the fighting front were considered vital to maintaining morale on the home front. A constant theme of *Mitteilungen für die Truppe*, a front newspaper distributed to every German unit, was the important task that *Feldpostbriefe* (letters from the field) performed in supporting the mental and spiritual well-being of those at home. Indeed, it characterized letters as "weapons" whose worth and value played a key role in sustaining the "attitude and strength of nerve" of the average civilian. Issue after issue screamed that "the field postal service is a weapon," that "letters are also weapons," even that they represented "a type of vitamin for the spirit" which would "lift tired hearts high again." They were compared to "important nerve fibers that [ran] from the exterior to the interior of the great body of the German nation," to the "blood circulation of a body." So important had letters from the front to home become that in August 1943 the commander of the third Panzer Army issued an order to his men that "the soldier must therefore be in his letters. . . . a blood donor for the belief and will of his relatives." And an order emanating from Army Group B decried, "It is necessary that every front soldier in his letters home radiate strength, confidence, and trust."[36] In what must have seemed to the *Landser* the ultimate irony of the war, then, in addition to his own concerns and anxieties he also had to help master those of the home front. Death knew no boundaries, and the task of coping while in the grip of overwhelming forces now encompassed the *Heimat* as well as the front.

Inevitably, as the war ground on and the various armies found themselves locked in a nervous embrace like wrestlers struggling for the final advantage, the strain of this everyday life of killing took its psychological toll. For at its most concrete, this was a war not of open combat but of waiting, hiding, creeping, brawling—a contest between small groups of men, each group trying to kill the other before they in turn were killed. In this continuous personal confrontation with death, every *Landser*—"we who are playing the walk-on parts in this madness incarnate," as one put it—had a breaking point. "The sight of comrades screaming and writhing through final moments of agony had become no more bearable with familiarity," Guy Sajer confessed, "and I, despite my longing to live or die a hero of the *Wehrmacht*, was no less an animal stiff with uncontrollable terror." All *Landsers*, the most seasoned veteran or a frightened replacement, felt a constant sense of anxiety and had to conquer themselves anew each day. As Harry Mielert noted, "Everything is agitated and in me there is only restless tension and anticipation. We must maintain our nerves. . . . Each second decides our existence." "The war, whose thin end we have behind us and whose thick we have before us, weighs very heavily on me," confessed Lieutenant W.T. in January 1944. "In moments of clarity" there was something "ghostly" about it, he admitted. "Although the facade still holds, how easily one can disintegrate at night."[37]

Many *Landsers* would have seconded the conclusion of an anonymous soldier at Stalingrad that the "suffering is greater than the possibility of assuaging it." During the Russian counterattack in December 1941, Corporal H.M. noted that the "retreat has really shattered us, the continually overstrained nerves sometimes want no more." In seeking a release, some men even turned to thoughts of suicide. "I have already thought often of making an end to my life," confessed Sergeant W.H. in January 1942. "And as a young man just to force myself to overcome this bridge from life into death costs inner strength that has nothing to do with courage or bravery." Some *Landsers* proved unable to refuse to cross the bridge between life and death. Admitted Sergeant K.H. ruefully in February 1942, "Unfortunately there are many men who cannot summon the energy to resist . . . and therefore face a certain death." As Harry Mielert well knew, "Here [at the front] you must be either brazen or shattered." And brazenness he defined as merely an "instinctive, egoistic self-defense," because you could have "no other attitude."[38]

For others, the strain of combat left them not so much resigned to death as simply indifferent, numb, and only occasionally roused to anger or hope or joy. "From time to time one of us would emerge from torpor and scream," recalled Guy Sajer. "These screams were entirely involuntary: we couldn't stop them. They were produced by our exhaustion. . . . Some laughed as they howled; others prayed. Men who could pray could hope." "Even death has lost all its horror," admitted Claus Hansmann. "It has become mundane . . . banal." Mielert betrayed the same indifference in May 1943, admitting to his wife, "My concerns are impersonal. . . . That here and there comrades lie dead or wounded is a part of everyday life." Later, he confessed, "I hardly know myself anymore. . . . I am so alone with my feelings, I cannot communicate them to anyone." And shortly before his death Mielert wrote, "The feeling will not go away from me that I am now an old man and have an illness that will accompany me until death." Similarly, Klaus Löscher confided in his diary that he "lacked concentration . . . because the feeling paralyzes me that after all, everything is in vain, without sense, without value. I once again have the strong feeling that I'm not coming back. . . . A vague listlessness has gripped me and immobilizes every activity."[39] Löscher fell three weeks later.

This all-consuming lassitude, in fact, often signified for a *Landser* the end of his struggle. "At the moment I am prepared," wrote Ewald H. "You see, I have seen life. I can no longer experience the happiness and the misfortunes of this world. War, you monster, this time you have crushed the whole earth. God, you have directed these events, why are you so inscrutable, so cruel and harsh? Build a new world, and allow this death to find an end." This despairing plea proved his last entry; he was killed four days later. As Max Aretin-Eggert explained in his last letter, this peculiar feeling was as if "we stagger in a whirlpool. . . . From the 'outside' no comfort and no relief and escape is possible . . . [for] one doesn't know if one is among the living or the dead."[40]

Indeed, the harrowing pressures of combat eventually affected virtually all *Landsers*. "During the last few nights I have wept so much that it seems unbearable even to myself," despaired a soldier fighting in Stalingrad. "On Tuesday I knocked out two T-34's. . . . It was grand and impressive. Afterward I drove past the smoking remains. From a hatch there hung a body, head down, his feet caught, and his legs burning up to his knees.

The body was alive, the mouth moaning. He must have suffered terrible pain. And there was no possibility of freeing him. . . . I shot him, and as I did it, the tears ran down my cheeks. Now I have been crying for three nights about a dead Russian tank driver, whose murderer I am. . . . I'm afraid I'll never be able to sleep quietly. . . . My life is . . . a psychological monstrosity." Another *Landser* writing from the doomed city on the Volga agreed: "Of my company, only five men are still around. . . . The others are all . . . grown too tired. Isn't that a nice euphemism for the horror?"[41]

"We felt like lost souls who had forgotten that men are made for something else, . . . that love can sometimes occur, that the earth can be productive and used for something other than burying the dead," Guy Sajer recalled as he and his comrades neared the breaking point. "We were madmen, gesturing and moving without thought or hope. . . . Lindberg . . . had collapsed into a kind of stupor. . . . The Sudeten . . . had begun to tremble . . . and to vomit uncontrollably. Madness had invaded our group, and was gaining ground rapidly. . . . I saw . . . Hals leap to his machine gun and fire at the sky, which continued to pour down its rain of flame and metal. I also saw the [sergeant] . . . beat the ground with his clenched fist. . . . [I] shout[ed] curses and obscenities at the sky. I had reached the edge of the abyss." At such a moment of extreme nervous exhaustion it was not uncommon, Sajer testified, for men to fall into a "paralytic sleep," a stupor so great that even the presence of the enemy could not rouse them. "When danger . . . continues indefinitely, it becomes unbearable. . . . After hours and then days of danger . . . one collapses into unbearable madness, and a crisis of nerves is only the beginning. Finally, one vomits and collapses, entirely brutalized and inert, as if death had already won."[42] Worn down by grinding fatigue, their reserves of energy exhausted, many men sank into this zombi-like state; their nerves shut down, and psychologically they withdrew from the battlefield.

Confronted with such overwhelming strain, then, even the toughest men and strongest nerves often disintegrated. Despite the motivation and self-discipline that sprang from the tight-knit nature of the small *Kameradschaft,* and the generally high level of confidence and cohesion between officers and men, the prolonged stress and dreadful casualties led almost inevitably to a breakdown in these invisible threads of discipline. As internal self-control wavered, Nazi and *Wehrmacht* officials quickly imposed external, often draconian measures to shore up the fragile shell of discipline. To a degree, Nazi practice reflected German military tradition, for harsh discipline had long been a staple of the Prussian martial heritage. For example, Frederick the Great had stated quite succinctly that "the common soldier must fear his officer more than the enemy." Still, in World War I the German army, compared to the British and French, had been quite sparing in its use of the ultimate punishment; in fact, between 1914 and 1918, German military authorities sentenced only 150 men to death, of whom 48 were actually executed. By contrast, the French handed down roughly 2,000 death sentences and carried out approximately 700, while the British sentenced 3,080 to death and executed 346.[43]

Hitler, among others, had bitterly criticized this sparing use of harsh punishment, claiming that feeble military justice was a prime cause of the deterioration of the German army at the end of World War I. Hitler, in fact, believed implicitly in the "stab-in-the-back" myth, the notion that Germany had lost World War I because of a collapse of discipline and morale on the home front. Once in power he was determined not only to toughen the army's code of discipline, but also to reshape civilian justice according to Nazi demands. Hence, military standards came to reflect those of civilian society, as for historical reasons Hitler aimed at creating a tight-knit *Volksgemeinschaft*, both civilian and military, which would do his bidding without cracking under the pressure of war. German military justice was thus fundamentally altered to create a strong link between the *Wehrmacht* and the Nazi regime. In place of the relatively lenient system of World War I came a harsh system of discipline at the core of which stood severe punishments for what were deemed "political crimes" against the National Socialist state: desertion and *Wehrkraftzersetzung* (undermining the fighting spirit of the troops). As the Nazi regime tied the *Wehrmacht* ideologically tighter to itself, behavior and discipline increasingly became political issues, and the *Wehrmacht* legal system in World War II proved quite willing to impose draconian punishments. Of the roughly 20,000 German soldiers executed by the end of the war, 75–80 percent had been deemed guilty of these "political" crimes.[44]

Not surprisingly, the growing harshness of discipline placed another burden on the average *Landser*. The infamous "punishment battalion," for example, was widely feared and resented as a virtual death sentence. In his searing and starkly realistic novel *Stalingrad*, Theodor Plievier described such a unit, placed in a dangerous sector of the Russian front:

It was a good post for the disciplinary battalion. The orders read: "The term of punishment is to be served in the farthermost front line. The punishment shall consist of the most difficult and dangerous work, such as mine clearance, burial of the dead, etc, under enemy fire. . . .

Pay: to be curtailed. Uniform: to hinder desertion, uniform without insignia. . . . Shelter: less comfortable than that of the other troops. Mail: at discretion of the officer in charge. . . . Association with other units or civilians is forbidden unless in line of duty. Lighting: none to be supplied. Privileges: will be granted in special cases only by the officer in charge."

Men sent to such posts were the chaff of the war, their principal "crime" deemed to be undermining the discipline or morale of the troops. "Fear of . . . the disciplinary battalion," Guy Sajer confirmed, greatly motivated him and his comrades.[45]

But the Landser soon learned that the punishment battalion was hardly the only thing to be dreaded. "So the Landser arrived," wrote one soldier to his wife following the German debacle in Rumania in the summer of 1944, "torn to pieces, filthy, unshaven, completely exhausted and with sore feet, many came without boots, with only cloths wrapped around their feet . . . and everyone, whether enlisted man or officer, had only salvaged their naked lives." But, he noted, the physical hardships proved to be the least of their worries: "There were no longer any organized formations, each sought only to save himself. . . . In Bessarabia we then reached a reporting station where the soldiers learned where they could again find their units. Also, at the crossroads and bridges stood officers who seized individual Landsers and used them to build new battalions. . . . There were also thousands who fell into bad company in this wild mess and didn't report . . . and drifted around for weeks robbing and plundering, for which many were given the death penalty and hanged." As Sajer confessed, the thought of "being incorporated into an impromptu battalion" struck terror into him, for these units were composed of men "already classified as missing or dead by their original units," so were "used as unexpected reinforcements whom there was no reason to spare."[46] A Landser caught in this human maelstrom was fortunate indeed to rejoin his old outfit, to escape being cast into one of the Wehrmacht's hastily organized units or becoming a roaming mercenary likely to end his soldiering days at the end of an army rope.

Nor was it only unruly soldiers engaged in illegal activities who found themselves caught in the wide net thrown out by the collecting officers. Following a disorganized retreat across the Dnieper in late 1943, Sajer and his fellow survivors were confronted by the dreaded German field police—who always inspired "desperate unease"—then in the process of restoring order and discipline. A corporal, Sajer recalled, "told us to get over to the tables to be screened. We should be ready to produce on demand the papers and equipment entrusted to us by the army. This reception only increased our sense of astonished unease," for as Sajer knew, "the most serious of accusations were leveled against anyone who returned without his weapons. . . . Our soldiers were never supposed to abandon their arms. They were supposed to die with them."[47]

Sajer's misgivings increased as he witnessed the interrogation of a lieutenant directly ahead of him in the line.

> "Where is your unit, lieutenant?"
> "Annihilated, Herr Gendarme. Missing or dead. . . ."
> "Did you leave your men, or were they killed?"
> The lieutenant hesitated for a moment. . . . [He] clearly felt caught in a trap, as did we all. . . . He tried to explain. But there is never any point in explaining to an M.P.: their powers of comprehension are always limited to the form they wish to fill.
> Further, it appeared that the lieutenant was missing a great many things. . . . The army did not distribute its papers and equipment only to have them scattered and lost. A German soldier is expected to die rather than indulge in carelessness with army property.
> The careless lieutenant was assigned to a penal battalion. . . .
> At that, he could think himself lucky.

Lucky, that is, as Sajer well knew, only because the alternative was to be shot on the spot.

> Then it was my turn. I felt stiff with fright. . . . Fortunately I had been able to reintegrate with my unit. . . .
> "You were retreating?"
> "Ja, *Herr Unteroffizier* (Corporal)."
> "Why didn't you . . . fight," he shouted. . . .
> "We were ordered to retreat, *Herr Unteroffizier*."
> "God damn it to hell!" he roared. "What kind of an army runs without shooting?"
> My pay book came down the line. My interrogator grabbed

it, and riffled the pages for a moment. . . . I followed the movement of his lips, which might be about to assign me to a penal battalion, to the life of a prisoner, to forward positions, mine clearing, infrequent leaves always confined to camps, so that the word "liberty" lost all meaning. . . .

   I held back my tears with difficulty. Finally the M.P.'s rigid fingers handed back my liberty. I had not been assigned to a penal battalion, but my emotion overwhelmed me anyway. As I picked up my pack, I sobbed convulsively, unable to stop. A fellow beside me was doing the same.[48]

So intimidating was *Wehrmacht* discipline that in the aftermath of a savage battle, in which he had only just escaped with his life, Sajer found himself overwhelmed with emotion not because of his recent ordeal but because he had narrowly eluded the more terrifying fate of the penal battalion or instant execution.

   The harshest discipline and greatest danger of execution came in the last months of the war, when "flying courts martial" and similar institutions likely executed 7,000–8,000 men, most immediately and on the spot, using the so-called political crimes of desertion and *Wehrkraftzersetzung* used to justify such draconian measures. The great majority of men thus summarily tried and executed had rarely exhibited any overt ideological or oppositional motivation for their behavior. Rather, they were simply men, usually young, poorly educated, and slightly bewildered, who just could not cope any longer with combat conditions. Guy Sajer related a dreary episode of a kind that would grow only too familiar in the months to come. During the disorderly withdrawal through the Carpathians in the summer of 1944, "someone up ahead shouted for us to come and see," Sajer remembered. "We looked down into a leafy ravine. A camouflaged truck . . . had crashed to the bottom." And to these ravenous men, some of whom had not eaten in days, the contents of the truck were "like a whole commissary. . . . Chocolate, cigarettes, wurst." But standing in the way of the enjoyment of such a bounty loomed the constant threat of the *Feldpolizei*, made more dangerous since many of these *Landsers* had lost or thrown away their military equipment. Sajer and his immediate comrades proved fortunate, however: "Like hungry beasts, we wolfed down the contents of the tins and the other provisions," he recalled. "'We'd better eat it all,' Lensen said. 'If we're caught with anything in our sacks that wasn't handed out, we'll be in trouble.' 'You're right. Let's eat it all. They won't slit us open to see what's inside, although it would be just like those bastards to check our shit.' For an hour we gorged ourselves until we were almost sick. When it grew dark, we returned to the road by a devious route."[49]

They had escaped detection, but others of their unit were not so lucky:

> We resumed our trek. . . . And then there was a tree, a majestic tree, whose branches seemed to be supporting the sky. Two sacks were dangling from those branches, two empty scarecrows swinging in the wind, suspended by two short lengths of rope. We walked under them, and saw the gray, bloodless faces of hanged men, and recognized our wretched friend Frösch and his companion.
> "Don't worry, Frösch," whispered Hals. "We ate it all."
> Lindberg hid his face in his hands and wept. I managed with difficulty to read the message scribbled on the sign tied to Frösch's broken neck.
> "I am a thief and a traitor to my country."

Poor Frösch had been one of those archetypal bewildered men who had never quite adjusted to life at the front, a nondescript individual whom Sajer had earlier described as "a foolish-looking fellow of angelic good will. . . . He always wore an expression of touching stupidity and banal good will."[50] For those like Frösch unlucky enough to have lost their units or equipment in the disorderly retreat that was the *Götterdämmerung* of the Nazi regime, such cursory "justice" loomed as a sobering reminder that the tentacles of the Hitler state still clutched them in a deadly embrace.

Landsers found without the proper documents or suspected of desertion also became victims of these summary trials. For maximum deterrent effect, those executed were normally left dangling from trees or poles with placards attached to them, warning others of the consequences of any perceived dereliction of duty. Max Landowski recalled such sights during his westward flight from Danzig in January 1945, remembering particularly that many of the hanged had been accused of "cowardice in the face of the enemy." As he put it, "There was no mercy." Reporting to *Wehrmacht* authorities in Cottbus, Landowski saw in front of the headquarters building "an executed German soldier [lying] on the grass, and he had a large placard . . . on his chest and on it appeared: 'That's how it goes for one who is a coward.' " Erwin Lösch recalled a similarly "horrific picture" in Danzig: "on the trees along the street hung

German soldiers, ropes around their necks. Some were barefoot and almost all had a sign on their chest on which 'coward' appeared. Not a few had decorations on their field uniforms. It took our breath away." And sixteen-year-old Hans-Rudolf Vilter still never forgot the picture of chaos in Berlin, especially "the deserters and apprehended soldiers that one saw hanging on the lampposts and trees with the sign: 'I hang here because I am too cowardly to defend my fatherland.' "[51]

As the front contracted in the final months of the war, terror menaced *Landsers* everywhere. Throughout Germany the field police, despised by the *Landsers* as *Heldenklau* (hero snatchers), diligently sought out so-called "enemies of the people." Max Landowski recalled that the army "guard dogs" patrolled the NSV (*Nationalsozialistische Volksfürsorge*, or National Socialist People's Welfare) centers, which had proved quite effective in dealing with displaced persons, searching for soldiers either to haul into the *Volkssturm* (people's militia) or to hang. All depended on a piece of paper, one's written authorization, and whether it had the proper stamps and signatures. Enterprising *Landsers* who, like Otl Aicher, had access to typewriters and stamped, blank forms authorizing various kinds of travel, successfully navigated the treacherous path to safety. In an ironic twist of events, Karl Grebe, a corporal, helped an officer reach his hometown by signing a travel document complete except for the authorizing signature. As Grebe recollected, "smartly I signed with swelling letters: Grebe, Colonel and Regimental Commander. Satisfied, he took the document. . . . I continued on." Often one needed not only luck but *chutzpah* to survive.[52]

Traveling with falsified papers remained highly dangerous, however, as the search patrols seemed ubiquitous. For the *Landser*, though, the field police were not the only concern. One recalled with bitterness that in the fall of 1944 armed German officers gave his unit no choice but to attack enemy lines. The other option was clear: be shot by your own leaders. Some units even established special formations whose instructions were "to make immediate use of their weapons in order to enforce obedience and discipline." As Helmut Altner wrote caustically, the situation many *Landsers* found themselves in was devilishly simple: "There were only two possibilities. Death by a bullet from the enemy or by the 'thugs' of the SS."[53]

Perhaps in order to spare those at home, the average *Landser* wrote surprisingly little about disciplinary measures in the army, and those who did referred primarily to deserters or common criminals. Nevertheless, the execution of fellow soldiers could be quite shattering. "As a sentry on a guard duty lasting several days, yesterday evening I had to [guard] a detainee sentenced to death [for desertion]," Friedrich Andreas von Koch reported from Holland:

> From 1:00 A.M. to 4:00 A.M. in the night I had the watch. After long indecision I entered the detainee's corridor. . . . and forced myself to open the door and look inside. Pain shot through my heart as I saw him suddenly bolt up from the bed. . . . "What is it?" he asked in a hoarse, quiet voice. I mumbled, retreated with a kind of horror, and once again left the cell corridor. Only after an hour was I finally able to gather some strength. I walked back there and said to the chaplain, while the condemned man slumbered, that I did not want to fail to carry out what I felt compelled to do. . . . I asked that he read the poems [that I had written down] to the convicted man and greet him for me.
>
> At 7:00 A.M. in the morning the field police appeared. . . . The shackled convict walked past me, saw me and nodded. He was quite steady, walked upright, and didn't appear pitiable. . . . While I am writing this, the sentence is being carried out.

Koch remained obviously troubled by the episode; in a letter some two months later he reported having heard that "the condemned man had died in a very composed manner, after he had rejected the proffered blindfold."[54]

Others, too, were upset by the apparent necessity of harsh discipline. "A member of our battalion stole a set of silver flatware and some other valuable items from a house," wrote Corporal J.S. of the Seventy-ninth Infantry Division. "The soldier came before a military court and was sentenced to death by firing squad. I myself was also ordered to be at the execution. . . . The condemned man, accompanied by a Catholic priest, was brought to the place in a car. The death sentence was read. The condemned, a twenty-two-year-old, said goodbye to the priest. To us he directed the words: 'Comrades, do your duty!' These were also his last words." Even a sentencing officer might express reluctance: "One thing is always difficult for me," noted Lieutenant Colonel H.Z. in August 1944, "namely, when for reasons of discipline I have to pronounce the final decision about life and death for a man and after the *most conscientious* examination . . . must sign the death sentence. This remains for me always the most difficult thing, but sometimes, thankfully *very seldom* with German soldiers, nothing else is possible."[55]

Perhaps to this officer the necessity of such discipline seemed rare, but to the average *Landser* the harshest punishment had become part of everyday life. As early as the end of 1941 one German division was taking steps to ensure discipline by instilling the fear that Ivan was less worrisome than the consequences of cowardice: "Lance-Corporal Aigner . . . was sentenced to death by court martial on the charge of cowardice," ran the special order. "Although he had seen his unit marching forward, he entered a house, drank a bottle of schnapps . . . and fled to the rear without cap or weapon, where he was seized in this ragged and drunken condition. Every case of cowardice will be severely atoned for with death. The troops are to be instructed on this by the company commanders personally." In the summer of 1943 the same division ordered that "every officer, NCO, and man . . . do everything to control . . . outbreaks of panic." Indeed, officers were expected "to make ruthless use of all means at their disposal against men who bring about occurrences of panic and who leave their comrades in the lurch, and, if necessary, not to refrain from using their weapons."[56]

Such pronouncements were taken seriously, both by the enforcers and by the men. "The news on the radio is really shitty and I believe it is five minutes before midnight, and now they will probably soon have us by the ass," wrote an obviously embittered Corporal B. in August 1944. "We will probably still have to work for the Russians. In any case it looks really ominous. . . . Accordingly, just none of us ask if you can or can't. We must, and if you don't want to, you get popped, and then you have no more worries."[57] Despite his none too subtle efforts at masking his true meaning, Corporal B. had his letter set aside by the censors and stamped "to be pursued further." He may well have become a victim of the harsh discipline he decried.

Discipline was not always uniformly applied, however. Whereas in the West the *Wehrmacht* tended to punish crimes such as theft, murder, and rape committed against civilians, German troops in Russia were often permitted to kill Jews and other so-called ideological or racial enemies without threat of punishment to themselves. Given the designation of the enemy as *Untermenschen* (subhumans) to be stamped out, it was rare indeed for a *Landser* even to be charged if his crime was committed against the Slavic population of the East, and those who were charged tended to get off lightly. Private H.K. furnished one example of this uneven application of military justice, noting in June 1940 the case of a corporal, "the father of five small children," who raped "a highly pregnant woman," raped a woman over age fifty, and attempted to rape two others—"25 June from midnight until 1:00 A.M.!" Although the eventual punishment was not as severe as the case warranted (the rapist received two years' imprisonment), what astonished Private H.K. at the time was that "the soldier in question already had an attempted rape in Poland behind him" and, far from being punished, had instead been promoted in rank. In another example of selective discipline, a *Landser* who had killed a Jewish woman in Russia received only six months' imprisonment for manslaughter.[58]

Given the constant elemental anxiety, the bleak sense that killing had assumed a life of its own, and the lurking fear that "only if I die will the war be over," even a moment spent in combat stamped a *Landser* for a lifetime. "In spite of the confusion swirling around the soldier in combat," claimed Siegfried Knappe,

> he still retained a clear sense of his own strength and the strength of the men beside him; he felt an almost palpable sense of solidarity with his fellow soldiers. This was the brotherhood of the combat soldier.
>
> Improbable as life in combat was, after a while it became the only reality, and the combat soldier soon found it difficult to remember anything else. He would try to remember the face of a loved one and he could not. The soldier on his left and on his right became the only reality and now, in truth, the only loved ones. To the combat soldier, life became an endless series of hard physical work, raw courage, occasional laughter, and a terrible sense of living out a merciless fate.

At the front, all shared this forlorn view. "I had often thought that if I managed to live through the war I wouldn't expect much of life," Guy Sajer admitted. "Terror had overturned all my preconceptions, and . . . one no longer knew what elements of ordinary life to abandon in order to maintain some semblance of balance. . . . I had already sworn to myself during moments of intense fear that I would exchange anything, fortune, love, even a limb, if I could simply survive." The very act of survival itself often seemed a daring blow against fate. "Who speaks of victory?" Harald Henry wondered bitterly in November 1941. "Survival is everything." Some *Landsers*, in fact, saw survival as the ultimate act of heroism. "In your last letter you thought I was a hero and even called me a hero," a twenty-three-year-old company commander chastised his wife. "Please don't write that again, for . . . I imagine a hero differently, and up to now I have still not met a man who was a hero; or, all of our soldiers here at the front are heroes." Each *Landser*, concluded Corporal O.S. sardonically, "should get the Iron Cross, but along with it most also get the wooden one."[59]

The hardships created by their daily existence and the capriciousness of death led many *Landsers* to adopt a certain fatalistic resignation that represented a way of coping with their situation. War, to Wilhelm Rubino, created "hard hours, where one stood small and helpless before a fate that decided your existence and nonexistence." Similarly, Bernhard Beckering despaired, "We stand time and again helpless and apprehensive before death." Gottfried Gruner put it more succinctly, remarking with pure resignation that "everything goes along because it must." Harry Mielert agreed, noting that it was "strange how you can occasionally let yourself be overwhelmed by lassitude. In actuality, it perhaps takes a threat to your life alone to overcome this debility."[60]

Still, this sense of fate as an independent creature, of having no control over one's destiny, of being in a situation where "the fate of the individual lay in the hands of blind chance," could be strangely comforting to some. "Fate is difficult, often incomprehensibly hard," explained Hans Pietzcker, "[but] we who often look death in the face wherever we go have learned to walk opposite him with composure. Certainly he will come sooner or later." Siegfried Knappe had "become fatalistic about [death] and assume[d] that eventually it would happen to me and there was nothing I could do to prevent it. I did not wait for it to happen . . . but I knew that I was going to be killed or badly wounded sooner or later. . . . I accepted my eventual death or maiming as part of my fate. Once I had forced myself to accept that, I could put it out of my mind and go on about my duties." Similarly, Lieutenant K. had come "to confront [death] with a manly courage, that is, with a quiet but steady resolve and a clear consciousness of the danger." Helmut Vethake believed that standing before the hard fate of death taught one "pure, total humility, . . . humility that compels me to contemplate the infinite purity, perfection, and patience of every plant and flower."[61]

Other *Landsers* seemed almost to glory in the strange mystery of chance. "The front lines, the entrenched riflemen have greatly impressed me," wrote Hans-Heinrich Ludwig in October 1941, "especially their attitude. These fellows are fabulous. A complete submission to fate." To Heinz Küchler there was no sense to the war—indeed, "its sense lay in its senselessness"—yet he maintained that "our greatness must lie in the ability not to master fate but rather to maintain our personality, our will, our love in defiance of fate and, unbowed, to be a sacrifice." Sacrifice and suffering as transcendent glory was a theme also emphasized by Siegbert Stehmann in September 1944: "How the horror of these times has affected us, that we accept the omnipresence of terror with an equanimity that we never could have imagined! The German people has almost surpassed the legendary capacity for suffering of Russia. Perhaps this is the greatness of its hour. 'Whoever tramples on his misfortune stands taller.' . . . For have we soldiers not already made the highest and last inner farewell and humbly take each day . . . as a gift of grace?" Willi Huber valued the fact that "this war, even as gruesome and atrocious as it is, has given us once again splendid examples of decent and upright men who sacrifice themselves." Trapped in Stalingrad, exhausted by the bitter fighting and lack of food, and nearing the end of his resistance, Lieutenant H.H. could still assert: "To maintain your loyalty with death before your eyes is a service that must prove us worthy," and Captain H. claimed to be "extremely proud to have participated in this unique heroic epic of history." Sacrifice, then, was seen as noble, especially because "individuals die, while the *Volk* lives on." After all, as many *Landsers* had been told, sacrifice was natural, because "an individual called to a heroic death was 'thereby furthering life itself.' "[62]

To Harald Henry, however, fate and the notion of a hero's death seemed merely a pathetic justification for continuing this "fight for our naked existence. . . . Only the absolute inevitability of our fate compels us to bear what otherwise would never be bearable." Likewise, Helmut Pabst raged against the capriciousness of death and those who said, "'It was fate, it was destiny.' But is that actually right? Is it not a miserable attempt to give a meaning to each event only because we are too cowardly to stare the senselessness of it in the face . . . ? War strikes without choice, and if it knows a law it is that the best are struck down. . . . Here no one surrenders to his fate. We are not lambs of God, but rather we protect ourselves, . . . and our confidence lies not in God but in the calm and attention with which we do what is necessary."[63]

This existential anguish, these "cries of damned souls," as Pabst put it, betrayed an almost desperate desire to believe, to give the war some sort of meaning. With frightening directness, Bernhard Beckering in his last letter confronted this loss of faith. "It is a lingering farewell. The gods have abandoned me. I have a frightful understanding . . . of what a central problem is the experience of being deserted by the gods."

Within the week, Beckering was killed. When, as Harry Mielert declared, "anger roars through all the cracks in the world," it was a rage based on fear that the war had no purpose. Still, Mielert insisted that there had to be some design to the war, even if he could not consciously grasp it. "I feel always clearer," he wrote, "that even my unconscious being and actions stand under the direction of positive values." Other *Landsers* too sought desperately to find some meaningful pattern. "Out of the chaos of terror I am building piece by piece concrete pictures," Günter von Scheven asserted. "The essential thing is that the inner structure remains solidly outlined."[64]

But the conflict between pattern and chaos persisted and led to inner haunting about the spareness of life. "I believe in a meaning, even if I cannot always detect it," declared Horstmar Seitz. "I know now certainly that my life must fulfill a spiritual purpose." But, he added tellingly, "you need much strength to remain hard and not to forget the larger issues in your own small fate." "What keeps me going," contended Gottfried Gruner, "is the consciousness that in the end everything must yet have a meaning." Imploring, pleading that there must be a pattern, a meaning to this chaos, some *Landsers* in their desperate search seemed to turn to a mystic romanticism. "To us lonely men in our hopelessness one thing has been revealed," wrote Siegbert Stehmann, "that reality is nothing, but miracle is everything. That keeps us upright. No man can help us, only God alone."[65]

Not surprisingly, many *Landsers* sought comfort in religion, but their faith was often tinged with arrogant self-pity, betraying anger at what they saw as both their own and Germany's undeserved fate. "The Germans, the eternal Job of world history, sit everywhere on the ruins of their silent, beloved world," moaned Siegbert Stehmann in September 1944, "and wait eagerly on the releasing word of God, who can heal the broken." To him, faith in God was at once straightforward and complex: "The present," he brooded, "is but a dark passage between God and God; for those who best know who God is sit in the grim fires of hell. We must not quarrel with our fate." Still, Stehmann could not finally accept such a judgment but proceeded to squabble over, if not his lot, the fate of Germany: "The material concerns weigh lightly when one thinks of the coming fate of our *Volk*. . . . A thousand-year Reich is going to the grave. . . . God will help us. For the sacramental grace that now for a millennium has flowed in our country . . . cannot be lost. . . . No one in the world is more blessed than our people, which even today still has its roots in the profound."[66]

Germany, at last, had to be rescued from destruction, if only because the Germans were uniquely profound. Audacious and presumptuous as it seemed, Stehmann's was not an atypical comment. "You must know to come to terms with your lot, even if it is tragic," wrote Rolf Hoffmann in February 1945. "Everything has an end, even the war. . . . Then we will again construct a worthy existence. As Eichendorff said: 'As long as I breathe, I'm not given up for lost.' So it is with our beloved Fatherland. We have held out for six long years against a world of enemies; we knew only battle and work and battle again. Do we deserve in the end to be smashed and destroyed? We want to trust in the Lord God, that He has not deserted our German people and will give back to it at the end of this mighty struggle its right to life on this earth. That means waiting until a better future is granted us."[67]

Others knew better, however, recognizing that despite their maudlin self-pity the Germans merited their fate. Wilhelm Heidtmann rued the fact that "many Anglo-Americans fight in the belief that they speak for Christ's cause when they defend the democratic form of state. . . . The Western powers have the advantage of an open profession of the Christian belief; thereby we are forced into the role of the opponent of the Christian faith. Furthermore, they are superior to us in that they have an unbroken belief in the practical consequences of the power of God in this world. . . . Perhaps in this we have something to learn from them. Who gives God honor, He helps. That you can see from history." Walter Wenzl came to a similar though more pointed conclusion. "We must never forget," he wrote at the end of March 1945, "that what has befallen us and is still descending upon us is deserved in its entirety. And only when we have served our guilt and when peace for us is again more than quiet and idleness, only then will this sacrifice come to an end. . . . Then what will also come will come from Him and He should find us ready."[68]

Some *Landsers* coped by maintaining a fierce will to live. After all, as Siegbert Stehmann noted, Rainer Maria Rilke had written that "'everything beautiful has a horrible beginning.' . . . And our life is beautiful, infinitely beautiful." At the front, "we are all alike," argued Helmut Pabst, "for we all have been shut off from a carefree life. But that does not lead to weariness or to resignation. . . . [Rather] we developed a powerful will to live. . . . One lives for the moment. . . . To live is alone happiness. But even in the serious hours one senses a life full of substance. It is bitter and sweet, all and one, . . . because we have learned to see the essential." Bernhard Beckering, before he fell into despair, insisted, "Our love of the lively and beautiful must become so great that the feeling of infinity envelops us. Then we will slowly come to the point that even suffering and death can be received as something proper and subordinate."[69] This love of life could become so intense that some, such as Wilhelm Spaleck, wondered, "Do we not love life all too much? Is our love not life, life, glowing life?" Harry Mielert confessed, "I hang on to my body so much, I love beauty so much . . . that the dead make no frightening impression on me."[70]

Whether fearful, fatalistic, or clinging to life, all *Landsers* struggled with a frightful harvest of emotions. As Harry Mielert remarked in November 1942, no one could understand or repay "the enormous mixture of fear, horror, and other unnamable feelings and their counterbalance, bravery and overcoming, that these men here must daily and hourly summon up." Despite everything, out of resignation, trust in some ultimate meaning, or belief in a better future, even the most discouraged and disillusioned *Landser* usually found the wherewithal to continue fighting, and to display an impressive willingness to sacrifice himself until the bitter end. "I know in my bones what . . . 'courage' means," Guy Sajer asserted, "from days and nights of resigned desperation, and from the insurmountable fear which one continues to accept, even though one's brain has ceased to function normally. I know what it means, remembering deliberate immobility against frozen soil, whose coldness penetrates to the marrow of the bones, and the howling of a stranger in the next hole. . . . German soldiers," he concluded, "would have to endure everything, in the world we had created. We were fitted only for that world, and were otherwise inadaptable."[71]

5. THE SEASONS OF WAR

Despite the perception of World War II as a mechanized *Blitzkrieg*, *Landsers* generally marched on foot into Poland, France, the Balkans, Russia, and most other arenas of battle. Hence, factors normally of secondary concern to historians forced themselves into the forefront of a soldier's everyday world: matters such as climate, terrain, disease, filth, and lack of shelter or privacy. Even though combat and the fear of combat loomed constantly in every soldier's consciousness, actual battle could be surprisingly infrequent, but no *Landser* could escape the unpleasant business of living rough, of coping with a harsh environment under conditions of extreme physical and mental exhaustion. For many *Landsers*, then, the real enemy often seemed to be the weather, the effects of living in the open, and the stresses and strains endemic to a group forced into proximity with an often unfamiliar natural environment. Getting accustomed to this primitive way of living often proved exceedingly difficult, especially for those from urban areas. War came to be seen as a dirty business, both figuratively and literally.

The most elemental of natural conditions—rain, mud, cold, snow, heat, dust—formed a leitmotif of the entire war for many soldiers. There were, of course, men from a farming background, working men accustomed to long hours of hard physical labor, and men who came from a wretched background of poverty for whom the physical conditions of war differed little from the grinding harshness of their everyday civilian lives. Most, however, would have agreed with Harry Mielert, who noted bitterly, "I sleep day and night in the same uniform, on the same plank bed, wrap myself in the same wool blanket. . . ; clay also hits me on the head and falls into my mess kit after each mortar round." Nor was this necessarily the worst of it. "We attempted to clean ourselves up," he wrote on another occasion. "In my cardigan I found after the first boiling 37 lice, thick and fat. The mud was removed from our uniforms first with knives, then with wire brushes and last through washing." Wrote Mielert three days later, "I know from experience that I am like an animal that can live as dead in a different element a year long and then be resurrected to a new life when put back into your own element."[1] The reality of the new environment experienced by most *Landsers* was made more difficult precisely because it seemed so alien, so out of touch with their normal circumstances.

One of the commonest complaints, perhaps because in their everyday civilian lives it had seemed so innocuous, centered on the persistent problem of rain. Especially in Russia, where paved roads were few, the *rasputitsa*—that wet period in the spring and autumn when drenching rains and melting snow turned the countryside into a swampy sea of mud—brought with it unending misery. "We spent the night in the open," lamented Wilhelm Prüller in July 1941. "We made ourselves dugouts and covered them with sailcloth. After midnight it began to rain, and we couldn't stand it much longer in these holes. Wet and shivering with the cold, we wait[ed] for morning." Just three days later, Prüller again expressed amazement at Russian weather: "When I see even at this time of year how our vehicles, after it's rained a little, can barely make the grade, I just can't imagine how it will be in autumn when the rainy period really sets in." But well before autumn, in late July, he noted, "Yesterday it began to rain, and it hasn't stopped yet. It's enough to make you desperate." The Russian rains impressed Friedrich Grupe as being of biblical dimensions. "The *Landsers* have built frames, laid pine branches and blankets on top in order to protect themselves to some extent against the dampness," he wrote. "So like a Noah's Ark emerged wood bunker after wood bunker in the swamp."[2]

Virtually every *Landser* in Russia, it seemed, complained of and suffered from the rain. "The constant thunderstorms have turned into a steady downpour," moaned Harry Mielert in July 1941. "Everything has become a sodden black mush. The swamps stink even more, filled up with carcasses and corpses, and the woods are awful." "The roads here are incredibly bad," wrote Corporal W.E., "at times of rainy weather hardly passable; fatiguing for man and horse. In general, you cannot get through any more with a motorcycle or auto." Little more than a year later, deep in Russia, Corporal H.T. complained, "The day before yesterday it rained the entire day and night, and all the afflictions have come to light today: rheumatism, aches [*Reißen*] and above all, that which rhymes with the latter [*Scheißen*, the shits]."[3]

Helmut Pabst noted similar discomforts in October 1942: "I'm in the back seat of the radio truck, holding my injured foot in the air, and watching how their clothes cling to the bodies of my comrades. Rain and snow beat against their faces, and an icy wind strikes sluggishly at the wet tents. The drivers on the box seats of the baggage carts sit with numb hands, with painful grimaces and heads held to one side. So they drive their wagons ... through water and mud like tragic ships, clumsy, laborious and burdened, pitching and rolling in the holes and ruts of the highway. . . . That is the highway . . . , a fruit of tough and continuous all-out effort and work."

Pabst's depiction almost perfectly exemplified conditions in Russia: a strenuous effort just to hang on while besieged by the harsh elements. And as if to prove that rain caused considerable misery elsewhere, Walther Happich wrote from Holland in November 1944: "With the incessant rain great demands are made on us. There are not enough adequate positions here; in a few water stands a foot deep." Forced by the war to live outdoors for the first time, many *Landsers* would readily have agreed that Henri Barbusse's comment from the First World War applied equally to the Second: "Dampness rusts men like rifles, more slowly but more deeply."[4]

Added to the rain was the monotonous horror of the mud it produced, a seemingly omnipresent, bottomless, glutinous concoction that clung tenaciously to everyone and everything it touched. Siegfried Knappe noted: "In late September [1941] it began to rain, and mud started to become a problem for us. . . . Everything turned to mud, . . . the earth was simply a quagmire of mud. Great clumps of mud clung to our boots and every step produced a smacking suction noise. It played havoc with [us]." Marching toward Moscow in late October 1941, Heinrich Witt was also taken aback by the all-consuming nature of the Russian mud. "The roads were again thawing," he noted, "so much so that the vehicles just sank down into it, so that each one had to be dragged out. We had to haul them out in snowy weather for two whole days, until the regiment had marched the pair of kilometers through the mud." To Hans-Heinrich Ludwig "the maddening mud" of Russia was "inconceivable" to anyone who had not experienced it—although Ernst Kleist might well have challenged that assertion, observing that "the Flemish mud is of course also famous." Ironically, the mud of "sunny" Italy proved perhaps most disconcerting and disheartening to the front soldier. "Everything is filthy," complained Helmut Wagner from Italy in late October 1943. "The mud clings in cakes to your hands, boots, pants and coat, as a heavy weight to your shoes. For the last five days I have not had dry feet."[5]

Still, it was the oozing mud of Mother Russia that inspired the most horror. Writing from Russia on the day he died in April 1944, Klaus Löscher referred to the hardship of the *rasputitsa*: "The mud in the trenches reaches to midcalf, and yet thick layers of ice still lie under the excavated dirt of the trenches. But at the same time yesterday there was the murkiest rainy weather. The sentries couldn't see their hands before their eyes." Similarly, Rembrand Elert described the Russian countryside during the *rasputitsa* as a

> sea of mud often stretching out for many hundreds of meters. Once [our vehicle] got stuck in it. Then all of us had to wade in water up to our calves and push, the men partially covered from top to bottom by clumps of mud. . . . It poured down in buckets, and the wind whipped through the treeless steppe.
>
> About 2:00 A.M. we finally got stuck for good. Each wrapped himself as well as he could in coats and blankets and attempted to sleep. But your legs, covered up to their knees in totally wet things and layered in many centimeters of thick mud, turned slowly to ice.[6]

In late October 1941, as the rainy season hit its stride, Wilhelm Prüller recorded: "The mud is now knee-high. . . . Many vehicles get stuck after the first few meters and can only be freed with the combined assistance of everyone present. Our drivers have now had experience in four campaigns. They mastered the plowed fields of Poland, the swift tempo in Holland, the breathless chase in France, the mountains of the Balkans; they drive in pitch darkness, without lights. . . . But the worst of the lot is undoubtedly the Soviet Union." It was the seeming bottomlessness of the Russian mud that inspired the sardonic joke about the man who is startled to discover a human face in the mud; the face tells him, "You'll be even more surprised when you learn that I'm sitting on a horse and riding."[7]

Of course, the very opposite of the cold rain and mud, heat and suffocating dust, also produced their share of laments, as the *Landser* quickly discovered that Mother Nature had stockpiled a treasure of torments. "We moved over deeply rutted dirt roads, through patches of loose sand and clouds of dust," noted Siegfried Knappe of the summer weather in Russia in 1941. "Our feet sank into the sand and dirt, puffing dust into the air so that it rose and clung to us. The horses coughing in the dust produced a pungent odor. The loose sand was nearly as tiring for the horses as the deep mud would have been. The men marched in silence, coated with dust, with dry throats and lips." "We are, enveloped in glowing clouds of heat and dust, again on the march farther eastward," confirmed Günter von Scheven of the conditions in August 1941. "There is no rest. Always the same advance through treeless plains, in thick clouds of dust along endless roads, column after column, horse, rider and artillery like ghosts." Similarly, Harald Henry marveled at how "the dust positively disguises all of us: the blondes have almost white, dully gleaming hair, the brunettes look like Frederician soldiers, brightly powdered . . . , and the military mustaches that many have . . . now, left untouched, turn gray." Marching through the Ukraine, Ludwig Laumen wondered at the "oddly strange landscape . . ., almost the entire trek we were under dust like a gigantic gray cloud, . . . dense, steep mountainous peaks [of dust]."[8]

Dust could torment the *Landser* everywhere. Writing from Egypt in September 1942, Martin Penck observed that after an artillery bombardment "clouds of dust and smoke crept ghostlike over the earth." Retreating through Rumania in late March 1944, Rembrand Elert complained, "The dust is so unbearable that now and again you cannot see anything at all." But it was while waiting for transportation deep in Russia that Claus Hansmann sat watching "supply and munitions columns tramp to the front covered in a massive banner of dust." He soon discovered that even a closed vehicle offered little relief: "The countryside was drier, sandy meadows alternated with parched fields," he noted. "In the column we now traveled as in a sandstorm. Clouds of dust penetrated through all the gaps in the windows. . . . The wheels churned up fountains of sand that blacked out the sun. Unbearably dry heat made sweat run from our pores. The dust burnt our nose and throat." Wilhelm Prüller, however, witnessed perhaps the most amazing spectacle of all, noting in his diary, "The shoulders of the road are all muddy from the previous rain, you sink up to your knees, but in the middle of the road there's dust already. The covers of the vehicles are rolled back, the men sit in them in their helmets, carbines in their laps, each vehicle surrounded by an impenetrable cloud of dust."[9]

If heat, dust, rain, and mud proved irksome and discomfiting, the legendary cold and snow of Russia inspired genuine fear and long hours and days of agony. Some *Landsers* were terrified merely by the approach of winter. In the autumn "the already flat rays of the sun, low in the horizon over the plains, misled us," said one. "But each evening . . . ominous black clouds would build up far in the distance, towering high above the steppe. These dark masses carried . . . the rain, the ice and snow of the coming winter." So menacing did the grinding approach of winter seem that a *Landser* might now and again turn his attention to an earlier winter campaign in Russia: "Now one can understand how Napoleon suffered under the still more primitive transportation methods and weather conditions of that time, and therefore no supplies came to the front," worried Private L.B. already in August 1941. "If we . . . were trapped into the winter, it would not go well for us either. If it only rains heavily for a few days, then that is a setback for many days, especially for the supplies. Unless you see it for yourself, you just can't imagine how chronic it is." Private H.S. admitted in September 1941: "The announcement that already plans are being made for the construction and organization of winter quarters weighs heavily on us. . . . In any case we might then count on a leave. But none of us wants to return to this gray and rainy country." "God save us from a winter campaign in the East," exclaimed Sergeant H.S. with fervent directness.[10]

New arrivals were particularly terrified by the prospect of facing a Russian winter. "Toward the end of [November 1943], we at last got some replacements," remembered Gustav Kreutz. "They were mostly young chaps from the training barracks. . . . In no time they were complaining about the cold. They kept fires going during the day as well as at night and were . . . [using] fuel which would have been valuable later. I had occasion to speak sharply to them about this and one of them answered that on that day the thermometer had fallen to ten below [Celsius], and was this not abnormal? I told him that soon he would count himself lucky when the thermometer was not ten but twenty-five degrees below, and that in January it would fall to forty below. At this the poor fellow broke down and sobbed."[11]

The autumn weather frightened Wilhelm Prüller as well. "It's very unpleasant now," he noted in his diary in late September 1941. "Terribly cold. You can't wrap yourself in too many blankets. . . . And who knows what's in front of us. . . ? The wind whistles through the canvas of the lorries . . . and blows the rain in. It's freezing cold." A few days later,

Prüller worried, "Autumn has made its appearance punctually. And then the question arises: which is better, to be moving and to sweat more *with* a coat . . . or to go on as we've been doing, without one?" He soon had his answer: "At night it gets really cold now," he noted in early October, "and we all think that it can't go on much longer. In this morass we shall soon be unable to move at all. . . . What will it be like in the rainy period?" The next night it was no longer the rain he feared: "Tonight we had the first real Russian snowstorm. . . . The wind whistled through every nook and cranny of our hut, and we expected the straw roof to take off at any moment. A nice foretaste of the coming winter. That can be a real mess!" A real mess: nice understatement in a diary. The reality soon proved paralyzing. "Icy snowstorms swept over the land and obstructed our vision," complained Lieutenant H.H. of the bitter weather that slowly ground the German advance to a halt in December 1941. "The ground was so slick that the horses had difficulty even standing up. Because of the cold our machine guns wouldn't work at all."[12]

"The snow blew almost horizontally in blizzards . . . with the wind piercing our faces with a thousand needles," recalled Siegfried Knappe. "The cold numbed and deadened the human body from the feet up until the whole body was an aching mass of misery. To keep warm, we had to wear every piece of clothing we owned. . . . Each man fought the cold alone, pitting his determination and will against the bitter winter." Yet this first onslaught, Knappe was stunned to discover, provided only a glimpse of what was to follow:

> A paralyzing blast of cold hit us. . . . Our trucks and vehicles would not start, and our horses started to die from the cold in large numbers. . . . We all now numbly wrapped ourselves in our blankets. Everyone felt brutalized and defeated by the cold. The sun would rise late in the morning . . . and not one fresh footprint would be visible for as far as the human eye could see. . . .
>
> The flesh on our faces and ears would freeze if we left it exposed for very long, and we tried to wrap anything around our heads to prevent frostbite. . . . Our fingers froze even in gloves. . . . They were so stiff from the cold that they refused to perform any function. We could not have fired our rifles.[13]

"The difficulty of getting under way," Guy Sajer agreed, "was almost unimaginable. We had to roll out barrels of gasoline and alcohol to fill the gas tanks and radiators, crank up the engines, an exhausting labor, and shovel out cubic yards of snow. . . . Heavy snowfalls buried the road so completely after the passage of each convoy that we needed a compass to dig it out again. . . . Ludicrous in our smallness, we continued forward into the immensity of white." In dismayingly precise terms Claus Hansmann recorded the unremitting natural horror of Russia: "Autumn: fog, rain, damp nights in a tent, wet clothing, cold food, mud, morass, freezing, hopelessness. And then winter: frost, brutal cold, raging icy wind, snowstorms, and snow, shrouding everything, white, broad expanses on which only the wind draws noteworthy figures. Snow-covered villages, loneliness." Not surprisingly, then, Hansmann concluded, "We are all so tired of Russia, tired of the war."[14]

Little did Hansmann know how much more brutal the winter would yet become. "That is the power of nature," he wrote later,

> when it rips at all your limbs, when you have to brace yourself not to lose your grip. . . . You're propelled like a withered leaf. . . . You forge on, and step by step you press on into the icy wall of snow that threatens you. Your head sunk low, a bit sideways with open mouth, snatching at breath, you carefully set one foot in front of the other. First you take a strong step, then tense your muscles powerfully, and you notice that slowly your body moves forward. So you fight against the elements, a small, tiny man all alone. . . . You go on, always forward. Forward? You must have reached the house at last? You carefully raise your face somewhat against the storm and squint for a few seconds into the white force. . . . But everything is a torrent, everything is snow in raging movement. You are alone. . . . Where are you, where is the house?[15]

Fear of getting lost in the snowy wastes was by no means unusual. Harry Mielert noted of "these crazy snowstorms" that "in a few minutes the most well-trodden paths and trails are obliterated, whole villages are totally snow-covered, you can't orient yourself on anything, . . . no one can find their way." Indeed, so obliterating were the snowstorms that Mielert wrote despairingly: "We are in a terrible situation. Nothing more is to be seen of our trenches. . . . You can only tell where the bunkers are by sighting a straw flag on a pole stuck above them. Every path, every trail is gone within a few minutes. . . . So here we stand on this front, lonely, without knowing what is to the right or left of us." On the day of his death, Günter von Scheven also described the horror, the forlornness, the sheer terror, of the "desert of snow" he was marching through. "Relentlessly the cold remains, −20 degrees Celsius with a constant east wind, long snowdrifts and deep, fine new snow envelop us. In the air swirl ice crystals, the universe appears to have fallen victim to congelation. We are sheltered, but we have also grown hard."[16]

Indeed, they had to grow hard. This brutalizing, demoralizing snow and cold, "the unspeakable agony of the cold," as Harald Henry put it, assaulted the sense of well-being of the *Landser*, who grappled with it in a solitary and seemingly futile effort to stay warm. "Our company . . . went into the woods until we were over our knees in snow, which filled our boots," Henry reported. "Across frozen marshes that broke open so that icy water ran into our boots. My gloves were so wet that I could not bear them any longer. I wound a towel around my ruined hands. . . . My face was contorted from tears, but I was already in a sort of trance. I stamped forward with closed eyes, mumbled senseless words and thought that I was experiencing everything only in my sleep as a dream. It was all like a madness. . . . Agony without an end." Others, too, noted the cold's drug-like effect. "The infantry," Helmut Pabst observed in February 1942, "which has remained outside for nine days and nine nights [and] which one can find at small fires under roofs of pine branches, sleeping in the snow, [appear] mute, frozen, without a flicker of emotions as under a heavy anesthetic." Dazed and overpowered by the cold, many *Landsers* slumped into a turgid resignation. "Nature demonstrates here its relentless strength," marveled Sergeant K.H. from Russia in February 1942. "Snowstorms, snow flurries, and the extreme cold . . . show here their true, death-dispensing face. Unfortunately, there are many men who can no longer summon the energy to withstand the strength of the winter and because of that face a certain death."[17]

"The fact of sleeping absolutely in the open in such appalling cold terrified us," agreed Guy Sajer. "In the biting cold which passed over us like a silent dream . . . , some men fainted as the cold struck them, paralyzed before they even had a chance to scream."

> We spent a fortnight in these bitter conditions, and it proved fatal for many of our group. . . . We had two cases of pneumonia, . . . we had frozen limbs and . . . a kind of gangrene from cold, which first attacks the exposed portion of the face, and then other parts of the body. . . . Two soldiers, driven mad by despair, left the convoy one night, and lost themselves in the featureless immensity of the snow. Another very young soldier called for his mother, and cried for

hours. . . . Toward morning . . . a shot jolted us all awake. We found him a short way off, where he had tried to put an end to his nightmare. But he had bungled his effort and didn't die until the afternoon.[18]

Many *Landsers*, as Martin Pöppel noted, withstood the Russian cold only by using alcohol. "We're no longer drinking for its own sake," he recorded in his diary in December 1941. "Now, you get as boozed up as possible, since the more you drink the better you can sleep." Guy Sajer confirmed the importance of alcohol at the front: "It's the easiest way to make heroes," he noted, and few would have disagreed with him. Ironically, Siegfried Knappe discovered that even trying to stay warm could be hazardous: "We learned now that getting warm in a peasant hut could be dangerous. The combination of newspapers on the wall and dried-out wooden walls set the stage for disaster. . . . If a fire was kept going in those peasant stoves for weeks on end the whole hut became extremely flammable . . . , and if the walls reached a flash point and someone struck a match to light a cigarette, the whole place would ignite." Sajer, too, remembered that even those lucky enough to find shelter in an intact peasant hut, an *isba*, faced constant danger, for "these men burned everything they could find. . . . The intense flames threatened to set fire at any moment to the structures themselves." Little wonder, then, that Sajer concluded, "Life in Russia for me was a perpetual shivering fit."[19] For the *Landser* who suffered through it, new words were needed to describe the experience of being cold in Russia.

The sheer misery of staying alive in Russia in the depth of winter proved nearly overwhelming; indeed, this invisible war often triumphed with deadly efficiency. In addition, as Harry Mielert reminded his wife, the *Landser* still had to face the prospect of tough fighting. "Yesterday we waged a real steppe-war," he wrote in October 1941. "We marched the entire night through a snowstorm; in the morning there was a sheet of ice. Thick fog lay over the fields. Russian horse-mounted reconnaissance troops . . . appeared everywhere from out of the fog. . . . At about four o'clock a Russian column with vehicles emerged from the fog. . . . We were a troop of twelve men, right in the middle of enemy country." But still worse was to come. "Think of an endless, cold field, frozen hard, covered with light snow," he wrote in the desolate winter of December 1943. "A terrible wind whistles across it and blows the thin snow behind the clumps of earth, so that the frozen topsoil is exposed. Our men lie solidly entrenched in this field. With the small infantry spade they hack and scratch at the stony earth until they reach unfrozen soil; there they dig a small hole in which one or two men can squat. There they stay, the one keeps watch while the other dozes. It is ice cold, they are warmed only by the heat of their bodies. The enemy quickly recognizes the line and shoots with mortars along the field. . . . The screams of those hit is frightful, without echo in the wasteland."[20] Little more than a week later, Mielert himself was the one struck, killed by shrapnel in the barrenness he so deplored.

Even routine daily tasks such as eating, bathing, and relieving oneself assumed monstrous proportions when undertaken in the midst of a biting Russian winter. "Those who could still eat," noted one *Landser*, "had to watch the axe rebounding as from a stone off the frozen horse meat, and the butter was cut with a saw." Still another claimed, "One man drawing his ration of boiling soup at the field kitchen could not find his spoon. It took him 30 seconds to find it, but by then the soup was lukewarm. He began to eat it as quickly as he could . . . but the soup was already cold and soon it would be solid." Indeed, with the breakdown of the supply system under the strain of the savage conditions, hunger loomed as a constant problem. "No trace of the mess convoy," Wilhelm Prüller recorded in his diary. "We bake our bread . . . using captured flour stores. Now we are getting used to the second, unpleasant side of the war."[21]

Gnawing hunger threatened constantly, and to the average *Landser* seemed more than merely disagreeable. "Something must be cooked," noted Claus Hansmann in his diary, "even if it's only a pot of water. . . . Only water, but even that already involves all the possibilities of what can be cooked in it. A pair of potatoes or some tea, a piece of meat or even a whole chicken. . . . The thoughts in our hungry brains produce bubbles already. . . . We think we smell the odor of bouillon. . . . We dream already of the pleasant activity of gnawing at the cooked chicken. . . . We glance wistfully at the knives and forks." As Hansmann knew only too well, however, often neither securing nor eating a meal proved easy:

> We are suddenly all hunters. On wary soles we creep toward the sound. . . . A quick grabbing for the knife: feathers fly, a hen, a goose lashed out with its wings, shrieking shrilly and was finished off. . . . Someone else has already dug after potatoes . . . and soon, mixed with cheerful clouds of smoke, certain odors float out.

I cook in a small barn on a ladder standing in a square entrance over a four-meter-deep cellar, for the smoke will not remained unnoticed for long. They out there are hellishly attentive, and their mortars will begin soon. The others sit underneath in a bricked cellar vault and give advice to me up above. They indulge in recipes and reminiscences. . . . A whistling sound. . . . Shrapnel slams into the boards. Then I surface again, concerned that something has happened to the food. . . . Now I take the pan with me when I must disappear. All around the courtyard creep the detonations of the light mortar. Peter crashes in between two explosions, breathless and happy that he has brought his onions with him. . . . But what wouldn't one do for such a meal? Warnings of danger appear laughable to us. . . . Finally we sit down. A stout soldier's knife cuts succulent pieces, and happy eyes full of expectation like those of children receiving Christmas presents follow the carving. . . . Excitement fills the room. The initial hunger gives way at last to blissful satiety. But when is such a soldier's stomach ever at its limit?[22]

A feast could indeed lift the spirits of even the most bedraggled *Landser*, providing both a sense of physical comfort and psychological uplift. Even in the midst of the fierce Russian cold, Guy Sajer remarked how "a large hot meal . . . produced an almost unbelievable sense of well-being, and raised our spirits to a remarkable degree."[23]

For many *Landsers*, though, getting enough—or anything—to eat was a constant struggle. "Food was our most difficult problem," asserted Sajer. "We became hunters and trappers and nest robbers. . . . Our eyes gleamed, like the eyes of famished wolves. Our stomachs were empty, our mess tins were empty, and the horizon was devoid of any hope. Murderous sentiments lurked behind our eyes, which glittered with hunger. Hunger produces a curious frame of mind." Sajer, in fact, witnessed a bizarre scene of famished Germans who "were no longer fighting for any spiritual motive, but were like wolves, terrified of starvation. . . . These men, who no longer distinguished between enemies and friends, were ready to commit murder for less than a quarter of a meal. . . . These martyrs to hunger massacred two villages to carry off their supplies of food. . . . Men were ready to commit murder for a quart of goat's milk, a few potatoes, a pound of millet. . . . Men died for very little, for the possibility of a day's food. . . . Like hunted animals intent on self-preservation, each man thought only of himself."[24]

Hunger could cause a *Landser* to engage in once unthinkable behavior, extending even to thoughts of cannibalism. Following a leg amputation, lying helplessly in a cattle car used for medical evacuations, the war nearly at an end and supply lines completely broken down, Hans Woltersdorf recounted:

> Here my war without weapons became a war without rations as well. . . . There was simply nothing at all to eat. . . . Rase still had all his limbs and was constantly out and about. . . . He brought leaves, grasses, and herbs and . . . knew what could be done with them. . . . Rase sized up my good leg and drew to my attention what a waste it was that I had not brought along the sawn-off leg as a reserve supply. . . . There would certainly have been a usable joint of some kilos left above the knee. . . . And so the only bit of hope remaining for me and Rase was that when the follow-up amputation was done on my leg, some extra kilos of flesh could be cut off and saved for consumption.[25]

Reduced by hunger and despair to the most primitive of states, Woltersdorf and his companion sustained themselves through the hope of eating amputated human flesh.

Even while the supply system was functioning, the quantity and quality of rations brought many Landsers close to despair. "The supply situation is again fairly normal," wrote Harry Mielert in August 1943. "Unfortunately the water is still polluted. The coffee tastes like piss, but it is still welcome." Likewise, Prosper Schücking complained in November 1943, "War and action by no means make you as tired as the strain of this uncomfortable foxhole, in which you cannot properly lie or sit, with lice and filthy blankets and cold coffee . . . and each evening potato or cabbage soup, for which you still must be very thankful." Of these "gluey soups," Guy Sajer commented drily that they "were nauseating but effective" at keeping them alive. Still, as the war wound down in the autumn of 1944, the quality of food deteriorated further: "Cellophane sausages stuffed with soybean puree, one for every two men. It goes without saying that these were cold." During the retreat back into East Prussia, Sajer witnessed "towns overflowing with starving refugees. People with the faces of madmen were wolfing down the flour which was the only food distributed to them. . . . Soldiers also had to stand in interminable lines, to receive, finally, two handfuls of flour apiece, and a cup of hot water infused with a minute portion of tea." Little wonder, then, that many *Landsers* often complained they had "too much food in order to die, but too little in order to live."[26]

Moreover, if the simple act of eating was a strain, relieving oneself at the front in winter proved at best irksome, at worst deadly. "The blizzards and the bitter cold seemed to stop most of our natural functions," noted a *Landser*, "but when it became necessary then a ravine, a dip, even a low snow wall would give that protection from the wind which was essential. . . . We had had, in that first year, also many cases of cystitis and the inability to urinate quickly as well as the intense burning sensation which accompanied the act. . . . Out of fear of frostbite most men wrapped that part of the body in a thick cloth that was used over and over again. Together with all the odors produced by unwashed bodies, feet and clothing, you can imagine that we did not smell very sweet." "Any desire to piss," Sajer remembered, "was announced to all present, so that hands swollen by chilblains could be held out under the warm urine, which often infected our cracked fingers." Indeed, General Heinz Guderian recorded that, as a result of the cold, "many men died while performing their natural functions."[27]

A byproduct of the cold, the inability to bathe and get clean clothing, led to incredibly filthy conditions, which inevitably resulted in a plague of lice. "While I am cheerfully writing to you," noted Harry Mielert in a letter to his wife, "the lice afflict me quite terribly. But you must also get over that. If you let yourself get driven crazy over such little things, how then could you cope with the big things?" For the *Landser*, though, the incessant suffering inflicted by the lice seemed anything but minor. "Unfortunately, many of the village houses we stayed in had lice," remembered Siegfried Knappe, "and we got them. Once we got lice, they stayed with us until we could be deloused. . . . The lice were a torment that was to stay with us for months. We scratched with increasing zeal. We scratched arms, legs, stomach, the small of the back, and it was a constant burning in the armpits. It was worst at night, and the men would thrash restlessly in their blankets." Ironically, as Knappe noted, "although we were freezing, we still provided enough warmth for the lice that fed on us. We had become, quite simply, frozen and exhausted men who were being constantly tormented by vermin. We felt like livestock rather than human beings. . . . I tried to imagine what it would be like to stand under a hot shower. . . . The image was maddening."[28]

Although Knappe dreamed of being clean and free of lice, the one did not inevitably lead to the other. "In Odessa we were given fresh underwear. Lice love fresh underwear," Hans Woltersdorf noted sardonically. "To lure them we wrapped fresh gauze bandages around our throats and thereby triggered off a Great Louse Migration. . . . The lice got on the move and crawled slowly over our calves and our thighs, our stomachs and our backs, higher and higher, until they made their way to the throat bandages. Then we threw the bandages into the fire. Morawetz presorted his lice. Those that were still too small he put back on his chest. One can get used to domestic pets." Similarly, Guy Sajer confessed that he "much preferred to keep my lice relatively warm between my gray undervest and my stomach," since then the maddening creatures would be less active. Most *Landsers* had less tolerance. "Truly, there are here only lice and filth," wrote Prosper Schücking in his last letter, "and for both we have the same horror." Kurt Reuber, trapped at Stalingrad and soon to be taken prisoner, declared: "You can hardly put yourself in our world of emotions. . . . We crouch together in some bunkers in a ravine in the steppe. . . . Filth and dirt. . . . I've not taken the clothes from my body since leave. Lice. Mice at nights on my face. . . . And yet everyone wishes for just one thing: life, to hold onto life!"[29]

Elsewhere, too, the *Landser* faced the travails of living with vermin that were both malicious and omnipresent. Writing from Italy in his last letter, Ernst Jünger—son of the famous author who had glorified war as a transcendent experience—complained, "Unfortunately I am stuck full of bugs now just like my comrades; each evening I go assiduously on the hunt [for them]." Theodor Kinzelbach wrote from North Africa of the "swarms of flies [that] sit on the meat that hangs in the open on door posts." Only in the evening "can one breath freely [in the desert]," Martin Penck noted. "The air is cooler and above all one thing is gone: the flies. You cannot possibly imagine what a plague of flies there is. . . . By the hundreds they buzz around each individual, crawl into your ears, nose, mouth, into your shirt and often bring you close to the edge of despair. . . . I myself cannot imagine a meal anymore at which everything was not black from noisy flies. . . . We have . . . also learned what thirst is. Since yesterday we have had no more water." In addition to thirst and a plague of flies, Walther Weber noted another problem common to the desert: "The stones that lie somewhat deeper," he wrote, "are enormously hard, mostly continuous rock, and that makes for great difficulty in constructing a position."[30]

Russia, too, had its share of pests other than lice. "Grasshoppers were plentiful," remembered Siegfried Knappe, "and could not seem to tell a moving soldier from a stationary tree, often hitching free rides. Swarms of gnats plagued us, and darting flies were everywhere." Complained Bernhard Buhl, "The gnats are a severe plague. Mosquito veils, green netting to be worn over the head, were distributed and are worn day and night." Siegbert Stehmann found the "myriad flies and buzzing insects" in Bessarabia extremely annoying. Still, he "preferred that to when after the rains we sat in mud up to our knees." Little wonder that for many *Landsers* Russia seemed less a place than a series of natural disasters. As Werner Pott lamented, "For weeks we have been in action without peace or rest, day after day a different billet, marches in snowstorms with the cold at minus 25 degrees Celsius, frozen noses and feet so that you would like to scream if you have to take off your boots, mud, vermin and other unedifying things." To which Harald Henry added, "It is no longer a given that you have a roof over your head, food, mail, that you spend the night in heated houses; all of these are special favors, gifts, Christmas presents if you like."[31]

As if to make the hardships complete, most *Landsers* suffered the travails of rain, mud, cold, and pests in a condition of extreme exhaustion. The average *Landser* experienced battle much as his ancestors had—after a long, grueling march. "When an infantryman at times gets to ride in a car," noted Claus Hansmann bitterly, "it means only a superficial relief, that somewhere it stinks, that they urgently need us and cannot wait long enough for us to come trudging along on tired legs." More typical of a *Landser*'s life—even in warm weather—was Hansmann's further observation: "We know no consciousness, forward, eastward through the painfully seductive fragrance of the early summer steppe. The war must lose itself in the sweetness around here, but the weight of the equipment . . . violently forces us back into the present. The painful feet, the exhausted muscles speak the words of our obligation. . . . Each step is made agonizing by the heat and sweat. A fight against thirst, a fight against fatigue as well, finding the strength against the sun, weariness, and despair."[32]

Marching through the "blazing heat" of Russia in June 1941, Harald Henry complained, "I don't know exactly how heavy my pack is, but on top of that there is a thick wool blanket, a munitions case which can make you nuts, and the miserable box with the books in it that I should have sent back." Nor did his burden get any lighter. "The next day was very strenuous," he wrote a week later. "In the afternoon an hour of rest, then in the evening we moved out. Forty-four kilometers, in the process we were shot at during our midnight rest and therefore we had to go with our equipment at the ready: that is, for me a thirty-pound munitions case . . . and as the second half of the forty-four kilometers came in the early morning, I was totally drained, exhausted to the last reserves." "A great many infantrymen *marched* to Tobruk!" Martin Penck emphasized in August 1942. "Who does not grasp that cannot imagine the strains of this infantry. Marching thirty kilometers a day under a blazing sun, combat pack, hand weapons and munitions cases or a machinc gun [weighing 75 pounds] or a mortar, and constant thirst." Similarly, Rembrand Elert noted of the hardship of the German retreat through the southern Ukraine, "Many walked the last 30 kilometers in their socks. I myself made the whole retreat in two right rubber boots."[33]

"It's strange how now and then you can be overcome by fatigue," Harry Mielert confided to his wife. "Actually it's likely that the only thing that allows you to surmount all these debilities is a danger to your life." Extreme exhaustion could cause even the strongest man to fall victim to a deadening lassitude. "There comes an hour," noted Helmut Pabst, "in which everything becomes indifferent, in which you are blind and numb because you cannot think of anything else but being allowed to sleep." Given no respite from the harsh strain of combat, Pabst lamented a few months later, "The fatigue presses down ever closer on my head, like a cap that numbs and deadens me, and finally there are only the feet totally alone that you put one in front of the other, step after step . . . like an old man. Behind me . . . rise the bitter cries . . . like the cries of damned souls." Struggling to keep pace with the rapid advance into Flanders in May 1940, Ernst Kleist admitted to being "dog-tired, falling down tired. But sleep will not come. All the images [of battle] rise up." The next day Kleist despaired of the furious exertion that he was "about completely sunk from the fatigue. Only through alcohol, nicotine and that never-ending, ear-deafening raging and roaring of the guns are you still able to remain upright." Other *Landsers*, too, found that they could overcome their fatigue only by using artificial stimulants, such as the Pervitin Hans Woltersdorf used to keep awake when he had "hardly more than twenty-four hours' sleep in ten days."[34]

Sooner or later, however, fatigue would win out, often with serious consequences. "We slowly limp into the next place," Wilhelm Prüller noted of the last exhausting days of the German advance in December 1941, "where we are assigned 3 small huts and 3 so-called Russian houses: one room for a platoon of 39 men. They can barely stand up inside, and that's where they are supposed to spend the night. . . . This isn't a war any more but a fight for billets . . . [with] no end in sight." The result of this numbing fatigue soon became apparent, even to so ardent a soldier as Prüller. "Our people are kaputt," he admitted on 19 December. "You've got to say it; and see why: one hour outside, one hour in the hut, watch, alarm sentry duty, listening duty, observer duty, occupy the MG posts, one thing after another. It wouldn't surprise me to see some of them break down. This has been going on since 28 November, . . . for weeks and weeks one hour of sleep, then one hour of duty, what that means!" A week later Prüller wrote, "We really can't take another march like this one. . . . We can hardly go on as it is. For the most part the men have only what they carry on their body. . . . All our shoes are ruined, our shirts and underclothes are black (they've not been changed for weeks). This is just a little hint of the way things are."[35]

The watch rotated in short intervals, of course, primarily because of the bitterly cold weather, but another reason noticeable to those at the front was stressed by Harry Mielert: the enormous casualties on the eastern front had so thinned the ranks that often not enough men remained to do the necessary tasks. "Every evening the Russians appear in front of our positions," he wrote. "But even though we are all bleary-eyed and our eyes burn, until now they have achieved no more success. But unfortunately through illness and so forth we are constantly fewer, and if a pair of men then come as replacements they are poorly trained folk or some other kind of scum."[36] With few available bodies and even fewer reliable men, those left had to endure to the point of exhaustion the constant cycle of sentry duty, work details, patrol, and combat with virtually no respite.

Extreme fatigue ultimately made it impossible for some men to continue functioning. "We hadn't yet encountered any of the real dangers of war," acknowledged Guy Sajer of his experience in a supply unit, "and we were all exhausted by the lack of sleep, the cold, this endless journey, and by our revolting condition of almost unbelievable filth." As Sajer noted, the initial effect of fatigue was more psychological than physical, for "the exhaustion we had been dragging about with us for days increased the fear we could no longer control. Fear intensified our exhaustion, as it required constant vigilance." Very soon, however, this fatigue gave way to a condition in which they were "too exhausted to react, and almost nothing stirred our emotions." Sajer and his comrades, in fact, soon reached a point of lassitude where "our overwhelming weariness was now affecting us like a drug," so much so that they could barely stir themselves even under fire. This "condition of near torpor," Sajer found, produced "the sensation of two simultaneous lives. Sleep and reality had become confused. I felt as though I were deeply asleep, dreaming of artillery fire, lost somewhere in time. My comrades went right on talking. I listened to them without really hearing what they were saying."[37]

Finally, even when he was not fighting, the *Landser* had to live in constant proximity to the same men, with little privacy or possibility of solitude. "Day and night standing guard, lying in ice and snow, defending against the attacks of the Bolshevik hordes, then for days no duty, no work, only a dull, introspective brooding, sleep and sleep again," complained Lieutenant H.G. of the Fourth Panzer Division of the monotony of his life:

> What, then, are you supposed to talk about time and time again? For the last few months we've lived together, know the other's life history, his experiences, know his thoughts and feelings. This country doesn't demand of us that we solve lofty intellectual problems. The only problem that we have to solve is the question of supplies. . . . This . . . makes us dull and shuts out all instinctive sentiments. Whoever at home occupied themselves with art or science now speaks here only of eating and drinking, of billets, of train connections, of supply provisions, and of mail. In the end is that all more important than dealing with an unworldly philosopher or a medieval singer or reading a poet? . . . Speaking with comrades of personal matters and feelings that concern you is not advisable though. You will be smiled at pityingly or mockingly comforted. Where, then, is there a person with whom you can share your sorrow and concerns, but also confide your small joys and happiness?[38]

As not a few men discovered, then, actual combat was not the only affliction of life at the front, or necessarily the most debilitating. The everyday confrontation with physical hardships, living a rough and mean life—this often hidden side of war proved a constant challenge and torment as well.

Yet if many *Landsers* struggled with the extreme demands of the most basic elements of nature in their daily lives, they also found themselves exposed to new scenes, panoramas, and vistas that they could hardly have imagined possible. Ironically, the strange juxtaposition of gruesome horror with natural beauty and alien landscapes contributed to a sensuous fascination with war which could be especially acute for urban soldiers unfamiliar with nature. "I wonder about my feelings," puzzled Harry Mielert in February 1943. "We have today a black day behind us [losing thirty men in an hour], and yet I am almost happier than usual because the sun is shining."[39]

This same sense of incredulity characterized many *Landsers* when surveying the landscapes around them, and none appeared more alien, and sinister, than Russia. "The steppes were wholly desolate and unpeopled yet filled with living menace," wrote the acclaimed Polish novelist Henryk Sienkiewicz in *With Fire and Sword*. "Silent and still yet seething with hidden violence, peaceful in their immensity yet infinitely dangerous—these boundless spaces were a masterless, untamed country created for ruthless men." A land filled with living menace, violent and dangerous, Sienkiewicz had written those words in the late nineteenth century, but they still resonated in Guy Sajer's description of the steppe as "that horrible landscape, indifferent to suffering, death, everything. There was nothing we could do about it, the screams of fear, the groans of the dying, the torrents of blood soaking into the ground like a vile sacrilege, nothing." "The swelling fruitfulness of the black earth," noted Claus Hansmann of the baleful contrast between the teeming life emanating out of the steppe and the death sinking into it, "elicits only a sigh for how sterile our existence has become." Not so blasé, Günter von Scheven concluded more pointedly that Russia was "a landscape characterized by death."[40]

But there was something else to the steppe as well, some inner spirit which fascinated men. "I ride on ugly wild *panje* horses over the steppe," Harry Mielert exalted, "fog and cold, filth and hunger accompany me. Finally a land that is wild and bold, a life without beauty, without ideas of spirit . . . , without sensation; a pure, barren, alien land." Russia—beguiling, capricious, heartless—represented to Mielert "a conflict between western spirit and eastern nature, but one that here does not result in a tension-filled but fruitful contradiction as with us, but rather in an incongruous phenomenon." For Mielert, in fact, Russia seemed less a place than an idea, even though "the idea is only a formal means of realizing a temporal bliss. But how fragile is this bliss!" Fragile indeed, for as he emphasized repeatedly, there was "a discomfiting barrenness" about the Russian steppe: "The character of this landscape . . . was the highest stage of loneliness." Still, Mielert admitted, "I am in a continual fierce struggle with this land and seek an inner contact [with it]." After almost two years in Russia, however, he was no longer so certain of his desire for a spiritual connection with the steppe, warning, "An evil spirit, demons hang over this land, which do not want to do evil to individual people, not you or me, but rather do evil in general. . . . We, with our peculiar exploring spirit of the Nordic people thirsting for danger, pushed our way in so as to fight it. Now we are embroiled in a howling, raging dance." Finally, just a month before he died, Mielert concluded that the turbulent dance had produced only "a comfortless landscape. No women's voices, no music, only the sounds of the front, detonations, artillery and machine gun fire."[41] It was a landscape, Mielert might have added, that made their hearts ache.

The ethereal yet seductive nature of Russia made a similar impact on other *Landsers*. "The yearning of the German mind after the spirit will never be stronger," claimed Wolfgang Kluge, then added ominously, "but also never bloodier, than in this realm of eternal horizons, where the land is like the sea." Not a few *Landsers*, in fact, feared that the eternally restless spirit of the Germans might well run aground in Russia, that it might prove to be the unattainable great white whale to their Captain Ahab. "We must defend ourselves against it, must overcome it," wrote Bernhard Ritter of the endless Russian landscape, "because it is the embodiment of the 'without a goal,' the infinite, 'the never to be able to achieve an objective.' In this country I am always in a conflict between the necessity of overcoming it and the foreboding of feeling its essence."[42]

The quintessence of the steppe, its vast, and solitary distances, seemed especially menacing to the average German soldier. Harry Mielert puzzled over "the endless space in which we feel after all eerily insecure, this mysterious Russian earth with its endless roads, where one spot looks exactly like another." Siegbert Stehmann complained that the immensity of Russia caused one "to lose the feeling of time," that it put one's "consciousness to sleep, while the body struggled forward." The steppe, it seemed, contained nothing but menace: "All around [was] a dismal landscape in great monotony and melancholy," wrote Kurt Reuber. In like manner, Günter von Scheven lamented, "The countryside always stretches further, barren, emerging more melancholy," while

Ludwig Laumen detected in Russia "a strange, closed land, the faces of whose people are also strange and closed. . . . We travel without rest along the great roads, but we will never get near this profound folk, in the soul of this land."[43]

Whether menacing or melancholy, the Russian landscape made an impression on all *Landsers*. "The spaces seemed endless," noted one, "the horizons nebulous. We were depressed by the monotony of the land-scape, and the immensity of the stretches of forest, marsh, and plain. . . . The villages looked wretched and melancholy. . . . Nature was hard, and within her were human beings just as hard and insensitive: indifferent to weather, hunger, and thirst, and almost as indifferent to life and losses, pestilence, and famine." "Nothing could have prepared us," agreed Siegfried Knappe, "for the mental depression brought on by this realiza-tion of the utter physical vastness of Russia. Tiny little doubts began to creep into our minds. Was it even possible that such vast emptiness could be conquered by foot soldiers?" The distances seemed so great and the spirit of the land so sinister that Harry Mielert concluded, "Only Vikings can wage war in this country." As individual hopes and actions seemed to disappear, Guy Sajer, too, confessed to a "feeling of revulsion toward the Soviet countryside" because "the immensity of Russia seemed to have absorbed us." For him, "the hostile indifference of nature seem[ed] so overwhelming it [was] almost necessary to believe in God."[44]

Often, in fact, the *Landser* conveyed a sense that nature gripped him in an embrace which threatened to overwhelm him. Not only the vastness of the steppe but the wall of the seemingly impenetrable Russian forests resembled to some the end of the human world. Willi Heinrich, himself a veteran of the eastern front, observed through a character in his novel, *The Cross of Iron*, "As far as the eye could reach, all the way to the purple-tinged mountains on the horizon, spread a tremendous forest. The bright, even green of the trees flowed on wholly unbroken; nowhere was there a sign of a clearing, of human habitation. The scene took their breath away." But Heinrich understood that though "at first it was all new and exciting for our *Landsers*, . . . the excitement didn't last long. These frightful spaces, monotonous and repetitious; you can't help feeling that one of these days they'll swallow you up." The alien nature, the silence, of the woods seemed, as Heinrich put it, "to radiate menace; they felt the danger like a pain that transformed their senses."[45]

Nor was Heinrich guilty of novelistic excess. "Since the day before yesterday we have come into a somewhat hilly area," Harry Mielert remarked in July 1941, but it wasn't the hills that merited his attention. "There are here endless woods, strange, mysterious, hidden. . . . But for us also dreadful because in them lie hidden terrors." Mielert felt such relief at finally coming out of the woods, in fact, that he said it was like "a rejuvenation." Another *Landser* stated simply, "We do not usually go very far into the forests. You can have no idea of what they are like."[46]

This haunting natural power was only intensified by the effects of war on the natural landscape. Friedrich Grupe described a forest south-west of Lake Ilmen as "a ghostly caricature of itself: mangled and charred trees stare like a reproach from heaven." And surveying the northern horizon one evening in January 1942, Siegbert Stehmann noted "a metamorphosis, something strange, the penetration of a new nature. In the distance out of the twilight rose a cloud. . . . It was blood red, on its edges flared golden flames. Steep pillars of light stood all around and supported the high, glowing vaults. That was no spectacle of nature. That was a warning, a conjuration of the future, a reaching into the unknown. . . . In this moment pretence was shattered. . . . Distant woods and villages burned and smoldered, and the smoke of disaster lifted itself dazzlingly upwards to accuse, warn, and communicate. The front came to us."[47]

In or out of battle, everywhere the *Landser* fought, the power of nature seemed to haunt him. "I felt the hot, still loneliness of Africa, where all life, desires, thoughts, and fighting is [*sic*] different," remarked Hans Schmitz in February 1941, although he did not fully appreciate just how different, and sinister, the desert landscape could be until a few months later. "We were . . . putting up our tent," he wrote in astonishment, "when suddenly from the west the world and the sky . . . were filled with dense sand that quickly raced toward us. In a few seconds the previously swelteringly hot wind was ice cold. The daylight became a sulfurous yellow. . . . Immediately the air was full of dust, the daylight disappeared, and an eerie black-gold night prevailed. . . . It was like before the creation of the world: one saw no beginning and no end." "So here we stand in magnificent, dangerous nature," mused Friedrich Gädeke, "small men, clinging to each other." Indeed, in this primal world many a *Landser* felt adrift and bewildered. "Technology no longer plays a role," Hans Pietzcker wrote in despair from Russia in December 1941. "The elemental power of nature broke the operation of our engines. What do we do?"[48]

Nature could indeed induce fright, but it could also offer a different vision. Advancing into the Kuban lowlands bordering the Sea of Azov, Fritz Trautwein portrayed a pastoral Eden:

> Wide fields of sunflowers stretch out in the glowing sun. The villages consist of thatched roof huts surrounded by fruit trees. One traverses deep gorges, passes by lakes in which water lilies offer up their blooms on the surface of the water. Then again comes the forest, then wide, golden fields of grain. . . . We are in a real paradise. Around the villages are fields of sunflowers, fruit trees, and small groves of beech and acacia trees. We sit here in a small woods surrounded by meadows with an infinite number of fruit trees, below in the valley "the lake smilingly invites one to bathe," and in the distance broad stubbled fields are visible, interrupted by great heaps of ripe fruit.[49]

Other *Landsers*, too, marveled at surroundings new to them. Walther Weber was struck by the brilliant contrasts in the African desert. "Early in the mornings it is mostly cool," he related of the sandy wasteland. "When the sun comes up the land is filled with a tremendous clarity. Because of the [lack of] humidity in the air one can see for unimaginable distances and all shadows are sharply drawn and dark on the dazzling sandy soil." "My first impression of the African continent was that it was yellow and sandy," remarked Hans Schmitz in February 1941. "Palms and small trees under whose miserly shade fields were laid out. . . . Solitary settlements, mud huts and mats, tents, caravan roads, dried-out riverbeds. Everything disappeared against the sandy horizon. Startled herds of wild goats and gazelles sprang about. A Bedouin with his camel stopped and waved to us like an image made from plastic." Contrasting with the yellow-brown of the desert, the towns of North Africa appeared to the *Landser* to be truly another world. "On Wednesday I was in the native quarter of Tripoli," reported Theodor Kinzelbach, "where there was a lively bustle in the narrow streets. There abounded a colorful mixture of Arabs, Berbers, Jews, and Negroes. . . . At the moment the oleander . . . are in full bloom. Going through an avenue with oleanders, dazzling white houses, and arbored passageways doesn't at all allow one to come to the realization that a hundred kilometers farther south the desert begins." Similarly, Wilhelm Heupel gave a vivid picture of human liveliness and tumult. "Sometimes on a bright, hot midday we sit in the piazza in Derna under the shadows of holm oaks and drink the almost intolerably sweet Arab lemonade," he wrote.

Young men and women come with baskets full of eggs and beg us to buy them. The kids are already sharp traders. . . . Others bring chameleons that they have captured in their gardens, also turtles and live chickens, to sell. . . . This part of Derna is full of life: Arabs, Jews, and Italians crowd about as buyers and sellers, among them the amber uniforms of the German air force and the green ones of the ground troops, tank grenadiers and infantry. . . . They buy the red Arab shoes or sandals, have small briefcases made from goat leather, and communicate with the Arabs through sign language. . . . The Jews bring soap, writing paper, English jam, and many other delicacies to sell in their shops, and the Arabs offer giant white and brown *Barakane* (rugs), up to five meters long, woven from the finest wool; next to them [are] tasteless, cheap, printed silk from Italy, bright silver bangles like the Arab women all wear, and colorful silver-embroidered velvet vests.[50]

Everywhere, the great diversity of people and customs the *Landser* encountered inspired amazement. "As we stopped in a village at noon I saw for the first time Russian peasant women in very fine costumes," wrote Ludwig Laumen. "Wide, heavy skirts with red stripes and small, heavily decorated red-black diamonds and hems. With them, white blouses with the familiar Russian embroidery and great, colorful babushkas. They stand there together: an elderly man with thick wool stockings around which he has wrapped black bands, large straw shoes, a thick gray jacket . . . with fur collar, on his head the indispensable earmuffs." Moving through a Tatar area on the Black Sea coast, Alois Dwenger was struck by the many small settlements strewn about but especially by the exotic-looking inhabitants. "The men are tall," he reported, "physically and obviously also mentally dexterous; their faces are often oval, hair and beard deep black, their clothes heavily influenced by the Russian style. The women are handsome, most with sleek, dark hair parted in the middle, with large, lustrous eyes like Turkish women." Anselm Radbruch was similarly astonished by a Kalmyk settlement:

I am now in the capital of the steppe, Elista, one of the strangest places that I have yet come across. Surprisingly plunked down right in the middle of this wasteland exists this "city" built out of colossal buildings of pinkish-red, sky blue, or snow white, and all around it the customary mud huts of the Kalmyks. This totally Lilliputian capital today has no more than 8,000 inhabitants. It makes an impression like an American city out of the picture books: huts and palaces, boulevards and sandy tracks, cow herds and snobs, camel wagons and heavy trucks immediately next to and among each other, a planless confusion of a not quite abandoned past and a too quickly invoked future.[51]

Nor was it merely the myriad peoples with whom he came in contact that produced sensations of wonder. In the midst of the destructiveness of war, a *Landser* might be struck by something so seemingly incongruous as the delicate nature of a flower or the natural beauty all around him. "The nightly marches through this unendingly melancholy, oppressively fragrant moonscape produces a strange mood," mused Harry Mielert of the Ukraine. "The village ponds lie low and sunk in between the squat houses, frogs croak, the moon gleams. . . . It is a wonderful experience. . . . When the sun comes up, it is immediately enveloped in a reddish brown dust cloud from the road, and it sparkles liquidly in the sweat . . . of the soldiers' faces." Crossing the Dnieper a few months later, Mielert marveled at its "absolutely grayish blue color. . . . There are strong colors, the blue river, the pale gray of the sand, the hazy woods on the eastern horizon, and the glassy sky above it all." Observing natural beauty could even, if only temporarily, ease the stresses of war. "Up to now the most beautiful [sight] was the trip here," Mielert wrote of a journey to the rear. "A valley was there, traversed by a roaring stream, beautiful, romantic hillocks with churches and ruins, at the same time the spring-like young greenery enchanted on all the trees and bushes, also the variety of green colors of the meadows and fields. Even the primitive clothing of the Russians, a reminder of earlier historical relationships, appeared romantic to me. . . . It was one of the most beautiful days of the war." Curzio Malaparte, an Italian war correspondent on the eastern front, left a vivid description of the vital presence of nature:

> Night falls, cold and heavy, on the men curled up in the ditches, in the small slit-trenches which they have hastily dug amid the corn. . . . Then the wind rises, a moist cold wind that fills one's bones with an immense numbing weariness. The wind that sweeps this Ukrainian plateau is laden with the scent of a thousand herbs and plants. From the darkness of the fields comes a ceaseless crackle as the moisture of the night causes the sunflowers to droop on their long, wrinkled stalks. All about us the corn makes a soft rustling sound, like the

rustle of a silk gown. A great murmur rises through the dark
countryside which is filled with the sound of slow breathing, of deep
sighs.[52]

During the bitter retreat from the Crimea in April 1944, racing to
get out before their avenue of escape was closed, constantly harassed by
Soviet partisans "who yapped at us like pursuing hounds," Hans Nicol
somehow found time to marvel at "the countryside. . . . Budding spring,
flowers everywhere, blooming bushes, tall, solemn cypresses; so went
the trip in the hills high above the light blue sea. . . . No rich greens and
no brown, rather a southern spring! Who still thought about it, that war
raged and our situation was really dangerous?" Likewise, while enduring
the fierce battles of that first German August in Russia, Will Thomas
could still note, "On the edge of the small thickets bloom tall thistles,
snow white daisies, and many other companion flowers. . . . A small
black cat comes to us in the trench, a pair of chicks peep near-by, . . . a
reddish brown calf comes to visit, . . . and then suddenly once again this
hellish noise [of battle]. . . . War is a strange thing." Just two months later
after the first autumnal snowfall, Thomas mused, "A thick snow cover
has fallen on the earth, as if heaven wanted to cover all evidence of the
blood and death that had scarred this field." Similarly, in March 1942 a
snowfall led Günter von Scheven to remark, "Now nature in reconcili-
ation has laid the purest white over the bloody evidences of the battle."[53]
Even the dreaded Russian winter could cause some *Landsers* to
marvel, as did Walther Weber, at the "broad, snow-covered land spanned
by a star-spangled sky such as no one in Germany knows." And Guy
Sajer, standing solitary guard duty on Christmas night 1942, could
remember it as "the most beautiful Christmas I had ever seen, made
entirely of disinterested emotion and stripped of all tawdry trimmings. I
was all alone beneath an enormous starred sky, and I can remember a
tear running down my frozen cheek, a tear neither of pain nor of joy but
of emotion created by intense experience." "Today was a wonderful day,"
rejoiced Harry Mielert in the midst of winter's grip, "clear as glass in the
farthest direction, cold winter sun, unreal silver blue of the river, . . . and
the desolation of the barren landscape with the cut-up ravines protruding
even sharper." A month later, Mielert marveled at "the crystal clear
nights . . . with the constellations twinkling like diamonds against the
dark backdrop of the sky." And on yet another of those frigid nights in
the eastern Ukraine near Kharkov, Mielert was again struck by the natural

drama taking place in the skies. "The crescent of the moon lay like a boat that swayed in a deep blue heavenly sea," he wrote in February 1943. "A shimmering, silvery reddish glimmer appeared on the horizon. The entire sky was starlit. . . . A totally silvery shine lay on the vertex of the sea . . . and there above on the vertex swayed a golden moon ship, half-sunk in the gleam. . . . It was a marvelous sight." Similarly, in the midst of the harrowing retreat out of the Caucasus, Prosper Schücking noted, "It was very cold, but a magnificent starry night. In the early morning hours we arrived at an empty clearing; in the distance the Black Sea shimmered and the entire eastern sky sparkled in the sunrise." And, amazingly, with the Stalingrad cauldron closing in around him and certain catastrophe approaching, another *Landser* could remark that "the soil here is very rich and soft. . . . Four days ago I lay in a hole a yard deep, and all day long I observed the soil."[54]

Some men even felt a sense of comfort and security as their daily existence came to depend on that soil and their reworking of it. "I'm crouching here in a rather miserable slit trench," complained Harry Mielert, "in which exactly two men can sit across from each other at a table made from a crate if the third man lies down. So we change between sitting and lying, just as long as we're in the hole." As Mielert knew well, burrowing into the earth offered virtually the only protection against the myriad flying objects trying to do in the *Landser*. "We are again under enemy pressure, for the time being only artillery fire and bomber attacks that make little impression on us," he wrote later. And why was this? "Because they have yet to hit our tiny holes in the great Russian earth." Mielert proceeded to reflect on the symbiotic relationship the *Landser* maintained with the ground around him: "We blast ourselves ever deeper . . . and soon with all our men have disappeared from the face of the earth. We infantrymen are regular moles. . . . These bunkers are on average 2.5 to 3 meters large, have a pair of wooden planks and a table. The *Landser* are indefatigable in their skill and inventiveness in building . . . within the shortest time the most charming bunkers. The walls are hung with strips of canvas. So many men sit around together that therefore it's not even cold inside."[55]

These bunkers could seem, in fact, almost like home, a comparison explicitly made by Mielert a few months later. "Every once in a while we go out into the Russian positions," he wrote to his wife, "that is, we creep and crawl behind bushes, through furrows, and instinctively feel the wild person in us. But it is certainly not nice. . . . When, totally filthy, you 'come home' to the warm bunker you just feel utterly happy." Guy Sajer, too, retained a powerful image of the bunker as a place of relative comfort and security in the storm of war. "The troops passed the time as best they could," he noted, "either sunk in sleep despite the discomfort, or playing Skat, or writing home with a pen precariously balanced between numbed fingers. The candles . . . were stuck into empty tins which caught the melting wax, prolonging their lives by as much as four or five times. The memory of those bunkers buried in the wildness of the steppe still haunts my memory, like a legendary tale heard in childhood."[56]

Some firsthand observers even made a study of the variety and individuality of the *Landsers* excavations. "Foxholes, slit-trenches, living relatives of the last hollows of the earth that have taken us in," mused Claus Hansmann:

> Primitive earth architecture of the soldier, a mirror of his soul. One of them, the eternally wary, digs a deep cellar with vaults in which he feels safe in his skin, into whose snoring mouth the crumbling earth falls when above the noise of the front he is permitted to sleep with full enjoyment. The other creates a sober four-cornered hole after the army service manual . . . and he lies flat with somewhat drawn-up knees, in the consciousness that he has completed the day in a soldierly fashion. With a sharp glance the crafty one scouts his surroundings and finds the bumps in the earth that with a few stabs of his spade allows him to prepare a suitable asylum, and he sleeps for a long time while the others, sweating, are still shoveling and digging. The individualist, on the other hand, wants a homestead: one that exactly fits his body, that becomes a lounge chair out of earth with special hollows for a cup of tea. . . . and for the pack of cigarettes with matches. Another values above all a roof over his head and covers it with a tent-half. . . . The parasite lies in wait until someone receives an order to go to the rear and is happy to get a cheap hole. Each prepares his nest like a bird. . . . And so we dig daily . . . , we birds of passage.[57]

Harry Mielert noted not only the way men transformed nature in order to gain a bit of protection from the deadly metal flying above but also how technology seemed to mimic nature. "Early in the morning today two fiery suns suddenly stood next to each other on the horizon," he recounted to his wife, "both enveloped in smoke, but the one thundered and roared and spewed fire like a thunderstorm." The rage bursting forth from the barrels of artillery proved a worthy imitation of heavenly fury, for as Mielert added, probably unnecessarily, "I knew that it was going to be a difficult day." Friedrich Grupe marveled as well at the entwining of nature and war. "In the evening as we lie in a valley in our foxholes, encrusted in the thick dust of our march," he recorded in his diary, "the sky . . . in front of us is blood red. This time it is not the impressive picture of a sunset, but rather the sinister backdrop of a burning munitions dump. It is a hellish concert, a bursting, cracking, and roaring. In the face of this inferno we drop off to sleep, exhausted and conscious of the fact that we have survived this day."[58]

He had survived this particular day, but the *Landser* knew that evidence of the relationship of man, nature, and technology often revealed the tragic. "First the dawning day brought clarity," reflected Claus Hansmann in his diary.

> Everything wrapped in the mantle of the night . . ., what the ears could only guess at, . . . slowly gained its frightful contour. . . . The morning began to breathe; in its shrouded twilight stretch the great expanses of snow, and ever more mercilessly the hesitant brightness gives certainty to the nightly atrocities. . . . Your glance slides over a small body, two hands pressed together in a violent loss of life, a profile full of clarity, gilded by the first rays of sunlight. The bullet hole, a dark red spot high on the forehead. . . . Not all die so softly as the young man on the snowdrift. . . . In places the snow is churned up, blood red, widely strewn weapons and hand grenades, lost gloves and fur hats. And red tracks lead to others: the bronze of their skin is pale, on their rigid corpses stand fiery signs of the war. Unreal eyes pop out of unshaved faces; cramped, bent limbs speak of war dead and polar cold. . . . Already snow crystals are gathering in the painfully wrinkled brows, fill the eye sockets, corners of the mouth, and uniform creases. . . . Only here and there is there still an arm, a thigh drawn up in the death throes jutting out of the glittering cover, last reminders of a night battle, on a segment of a gigantic front of death.[59]

Like Hansmann, Harry Mielert was struck again and again by the connectedness of the icy, black, sparkling night and the weapons. "Another world, also truly strange to me, reveals itself in these . . . impressions of ice and iron, metal and stars, black sky and white-covered earth."[60]

Whether they were struck by its beauty, by the incongruity of images of death alongside pristine panoramas, or by its awesome power, for most *Landsers* nature intimated something both substantive and mysterious. "Yesterday evening there was a wonderful sunset to see," Mielert brooded, "and around midnight the slender crescent of the moon stood almost theatrically translucent between two brown wisps of clouds . . . like a miraculous apparition, a delightfully wistful reflection of my own yearning. . . . I have become so full of longing and melancholy at heart." Surveying the summer beauty of southern Russia just before the fearsome slaughter at Kursk, Helmut Vethake noted reverently, "Flowers and grasses, and the blooming, growing, and ripening of the harvest: [nature] is a part of my day, my thoughts, constantly full of new experiences, of deep astonishment, and of a harmony and fulfillment as I have hardly ever so quickly and so strongly felt." Wolfgang Döring claimed simply, "No one can feel the beauty of nature as a soldier can." The unexpected impact of the natural world was perhaps best summarized by Horstmar Seitz, who asserted, "Even if we lose everything in this war—home, innocence, virtue, our boldest dreams and ideas—we have still found something, to be sure not gods and worlds, rather that which we can grasp with our hands, sense with our eyes: the damp earth, the light, the sun, a solitary pine or the laugh of a young woman. Those who face death learn to love life. . . . This truth is the maternal pain of nature."[61]

Largely unaccustomed to the ways of nature, intrigued by its mystical essence but harassed by the suffering it inflicted upon them, both awestruck and frightened by its power, the typical *Landser* would likely have agreed that the hardships and frustrations produced by nature often seemed more onerous than the rigors of combat. "This primitive existence," concluded Günter von Scheven, expressing a thought likely shared by many others, "imparts a new oneness with nature, you are continually exposed to the wind, sun, and all the elements." But, he hastened to add, "don't let yourself be frightened by what I've said; for us who experience it, it is normal."[62]

6. THE MANY FACES OF WAR

Through long hours of boredom and loneliness, deprivation and hardship, horror and agony, the *Landser* soon became familiar with many of the myriad faces of war. Still, as Günter von Scheven observed, "This endless, sinister war brings the deepest layers of our being into turmoil." Conscious of "an enormous . . . change," Scheven wrote that "individual fates evaporated in the limitless expanses [of Russia]." But this, he added pensively, was both "a painful and yet a pleasant experience." For the anonymous soldier, the real war was intensely personal, tragic yet ironic, agonizing but also magnificent, a frightful harvest of emotions, and, above all, deeply sensory. "We are branded in our strengths and passions," noted Siegfried Roemer in December 1941, "by war and its demands."[1]

Fear was the real enemy of most *Landsers*: fear of death or of cowardice, fear of the conflict within the spirit, or, echoing Montaigne's claim, a simple fear of showing fear. Men felt haunted, hollowed on the inside by pockets of fear that would not go away, caught in the grip of something enormous about to overwhelm them. Still, the notion that combat constituted a test in which mistakes were counted in blood, and which one dreaded to fail, served as a motivating force for countless soldiers. "We fought from simple fear," Guy Sajer maintained, "which was our motivating power." Whether assured ("I go into battle confident, happy, and undaunted and take up the test of life with pride"), hopeful ("These tests must have a blessed effect on us"), or doubtful ("Who among us knows if he will pass the test"), many *Landsers* would have agreed with Karl Fuchs, who maintained that "a man must prove himself in battle." In a letter written to his wife on the eve of his initiation into combat, Fuchs claimed: "A man . . . has two souls in difficult times; indeed, he must have two: The one soul expresses the sincere wish to be home with his beloved; the other soul wants to be engaged in battle and to be victorious. This feeling for battle and victory must be the more important in a man. . . . Life, by definition, means struggle and he who avoids this struggle or fears it is a despicable coward and does not deserve to live."[2]

A harsh, Nazified social Darwinism, perhaps, although most *Landsers* would have agreed with the more prosaic judgment of a captain who ruefully admitted that it "would certainly be easier to experience the war from at home, but I would be ashamed of myself if I were not here." Similar thoughts were betrayed by Harry Mielert. "If I have to be in the war," he concluded, "I want . . . to belong to the frontmost men, to the little men who carry on the real war with only their weapons and physical strength." Still, he acknowledged, "it is difficult to preserve oneself."[3]

Most men knew full well which foe they had to steel themselves against. Preparing for his first action, Guy Sajer watched his closest friend "trying to build up his nerve. In reality everyone feels considerable emotion. . . . The idea of war terrifies us." Similarly, on the eve of the invasion of the Soviet Union, Claus Hansmann observed: "Interwoven desires, fears, and uncertainties are the content of this night. . . . There on the border bridge is the first man that this day will demand. We know already how long his life is still to be measured." Others feared not war in general so much as their specific response to it. "Anxiety often seizes me," Ernst Kleist admitted in May 1940, "not anxiety about battle or death. But events have grown so gigantic that I feel myself much smaller than nothing." "I will not be a coward, so I pray a lot to God," wrote Walther Happich. "I know against which opponent I have to fight." In the last lines written in his diary, Klaus Wilms asserted, "There must be fighting and searching in life; fighting for the necessities of life, yes, even with the dark powers within yourself." Friedrich Grupe, before going on patrol in a dense thicket teeming with Russians, found it necessary to struggle with his fear, "to overcome the inner *Schweinehund*." As Private H.S. put it succinctly, "We must often conquer ourselves."[4]

This was a conflict of the spirit, "a frightful fact that must be endured," as Harry Mielert put it. "The battlefield constantly provokes a shudder in me," he wrote. "I would like no longer to see the dead and the squirting, streaming blood. But I must hold out next to that like one who has been given this as a task." In eerily Nietzschean tones, Eberhard Wendebourg tried to come to terms with this spiritual struggle by asserting, "When the spirit and body are healthy, suffering can only make one stronger and harder." Less positively, Günter von Scheven maintained, "The essential thing is to keep one's inner structure firmly outlined." Sergeant W.H., however, knew precisely what this internal struggle cost: "It is no stroll, to make war here in Russia; rather, hardship follows hardship. I myself saw my life more than once hanging by a thread. . . . I have already thought often of ending my life. And just to force myself to overcome this bridge from life into death as a young man costs inner strength that has nothing to do with courage or bravery."[5]

Some *Landsers* failed in this struggle to preserve their inner spirit, glimpsing, as did Kurt Reuber, only "anxiety, fear, and terror, . . . a life without return along with terror without an end." "The heart is overwhelmed," as Gerhard Meyer put it, at the unbearable thought that "the smell of dead bodies is the beginning and end and ultimate sense and purpose of our being." Horstmar Seitz spoke of "a powerful loneliness," of "always being on the edge of despair." "The war," he concluded, "strikes wounds to my soul that perhaps will never again be healed." Harry Mielert noted the "uncultivated primitive self" within each man: "Here now . . . I am again experiencing my own particular primitive self even up to a simple inner scream. I must think of poor R.M. Rilke, as he began his Elegies . . . , 'Who, when I scream, will hear me then!' " Nor did Mielert have any illusions that this inner struggle would not remain a constant concern, writing later, "I must sit here in this unsurpassed filth, this abhorrent cruelty, this psychological strain. . . . One must wait, sit, plan, and do the worst, act mechanical and hard, look at and watch the inhuman, without flinching." "The war experience," he concluded, "has put my nature into a turmoil. Never have I so energetically reflected over and fought the evil in myself as in this year."[6]

Although few could express their despair as well as Mielert, the ordeal of war pushed many men to the edge of desperation. In hauntingly stark words, Private K.P. observed simply, "I have forgotten how to laugh," and a fellow *Landser* trapped at Stalingrad remarked mournfully, "During the last few nights I have wept so much that it seems unbearable even to myself." Most distressing, those who uttered what Helmut Pabst termed the "cries of damned souls" at the landscape of horror and death could find little internal relief, for according to Ansgar Bollweg, "The realm of destruction was no longer restricted to the front but extended . . . even to within ourselves. Where is the realm where the demons can no longer reach us?" For many who had already made an "inner farewell," who sat in "the dark fires of hell," the damage to their souls was complete; they "lay as in a sarcophagus," said Siegfried Roemer, "but were still alive." "Russia," concluded another *Landser*, "is like a cold iron coffin."[7]

All men wrestled with this primal fear, struggled, as did Meinhart Freiherr von Guttenberg, with a "turmoil of emotions, feelings, even knowledge, which attempt to assault one's psychological balance, which must be mastered." Will Thomas also emphasized the mental strain that fear exacted, writing, "The psychological load presses harder than the burden of the almost superhuman physical exertions," admitting that only "a piece of me remained which could not be changed by the horror and suffering." Harry Mielert spoke in similar tones of the "enormous amount [of] psychological strength demanded of each individual soldier. The physical is the smallest part of the strain." Kurt Reuber noted that "everything suffers, body and soul. I must tap some psychological and physical reserves." As Harald Fliegauf put it, this was "a test of endurance."[8]

Inner conflict proved debilitating for many *Landsers*. The worst things were "not death that is lurking around you, not the fatigue and discouragement that accompany you," according to Siegfried Roemer, "but rather the standing before a cold, dark eternity, daily, hourly, in order to win a little piece of finiteness in which your yearning and love have a sense and goal, beginning and end." Indeed, the effort to conquer the inner self could be achieved only at great price, for as Harald Henry noted, it "demanded an enormous strength, something like heroism." "There is as yet no name for that which is sweeping over us, happening to us," puzzled Max Aretin-Eggert in his last letter. "We stagger in a whirlpool whose force is not stirred up by a human power." This power might have been inhuman, but it had human consequences: "I see [nervous collapse] in many simple men . . . who lacked the mental strength of a stoic self-consciousness," wrote Harry Mielert. "These are very dangerous hours for themselves and for their comrades." "There are some," noted Wolfgang Döring, "who simply hide away in animalistic anxiety." In more prosaic language, Sergeant Steiner, the protagonist of Willi Heinrich's novel *The Cross of Iron*, declared: "We're all miserable bastards. . . . We're all sick to death of it and scared to death, all of us." As Harald Henry put it, with frightening directness, "I am broken in every fiber."[9]

Nor did one ever become accustomed to the fear. The continual confrontation with death or mutilation left many men on the edge of nervous collapse. "Our fear reached grandiose proportions" during a Soviet tank attack in February 1945, admitted Guy Sajer, himself a veteran of three torturous years on the eastern front, "and urine poured down our legs. Our fear was so great that we lost all thought of controlling ourselves." "I had never really known anxiety before," claimed a *Landser* in August 1944. "But a few days ago our company was led into a rye field, and shortly thereafter the Russians pounced on us from all sides. Since then my entire body shakes if I only hear the Russians coming. It is dreadful. I was so far gone that I wanted to stay lying on my belly and let myself be taken prisoner." Returning to the Russian front from home leave, Klaus Löscher felt "a strongly symbolic experience" when his troop crossed, in the moonlight, from one bank of a river to the other, from "the joy of the spent days of furlough to the uncertainties and dangers of the future. Who among us," he added somberly, "might again cross the bridge in the reverse direction? And how?" Löscher's gloom was well-placed: two weeks later, on his mother's birthday, he was killed.[10]

Writing to his wife in April 1943, Harry Mielert attempted to explain the power and the intricacy of this fear: "You often admire my strength . . . but you probably don't know the whole, what I allow to build up, erupt, and inundate me in the miserable nights like tonight, when the howling storm swept over the raven-black heights, when it lured me out . . . against the Russian positions, because there a real danger threatens, there life and death are demarcated by a thin line. You cannot know how my heart then wailed and cried. . . . It is not easy to live life as I must live it." Even the veteran like Heinrich's fictional Steiner could succumb to the omnipresent terror:

Cautiously he climbed up the other side of the trench, clambered over the rampart and waited until the next flare came. When it faded, he straightened up and tensed his body. His heart suddenly began to pound like mad, and he sank back on the ground. "Stand up, you son of a bitch," he told himself, "stand up!" His legs were trembling violently; he panted, gasped for air and dug his fingers into the soft earth. For a few seconds he fought desperately against his fear, against the sheer terror that pinned him to the ground. . . . His face was contorted and he stared wide-eyed. . . . He groaned between clenched teeth; he tried to force his body into motion. . . . [Fear] constricted his throat until he felt that he was choking; a sound like a death rattle emerged from his mouth, and spittle trickled from his lips onto his hands.[11]

Moreover, this fear could surface at any time. The anticipation of an enemy attack, for example, could leave a *Landser* trembling. "Wild animals, even ferocious ones, always flee armed men," Guy Sajer reflected on the eve of a massive Russian attack in the winter of 1943. "We all felt extremely nervous. . . . Some of the very strong had even managed to persuade themselves that since no man is immortal . . . the hour of death was unimportant. . . . Others, strong but not that strong, lived to delay that moment. . . . The rest, which is to say the majority, were pouring with a cold sweat. . . . Those men were afraid with an intense fear that reduced every conviction to nothing. . . . They were afraid before every operation, . . . assailed by fear as persistent as the daylight."[12]

As Sajer admitted and thousands of other *Landsers* would confirm, before every attack, no matter how large or small, the same welling fear made an appearance: "A heavy sense of foreboding settled over us, and the knowledge that soon some of us would be dead was stamped on every face. . . . In fact, none of us could imagine his own death. Some would be killed, we all knew that, but . . . no one . . . could think of himself lying mortally wounded. That was something which happened to other people. . . . Everyone clung to this idea, despite fear and doubt. . . . And each of us was obsessed by the particular question: 'How shall I come through this time?' " Indeed, Sajer insisted, experience of combat lent scant comfort. "The sight of comrades screaming and writhing through final moments of agony had become no more bearable with familiarity, and I . . . was no less of an animal stiff with uncontrollable terror." "The experience of the battle itself," he concluded, "had been as always, more fear." Everyone was afraid, awash in a sea of anxiety. "What might Ivan be thinking?" Harry Mielert wondered in late March 1943, then answered his own question: "We all have the same [fears]."[13]

Sajer also noted another common manifestation of fear: "When anyone is afraid, he thinks of his family, especially of his mother, and as the moment of attack drew closer, my terror was rising. I wanted to confide something of my anguish to my mother." Some men found comfort in these thoughts of home. "We could not ward off our anxieties," noted Friedrich Grupe before an assault. "Who will get it tomorrow. . . ? Images whirled through my thoughts: my hometown, the old castle high on the sandstone cliff, the colorful fields of flowers on the edge of the city, my father and sister at home. . . . My heart is pounding into my neck. I again turn my thoughts to home. . . . In the next minutes there will be no more sentimental thoughts."[14]

As unbearable as the prospect of an attack could be, for many *Landsers* the nights—those "frightful . . . , terribly long nights," as Harry Mielert called them—proved even more agonizing. "The nights are the most taxing," said Mielert, for as he noted in another letter. "One has the feeling that a wild animal is menacing us." "The nights are the worst," confirmed Friedrich Grupe. "To be sure the guns are then silent, to be sure it is uncannily still, but this stillness tugs at the nerves, because each knows that the enemy lies only a few meters before us. The continual crowing of roosters . . . makes us even more nervous, for we hold these noises to be the communication signals of the Russians." Action carried out in darkness was equally fearsome. "There is nothing more terrifying than moving at night through a piece of wooded or bushy country," Sajer asserted, adding that the experience "kept us in a state of prolonged tension." Wilhelm Prüller agreed: "A battle in the woods [at night] is the worst possible thing." Martin Pöppel commented more colloquially in his combat diary, "Everybody is frankly shit-scared in this eerie night, and I have to curse and swear at them to get them to move." "One must have nerves in this modern war," Martin Lindner concluded, "nerves like steel!"[15]

If not totally broken by the general fear of battle, the *Landser* struggled daily with the worry that he might be permanently maimed. Corporal A.K. expressed the concern of many to "make a strong effort to come out of this affair and to be sure with healthy bones, for I would not like to eke out a living after the war by going with an organ and begging." Harry Mielert commented on a sergeant "so badly burned that his head resembled more a skull than that of a living person. An officer was also just as badly burnt. These injuries are actually seen with more fright than many wounds. These men are married. How will they put it to the wives . . . ? These are probably the worst cases that the war can bring about."[16]

The sight of the dead and wounded often frightened men more than being wounded themselves. In a letter in early December 1941, Harald Henry matter-of-factly dismissed his own wound, noting dispassionately, "The thing looked so gruesome, my coat was so ripped to pieces and splashed with blood, [but] nothing happened, it was only a small flesh wound." Similarly, Siegfried Knappe noted, "The first time I had been wounded . . . I had been surprised, but when it happened the second time I just thought, 'Okay, it has happened again and I am still alive.' "[17] Henry and Knappe, in surviving, found their sense of invincibility reinforced.

But the stark realization that his comrades lay dead or wounded forced the *Landser* to confront his doubt and fear. Richard Holmes has pointed out that the sight of a corpse provoked feelings akin to that somber message often chiseled on medieval gravestones: "As you are now, so I once was; As I am now, so will you be." As Hans Woltersdorf remarked laconically, "It wasn't good to look into the [destroyed] tank . . . , to look at the gruesome reality. One always sees oneself sticking to the walls in a thousand pieces like that, without a head." Although death remained a commonplace occurrence, many *Landsers* never got accustomed to the sight of it. Hans-Friedrich Stäcker confessed that a "dizziness again and again flashes through me when I see dead comrades. " "The pictures of fallen comrades move before my eyes," wrote Günter von Scheven. "Covered by gray coats, prematurely stiffened by the cold, silent and lifeless they lay there, with their faces decomposed from the frost and their lifeless eyes. . . . [It is] a merciless, hard death. After many days of battle long rows lie next to each other. . . . What we see here is the face of the Russian war."[18]

"We marched by a strange place," noted Friedrich Grupe of his first encounter with the sight of large numbers of German dead, "where in the faded twilight German *Landsers* lay in rows under their tent halves, out of which only their stiff feet showed. Everywhere graves were being shoveled out. That shocked me and made me feel cold. Go on, just go on. Don't think." Numbness also gripped Harry Mielert, who noted dispassionately after a night attack: "No tears flowed for our [fallen] comrades. They were laid on the stretchers and transported rearward. . . . It is a strange sight, when the men from the burial units come trembling to the front, always at dawn, to pick up the fallen. Quickly, a bit too quickly, they then stagger back to the rear. . . . It has something of the theater about it, it is done with many gestures and formal expressions [but] few words." This detached attitude, however, proved hard to maintain. "Under the snow melting away appear more and more corpses of fallen Russians. When you see these cadavers," Mielert later admitted, "you involuntarily think . . . that you yourself could also look like that." Indeed, Mielert betrayed the secret fear of every *Landser*: "When my comrades fall or are wounded, I am always surprised and ask: 'when will it be me?' " Two weeks later, Mielert got his answer: he was killed in action in southern Russia. Imagining these scenes today, one could well understand what Friedrich Böhringer meant when he wrote, "Death is perhaps not the worst thing, but we must suffer it!"[19]

Prevalent always, of course, was this fear of death, a "fear that had been with [Sergeant Steiner] for so long that it had become a living part of himself [and] was gradually smothered by dull indifference." So wrote Willi Heinrich in *The Cross of Iron*. For others, however, the fear took a more active form. Even before his first encounter with the enemy, Friedrich Grupe wrote in his diary, "A premonition of death on the battlefield overcame me, of mutilated bodies that could only be identified by their identity tags." "I suddenly felt terribly afraid," recalled Guy Sajer of an episode in the autumn of 1943. "It would probably be my turn soon. I would be killed, just like that, and no one would even notice. We had all grown used to just about everything, and I would be missed only until the next fellow got it. . . . As my panic rose, my hands began to tremble. I knew how terrible people looked when they were dead. I'd seen plenty of fellows fall face down in a sea of mud, and stay like that. The idea made me cold with horror."[20]

One *Landser*'s wife rebuked him for "always mentioning death in [his] letters," enjoining him "to want to live, always live." But who could blame a *Landser* for being obsessed with death, since, as Harry Mielert noted, "death . . . belonged to our everyday life." "Death lurked every-where," Friedrich Grupe confided in his diary. "All around, the bushes shone in delicate May greenery, the sun brought a glow to the few remaining birch trees. But death triumphed here." Explained another soldier to his wife, "Life goes on until one day you yourself stand at the place at which there is a dark door from which no one returns. . . . For us soldiers death of course has a different look than for those people in middle-class lives; we are more familiar with it and it also comes inwardly closer." Likewise, Bernhard Beckering observed, "Death is always around . . . and before him goes worry and anxiety and suffering and animosity." And in another letter, "We always stand perplexed and apprehensive before death," which to him appeared to be an "endless expanse of inscrutability."[21]

"Death isn't something you realize," remarked another character in *The Cross of Iron*. "It comes like the night. When the twilight falls among the trees, it's there already and you can't avoid it." Indeed, to

Günter von Scheven, "every hour was filled with the twilight of death." Death was a natural, predictable, if inscrutable phenomenon, as reliable as day and night, something that could not be avoided; with justice, Reinhard Becker-Glauch referred to "the indivisibility of life and death." The sense that life and death were woven together in a frightening pattern, that beauty and horror constantly intermingled, struck Claus Hansmann as well. "You might already have marched for a long time . . . and passed through villages and fields full of destruction and evidences of the tumult of battle. But there are also bucolic landscapes that have been spared: farmer's gardens with brown, sturdy girls and women. And you see fruit trees amid the green shade. . . . With luck and the sharp eyes of a soldier you find just the right tree. . . . Then you don't concern yourself over anything else and [grab] . . . ripe plums . . . laden with sweetness. . . . You are almost unconscious and enjoy again and again sliding the sweet flesh of the fruit back and forth through your parched throat." But while strolling through the village and enjoying this unexpected bounty, Hansmann stumbled upon "an everyday sight, a shattered tank. . . . You see a man there, the man is burnt. He lies in such a strange position on his back, his arms raised in frozen defense . . . and his feet trapped under the tank . . . ! Burnt human flesh there before you, and you throw the plum away, for in your hot fingers it has become too soft, and you are for a thought-provoking moment too soft yourself."[22]

If some *Landsers* viewed death as an everyday part of life, for many others its capriciousness and random appearance engendered fear and apprehension. "Five days ago in our firing position, just short of the path to the observation position, I sat together with our intelligence chief and talked of Würzburg with him," wrote Gerhard Meyer. "He then fetched his shirt, which lay drying fifteen meters away and waved to me. There a piece of shrapnel hit him in the head. Today I am . . . at his grave. . . . Whoever is not a soldier cannot understand this."[23]

The fickleness of death impressed many men. "We observed from the bunker the explosions that threw a comrade to the ground, as new shots whizzed," Friedrich Andreas von Koch observed in dispassionate tones. "Heavy shrapnel flew thick over him; if he had held his head a little higher, well it didn't hit him and he came into the bunker and wrote further on the letter that he had begun." Koch's earlier comment that war "is all so profane, so impersonal" certainly applied to this episode of daily life. The mystery of survival in the face of sure death impressed Klaus Löscher, who sent his wife "a shot-up note that I carried folded in my pants pocket when the shot passed through my leg. Praise God, this time it whizzed over the hand grenade that was also stuck in the pocket." Prosper Schücking was less impressed, however, mentioning almost indifferently, "Yesterday I sat behind the house peeling potatoes, when a mortar happened to hit five meters from me and a giant cloud of dirt and powdery dust fell on me."[24] That was it: no mention of casualties, no reflection on life, just a routine daily occurrence that netted three sentences in a page-long letter.

Harry Mielert also professed nonchalance: "I stood immediately next to him [Captain O.], about 150 meters opposite an undergrowth in which Russian sharpshooters lay. He was hit, I had the luck instantly to have thrown myself down. . . . as soon as I saw the fellow lying there before us. The captain reacted a fraction of a second later and was wounded." Siegfried Knappe assumed a similarly fatalistic attitude after a stray artillery shell struck his group. "The *Oberleutnant* (First Lieutenant) killed beside me was a reserve officer," he recalled. "One moment we were discussing our plans, and the next moment we lay side by side in the dirt, one dead and one unharmed. That I happened to land where I did and he landed where he did was just a throw of the dice. . . . I knew the next time I might very well be the unlucky one. . . . I accepted my eventual death or maiming as part of my fate."[25]

But every *Landser* spared this time knew that his luck might run out next time. Certainly Franz Rainer Hocke must have felt that his quota of good fortune had been used up in one episode: "Recently the English three times shot me out of a house in which I was observing. First came a tank and cracked off five or six shots at me from a thousand meters away which went crosswise through the hut. Then followed artillery shells, and finally a mortar knocked me off the roof. This last time I was saved only by the circumstance that the shell struck directly on a thirty-centimeter-thick roof beam." Little wonder that Hocke felt as if he were "in a wreck in a heavy, stormy sea." Certainly most *Landsers* would have understood Konrad Wilhelm Henckell's diary reference to "men alone, who daily stand facing the gruesome arbitrariness of war." The sense of isolation and helplessness in the face of random, impersonal death could eventually crack even the strongest nerves. As Harry Mielert acknowledged, he had come to realize, instinctively, involuntarily, the truth of "the old war saying that one must be completely aware of death, must completely absorb it, in order . . . not to be concerned with it any more."[26]

For many *Landsers*, war produced a feeling of release not in the embrace of death but in indulging the violence that led to death. The thrill of war, the beauty in terror, lay in giving vent to the dark, emotive, and irrational within the individual, to unchaining the chaotic and inexplicable, to losing oneself in the fascination with absolute freedom. The sudden onrush of danger and elemental forces, of a destructive passion, often proved unexpectedly intoxicating. "These men out there have discovered that their lives were not fulfilled," mused Helmut Pabst in April 1942. "All their petty reasons paled before the force of nature, the cry of the blood: to have committed the ultimate violence." The ultimate, to experience everything: Harry Mielert claimed that it was "sentimental and fastidious to feel a horror about corpses. . . . It is not the ugliness, rather the desire produced in you by the sight that is repulsive. This hazy in-between feeling . . . is never betrayed by us; but the soul always . . . suspects something." Hidden in our psychic depths, a secret that most of us would prefer to keep buried, lies the awareness that many men come to enjoy war, not only for what Pabst called the primal "cry of the blood" but for the sense that one experiences ultimate freedom in battle. Though distressed by his feelings, Mielert nonetheless confided in his diary that "soldierly cruelty is sensual." This sensuality seemed to him "terribly demonic," even as he admitted that the result of it was "a sensual aesthetic." For others, too, there seemed something seductive, almost wicked but beautiful, beyond morality, in doing everything in life, even killing. "It is so easy to kill," agreed Guy Sajer, "especially when one no longer feels any particular link with existence."[27]

"These twenty-four hours are among the most unforgettable and really most stirring and beautiful of my life," confirmed Wolfgang Döring as he reflected on a recent attack. "How such experiences affect individual men is totally different. There are some who simply hide away in animalistic terror. There are often those who then just meet with some kind of accident. There are others who are completely panicked and incapable of any kind of decision. . . . There are also the reckless mercenaries and natural adventurers who enjoy such moments and fall into an almost euphoric state." Döring left no doubt as to his own category, concluding that in those moments he felt possessed of "a cool calm and almost an instinctive sureness."[28] To him, the sudden sense of power and liberation from conventional restraint proved intoxicating.

This heightened sense of awareness, the exhilaration of peering into the abyss, often acted as a stimulant, producing an experience "quite different from that portrayed in the World War books," a sensation of "a new baptism." "There is a strange joy in war," Heinz Küchler remarked with little attempt at elaboration. Others, however, sought to give expression to the peculiar sensations war produced in them. "In life, pain and joy, despondency and happiness often come together," asserted Rudolf Bader. "Their collision is painful, but can also be fruitful. Great things and deeds come into the world only with pain. Whoever seeks life must suffer the bitterness of death." To Rudolf Halbey, it all seemed so obvious. "Life is no longer a given," he remarked in January 1943, "it is a gift." Guy Sajer neatly combined both explanations in deciphering the attraction of war. "Peace has brought me many pleasures," he reflected, "but nothing as powerful as that passion for survival in wartime . . . and that sense of absolutes."[29]

Some insisted that one could appreciate the intensity of life only next to the horror of death. To Wolfdietrich Schröter, the exhilaration of war resulted from living "as if this were the last night, the last day . . . ; this continual standing immediately before eternity awakens a great joy." "For us men this war is perhaps an indelible experience," mused Wolfgang Döring, "that can once more let us experience and live in a completely original sense the deepest law of our being. There is no question that the war has transmitted a new immediacy to everything and directed a totally fresh look at the few great and most important things of life." "Only those who have experienced [war] can measure the range of human existence," claimed Horstmar Seitz. Helmut Pabst noted, "Even in these grave hours one feels that life is full of content. It is bitter and sweet . . . because we have learned to see the essential. . . . In such hours the desire emerges . . . to form a second life out of our insights." Similarly, Harry Mielert reflected: "We exist in a hard fate which daily puts the truth of this earthly existence relentlessly before our eyes, that out of that death and transitoriness springs as a blessed illuminating happiness an enjoyment of beauty, that only one who has experienced and grasped this existence between transitoriness and death can properly understand such a source of happiness." Soldiers, Mielert concluded, were "members of a vital dimension." Wolfgang Kluge agreed: "We who must walk on the shadowy side of life cling more to the beauty of life than those who possess it." Indeed, some men came to believe, along with Martin Lindner, that "only one who has gone through the abyss and horror of many battles can experience how peaceful, how infinitely beautiful the earth and life is [sic], how beautiful flowers are, how moving music or how heartfelt a picture can be. . . . One feels the love and warmth of God strongest after a battle, and a great thankfulness and joy spreads through a person."[30]

Other *Landsers* asserted, along with Reinhard Becker-Glauch, that war brought a "consciousness of the limits of things, where the false values sink away and the true things remain." "Nature," declared Rolf Schroth, "has created us so that we sink into habit," a tendency he saw as "not only false, but also weak, comfortable." The value of war, then, was that it "demanded a constant proving of oneself, that again and again one had to conquer the obvious. . . . It is, after all, happiness that I experience here: I want to look more powerfully into the depths of life." Some, such as Eberhard Wendebourg, valued war because one came "to judge men not by their rank and position, name and honors, but only by their character and performance. . . . War teaches the true worth of men." Finally, a few, such as Hans Pietzcker, purported to be proud to have "lived" in this misery and distress and "not just gotten through it." In a letter just before Christmas 1942, Pietzcker reflected: "Fate is difficult, often incomprehensibly hard . . . , [but] we have truly learned to treasure life more than someone at home. . . . We love this life of danger because the border between life and death illuminates the pure truth. Danger no longer means more terror for us, and death is no longer a threatening darkness. He belongs to life like a brother. . . . It's only a pity that we won't be able to apply to life what we've experienced in these hard hours. To pass on this experience to others, that may well be the finest thing."[31]

The "horribly beautiful power of war," its "terrible splendor," also flowed from an excitement released by the conquest of fear. As Reinhard Goes confessed, "I feel closest to life when death is at its worst and is mowing and destroying all around me. . . . This dangerous life is the best and the most liberating. When one has only the goal and task before one's eyes, the fear disappears and the exhilaration carries along even the weakest." Life interposed with death, danger with liberation, exhilaration with the accomplishment of the task—combat indeed released a complex jumble of emotions. As Hans-Friedrich Stäcker noted, "I have literally felt how in a hard moment a hot wave of blood shot through my heart and pulled me forward." Some men indeed came to believe, parroting the words of Ernst Jünger, that war was the "father of all things," creating a situation like that "before the creation of the world."[32]

Even men not consciously gripped by the "foolhardy magnificence" of war could betray similar sentiments. Caught in the whirlpool of battle on the eastern front, Guy Sajer felt "an almost drunken exhilaration," filled, as he was, "with the spirit of destructive delight." Confronted with seemingly endless combat, Sajer nonetheless remarked on the "hitherto unsuspected acuteness [that] sharpens every sense," while "at the moment when our mission was about to be accomplished" he noted a violent feeling of nervous energy and release of tension.[33] Mastering fear, living on the edge of danger, being liberated from tension, accomplishing the task—all of these produced that great intensity of sensation which caused some men to see combat as a drama of horribly beautiful power.

Still other *Landsers* were struck by the strange beauty of battle in the midst of horror and destruction. "Smolensk was burning," exclaimed Hans August Vowinckel in June 1941. "It was an enormous drama. . . . With magical power the flame drew one to glance into its depths, as if it wanted to pull in men and machines." In similar awed tones a *Landser* described his first experience of a *Nebelwerfer* (rocket artillery) attack during the German advance on Voronezh in mid-1942: "The night was dark but clear. . . . Three batteries of *Nebelwerfers* opened fire. . . . The sight was as awe-inspiring as the sound was nerve-shattering. A low-pitched howling rose quickly to a screaming crescendo and then huge gouts of flame erupted, firing the rockets and sending them like huge comets hurtling through the air. . . . Lines of flame escorted by trailing clouds of red-lined smoke marked their route as they streaked across the sky."[34]

Helmut Pabst was similarly gripped by the beauty of battle. "To the south a gigantic fire threw slender beams of light straight up into the sky like a searchlight," he marveled in March 1943. "The redness colored the snow soft and warm. . . . Fine snow crystals and broken tatters of clouds swirled against the clear sky of the sparkling night. At 20.30 some lightning flashed behind us and filled the area from horizon to horizon. The detonations rolled muffled over us. It was a drama of horribly beautiful power." In one of his last letters, written in the midst of the appalling devastation during the German retreat toward Kiev in the autumn of 1943, Pabst again betrayed his fascination with destruction:

> Two Pioneers [combat engineers] ran here and there, placing explosives under the rails, . . . [then] blew the white, thin beams out of the earth. . . . But that was only a part of the destruction, a laughably small part. . . . The villages burned. They burned with raging power. The embers covered the street. We went through in a gallop, our

faces covered against the shower of sparks. . . . The smoke mingled with the thick dust to form a compound so thick that we were wrapped in a double coat. Long before evening the sun was already red, as it hung sick and thirsty over the march of destruction. The clouds over the army column, illuminated by a double light, gave the most splendid, beautiful colors that I have ever seen: it unfurled war in its whole terrible splendor. We saw houses in all stages of destruction . . . , the first outbreak of red flames that battled the black smoke clouds, the victorious dance of the red rooster over the roofs. We raced through the white-hot dying streets.[35]

Harry Mielert perhaps best described the jumble of sensations produced by battle, the sense of pure exhilaration at the realization that all limits were off, that the normal range of human possibilities had expanded to include wanton destruction:

The Russians shot into [the town] with artillery, nearly all the houses were burning, in between large stores of munitions detonated and buildings and facilities were blown up by Pioneers. Everything roared, flamed, shook, cattle bellowed, soldiers searched through all the buildings, kegs of red wine were taken away on small *panje* wagons, here and there was drinking and singing, amid that again the explosions and the new fires roaring out. . . . But the strangest thing is the colorful confusion. . . . It is magnificent. All barriers are broken. . . . Anger roars through all the cracks in the world.[36]

The sensory fascination with war was not limited to visual images; many *Landsers* remarked as well on the peculiar sounds and smells of their surroundings. "The roar of combat alone was enough to shatter a soldier's will," claimed Siegfried Knappe. "But combat was a great deal more than noise. It was a whirlwind of iron and lead that howled about the soldier, slicing through anything it hit. Even inside the roar of battle, strangely, the soldier could detect the whistle of bullets and the hum of slivers of shrapnel, perceiving everything separately: a shell burst here, the rattle of machine gun fire over there, an enemy soldier hiding behind cover in another place." Günter von Scheven, too, was struck by the whirling tumult of sounds that characterized battle. "You could not have any idea of this landscape that is characterized by death," he wrote in March 1942, "with cries and groans, jubilant cheers of the attackers and the wild, piercing roar of the enemy infantry. Nearby the reverberation of bombs dropped from softly droning airplanes; along with it the rumble of artillery. We live in bunkers in the trembling earth." Hans-Heinrich Ludwig noted with fear and amazement the "crazy attacks" of the Russians, accompanied by "a wild choir of stormy Russian 'hurrahs.' " The tendency of the Russians to trumpet their assaults with bloodcurdling screams unsettled many *Landsers*. Leopold von Thadden-Trieglaff, in his last letter, wrote of the terror of the "fanatical [Russian] cries of 'hurrah'. . . which shattered us." The sound of Russian partisans "yelping at us like pursuing hounds" also unnerved Hans Nicol. Still others recoiled from what Kurt Reuber, at Stalingrad, termed the "frightening din of annihilation." Rudolf Halbey was struck by the profusion of sounds: "bullets whistling, screams, orders, shots." while Harry Mielert was haunted by "the awful cries of the wounded, without echo in this wasteland."[37]

The cries of the injured could be especially unnerving. "Terrifying screams drowned the sounds of engines," Guy Sajer recalled after one battle, "screams so prolonged and horrible that my blood froze. . . . We heard the sounds of gunfire and explosions coming closer, punctuated by bloodcurdling screams. . . . We felt petrified by fear." In another engagement he noted "the cries of the wounded, of the agonized dying, shrieking as they stare at a part of their body reduced to pulp, the cries of men touched by the shock of battle. " On yet another occasion Sajer flinched at the "the death rattle of thousands of dying men, which filled the air with a horrible sound." An anonymous soldier writing from Rumania in June 1944 described how "next to me lay comrades who had had it. They could no longer walk, and shrieked dreadfully, as I have never before heard humans scream. . . . You vacillated in your feelings and asked yourself if you should stay with the wounded, or should go on. To stay would be suicide and therefore I went on." The screams of the wounded could shake even the strongest men; as Rudolf Halbey noted numbly in his diary, the "cries and groans of the wounded strain the nerves."[38]

Aside from human cries, the sounds of war seemingly became commonplace to some. Friedrich Grupe recorded in his diary that the Russian artillery "hammered at the edge of our positions. An unpleasant and threatening musical accompaniment," but then remarked, "In the evening I sat in the battalion command post and listened on the army radio to music from home. In the course of this one forgets the reality, the gray earth, . . . the desolate villages, . . . the noise of battle." "We have had heavy artillery fire for over twelve hours," noted Walter Happich in a letter to his mother in February 1945, "but that doesn't bother us. . . .

These hours during the bombardment are sometimes quite nice. . . . They are the only hours of rest except for the meager sleep we get in the night."[39]

Some commented as well on the variety of rhythms produced by war. Grupe was struck by "the sharp crack of the hobnailed boots on the asphalt and cobblestones, the tramping of the horses, the clatter of their hoofs, and behind them the sounds of the rubber-treaded combat vehicles; now and then we just have to sing, then one of the old or new soldiers' songs rings out from hoarse throats." A few months later, Grupe again noted in his diary how "the resounding march rhythm of a thousand army boots on the cobblestone rang out" as his unit paraded through the streets of a town. On the day of the invasion of Poland, Grupe recorded the noise of "military march music on the radio," the "continuous fresh cries advertis[ing] special editions," the "national anthem ringing out of the loudspeakers." Indeed, Grupe's diary registered the cacophonous sounds of war in all their discord: "Rain drummed on our steel helmets"; "Motors drone on the forest paths"; "The steps of ten thousand men ring over the sodden earth. They move past like silent shadows . . . , disappear into the dark, accompanied by the patter of horses, the rattle of wheels, . . . then the loudspeaker clangs like something out of a far, far world. . . . Company after company stamps past, the melody wafts back over the soldiers, blows away, is swallowed up by the marching steps."[40]

In addition to the din of combat, virtually all *Landsers* noted the unique odors of war. "One smells a curious odor," Harald Henry wrote of Russia, "that for me will probably always stick to this campaign, this mixture of fire, sweat, and horse corpses." Another veteran of the Russian campaign also claimed that he would never forget the "compound of smells: stale urine, excrement, suppurating wounds, and the most unpleasant smell of *Kasha*, a sort of buckwheat porridge." Friedrich Grupe was struck by the "repulsive stench of powder, burning iron, and earth." Similarly, Siegfried Knappe "learned that the smell of rotting flesh, dust, burned powder, smoke, and gasoline was the smell of combat." During a night attack, Knappe also observed the role played by smell in his unit's success: "The surrounded Russians . . . were attacking my battery . . . and my men were defending themselves. . . . They could not see the Russians they were shooting at, but they could . . . smell them! The Russian soldiers smelled of *makhorka* tobacco, which had a very strong unpleasant odor. . . . This awful smell got into their thick uniforms and could be smelled for quite a distance."[41]

The Italian war correspondent Curzio Malaparte noted, in the early months of the Russian war, that the "odor of rotting things rose from everywhere. . . . The smell of rotting iron won over the smell of men and horses. . . . Even the smell of grain and the penetrating, sweet scent of sunflowers vanished amid that sour stench of scorched iron, rotting steel, dead machinery. . . . The smell of iron and of petrol grew stronger in the dusty air . . . as if the smell of men and beasts, the smell of trees, of grass and mud, was overcome by that odor of gasoline and scorched iron." Siegbert Stehmann commented on the "sweet smell of decay" that filled the air after a battle, as did Wolfgang Kluge, who noted "everywhere the disgustingly sweet smell" of rotting bodies. Johannes Huebner claimed that the worst aspect of the war was the "noxious odor of fire . . . , corpses, the wounded, [and] the burnt cattle." Guy Sajer explained simply: "We could smell the presence of death, and by this I don't mean the process of decomposition, but the smell that emanates from death when its proportions have reached a certain magnitude. Anyone who has been on a battlefield will know what I mean."[42]

For many men one of the sharpest and most agonizing sensations of the war resulted from its awful impact on horses. "On the way lay a wounded horse," wrote Harald Henry in October 1941. "It reared, someone gave it a mercy shot, it sprang up again, another fired . . . , the horse still fought for its life, many shots, but the rifle shots did not quickly finish off the dying eyes of the horse. . . . Everywhere horses. Ripped apart by shells, their eyes bulging out from empty red sockets. . . . That is just almost worse than the torn-away faces of the men, of the burnt, half-charred corpses with their bloody broken chests." Despite all the bloodletting and mutilation of one battle, Friedrich Reinhold Haag was most shaken by the sight of a "beautiful white horse grazing by a ditch. An artillery shell . . . had torn away his right foreleg. He grazed peacefully but at the same time slowly and in unspeakable grief swayed his bloody stump of a leg to and fro. . . . I don't know if I can accurately describe the horror of this sight. . . . I said then . . . to one of my men: 'Finish that horse off!' Then the soldier, who just ten minutes before had been in a hard fight, replied: 'I haven't got the heart for it, Herr Lieutenant.' Such experiences are more depressing than all the 'turmoil of battle' and the personal danger."[43]

Some *Landsers* were gripped by odd historical sensations, treading as they were on ground fought over by their fathers in World War I, or by Napoleon's ill-fated troops in 1812. Fighting on the Belgian-French border, Helmut Neelsen was stunned to discover that his "company commander [was] wounded in the same place where twenty years ago his father gave his life for Germany." Hans-Heinrich Ludwig remarked in a letter from Russia, "I am living for the first time in a bunker just like father in 1914–1918," adding, "I often think about that." Marching through the Chemin des Dames area of Champagne, much contested in World War I, Private H.B. mused that it was "a historic region, whose soil was soaked through with the blood of our fathers in the world war." The bloody fighting near Sevastopol in June 1942 caused Alois Dwenger to admit that "many times we think about Verdun."[44]

Images of the Great War were even more pressing for those who fought in both wars. Private A.M. noted dispassionately, "Now for the second time I am conscripted to France as a soldier and find myself not far from my old battle grounds of the year 1918." Similarly, Captain F.M. observed: "Our company is now located almost in the area where I was situated in the world war. Many times I cannot believe whatsoever that twenty-three years have passed since I experienced those stormy days. . . . Certainly it would have been more comfortable to experience the war from home, yet I would have been ashamed of myself if I were not also there this time, in order later to say with satisfaction: 'I was there in the world war, when we lost the war, but I was also there again when we won in an unheard-of rapid fashion.' " Corporal E.B., marching through Flanders, was surprised that "the trenches and dug-outs [of World War I] were still there, duds still lay about, as did large heaps of corrugated iron that had been removed from the bunkers." Less surprising was the fact that when the first snows of that terrible Russian winter of 1941 descended on the German soldiers, some remembered an earlier attempt to conquer Russia. "One really cannot conceive why we have not received any winter things," wrote Private L.B. in November 1941. "If it goes on this way, it'll go like Napoleon. . . . But I believe that in 1812 they were better prepared against the cold than we were. Almost everyone's socks are worn out, no one has earmuffs. . . . So little concern for us! In the year 1941! (not 1812!). . . . If I was not in the military myself . . . I would not believe it. But I have seen and experienced it."[45]

Ultimately, it was precisely this sense of wonderment, the diverse sensory knowledge gained from personal experience and observation, that fascinated the *Landser*. "Those who haven't lived through the experience may sympathize," Guy Sajer declared, "but they certainly will never understand." The myriad sensations felt by the *Landser*, the intense feeling of living for the moment, produced a sense of affirmation, validating his existence and at least temporarily stifling the pervasive fears of death. Hans Pietzcker quoted Goethe in an attempt to convey the impact of the sensory experience of war: "I am happy, and when I am not, at least all the deep feelings of joy and sorrow dwell in me. The main thing is that you have a soul that loves the truth and that you absorb it where you find it." And where had Pietzcker found such truth? "In the midst of distress and death," he confirmed, "how . . . much we have first learned here about living life." To some *Landsers*, in fact, the sensations produced by war proved all too authentic: they wondered what life would be like without them. "In the final analysis," Kurt Reuber conjectured, "after all the profound experiences [of the war] our further lives will not have much worth."[46]

7. THE BONDS OF COMRADESHIP

Writing just a month after the invasion of the Soviet Union, Gerhard Meyer had already been reduced to near hopelessness by the savage fighting taking place along the Dnieper: "To believe that the rotten smell of dead bodies is the beginning and end of life and the final purpose and meaning of our existence is unbearable to me." Just a few days later, however, he spoke of a sense of renewal: "I have been directly at the front for five days and nights, and at night, despite the nearness of the enemy, have rejuvenated my soldier's heart by roasting chickens in the bunker [with my comrades]."[1] For the *Landser*, life in the midst of terror and uncertainty often seemed bearable only because of the intense feeling of camaraderie forged in the fiery furnace of battle. Comradeship provided a sense of affirmation of life amid the prevalence of all-consuming death and a confirmation of community, even as these tight-knit groups disintegrated. It sustained a feeling of invulnerability and well-being, even when all understood the tenuous nature of life at the front.

Willi Heinrich, himself a veteran of the eastern front, summarized well in his novel *The Cross of Iron* the mixed emotions of many German soldiers:

> It's the *Landser* I'm most sorry for. You know, he's the unluckiest invention of this twentieth century of ours. . . . Our men no longer have any ideals. . . . They're fighting for nothing but their naked lives, for their bedeviled, unfortunate flesh. . . . Flesh is patient. It will suffer anything that is put on it. It can be used; it can be abused.

And it has suffered abuse because it has been lured with the bait of so-called ideals. It has been killed and it has been allowed to kill, until it seems to exist only for its own sake. But behind all that there is the common soldier's fundamental decency which doesn't permit him to leave his comrades in the lurch.[2]

Amid the despair and cynicism, that affection for those enduring the same horrors created a sense of unity and pride, an intensity of feeling that rose to a level rarely achieved by mere friendship. Loyalty, mutual obligation, a willingness to sacrifice, pride, a sense of duty, even love—these constituted comradeship for the *Landser*.

The *Wehrmacht*'s stress on camaraderie was an essential element in the production of a cohesive and resilient band of front fighters, but it aimed at something else as well: nothing less, in fact, than transforming the *Frontgemeinschaft* (front community) into a *Volksgemeinschaft* (national community), an ideal of harmony and social unity that supplied the vital principle around which a new German society was to be organized. Comradeship thus served as both cause and effect, a means by which to create a new sense of community, as well as the inevitable by-product of such a community-based society.

Precisely in order to nurture and instill this fierce sense of camaraderie, the German army had long emphasized the creation of primary groups. From the regiment to the battalion down to the smallest rifle squad, tradition and practice encouraged the men to develop a special bond and fierce loyalty to their unit. Karl Fuchs put this feeling succinctly when he wrote to his father in February 1941, "I've become such an integral part of my company that I couldn't leave it ever again." According to Martin van Creveld, German army tradition, training, organization, recruitment and replacement policies, leadership ideals, and tactical expectations all aimed precisely at creating, "especially at the lowest levels, . . . tight bunches of men who suffered, fought, and died together."[3]

In practice, this meant that the Army attempted to recruit and keep together men from specific regions and even to supply replacements from the same area of the country. Fuchs himself spoke of his intense joy at being in a unit with men from his region and village, a pleasure that contributed to the growth of a close fighting spirit. Moreover, replacements never traveled to their units as individuals—as in the American army—but as coherent groups (*Ersatzbataillone*, or *Marschbataillone*), commanded either by officers sent by the parent division or by men wounded in that unit who had recovered and were on their way back to the front. This practice gave divisions an incentive to look after their own replacements' training, and the replacements themselves could begin the process of generating group loyalty even before they arrived at the front, a factor that greatly enhanced their chances of surviving the first deadly days of combat.[4]

The *Wehrmacht* also expected its officers to look after the physical and emotional needs of their men, thus creating in them a sense of belonging to a tight-knit family. In a diary entry from the spring of 1939, Friedrich Grupe described the stress of military training by day, then marveled, "In the evenings 'big-mouth' Schmidt [our drill sergeant] comes into the barracks room, sits informally with us, and laughs and jokes and sings with us just like a good comrade. . . . You get accustomed to it, especially the companionship with the comrades, which helps you get over much." Harry Mielert, on his birthday in December 1942, reflected in a letter to his wife on the curious interplay of comradeship and company life: "I can well say that I feel myself to be . . . at the fullness of my creative possibilities. . . . It appears to me to be symbolic that I am experiencing this period of life just as a company commander. . . . To be responsible for about 100 men is a wonderful task worthy of a man." The emphasis on creating a sense of family, of community, was pervasive. Just a year later, in Berlin, Grupe was struck by a speech Hitler made to officer candidates in which the Führer "emphasized that the German soldier should . . . always see in our [fellow] soldiers national comrades. That is our task; always we should trust the worth and the strength of the German workers. With them he would give our world new meaning, new powers."[5] Thus, the camaraderie of soldiers was to be made the basis for a transformation of Germany.

During the Nazi period, vigorous efforts were made as well to promote a sense of egalitarianism by opening officer careers not only to men of elite background but to those who showed talent. Many front soldiers, among them Hans Woltersdorf, remained convinced even after the war that the Nazi regime had produced a veritable revolution by promoting equality of opportunity. "The real background to our elite combat record," he claimed, resided not in ideological fanaticism but in "the special leadership principle. . . . The necessary qualification for an officer's career was not the high school diploma but exemplary ability, the true authority. Everyone who led a unit had to be the best man in his unit as well; not the uniform, not being in command, but example made the leader." The army also hoped to nurture a spirit of camaraderie through measures such as the equalization of food rations, the relaxation of traditional military protocol, and the encouragement of personal relationships between officers and enlisted men. Finally, German army doctrine stressed tactical initiative (*Auftragstaktik*), which placed emphasis on independent action at the lowest feasible level, thus contributing to a strong sense of personal as well as group involvement in the outcome of a mission.[6]

So impressive were the results of this system that in the immediate postwar years many Western analysts focused almost exclusively on comradeship as the reason for the remarkable cohesion and effectiveness of the *Wehrmacht*. "The extraordinary tenacity of the German Army" did not depend on Nazi ideological convictions on the part of the average German soldier, Edward Shils and Morris Janowitz asserted in 1948; they claimed that "the unity of the German Army was in fact sustained only to a very slight extent by the National Socialist political convictions of its members, and that more important in the motivation of the determined resistance of the German soldier was the steady satisfaction of certain primary personality demands afforded by the social organization of the army." Writing more than three decades later, van Creveld agreed: "The average German soldier in World War II . . . did not as a rule fight out of a belief in Nazi ideology. . . . Instead, he fought for the reasons that men have always fought: because he felt himself a member of a well-integrated, well-led team whose structure, administration, and functioning were perceived to be . . . equitable and just."[7]

Although much anecdotal evidence seems to support such assertions, the ideological dimensions within the German army should not be understated. Ideology can be understood on a number of different levels, and the average German soldier, perhaps to a surprising degree, exhibited and embraced various forms of ideological commitment to Nazism. The very emphasis the Nazis put on comradeship and community, in fact, can be viewed as an aspect of ideology, since in many respects the close-knit infantry company was to be the model for the larger *Volksgemeinschaft* envisioned by Nazi ideologues. Camaraderie was seen as a vital component of the *Wehrmacht* not only in order to enhance fighting efficiency but also to break down the economic and social barriers hindering the establishment of a genuine national community. And in practice, the National Socialist leadership began almost immediately to establish the preconditions for this new community.

"I am beginning with the young," Adolf Hitler exclaimed soon after coming to power in 1933. "We older ones are used up. . . . We are rotten to the marrow. We have no unrestrained instincts left. We are cowardly and sentimental. We are bearing the burden of a humiliating past. . . . But my magnificent youngsters! Are there finer ones anywhere in the world? Look at these young men and boys! What material! With them I can make a new world." Nor was this mere hyperbole. Hitler intended, with a desperate seriousness, to create a new man and a new society. "We must educate a new type of man," he proclaimed at the Nuremberg Party Rally in September 1935, and in a speech in Reichenberg in December 1938 the Führer outlined what he meant: "These young people learn nothing else but to think as Germans and to act as Germans; these young boys join our organization at the age of ten, . . . then four years later they move . . . to the Hitler Youth. . . . Then we are even less prepared to give them back into the hands of those who create our class and status barriers. . . . If they . . . have still not become real National Socialists, then they go into the Labor Service and are polished there. . . . And if . . . there are still remnants of class consciousness or pride in status, then the *Wehrmacht* will take over for a further treatment. . . . They will not be free again for the rest of their lives."[8] Hitler intended early on, then, to create a new Nazi society through intense efforts at socializing the young and eliminating what he regarded as ruinous vestiges of the class conflict that he believed had brought Germany to a state of weakness and degradation.

Much of the passionate energy and idealism associated with Nazism stemmed from these young people, exposed as they were to relentless National Socialist ideological indoctrination and training. Many of them were attracted by the rebellion against seemingly failed old norms and traditions, as well as by the promise of building a new classless, harmonious society in which internal divisions would be eliminated and a spirit of community would prevail. The Nazi stress on comradeship, achievement, and constant action produced a restless dynamic that drew many fervent followers into the circle of belief. "What I liked about the HJ was the comradeship," remembered one Hitler Youth leader after the war:

> I was full of enthusiasm when I joined the *Jungvolk* at the age of ten. What boy isn't fired by being presented with high ideals such as comradeship, loyalty, and honor. I can still remember how deeply moved I was when we learned the club mottoes: "*Jungvolk* boys are hard, . . . they are loyal; *Jungvolk* boys are comrades; the highest

value for a *Jungvolk* boy is honor." They seemed to me to be holy. And then the trips! Is there anything nicer than enjoying the splendors of the homeland in the company of one's comrades. . . . And it always made a deep impression to sit of an evening round a fire outside in a circle and to have a sing song and tell stories. . . . Here sat apprentices and school boys, the sons of workers and civil servants side by side and got to know and appreciate one another.

Indeed, remembered Gustav Köppke, a worker from a Communist family in the Ruhr and himself a communist after the war, "Our workers' suburb and the HJ were absolutely not contradictory. . . . The HJ uniform was something positive in our childhood."[9]

This attempt to bring together Germans from differing social, educational, and occupational backgrounds made a deep impression on many young Germans. "The creation of that *Volksgemeinschaft* in which the workers would be fully integrated," Friedrich Grupe remembered thinking, "the end of the destructive class struggle, the realization of the principle 'common good before individual good,' was that all not really revolutionary in comparison to that which had been before?" To serve a *Volksgemeinschaft,* to live a life of camaraderie, to believe in the German people and Hitler as the German Führer—these were ideals pressed into the minds and souls of German youth. "Our freedom was service": this line from a Hitler Youth song reflected the ideal of devotion to the community—even to the point of death; as Grupe acknowledged, hardly any song sung by the youth of the HJ did not celebrate death in the service of the community. "Laugh, comrades," one such song proclaimed, "our death will be a celebration." And why? "Germany must live, even if we must die," went the refrain. "We dedicate our death to you as the smallest deed." Nor did such songs denote empty ceremony. "We believed in a new community, free from class conflict, united in brotherhood under the self-chosen Führer . . . , national and socialist," Grupe claimed. Further, like many of his generation, he believed that "this new society should grow out of the youth movement. Our struggle above all aimed at the profiteering 'plutocrats' and the vain, egoistic bourgeois materialists." The group's motto, Grupe recalled, was, "Down with these external signs of class snobbery. We are all comrades!"[10]

As Hitler had foreseen, the Labor Service (*Reichsarbeitsdienst*) appeared to many young men, as Grupe put it, "the embodiment, the realization of the *Volksgemeinschaft.* . . . Everyone had to perform work with the spade in the German earth, everyone became a worker belonging to the great national community over and above rank, status, and class. . . . That was living comradeship." This enthusiasm was no mere romanticized sentiment, for Grupe wrote in 1937 during his own stint in the Labor Service:

> This community of working men is something unique. From all sections of society we come here together. . . . Often we sing the song that characterizes this new compulsory labor service in the Third Reich:
>
> > Yesterday in class and rank divided,
> > yesterday one from the other avoided,
> > today we dig together in sand,
> > loyal to our Führer's command.
>
> Because of our burdens borne in common the feeling of comradely identity grows rapidly. . . . We're experiencing here what we understand to be *Volksgemeinschaft*. And we're putting our conception of National Socialism into action: We are all the same in our service for our people, no one is asked his origins or class, whether he is rich or poor. . . . Snobbery, class consciousness, envy, and idleness are left out on the street. This is the way from "I" to "We."

An obvious Nazi enthusiast as a young man, Grupe provided a hint of the seductive force of the notion of national community, relating in his diary a contemporary episode redolent of the enthusiasm generated by this idea:

> This excitement has also infected those men who obviously did not believe in National Socialism. Just a short time ago one of my roommates, who openly admitted to still being a communist, confided to me that he would never, absolutely never, belong to our *Volksgemeinschaft*. Afterward as before there would be no doubt as to the reality of the class struggle. . . . But now, situated in our special train on the return trip, which is filled with a happy din, he has also put a flower in his buttonhole and appears to be visibly moved. And I ask him: "Have you now felt it, the National Socialist *Volksgemeinschaft*?"[11]

To Grupe, as to many young Germans, the Labor Service represented true socialism in that everyone wore the same uniforms and performed similar tasks in service to the nation. But just how representative Grupe's emotional attachment to the concept of a national community was remains a matter of conjecture. The Hitler Youth's success in indoctrinating young people in Nazi ideology probably proved less than its founders had hoped. The quality of leadership in the HJ was generally poor, and the war served further to remove talented section leaders from the organization. Nonetheless, the Hitler Youth and the Labor Service almost certainly reinforced specific values important to the Nazis: camaraderie, sacrifice, loyalty, duty, honor, endurance, courage, obedience; and perhaps as well a certain contempt for those outside the bonds of community.

The Labor Service seemed to many young Germans a statement of commitment to building a new society in which everyone, regardless of social position, was expected to work for the good of Germany. The "socialist" aspect of National Socialism could and did have a significant impact on Germans of Grupe's generation. Although the Nazi revolution stagnated once the war began, the vision of a *Volksgemeinschaft* endured with great tenacity until the end of the war. Just as important, those who had participated in the Hitler Youth or Labor Service had instilled in them both a general spirit of camaraderie and the expectation of a continued comradeship as they flooded into the army. Grupe expressed this connection well, writing in his diary of a night march in October 1939, "We fought against the fatigue. So we sang at full volume, and . . . the song spread from company to company and echoed thunderously against the bare facades of the houses." And the song they sang was one that all the men knew:

> Now the dark night is over
> and magnificently the day is breaking!
> Comrade, lend a hand, work is liberating.
> Let's go, let's get cracking!
> Gray as the dust is our clothing,
> gray solders in a storm-swept time!

"That is actually a song of the Labor Service," Grupe added revealingly, "but we sing it often, it fits so well: 'gray soldiers in a storm-swept time.' "[12]

Nazi ideological practice thus reinforced *Wehrmacht* goals, contributing to the creation of those tight groups of men who would fight, suffer, and die together. If in the Labor Service a young man felt a general sense of comradeship, in the army his world was his ten-man rifle squad. The close relationships that sprang up between the men in such a *Kameradschaft* (the original Prussian term for a small unit) proved vitally important in promoting both cohesion and resilience in the face of the punishing reality. The *Landser's* world was circumscribed; what mattered most to him was the small group of castaways with whom he sought to weather the storm of war. If comradeship depended on trust, respect, and mutual loyalty, nothing was better suited to create it than being thrown together with a small group of men each of whose lives depended on the reliability of the others. "My unit was my home, my family," wrote Hans Werner Woltersdorf, "which I had to protect."[13]

Indeed, the notion of family became a leitmotif in the reminiscences of many men. At the end of his arduous training period, Martin Pöppel wrote in his diary, "From the officers down to the last driver, we had become a family. We were ready." Friedrich Grupe recorded a scene in his diary in 1939 that could easily have been that of a father reflecting on his brood: "Now once again the intimate life reigns. In the washroom the water is running, in the shower room the showers are splashing. Then the comrades finally lie in their freshly changed beds, fall asleep quickly and snore in the manner of *Landsers*." In fact, Grupe and his comrades, perhaps in conscious imitation of the motif of family, referred to their respected and beloved commander as "Papa." Reflecting after the war on "the community of those accustomed to war and those comrades sworn to each other," he claimed: "Among them I felt, hardly to be believed, again something like security." In similarly embracing this close-knit life, Helmut Vethake spoke of "a rewarding joy" when his men assembled before him, seeing in them "a large family that knows they will stay together in happy as in serious situations." For Vethake himself, this sense of comradeship made his responsibilities easier, since he was "freer to do the important things, the entirely personal matters of contact that are so necessary." To Wolfgang Döring it seemed self-evident that in these "pitilessly . . . revolutionary times . . . the only support lay in the love, loyalty, and reliability of the men next to you."[14]

An awareness of support and security within the group was a principal feature of camaraderie. Many *Landsers* drew a profound sense of importance from being a member of a tight-knit band, a feeling that revealed an acute longing for community. Upon being reunited with his comrades after a brief separation, Guy Sajer remarked: "Our sense of happiness and relief at meeting again was so great that quite spontaneously we grabbed each other by the shoulders and mimed an exaggerated polonaise, shouting with laughter. . . . Knowing that my friends were there . . . made me feel a great deal better." Friendships, he reflected later, "counted for a great deal during the war, their value perhaps increased by the generalized hate, consolidating men . . . in friendships which never would have broken through the barriers of ordinary peacetime life." Sajer remembered a sergeant's claim that "a genuine soldier's life [was] the only life which brings men close to each other on terms of absolute sincerity. Here, a sense of comradeship exists between each and every one of us, which might be put to the test at any moment."[15]

The moment of acceptance into the group, of belonging to the *Frontgemeinschaft,* often proved a revelation. Willi Heinrich, in *The Cross of Iron,* described the sudden realization of a replacement named Kern that he had become one of the community of men:

> The thought filled him with pride. Suddenly he felt a part of the platoon, as though he had been with it for ten years. It's a damn fine thing to belong to a crazy bunch like this, he said to himself. We all belong together. All for one and one for all. He no long remembered where he had picked up the phrase, but it sent chills down his spine. . . . It was a great thing to have comrades. . . . Comradeship is everything, he thought. It didn't matter if you pitched into one another once in a while; what mattered was that you could depend on the others when you were in trouble. And, by God, you could depend on these fellows here! You really could, and he was damned glad to be in their platoon.

"I soon felt really at home," Martin Pöppel confided of his early war experiences, because he had been "accepted into that special circle of men. . . . From the officers down to the last driver, we had become a family." Even those outside the front community readily understood the importance of it. "Comradeship must grow quickly," wrote Karl Friedrich Oertel, a student sent hurriedly to the front in January 1945, "so that [my heart] does not burst from anxiety."[16]

For many men the feeling of camaraderie affirmed their existence in the midst of war's cruelties and provided a positive ideal to balance the uncertainties of their daily life. "Here among these men I have finally found my inner peace," wrote Rolf Schroth in the autumn of 1942. "They are a strange breed, these men fighting in Russia, and it had bothered me ever since I'd had to leave them. I could not rest until I had received my marching orders to go back there. This experience of growing loyalty . . . gives me inner strength"[17] Moreover, this feeling of camaraderie could be almost tangible even in the humblest of circumstances. In a haunting and evocative letter, Helmut Pabst recorded one such incident in October 1942:

> I went early in the morning through the trenches and found a sentry. He was a small fellow with a round face under his helmet. He stood alone. It was cool. He was freezing, drew his shoulders up, and jumped from one leg to the other. Then a tall, gaunt man with a full red beard slipped out of the dugout for a moment. They greeted each other warmly: "You, do you still have a cigarette?" asked the small man. "Yeah," beamed the tall one, "wait, I'll get them right away." "Do you know," said the sentry, and one felt that he just once had to say this, "we are really friends, we two." His round face beamed genuinely from within, and he wanted a confirmation for this great and good thing. . . . A demonstration, I thought, that there is no greater pathos than in the act of one man giving another a light: it is totally simple, absolutely natural, and it was something grand that took place before me in these early hours in a quiet trench, this friendship between two men.[18]

This need for friends—to lessen the personal danger, to provide comfort in the midst of distress, to combat the loneliness, to dampen the inner fears—served as a powerful magnet that drew and held men together even under the most adverse circumstances.

It was particularly important for a *Landser* to get close to those around him, to have a sense of personal contact, in order to lessen the feeling of loneliness once he was in battle and, not least, to know he could rely on the strength of others during this most trying time. "Many times my nerves want to get the better of me," confessed an anonymous soldier. "Then you think you must throw all the crap away, you can't hold on any longer, and only in the circle of your comrades and with a glass of beer can you again find a diversion." Otherwise, the overwhelming sense of being forsaken struck at all *Landsers*. "The old experience of every earnest soldier out here is awakening in me again," Harry Mielert reflected in November 1942, "how totally alone . . . a man is placed here immediately on the front. There is no relying anymore on your own strength or the power of your weapons. I have been forced to learn it again this evening."[19]

The constant feeling of being threatened, the sense of being stalked, the fear of being killed or captured at any moment produced intense feelings of terror and a consequent desire to be part of the security of the

Kameradschaft. Mielert himself revealed the power of this feeling of belonging, writing in his next to last letter, "I shall never be so enraptured by the atmosphere of this war as in this year. . . . There where men, freezing, trembling, shaking, throw a bundle of straw in their hole and huddle together in there as in a nest, commences a different . . . principle. And this is also [revealed] frequently in conversations, feelings and thoughts. In the night I crawl from hole to hole [because] the men need strengthening." In a previous letter Mielert had expressed, in searing fashion, precisely why the men needed support: "No one in the homeland will later be able to give the front soldier a 'reward' for his suffering. None of them can repay this enormous mixture of fear, horror, and other unnamable feelings and their counterbalance, bravery and the will to overcome, that these men here must daily and hourly summon up."[20] Only a profound sense of camaraderie, of being part of the group, allowed men to cope with these overwhelming pressures and the creeping sense of despair felt by all.

Camaraderie, for most men, did develop quickly. "I have assimilated myself amazingly," Mielert wrote wonderingly in May 1941. "Sometimes I am like an old *Landser* and yet it has been just four weeks. I have gained more interest in many military things that earlier I not only did not have but also fought against. But now I see much that is positive in [the soldier's life]." The spirit of comradeship, in fact, bound men to their front-line officers as well. "It's our commander's birthday today," Martin Pöppel recorded in his diary in October 1943, "so my last sausage and the last bottle of Vermouth are sacrificed for a present. However, we're all happy that we can give the 'Old Man' something at least."[21] This sense of belonging, this bond between men facing danger, constituted one of the fighting man's few rewards.

To the intense pleasure in belonging was added the sense of participating in a shared experience and a perhaps perverse pride at enduring common hardships. The very intensity of their suffering welded *Landsers* together in a community of fate without parallel in civilian life, for this was a group bound by a common effort to endure the unendurable. "Finally I have now landed at the division and march immediately to the regiment," Harry Mielert wrote in November 1942 following an extended furlough. That it was his old regiment was "naturally very agreeable, because one gladly returns to a group of men with whom one has gone through many hardships." In May 1943 Mielert claimed, "The front is . . . like a homeland. . . . There is a 'solidarity of fate' that probably exists only in the closest relationships, between lovers or friends. This comradeship in war still has too much accidental about it . . . [but] admittedly the objective of soldierly comradeship is also a higher ethical value."[22]

Few *Landsers* expressed the notion of camaraderie as metaphysically as Mielert, and many would have been embarrassed by talk of a higher ethical value, but virtually all understood the notion of the solidarity of fate among soldiers fighting in the same cause. "At regular intervals on the tracks there are little huts occupied by German railway soldiers," Martin Pöppel recorded of his journey into Russia in 1941. "They are doing their lonely duty there. . . . As we pass we are delighted to exchange greetings, and salute these men we regard as brothers. Out here we really feel the force of the destiny which binds us together as Germans. Here a man looks at other Germans and sees his brother, his home. At home things are different, people walk straight past each other and only take any notice at marches or rallies."[23] As Hitler had anticipated, and as Pöppel's statement makes clear, the development of a *Frontgemeinschaft* was clearly preceding that of the domestic *Volksgemeinschaft*.

Similarly, even as he sought to explain the mixed emotions that the "unforgettable images" of the bitter fighting produced in him, Siegfried Roemer emphasized his "pride and furious joy when I see a German company marching over the still-frozen roads of the Russian early spring." More directly, without puzzling over it, an anonymous soldier wrote from Russia, "It is a magnificent front camaraderie that binds us here." Trapped by Russian forces in the autumn of 1943, Guy Sajer remembered, "We had to attack, or die. At that time, there was no question of captivity. As always after a hard knock, we rediscovered a kind of unity, and seemed to be held together by tighter bonds. What provoked the sentiments of generosity which brought out the last cigarettes, or the chocolates so rare they were usually devoured in secret?"[24] The source of these deep bonds puzzled even one so reflective as Sajer, but behind them lay an intense human desire to share the suffering and hardships of war and an equally strong impulse to see in human contact an affirmation of life. Quite simply, comradeship provided a feeling of well-being in the midst of a dangerous life.

Moreover, in a situation where men had become mere implements of warfare, the constancy of their misery hammered the *Landsers* into a community of suffering, creating a compassion and affection for those (on their side) who had to endure the same horror. While acknowledging his distress at the crushing physical and psychological burdens imposed on him during the terrible weeks of fighting in the Russian winter of 1941–42, Will Thomas nevertheless recognized the importance of camaraderie in bolstering fighting spirit and providing meaning in otherwise desperate or hopeless situations: "Now that the last and dearest of my old comrades are gone I can no longer get rid of the feeling of loneliness. I am now the only remaining officer of the regiment present since the summer and the only one of the company commanders who were appointed in the fall. But I still have my company, and that means infinitely much."[25]

Although trapped in the Stalingrad pocket, Kurt Reuber clung to his sense of comradeship as a way of conferring meaning on this misfortune, claiming that distress "taught true human comradely love" and professing a "genuine joy for his comrades." Disappointed at not being granted leave in the winter of 1943, Guy Sajer nonetheless "suddenly felt the full strength of my attachment to all the friends . . . nearby, an emotion which struck me as both idiotic and profound." It was because of attachments such as these that Sajer never regretted volunteering for a combat unit, because there he "discovered a sense of comradeship which I have never found again, inexplicable and steady, through thick and thin." At the end of the war, reflecting especially on his friend Hals, "the man who had so often carried my load when my strength was failing" Sajer realized, "I would never be able to forget him, or the experiences we had shared, or our fellow soldiers, whose lives would always be linked to mine." Indeed, he concluded, comradeship was "my only incentive for life in the midst of despair."[26]

Each *Landser* well knew what fear and terror confronted his comrades, for he felt them himself, and all understood that it was essential to share this burden with friends rather than bear it alone. One simply could not leave a comrade to face the uncertainties and horrors of battle alone. As a result, the *Landser* felt a profound sense of duty, responsibility, and mutual obligation to his fellow front fighters. In March 1943, Harry Mielert attempted to sort out this complex web of ties. "Do you understand," he wrote to his wife in an urgent, almost pleading tone, "that now and then we out here can also laugh, when there is occasionally a bit of schnapps and we jovially and in the manner of soldiers of fortune tackle the 'great' questions of politics. . . ? This comradeship that rules here is actually primitive. One knows just the name of the others. Nevertheless, one would not hesitate to stand by them in the heaviest fire. One risks his life for the others, and yet there exists no 'emotional' relationship. Understand that who may, it's beyond me. But that is an important element of a soldier's existence."[27]

In like manner, Friedrich Grupe reflected after the war on the almost mystical nature of comradeship: "A comrade always stood by our side, a comforter and a helper, often endowed with a natural wit and always full of sympathy and understanding for the others. He made the unbearable bearable." Then, as if uncertain that modern readers would really grasp his message, perhaps fearing that the notion of camaraderie had been overused and worn a bit thin, Grupe pointed to a song—the "song of songs of comradeship," as he put it—that had been sung by German soldiers and had put new heart into millions of them:

> If one of us grows tired,
> the other stands watch;
> if one of us should doubt,
> the other faithfully laughs.
> If one of us should fall,
> the other stands for two,
> for to every fighter God gave
> a comrade-in-arms![28]

Guy Sajer provided perhaps the best example of the emotive power, compassion, and sincerity of this spirit of comradeship, which rarely degenerated into bathos. The sudden prospect of leave in the autumn of 1943 brought forth a jumble of emotions long buried, feelings that illustrated the sense of mutual obligation and responsibility the *Landser* felt toward his comrades: "My head was spinning with the thought of a leave, and with the anguish of the possible loss of my special comrades. Perhaps I had already walked past their burnt bodies. . . . Would I also have to renounce the friendships which had seen me through so much? I knew that they also were so close to being stripped of everything that the sentiment I had for them seemed permissible. . . . Must I also obliterate. . . . the memories of Hals, and Lensen, and even that bastard Lindberg?" Even in the midst of dreadful hardship, this camaraderie yielded inspiration. During the retreat of the winter of 1943–44, with rations scarce and the troops desperately hungry, Sajer noted almost in awe how the men divided the food they had just secured: "No one was cheated; the amazing sense of comradeship and unity of the Wehrmacht held, and everyone received a fair share. The war had brought together men from many different regions and walks of life, who would probably have mistrusted each other under any other circumstances; but the circumstances of war united us in a symphony of heroism, in which each man felt himself to a certain extent responsible for all of his fellows."[29]

It was when he lay ill in his foxhole, however, with his closest friend at his side, that Sajer came to understand the pure essence of comradeship:

> "Go to sleep, I tell you. You're sick," [said Hals].
>
> "No!" I was shouting now. "I'd rather be killed and get it over with right now."
>
> I jumped up, and left our hole. But before I had taken more than two steps Hals had grabbed me by the belt and pulled me back.
>
> "Let go, Hals," I shouted, louder than ever. "Let go, do you hear."
>
> "You're going to shut up . . . and calm down," [Hals replied]. . . .
>
> "Let the hell go of me. What business is it of yours anyway? What difference does it make?"
>
> "The difference is that I need to see your face from time to time, the way I need to see the veteran, or that bastard Lindberg. . . ."
>
> A violent shiver engulfed my whole body. Tears continued to pour down my cheeks, and I felt like kissing my poor friend's filthy face. . . .
>
> We began another interminable night of fear, in a dark hole, with . . . an exhaustion so heavy one wished to die. . . . We listened to the cries of our fellow combatants. . . . We hardly spoke during that night, but I knew that I should try to live for the sake of my friend.[30]

One should live, Sajer realized—and a significant insight it was—not merely for one's own selfish reasons but, more important, because one's comrade needed someone to sustain him.

For some *Landsers* the lure of camaraderie overrode even their fear of death; indeed, the dread of appearing weak and earning the scorn of their comrades led some to heroic deeds of valor—and to death. During the savage and lethal fighting on Crete in May 1941, with many German units broken up, new battle groups were hastily thrown together out of the remnants. "Tired and dispirited, we sit there with bowed heads," Martin Pöppel recorded in his diary. "To top our astonishment, we discover that our East Prussian *Leutnant* Rikowski has turned on his heels and escaped here without his weapons and hardly any uniform. Well, we can understand most of it, but how the hell did Rikowski (who's normally so reliable) ever leave his gun behind?" But once the new units are assembled, Rikowski was accorded the opportunity to redeem himself: "Patrols are sent out, some through a deep ravine to a town which has apparently been evacuated by the enemy not long before. It's here that Rikowski gets his chance. He's allowed to go into the village alone while we cover him, so that he can recover his self-respect. He completes the job successfully, and after that his inglorious flight is forgotten."[31]

The significance here is not just that Rikowski did in fact recover his self-respect but that he was "allowed"—indeed, expected—to redeem himself so that the group could be made whole again. Some men, in fact, saw even being wounded as a betrayal of the group, as leaving one's comrades in the lurch. "It's a long time before I can sleep," Pöppel wrote while lying wounded in a field hospital. "My thoughts keep returning to events at the front and to my comrades there." A casualty once again in Italy, Pöppel could only remark disgustedly, "It's such a damned stupid way for me to be put out of action, especially when the men are having such a hard time." Such powerful attachments help explain how Bernhard Buhl could confess in his diary in July 1942 that the "reason I feel myself today in the right place as a soldier [is] to be worthy of my friends who are also in the field and at the front."[32]

Virtually all *Landsers* understood the importance of gaining, and maintaining, the respect of their comrades and the price that occasionally had to be paid in order to redeem oneself in the eyes of the group. Writing to his wife in July 1943, Harry Mielert noted that "a sergeant, who in the last attack was accused of cowardice, really conducted himself with heroic courage. With another man he stormed totally alone a heavily fortified bunker, and fell there in the trench fighting. There are many about whom songs should be sung and great deeds should be praised. But it is not the time. . . . Later we will again have the courage to talk about the details. . . . Now we are quiet and gather ourselves inwardly."[33] This was a serious business, as Mielert indicated, for every man knew that he had a breaking point beyond which he too might be accused of cowardice and for which he might be expected to seek redemption in personal valor, and possibly in death.

This tug of comradeship could be frighteningly powerful, especially, as Guy Sajer realized, in extreme circumstances. "I knew that the struggle was becoming more and more serious," he wrote in the autumn of 1944, "and that we would soon be obliged to face appalling possibilities. I felt a strong sense of solidarity with my comrades, and I could think of my own death without too much flinching." Shortly thereafter, feeling that he had trapped himself and his men in a situation from which there was no escape, overcome by the sense that he had failed his comrades, Sajer asked one of his companions to shoot him: "On that day, at a critical moment, I failed. I failed in everything I had hoped for, from others and from myself. . . . I shall never forgive myself for that instant."[34] In appearing weak and indecisive, Sajer not only suffered a blow to his own ego but, more significantly, feared the scorn of his comrades. To be judged a failure by your buddies counted as the ultimate blow, something for which you could never forgive yourself, something to which death might be preferable.

For many *Landsers* the strong cohesion of the battle group forged in the fire of combat served as the prime compensation for a life lived on the edge of death. As a consequence, an individual soldier could invest an astounding degree of loyalty and pride in his squad or company, which functioned as the focus of his world. Richard Holmes has referred to a sense of "group narcissism" whereby a soldier with doubts about his own ability submerged them beneath his devotion to his unit, thus producing both immense satisfaction for the individual and a stiffening of his resolve to fight on. Helmut von Harnack, writing from Russia in October 1941, exclaimed with pride that his unit was "a real fighting company, which had successfully come through the most engagements with the heaviest losses in the regiment. The young soldiers are overwhelmingly good guys . . . who . . . radiate a vital energy that is unshakable despite the bitter hours. Out of the eyes of these men speaks an invincible strength." While describing fierce fighting around Vitebsk in January 1944, in which he was wounded for the third time, Klaus Löscher nonetheless wrote with barely concealed pride, "My good old company is badly battered, as in general is the proud regiment." Writing from a field hospital a few days later, he could still proclaim his pride that "despite heavy losses my company achieved the greatest success." All in all, he concluded, his men were "golden fellows and courageous soldiers."[35]

So intense could this feeling of pride become that it often verged on hubris. "The incredible pride we have simply doesn't allow us to retreat," Martin Pöppel bragged from Russia in early 1942, "and makes us a legendary force." "I find it simply fabulous," boasted a *Landser* similarly in a July 1941 letter from Russia, "that we are settling scores immediately with all our enemies. But of course the whole world must now also recognize how splendid and powerful our German *Wehrmacht* is. No other force in the world is a match for us." This, of course, was written during the heady first days of triumph in the war on Russia, but amazingly, this intense pride persisted even in the latter stages of the war. An anonymous *Landser* trapped in the Falaise pocket at the end of the Normandy campaign wrote in August 1944, "It doesn't look very good ... but nonetheless there is no reason to paint too black a picture. . . . There are so many good and elite divisions in our near-encirclement that we must get through somehow." In the same vein, Siegfried Roemer declared in March 1944, during the savage combat along the Dnieper, "When I look over the past week, the work, the exertions, the danger, sweat, blood, and privations, in the midst of the worst jams we still have the feeling of superiority. The mood of our soldiers was like a plant that always climbs to the light."[36]

And what was the light, the factor that could so elevate the morale of the *Landser*? Often it was nothing more than a stubborn pride in resisting the fierce enemy assaults. "It is a mockery if one still speaks of us as the twenty-fourth Panzer Division," grumbled Rembrand Elert, writing at roughly the same time as Roemer. "The whole division moves by foot. It has no more tanks, four whole SPW [armored scout cars], three laughable field guns with no ammunition, two anti-tank guns and [one anti-aircraft gun]. No more mortars, sMG [heavy machine guns], or IG [artillery]. . . . And yet our division kept its thrown-together units firmly under control, again and again formed a front, and in numerous battles smashed all enemy attempts at encirclement."[37] Despite the disintegration of his unit, Elert took deep satisfaction in its having stood the test. Overwhelming pride in his unit and in the men around him, a sense of membership in a special organization that was tenacious and proficient, satisfaction from performing a difficult task under onerous conditions— all of these things stiffened the resolve of the *Landser* and caused him to fight on even in desperate situations.

Helmut Vethake, amid the wreckage of the eastern campaign, expressed not the arrogance often generated by this fierce group loyalty but rather the support it provided in difficult moments. "We have gradually been forced into a renunciation of everything that was formerly valuable and important to us," he mused. "Only a few simple things remain intact: pure dedication and a plain, loyal standing side-by-side and helping out in the common work: comradeship! We experience it most strongly as we are standing ready on the eve of a heavy attack. Then nothing else is worth more, not even one's life, which each is willing to give up." "Duty calls," Siegbert Stehmann concluded in a letter in October 1943. "One must bear it and hold on to that which remains: the good spirit of comradeship which surrounds me with much love." The sense of duty to one's comrades not infrequently served as a motivation for fighting on, as an anonymous soldier revealed in June 1943: "Shoulder to shoulder we fulfill our duty, like the old comrades, and are firmly resolved to fight and to triumph, so that our models, the fallen comrades, will not be sacrificed in vain. Their death is my duty. . . . Better to fight honorably and die than to steal life."[38]

In the carnage and chaos of war, when many *Landsers* came to regard this camaraderie as the one true or pure relationship, the death of a comrade could be agonizing. "Tomorrow we have a sad job," lamented an anonymous soldier. "We must bury a comrade from our company. . . . He is the first out of our midst. When you are together for almost a year, it is a real misfortune." Bernhard Ritter was but one of many who noted a similar sense of loss: "In the march to the rear we went by the graves of [two] comrades who had been killed. . . . One now suddenly understood just what that meant: They stood by my side, as if they were a piece of me. One felt that totally unsentimentally, naturally, even when one barely knew them. The graves remain back there, and a piece of one's self remains there as well. That is one of the secrets that the war has taught us, and it is all very simple."[39]

"It is serious," agreed Claus Hansmann of the loss of a friend, "so terribly, inevitably pointed in the direction of one question: life or death. . . ? The pain of our buddies comes alarmingly close to us, the eternal same thoughts of such an hour: why him, why not me?" And later, in reflecting on the death of a friend, Hansmann admitted, "I know and feel nothing but the old refrain: 'as if it were a piece of me. . . .' Certainly a piece of me." Another *Landser*, reading that a friend had been killed, remarked sadly, "As I read the lines, it was as if I myself had been struck." Similarly, after seeing some of his comrades killed, Guy Sajer raged:

> At that moment, I suddenly understood the meaning of all the cries and shrieks I had heard on every battlefield. And I also understood

the marching songs, which so often begin with a ringing description of a soldier dying in glory and then suddenly turn somber:

> We marched together like brothers,
> And now he lies in the dust.
> My heart is torn with despair,
> My heart is torn with despair.

Once again I learned how hard it is to watch a comrade die: almost as hard as dying oneself.[40]

Learning that lesson could involve more than a moment of agony especially when death did not come quickly. In an intense and emotional passage in *The Forgotten Soldier*, Sajer allows a glimpse of the almost frightening power of comradeship:

"Anybody hit?" one of the noncoms called out. "Let's get going then. . . ." Nervously, I pulled open the door [of the truck]. Inside, I saw a man I shall never forget, a man sitting normally on the seat, whose lower face had been reduced to a bloody pulp.

"Ernst?" I asked in a choking voice. "Ernst!" I threw myself at him. . . . I looked frantically for some features on that horrible face. . . .

His coat was covered with blood. . . . His teeth were mixed with fragments of bone, and through the gore I could see the muscles of his face contracting. . . .

In a state of near shock, I tried to put the dressing somewhere on that cavernous wound. . . . Crying like a small boy, I pushed my friend to the other end of the seat, holding him in my arms. . . . Two eyes opened, brilliant with anguish, and looked at me from his ruined face. . . .

In the cab of a gray Russian truck, somewhere in the vastness of the Russian hinterland, a man and an adolescent were caught in a desperate struggle. The man struggled with death, and the adolescent struggled with despair. . . . I felt that something had hardened in my spirit forever.[41]

The death of one's comrades could sometimes seem too hard to bear. "Tonight we again had some heavy losses," admitted Harry Mielert in October 1943, "among them a really old veteran, a sergeant who was the pillar of his men. He died before our eyes. Our staff doctor, who . . .

is usually without exception drunk, was sober on this night, and he revealed himself as a man . . . lacking the strength to hold on in this war. He cannot bear the strife and deadens himself with nicotine and alcohol. . . . He longs for reality and yet must always shut his eyes when it becomes very real, as this evening with the poor comrades." Returning from an action against Russian partisans, Sajer witnessed the lead car in their column go up in flames. Among the victims was their beloved Captain Wesreidau, who "was covered with wounds, and his body seemed broken. . . . We did everything we could for him. The whole company thought of him as a friend. . . . In a very weak voice he spoke to us of our collective adventure, stressing our unity, which must hold in the face of everything to come. . . . The silence was terrible. . . . We felt that we had just lost the man on whom the well-being of the whole company depended. We felt abandoned."[42]

Yet to a comrade the dead never left the battlefield; their spirit always remained. Given the bonds of comradeship, it is hardly surprising that Hans Martin Stählin, reflecting on the nature of death, noted, "In death the realms of God and man border one another and the issue of death is a questioning after God, just as one would inquire at a door if one wanted to know something of the expanse behind it. Soldiers know that. Can you understand it if I say that it is not immaterial how we think on our dead. . . . It is not empty talk when one says, the dead are always with us." The air might well be heavy with death, with the impermanence of life, but Mielert asserted in July 1943, fallen comrades "live immortally in that spirit which shapes a common spirit of the nation."[43]

The impulse to grieve for the fallen proved so powerful that even in the aftermath of a winter battle, with the ground frozen solid, one's comrades still saw to a funeral service. "The grave had to be hacked out of the frozen earth like out of rock," Ernst Friedrich Schauer wrote in February 1942:

> It was a brilliant, bright winter day. The birds twittered, as if spring wanted to begin. . . . The bodies of both fallen [comrades] lay there, rigid and lifeless, wrapped in a brown tent. The bloody emergency bandage still clung above Hans-Jürgen's right eye. His expression was indifferent . . . , as if wanted to say: "What's going on with me?"
>
> We laid the bodies side by side in the grave. Then I said a few words. . . ."They cared for us as comrades and brothers and friends in past times. They fought with us, starved and froze with us, shared

the concerns and distress of the *Landser* experience with us. . . .
They marched next to us and now they've fallen next to us. . . . Not
only your spirit and your memory lives on, no, you yourself, you
live in another, better world. . . ." We took the shovel and threw dirt
over the bodies, I first, then Ewalt, then Kurt Link, then the others.
Then we went back to the front.[44]

"All over the burning steppe, in the blank, unending expanse of
Russia they lie," an anonymous soldier reflected in June 1943, "our
comrades, who caroused with us, sang, marched and fought, starved and
fled with us. In the woods, in villages, on the roads, their graves are
everywhere, a mound, a white birch cross, the steel helmet on top, silent
reminders for us who still remain to fight on further for those who have
fallen."[45] In burial ceremonies such as these, repeated a thousandfold
throughout Russia and elsewhere, the *Landsers* not only honored and
thereby reaffirmed the fragile ties of comradeship, which could be
exploded with the next shell, but also exorcised their own collective grief,
fear, and vulnerability, if only for a brief instant.

This almost mystical, spiritual closeness, so like love, perhaps also
explained why so many *Landsers*, when away from the line, felt an irresistible tug from their buddies at the front. "I [voluntarily] reported to the front,"
wrote Private K.B., "because it is better for me. It is a funny feeling to sit
around in the rear while others must lie out there in that crap." An odd
feeling indeed, mingling guilt at living in relative comfort and safety with
the acute sense that a vital spirit, one that you loved and in which you
wanted to immerse yourself, was missing. The bonds of comradeship
defined the *Landser*'s world. Within this circle, he knew intense loyalty
and emotion; outside the union, he felt isolated and rejected. While
recovering from his second wound, Helmut von Harnack speculated
about this mysterious attraction: "Why do I feel so pressed to go back
there so soon, back to the troops at the front? For a long time it's had
nothing to do with ambition and personal impatience; it's a feeling of
duty, that you cannot leave your comrades stuck in that crap but must
help, that you simply belong up there, that you cannot get over it because
you almost feel at home there." After being rotated away from the front,
Bernhard Buhl complained that in the rear areas all sense of comradeship
disappeared, that there the war seemed only "a battle against dirt, vermin
and illness, chaos. . . . I want out of here . . . to go forward, back to the
front."[46]

Harry Mielert vented similar frustrations with the revolting nature of life in the rear, writing of a period of training behind the front, "Tomorrow is the last day of this repugnant instruction. I am already downright glad to be going back to the front. . . . At the front, where I do really necessary work, I feel myself in the right place." "Don't worry about me," one eighteen-year-old soldier reassured his parents, "I've never been so carefree in my life," because, he explained, with one's comrades at the front one is "really free."[47] As Buhl, Mielert, and many other *Landsers* discovered, without the rewards of camaraderie the war appeared merely a sordid and meaningless affair.

Home leave and a chance to get away from the misery of the front were certainly welcomed by the *Landser*, but the pull of the front remained irresistible. "There I sit now. Am I happy?" puzzled Hans Pietzcker in October 1942, while enjoying art exhibitions and Beethoven concerts in Berlin. "I have homesickness just now; but I yearn not to go home but out there; my comrades are out there in the Russian mud. . . . With my old companions I stood sentry in the evenings. . . . We talked of art, of music. The rain trickled over the mud. It was cold. It snowed, the winter came. Ah, forget, forget! But still, was it not beautiful?" Even though stationed in France, which was regarded almost wistfully by those in Russia as a radiant paradise, Reinhard Goes betrayed sentiments similar to Pietzcker's: "I could no longer live any further in France amid this quiet and richness, I had to get back to my friends and brothers at the front. Perhaps it was the call of the dead comrades that compelled me to return here. . . . I am proud to be at the focus of the battle."[48]

Not even a wound would necessarily break the magic spell of the *Fronterlebnis* (front experience). Recovering at home near Munich, Martin Pöppel turned a deaf ear to all entreaties from friends and relatives and returned to the front with his arm still in a sling. "No, it's better by far to be out there," Pöppel recorded in his diary. "I had to get back to the front. I couldn't bear to sit around . . . when I knew what my comrades were going through. I had to get back." Klaus Löscher felt the same tug. He had already been wounded five times; he considered the war nonsensical and hideous; yet despite his never-ending fatigue and earnest conviction that he would not return alive, Löscher still delighted in being sent back to his old unit, in which he took enormous pride. Shortly after rejoining his comrades at the front, Löscher fell victim to the blast of a hand grenade. In his wallet lay Manfred Hausmann's poem "Path in the Twilight," with the closing lines marked:

> Who covets light, must go in the darkness;
> Let salvation begin in that which horror multiplies,
> Meaning only rules where sense is missing;
> The path begins where there is no longer a way.[49]

Who coveted light had indeed to proceed in the darkness; many *Landsers* found that away from the front they seemed overtaken by a soul-destroying emptiness, and that there existed no equivalent feeling of comradeship, no strong sense of unity, no meaning, in the rear.

Tension between front and rear has always been a feature of military life, of course, with soldiers on the front line typically contemptuous of those stationed behind it, and the front soldier's definition of the rear could be extremely harsh. As Harry Mielert wrote from a retraining center: "Only the front has a right to exist. Everything that is carried on here [in the rear] is without urgency, it can just as well be discontinued, for no person would notice. The front on the other hand cannot simply be abandoned; it is necessary."[50]

Martin Pöppel, in his war diary during the desperate early days at Normandy, expressed the same contempt and illustrated as well the very different feelings the men had toward upper-echelon officers in the rear as opposed to those who shared the front-line hardships with them.

> Rrriing. Yet again. The Commander! Why am I providing harassing fire with my big gun and not with the machine guns? Crazy question from the Old Man. Because machine gun fire is completely ineffective . . . and because the Battalion has ordered me to provide harassing fire with all the guns I can. As a result of telling the truth I get a dreadful dressing down. . . . Rrring. Now there's chaos, the Old Man is back on the line, even more furious with me than before. Now the word is that my mortars are firing too short. But that's not possible, since the firing data has been precisely calculated and checked. As I've been firing for two hours, and accurately at that, then I can't suddenly be firing too short using the same calculations. It's enough to make you puke. The Old Man has suddenly gone crazy. . . .
>
> The Old Man is on the telephone again. Why am I firing with my big heavy gun again, after he expressly ordered me not to? Because a curtain barrage is the warning sign to the infantry that the enemy is making a major attack. . . . In such a case all heavy guns are to fire. . . . But the Regimental Commander is always right, or at least he thinks he is, and I'm removed from my company

immediately. . . . It's easy to imagine my bitterness. My platoon leaders . . . are furious as well, but there's nothing to be done. The scum up there always stick together.

A few weeks later, during a temporary lull in the savage fighting, Pöppel got a measure of revenge, of *Schadenfreude* (malicious glee) at those in the rear: "The weather is still warm and beautiful. Most of the men are sitting in front of their dugouts to enjoy the sun. . . . A sudden concentration of fire from the enemy, but it lands behind our lines. And why not, why shouldn't they get their share of our daily torment back there?"[51]

Gottfried Gruner, a medical doctor serving on the front lines on the Black Sea coast, wrote scornfully in June 1943, "Recently I have even hauled around the Corps doctor. I think it was new to him to find that the war also took place there where he could not drive his car to it. Similarly, a professor from Königsberg, who had come . . . with his fly-net in search of malaria flies and larvae amazed us. The *Landsers* just laughed." Similarly, Hans Woltersdorf raged at "those civil servants . . . [who] wore our uniforms, decorated themselves with our ranks, and considered themselves far too valuable to be wasted at the front, too good to be expected to end up as shreds of flesh on the bulkhead of a tank or even to have to see this. It was they who, with their signatures and a few strokes of a pen, sealed our fate, the fate of soldiers."[52]

These comments, accurately expressing the contempt for the *Etappenschweine* (rear swine) felt by the *Frontkämpfer*, also demonstrate that those at the front saw themselves as a lonely band of men exposed daily to the hardships and dangers of war; naturally, they resented those who were not. Most *Landsers* were convinced that neither officers and men stationed in the rear nor the folks at home could or would understand what they lived through, what the front was really like. Responding to a letter from home that had complained about a drunken soldier, Helmut Kniepkamp exclaimed:

But did you know his fate? Did you know what he had gone through? A year ago I was on Capri together with a comrade: 22 years old, a student, a corporal, 23 months without leave in Africa. What that means can only be appreciated by one who saw this man. Twenty-three months without trees and bushes, only desolation and emptiness! Physically he was a wreck and psychologically precarious. I will never forget him. His parents were killed in a bomb attack on Duisburg, his bride had cheated on him, his only brother had fallen in Russia. A fate that must leave us silent. . . !

Another comrade who was in the same regiment as I in Africa told me his life story: Wounded and taken prisoner by the English, escaped, handed over by Gaullists to the Americans, jumped from the train while under way, smuggled by Arabs to Spanish Morocco, then returned to Germany via Spain. So I would like it if you would just see a human in every soldier, even if he should misbehave, a man who, also for you, is giving his last unconditionally.[53]

"It actually looks as if those at home want to lose their nerve," complained a *Landser* furiously in August 1941. "If that is so, what should we at the front then say? Do you then believe that this acts as an encouragement for the soldiers?" "Whoever makes a soldier's life miserable," he continued in another letter, trying, perhaps vainly, to explain the mystique of camaraderie to an outsider, "and has not properly savored it, does not belong among humans." "The impression that I had during my last leave was shattering," concluded Lieutenant W.T. miserably. "The distance between those at home and those out there at the front has grown so much wider in the course of the year that there is hardly a bridge any longer."[54] Their fierce pride at being able to endure harsh situations, as well as their sense of being at the focus of battle, produced a feeling of exclusivity among the *Landsers* which blossomed into a deep loyalty to other members of this elite fraternity but generated an inevitable hostility between those who served at the front and anyone who did not.

It is hardly surprising, then, that their bond of comradeship often impressed *Landsers*, just as it had their fathers following World War I, as a valuable organizing principle for civilian society. Camaraderie, as Helmut Vethake noted, was something we "would certainly like to bring back home from here and there preserve, namely the view for the essentials and the satisfaction in simple things: 'simple people and simple happiness.' " Karl Fuchs thought the future would surely be based on the lessons learned at the front: "A great friendship binds us German soldiers together out here. It is this comradery [*sic*] and the support that we're able to give each other that is, in my opinion, the secret behind our incredible successes and victories. This loyalty and devotion to the cause again and again was the decisive factor in many a battle . . . , and this comradeship has been one of the most magnificent experiences out here. This loyalty is the essence of the German fighting spirit. We can depend on each other unconditionally. . . . Let this loyalty which I've experienced out here in comradeship be the foundation of our future life."[55]

Writing from Russia in September 1943, an anonymous soldier asserted, "We can only feel ourselves to be preparing the way for our future nation. And that as *Landsers*. There is no individual destiny here." Friedrich Grupe recalled being overwhelmed by the idealistic dream that a new vision of life based on comradeship might form the basis for a new society. After the war, he wrote, "the front soldiers, purified through the great experience of comradeship in the face of death, will decisively undertake the fashioning of the National Socialist Germany and life in the Reich. You, the true *Volksgemeinschaft*, who have lived in distress, will be called first to be a model and example for the *Volk*."[56] The experience of comradeship in the trenches thus proved an intoxicating force, leading many to believe that the *Frontgemeinschaft* could be transferred to a genuine *Volksgemeinschaft*.

Amazingly, some men even saw in the spirit of comradeship the hope of transcending Nazi racial ideology. Paul Kaysel, a part-Jewish soldier from Berlin, wrote in February 1940: "For the first time since 1933 I have forgotten the curse that otherwise burdened me and in some form was always with me. Now I have the feeling that it only matters what kind of a person you really are, not on what things are written on a piece of paper." Others, too, felt the tug of this rough democracy, this meritocracy based on character and achievement. Eberhard Wendebourg wrote from Russia that the war had taught him "the true worth of men," for he had learned "to judge men not by their rank and position, name and honors, but only by their character and performance." And to those at home, despairing of the final outcome of the war, the spirit of the front soldier often offered a glimmer of hope and meaning. Bernhard Beckering, in the retreat into Germany in December 1944, noted in amazement that the civilian population ardently sought hope from the comradely attitude of the soldiers, an observation confirmed by Martin Pöppel. So powerful and so positive was the impression made by front soldiers on the civilian population of Germany that the *Wehrmacht* in the latter part of the war even attempted a systematic propaganda campaign using front soldiers to buttress the morale of the home front.[57]

The integrating power of the *Volksgemeinschaft* ideal kept many in its grip until the very end of the bitter fighting. "Only one thing seemed certain to us," Melita Maschmann recalled, "that no power on earth would succeed in destroying our community." Out of the earlier crises of World War I and the social and economic upheavals of the Weimar years had come a new ideal: a notion of salvation based on community, an idea that was promoted—especially by the young—with a dynamic intensity and for which many were prepared to make individual sacrifices. The ferocity with which many *Landsers* clung to a sense of camaraderie reflected not only the experiences of war and the workings of the front but also a persistent belief that this very comradeship signified a new and more positive organizing principle for German society as a whole. The realization, at the very end of the war, that this ideal lay in ruin was devastating; as Friedrich Grupe noted in his diary in April 1945, "In these hours and days for me and for millions a world is sinking, a view of the world is shattering." For many *Landsers*, the holy grail remained comradeship, possessed during the hard days and hours of war but lost at war's end and, many feared, irretrievable. As Guy Sajer recalled regretfully, during the war "we discovered a sense of comradeship which I have never found again, inexplicable and steady, through thick and thin."[58]

Undoubtedly, the romanticism of comradeship was seductive, and many *Landsers* fell under its spell. But in the end there was something deeper, more intense, less shallow and sentimental, to this feeling. "Timidly I once again stroke his cold hand," began Claus Hansmann in an entry in his diary entitled "Letter to a Mother":

> The canvas strip falls back and in a disembodying way the cloth blurs his familiar face. Dead. A few minutes ago, as we still shouted our acerbic jokes from foxhole to foxhole . . . , a bit of shrapnel struck him in the heart. . . . Dully I crawl back into my foxhole and search for a piece of paper.
> "Dear Frau X. . . ?" or simply "To the mother of a comrade. . . ." May it be a comfort to you to hear this terrible news from us comrades, instead of through an official notification. He fell on 25 July in Voronezh, your young son Ernst, lifted out of the midst of the sacrificial life of a soldier. His fate overtook him, and for you as with us opened an awful, painful void. Yet amid all the incomprehensibility, at least a bit of comfort: he was granted a good death, good like the pitiless crack with which a young tree breaks and is not crippled. . . . But such poor comfort for a mother, for the continual loving concern, for the gladly borne sacrifices, the shattered hopes. . . . How small are the emotions that a man spends on friendship and love against that which is a mother's love. . . . We [are] detached in this hard world of men full of high-sounding

notions of "fulfillment of duty. . . ." Yet we also have the reminder of a shattered friendship, of an empty place in the ranks. A place in our hearts is deserted as the days at the front become more difficult. Seeing all the suffering has not made us so numb that in our carefully protected inner being we don't also feel the pain.[59]

Yet for Hansmann, even this heart-rending letter failed to explain his thoughts on the essence of camaraderie sufficiently. In his next diary entry, made at a field hospital, he again returned to the theme. "Comrades?" he puzzled. "Yes, now, here where we everywhere stand alone, they are more important than perhaps otherwise, where human weaknesses would sometimes be unbearable through the crowding together." Spotting a buddy, Hansmann inquired about his squad, which had been scattered in a recent battle. "What about the rest?" he asked anxiously. What about

Karl, Hansl, and Willi? You hang on his words as if it were your own fate you must hear. A tired, vague movement of the hand underscores the definitive "dead." You can't comprehend it. . . . You look at each other, you survivors, with whom you lay together in the same foxhole day in and day out, at night stood watch shoulder to shoulder, with whom you laughed together, cooked, ate, slept, fought with and made up with. Within you something aches impulsively, that you were not with them, although reason says: Probably never again will luck so clearly favor you. . . . What binds you together under the rough surface? [Men whom] chance has thrown together, certainly not meant for one another? What binds the living so strongly and so loyally to those who are dead? How are we tied in common? Often misinterpreted, by a few completely understood, bound by chains of necessity: Comradeship?[60]

Aware of its power but still unable to articulate this force, Hansmann was ultimately defeated in his attempt at definition; he could only conclude that comradeship was its own explanation. What did tie these men together, produced the void, the feeling when a comrade died that a bit of yourself had also gone to the grave? "I had looked for Hals," remembered Guy Sajer of the chaotic days at the very end of the war, "but hadn't been able to find him. He filled my thoughts, and only my acquired ability to hide my feelings kept me from weeping. He was attached to me by all the terrible memories of the war. . . . Hals and all the others, the war, and everything for which I had been obliged to live;

all the names of all the men beside whom, my eyes huge with terror, I had watched death approach; and death itself, which could have overcome us at any moment; the names and faces of all the men without whom I would never have made these observations. . . . I could never forget nor deny them."[61]

To Sajer, then, comradeship loomed larger than life because it had bestowed life itself. A soldier solitary and alone, without friends, would quickly have been overwhelmed by despair at all he saw and did, would certainly have fallen victim to the insatiable appetite for death that ruled the battlefield. Only with the aid of a comrade could one hope to conquer the anguish and endure; only by sharing the pain could one live. Comradeship not only enabled Sajer, and many others, to survive; it allowed him to make some sense of the hurricane of events, to achieve a measure of comprehension of the deep human reality behind the impersonal facade of the war.

8. TRYING TO CHANGE THE WORLD

Observing the scene in Berlin upon the outbreak of hostilities with Poland, Joseph Harsch, the correspondent for the *Christian Science Monitor*, claimed with only a trace of exaggeration that "the German people were nearer to real panic on 1 September 1939 than the people of any other European country. No people wanted that war, but the German people exhibited more real fear of it than the others. They faced it in something approaching abject terror." Indeed, as Adolf Hitler motored through the streets of Berlin to the Kroll Opera House, where the *Reichstag* met, to deliver a speech at ten o'clock that morning, the crowds were thin and noticeably sullen. Nor did Hitler's words on the occasion of the outbreak of war generate much enthusiasm.[1] German soldiers, in fact, marched off to war accompanied by none of the wild hysteria and excitement of 1914. Quite the contrary: in 1939 the *Landser* did not go joyously off to battle in search of an adventure, confident of his purpose and innocent of war's punishing reality. But go to war he did, however much cynicism and intellectual wariness he carried as baggage. And still the *Landser* not only bore the brunt of the war's frightful harvest but withstood its terrible fury for six long years, taking ground swiftly and giving it back only grudgingly, until Germany, as the focus of battle, ceased to exist.

Why, then, were these soldiers fighting? Did they fight for National Socialism, against Bolshevism, out of racial hatred, because of love of country, merely for themselves? Had the Nazis constructed a new creature invigorated by death? Might the *Landser* simply have been following in the tradition of absolute duty and obedience, the famous *Kadaver-gehorsam* of Frederick the Great? Or had the Nazis succeeded in creating a *Volksgemeinschaft* for the maintenance of which the *Landser* fought tenaciously? Since an army tends to reflect the society from which it sprang, if the men of the *Wehrmacht* fought steadfastly in support of Hitler and Nazism, something within the Hitler state must have struck a responsive chord.

In order to begin to understand the motivation of the average German soldier in World War II, one must look back to the impact of the Great War. Men had been transformed by the horrifying experience of the trenches. The very concept of the hero was redefined in World War I, when, as Jay Baird put it, "bare-chested men stood against the full force of the weaponry of a technological age." The ideal of creating a new man after the bloodletting of the trenches stemmed from the belief that this sort of war had produced a new type of individual, a "frontier personality" who served as an agent of rebirth, regeneration, and new life, a person who journeyed to the limits of existence seeking renewal out of the destruction of war. This new man was not a fighter who enthusiastically sacrificed himself for glory and honor, as had the soldiers of 1914. Instead, driven by will, amoral, cool, functional, and hardened, he could withstand the ultimate test of battle without cracking. At the same time he was a technological warrior who understood that the war expressed the very rhythm of industrial life, as well as a man of steel who gained personal fulfillment through a narcissistic dynamism of will and energy. "All is permissible," Gottfried Benn remarked in the late 1920s, "that leads to experience." A certain matter-of-factness thus marked the new man, who replaced the romantic relics of a failed bourgeois age with the image of mechanical precision, a man who functioned to the rhythm of the machine. "The German factory," despaired a French soldier in 1917, "is absorbing the world." The Great War thus proved a breeding ground for the post-bourgeois man, as these workers of war fashioned a true revolution.[2]

More than any other writer, Ernst Jünger expressed and popularized this image of the new man. In the *Fronterlebnis* Jünger discerned the glimmerings of a new society, a world in which the worker and soldier, made one by the energy of technology and the vitalism of war, fused to create a new being who combined "a minimum of ideology with a maximum of performance," intellectual mastery of technology with primordial soldierly qualities. War, Jünger asserted, afforded personal rebirth through passage into the intoxicating world of instinct and emotion, where men thrown together in the hurricane of battle rediscovered courage and passion. "Perhaps one must lose all in order to gain one's self," wrote, Horstmar Seitz in October 1942, his tone certainly that of Jünger. "We must throw away all culture and education, all false pretenses that hinder us from being ourselves. . . . For us there is only one thing: to begin completely anew, to erect new values and create new forms." War thus fostered both transfiguration and redemption, forging a community of men who shared a great destiny and encompassed a higher mission, a *Gemeinschaft* whose merits of action, decision, and existential commitment resulted in genuine self-realization.[3] Inner truth, then, flowed from collective experience.

Modern war, Jünger proclaimed, transformed life into energy, so that it resembled a gigantic labor process. The new face of war, human mastery of the machine, led to the development of soldiers with steel armor and ruthless will, men who were resilient and malleable under the new conditions of battle, men who were "day laborers of death . . . for a better day." Overblown rhetoric perhaps, although in a letter written in November 1944 Sebastian Mendelssohn-Bartholdy claimed that he "would like to be one of the nameless in the greater community who takes on every sacrifice for the war in order to serve a future that we don't know and yet in which we still believe."[4]

To Jünger the front soldier, whose face was "metallic, . . . galvanized," and who stoically accepted pain, was a fighter made of modern material: amoral, dispassionate, hard, and functional, a man who had become a fighting machine. "You must wait, sit, devise, and do the worst things," Harry Mielert explained unemotionally in the tones of the new man in March 1943, "act mechanical and hard, look and see the inhuman without batting an eyelid." "We don't cry," Mielert noted a few months later, "and our exteriors appear hard and like a bizarre personification of the pure manly, cold, warrior." "This war has shaped us soldiers into something else," Ansgar Bollweg mused in November 1943. "With the sharpness of a predator's eyes we recognize that the remains of the old world will be crushed between the millstones of this war. . . . Out of 'total mobilization' . . . comes the form of the worker. In 1933 I read a book of Ernst Jünger's: *Der Arbeiter* [The Worker]. It left a great impression on me, but only now do I recognize the consequences. . . . I see how in the epoch of masses and machines each individual life will always become more explicitly that of a 'life of a worker' and how because of that the war gets it cruel character." "You can't afford to be soft in war," Karl Fuchs explained in a letter to his wife in June 1941. "No, you must be tough; indeed, you have to be pitiless and relentless. Don't I sound like a different person to you?"[5]

A different person indeed, Jünger's modern warrior, one who was steady, precise, a fusion of steel with flesh, a center of technological and human coordination, able to move freely and instinctually in an environment suffused with death, a man whose morality meshed with technology to produce a modern fighting machine. Personal satisfaction came from the individual's identification with and performance of his task. For the "anonymous soldier" the standard was matter-of-fact achievement; proficiency replaced romantic notions of sacrifice. In a post-bourgeois world where the worker and soldier were becoming identical and where technology resulted in the penetration of the dangerous into everyday life, combat seemed merely a factory job: the machines of destruction were fed and let loose, and the tight web of the machine and its routine determined a man's life. Consciousness of the "iron necessity" of duty dogged many a *Landser*, for as Sebastian Mendelssohn-Bartholdy put it, "We soldiers have no choice but duty and obedience. We claim to sacrifice for us and nobody else, and to continue to sacrifice."[6]

Jünger argued as well that pleasure and horror were inseparable in war, horror at the destruction but pleasure in the will to sacrifice. Indeed, he asserted, "the deepest happiness of man lies in the fact that he will be sacrificed." To Jünger, domination and service were identical, or as Reinhard Goes put it in November 1941, "I have learned that one is free not only when one can give orders, but also when one can take orders." The key issue, then, was not improving one's life but imparting the highest, decisive meaning to it. "The pull of destiny," Jünger asserted, "is indicated by a feeling for the necessary, a compulsion that often leads us to act against our own interests, against tranquillity, happiness, peace, even against life itself." Echoing Jünger's contention, Heinz Küchler wrote from Poland in September 1939, "Our greatness must lie in the ability not to master fate but rather to maintain our personality, our will, our love in defiance of fate and, unbowed, to be a sacrifice to a world order that is not ours." After all, Jünger asserted, war was "a matter of taste."[7]

To his taste or not, for the *Landser* sacrifice and massive loss of life became the most striking reality of World War II, especially on the eastern front. "After a week-long, extremely exhausting march, my division went into action at the Dnieper," wrote Gerhard Meyer in late July 1941. "The first encounter of our side with a superior force without artillery preparation cost blood on top of blood. . . . The positive strength of the division had now sunk under half; 80 percent of the officers had fallen, but we remained engaged." Nor was his outfit unique. By mid-September 1941, Corporal E.K. of the Ninety-eighth Infantry Division reported "In our company we have 75 percent casualties. . . . If the replacements don't get here soon . . . we will be lost." A few replacements trickled in, but German units continued to melt away during the lethal advance on Moscow. "At the moment we're lying in defensive positions north of Moscow," wrote a corporal in late November 1941. "We few remaining soldiers of our division long terribly for the hopeless relief. In our company on October 26 there were only 20 men." This sense of isolation, of having been forgotten, was intensified by the grim reality of profligate death on a battlefield far from home. Despaired a *Landser* in the midst of this carnage, "When will they at last pull us out of the line. . . ? When will we ever get back home?" As a divisional chaplain put it, "When one asks after somebody, the same reply is always given: dead or wounded."[8]

Similarly, in January 1942, Sergeant W.H. lamented, "The soldier's luck has really abandoned our company. We marched off with 200 men, and now our company is only 140 men strong. . . . I myself saw my life more than once hanging by a thread." In early July 1942 a chaplain of the Eighteenth Panzer Division noted sorrowfully in his diary, "The number of dead is increasing, the number of wounded is frightful. In my black book there is already one black cross after another. My whole congregation is almost completely dead or wounded." Martin Lindner commented dryly in September 1942 that his unit had been placed in the most dangerous position in the line, "therefore we also have high losses, and our fate is once again to be slowly ground down. . . . In my company there are only a few, which you can count on your fingers, who have been in action as long as I without being wounded. . . . Since 28 June 1942 alone our company has lost 190 to wounds and death." Little more than a month later, just back from leave and plunged immediately into battle, Lindner noted, "Two-thirds of my platoon have become casualties."[9] He himself was killed three days later.

After the first brutal year of the war in Russia, then, the *Wehrmacht* had already suffered crippling casualties. In the midst of the savage fighting around Sevastopol in July 1942, Friedrich Haag reflected on the stark reality produced by this enormous loss of life: "I have recently experienced how difficult it is to lead a company into fire and to sacrifice men whom you hardly know from one another. They fall next to you, and perhaps one cries: 'Herr Lieutenant, you must write home,' and you don't even know what his name is." All so commonplace, this anonymous death on an obscure battlefield. "A letter to an unknown soldier of the company arrived in which a girl asked to have information about her dead fiancé," Wilhelm Prüller noted in his diary in February 1942. "No one wanted to answer it, because there's no one here any more who was there when he fell."[10]

Certainly from 1942 on, despair is palpable in many letters. "The war has ripped my joy away from me," wrote Horstmar Seitz in July 1942. "One can lose one's beliefs, one's love, one's reverence. Today I stand in external and internal struggle. Of my friends the best have fallen. . . . I don't know when I will again have peace." Bitter at the loss of a close friend, Helmut Pabst complained that one hears, " 'It was fate,' it was destiny. But is that really true? Is it not a miserable attempt to give meaning to each event only because we are too cowardly to stare the senselessness of it in the face . . . ? War strikes without choice, and if it knows a law, it is that the best are struck down." "Here it is a matter of life or death," Corporal F.B. emphasized in a letter from Russia in January 1943. "Russia is our fate. . . . The fighting has reached a harshness and relentlessness that takes away all words. 'None of us has the right to come back alive!' We soldiers often repeat this saying, and we know that it is meant seriously." War, Harry Mielert concluded, "is not an experience, but only a frightful fact that one must endure."[11]

And yet the dominant theme running throughout the letters of these *Landsers* was not so much disillusionment as a stubborn resiliency. "In deep darkness I sit among the vacationers who are returning from [leave in] the homeland," wrote Siegfried Roemer in March 1944 while traveling in a freight car from Orscha to Vitebsk. "Many are concerned about the aerial bombing damage. They speak bitterly and out of deep resignation, yet I am convinced that at the front each of them will continue to do his duty." In the midst of his misery, Hans Pietzcker stressed, "We stuck it out true to our duty and responsibility . . . [and] we were still undefeated, knew our goal and orders." And even as he expressed his loneliness at the loss of old comrades, Will Thomas went on to note proudly, "The attitude of the men is also wonderful despite all the difficulties and all the privations, which you at home cannot imagine."

Horstmar Seitz, noting that "the past is distant and dark and deadened by the blows of shells," nonetheless marveled, "and yet we stand here for women and their laughter, for beauty, for the homeland, and for ourselves." Similarly, Helmut Pabst threw off his acrid cynicism, declaring in a later letter that in the struggle for Germany's existence, "duty was not good or evil, but rather an inviolable attitude until the final consequence."[12]

The war in Russia, with its horrible slaughter and characteristic smell of fire, sweat, and decaying corpses, prompted Harald Henry to observe: "On the whole I experience the war as totally different from how it was portrayed in the World War books, unemotional, nowhere as an unshakable uplifting song of 'loyalty and courage in the face of death,' as a steely rhythm of 'fire and blood,' . . . as a 'stirring and formative life force,' [but] rather as a pessimistic caricature of overall life, as exactly the same mixture of tribulation, anger, joy, and passion, full of sacrifice and courage, full of egoism and malice. Only a German visionary could regard this as the best of all possible worlds." Still, Henry did admit to a certain Jüngerian functionalism:

> What I am living here is idealism. The idealism of "in spite of it all. . . ." What we must do here, suffering until madness, holding on with clenched teeth . . . and yet then in the most gruesome misery, in the abysses and dark sides of life to preserve a belief in the bright and beautiful sides, in the meaning of life . . . , in the whole rich and beautiful world of idealism, how should we call it? It is that "in spite of it all," that inner indestructibility, that unconditional will finally to comprehend even the most horrible as part of the whole, to see it within the "good" total cycle of life. . . . An enormous mental strength goes into this attitude.[13]

Had the anonymous *Landser*, then, become the embodiment of Jünger's worker-soldier, who thrilled at the dark, chaotic, inexplicable beauty of war and for whom ideological motivation was superfluous? Certainly one can find examples of nihilist bravado among the letters written by the *Landsers*, many of whom seem consciously to have adopted a Jüngerian attitude. "The front line, the entrenched riflemen, have deeply impressed me," wrote Hans-Heinrich Ludwig from Russia, "especially their attitude. These fellows are fabulous. A complete resignation to fate." Seeking to explain this feeling to his wife, Harry Mielert claimed, "There forward in my foxhole I was a free man. . . . Can you understand that I yearn somewhat for the freer life in the dangerous trenches?" During the retreat out of Russia, Mielert again emphasized this sense of existential freedom. The war, he claimed, "is again a great selection process. Whoever is not able to come along is left behind. The men abandon all their belongings and possessions in order to save their naked lives." Similarly, Harald Henry admitted to distress but went on to claim, "Our suffering is . . . an infinitely beautiful, colorful, painfully lively suffering." Confessed Hans-Friedrich Stäcker, in a reference to Jünger's most famous statement, "I have slowly come to the understanding behind the words: 'war is the father of all things.' "[14]

Others also closely mimicked Jünger. "Men die daily, and daily rise from the dead," wrote Wolfgang Kluge, reflecting Jünger's notion of rebirth through war; in a later letter he touched on the notion of affirmation, arguing, "We who must walk on the shadowy side of life hang on to the beauty of life more than those who possess it." War affirmed life, as life seemed to Siegfried Roemer to affirm war: "But to us the war has now become a life form, to be sure full of danger and filth and blood, but we stand in the middle of it and affirm it to a certain degree." Similarly, Siegbert Stehmann sought to understand the war "not as a refuge from our passionate time, but rather as a door into it." To Heinz Küchler, it was "really curious to go marching into war with the attitude that we must have: without hate, without passion, . . . without a feeling for this war. And in spite of it we 'fight.' " Küchler noted later, "The war here [in Russia] is being carried on in a 'pure cultural' sense; every evidence of humanity appears to have disappeared in deed and in heart and conscience."[15]

At first glance, then, the Jüngerian worker-soldier, the so-called new man glorified in the years following the Great War, seemed to be personified in the anonymous *Landser*, who endured the grim everyday life of war and persisted in his job despite objective considerations of victory or defeat. "To have created the new warrior," boasted *Signal* magazine, a slick wartime product of Joseph Goebbels's propaganda apparatus in 1942, "who dared to advance against the products of war techniques, was the proud achievement of the German Infantry [of 1918]," and those front fighters had "passed on to the coming generation a legacy of the spiritual kind, the science and teaching of the new man."[16] So strong was this attempt to link the so-called new soldier of World War II with the much-glorified trench fighter of the Great War that the Nazis even produced a series of picture postcards depicting the stern, dauntless visage of the stormtrooper of 1918, no doubt to remind the *Landser* that he stemmed from mythic material. Still, this image of the dispassionate, functional warrior obscures the complex interplay of forces that was the reality of the *Landser*'s motivation. The image is not so much incorrect as it is incomplete.

Although some *Landsers* seemed to validate Jünger's contentions that modern war produced an emotionless, assembly-line soldier, a man acting in harmony with the machine but lacking any ideological motivation, such a reading of the average German soldier would be misleading. The typical *Landser* did not function as a robot devoid of a sense of purpose but was in fact sustained by a broad spectrum of values. "How then, I ask myself," mused Friedrich Grupe, himself a front soldier, after the war, "were the enormous achievements of the German *Wehrmacht* possible, if the majority of the young soldiers thought only about saving their own heads?" As Hans Woltersdorf admitted, "We threw ourselves into national tasks with National Socialist idealism, redeemed ourselves."[17] Anti-Semitism, anti-communism, *Lebensraum*—these central tenets of Nazism were all inextricably linked with the *Landser*'s conception of duty, with his place and role within the vast machinery of war.

Indeed, the notion that Germany was under assault from an alleged "Jewish-Bolshevik conspiracy" served for many as the prop that sustained them under the burden of war. "Now Jewry has declared war on us along the whole line," wrote Corporal A.N. the day after the German attack on the Soviet Union. "All that are in bondage to the Jews stand in a front against us. The Marxists fight shoulder to shoulder with high finance as before 1933 in Germany. . . . Through our preventive attack, we again have the Reds by the nose. . . . We ourselves know exactly what is at stake in this game." This sense of combatting a heinous conspiracy was seconded by Private H.K., who asserted, "We are . . . fighting against the Bolshevik world enemy." "The great task that has placed us in battle against Bolshevism lies in the destruction of eternal Judaism," thundered Corporal K.G. "When you see what the Jew has brought about here in Russia, only then can you begin to understand why the Führer began this struggle against Judaism. What sort of misfortunes would have been visited upon our Fatherland, if this bestial people had gotten the upper hand?"[18]

Pure Nazism, this equation of Marxism with Judaism, and the formula recurred often in soldier's letters. "Adolf and I are marching against our great enemy Russia," exclaimed Private F. in the heady days of victory in July 1941. "Consequently one of my wishes has been fulfilled, as I was gladly drawn into this blasphemous country. This time we will certainly make an end of this power which is hostile to God. . . . You see evidence of Jewish, Bolshevik cruelties which I can hardly believe possible. Yesterday we marched into a large city, past a prison. . . . Inside lay 8,000 dead civilian prisoners, slain, murdered . . . , a blood-bath done by the Bolsheviks shortly before their withdrawal. In another city absolutely similar cases, perhaps even crueler. . . . You can imagine that this cries out for revenge, which will also be carried out." Even *Landsers* initially dubious of Nazi propaganda claims concerning the threat of Soviet attack could admit, as one did in a letter to his parents, "If until now I have taken the declarations of the government rather skeptically and critically, so today I can actually acknowledge the truth of these reports totally."[19]

This racist ideological hostility, when mixed with the notion of a preventive war, often produced a strange sense of relief mingled with the notion of performing an indispensable task. "The German people have a great obligation to our Führer," claimed a corporal in mid-July 1941, "for if these beasts who are our enemies here had come to Germany, murders would have occurred such as the world has never seen before. If uncounted thousands of their own citizens have already been murdered by the Soviets . . . , how would it have been for the Germans? No newspaper can describe what we have seen. It borders on the unbelievable. . . . And when one in Germany reads *Der Stürmer* and sees the pictures, that is only a small example of what we here have seen and what crimes the Jews have committed. Believe me, even the most sensational newspaper reports are only a part of what is happening here." To Private M.M. the purpose of the war became self-evident once he "realize[d] how it would have been with our women and children if these . . . Russian hordes had invaded our Fatherland. I have had here the opportunity to see and observe these uncultivated, mongrel people. Thank God that they were thwarted, that they could not plunder and rob our homeland." Indeed, "a complete destruction [of Bolshevism] is . . . required," asserted Corporal W.F. in November 1941, "[for] if these bestial hordes of soldiers were to fall upon Germany all would be gone that is German." "The battle against these subhumans, who've been whipped into a frenzy by the Jews," claimed Karl Fuchs, "was not only necessary but came in the nick of time. Our Führer has saved Europe from certain chaos. You at home," he admonished, "must always keep in mind what would have happened if these hordes had overrun our Fatherland. The horror of this is unthinkable."[20]

These were not isolated sentiments. Writing from the front in mid-July 1941, Fred Fallnbigl asserted, "We had been forced into the war against the Soviet Union. For God have mercy on us, had we waited, or had these beasts come to us. For them even the most horrible death is still too good. I am glad that I can be here to put an end to this genocidal system." Indeed, the fighting was tough, admitted one soldier, but "to those in the homeland we soldiers can only say that Adolf Hitler has saved Germany and thereby the whole of Europe from the Red Army." Another *Landser* wondered, "What would have happened to cultural Europe, had these sons of the steppe, poisoned and drunk with a destructive poison, these incited subhumans, invaded our beautiful Germany?" "Every *Landser* has seen the strange character of Bolshevism," claimed a soldier in a letter to his mother, "[and] knows what will happen if it comes to Germany." "Praise God that the German people now has summoned the calmness and strength to give the Führer the tools that he needs in order to protect the West from ruin," concluded Captain E.P., "for what the Asiatic hordes would not have wrecked would have been annihilated by Jewish hatred and revenge." This popular sentiment was seconded by Corporal H.H., who stressed, "We must win the war in order not to be delivered over into the revenge of the Jews." That the initial fear of a vague "Bolshevik-Jewish conspiracy" thus gave way to real concerns about the possibility of Jewish revenge indicates a recognition on the part of average *Landsers* that horrible atrocities, committed in the name of Nazi ideology, had been visited upon the Jewish population of Eastern Europe. As Corporal H.G. acknowledged, "This is not exactly a struggle of country against country, but rather one between two fundamentally different ideologies."[21]

Not surprisingly, since both Nazi propaganda and ideology hammered at the notion of an identity of interests between Bolsheviks and Jews, some *Landsers* displayed a murderous anti-Jewish attitude. "The political doctrine of Bolshevism . . . is but a purely political act of world Jewry," claimed Wilhelm Prüller. "And just as the Talmud teaches nothing except murder and destruction, so Bolshevism knows but one science: murder and destruction, cruel and barbaric murder." "Only a Jew can be a Bolshevik," agreed Paul Lenz, "for this blood-sucker there can be nothing nicer than to be a Bolshevik. . . . Wherever one spits one finds a Jew." This allegedly omnipresent, sinister Jewish force was held responsible by Reinhold Mahnke for terrible atrocities against the Lithuanian population: the Jews had supposedly "cut off their feet and hands, tore out their tongues. . . . They even nailed men and children to walls. Had these criminals come to our country, they would have torn us to pieces and mangled us, that's clear. But the Lithuanians have taken revenge," for as Heinrich Sachs noted approvingly "the Jewish question was solved with impressive thoroughness under the enthusiastic applause of the local population." To Hans Kondruss Russia furnished ample evidence that "a whole people has systematically been reared into subhumanity. This is clearly the most Satanic educational plan of all times, which only Jewish sadism could have constructed and carried through." Kondruss too observed with satisfaction that the "wrath of the people has . . . been turned upon this people of criminals." It will be necessary," he asserted, "to scorch out this boil of plague radically, because these 'animals' will always constitute a danger . . . [since their goal] was the brutalization of a whole people in order to use it as an instrument in the war for Judas's world domination."[22]

Others, too, denounced the Jews. "Overall this country makes a ghastly impression on me," wrote a soldier from Poland in September 1939. "Beginning with the roads, which were indescribably bad and dusty, then this dump with its many pests, and finally the endless great number of Jews, these disgusting Stürmer-types." To Lieutenant H.C., the "mass [of Jews] are filthy swine," a sentiment readily accepted by others. "I long ago recognized the Jewish poison in our people," claimed Corporal F.K. in mid-August 1942. "How far it might have gone with us, that we see only now in this campaign. We see every day what the Jewish regime has done in Russia, and in view of the facts even the last doubters are likely cured. We must and will be successful in liberating the world from this plague; that's why the German soldier protects the eastern front, and we will not return before the root of all evil here is torn out and the center of the Jewish-Bolshevik 'world benefactors' is destroyed."[23]

Russia thus served as a great ideological proving ground where many *Landsers*, previously skeptical of Nazi propaganda, confronted what they accepted as the reality of the Jewish-Bolshevik destruction of a whole nation. Some gleefully noted that the Jews were now being shot—were, in a favorite phrase of Hitler's, being "eradicated root and branch" through the "toughest punishment conceivable." In Russia "the Eastern Jew now reveals himself in all his brutality," observed Corporal H.K., himself an avid *Stürmer* reader, then enthusiastically referred to Hitler's famous prophecy concerning the fate of the Jews: "As our Führer in his great speech on the outbreak [*sic*] of this struggle of world Jewry predicted: 'should the Jews once again bring it about that the nations are plunged into a world war, it would be the destruction of their race and not ours.' Gradually this race is more and more remembering these words. . . . But all their nagging and all their exertions may no longer alter their fate."[24]

Certainly the average *Landser* was encouraged in this racist hatred by the *Wehrmacht* high command. Even before the invasion of Russia, in March 1941, Hitler had informed his generals, "The war against the Soviet Union will be such that it cannot be conducted in a knightly fashion; the struggle is one of ideologies and racial differences and will have to be conducted with unprecedented, unmerciful and unrelenting harshness." Hitler's words obviously fell on receptive ears. "The most important goal of the campaign against the Jewish-Bolshevik system," Field Marshal Walter von Reichenau, commander of the Sixth Army, wrote in a general order on 10 October 1941, "is the complete smashing of its means of power and the eradication of Asiatic influences in the European cultural sphere. . . . The soldier in the East is . . . a carrier of an inexorable racial idea and the avenger of all the bestialities that have been inflicted on the Germans and related peoples. Therefore the soldier must have complete understanding for the necessity of the severe but justified atonement of Jewish subhumanity." Just over a month later General Erich von Manstein, commander of the Eleventh Army, similarly urged his men to harsh measures: "The German soldier . . . marches also as the carrier of a racial idea and avenger for all the cruelties that have been inflicted on him and the German people. . . . The soldier must summon understanding for the necessity of a harsh atonement on Judaism, which is the spiritual carrier of the Bolshevik terror." In order to execute this "harsh but just atonement," other commanders urged their troops to be merciless "against the Muscovite-Asiatic flood," to conduct the campaign against "Jewish Bolshevism" with "unprecedented severity," as "compassion and weakness" were out of place in this struggle between two "spiritually unbridgeable conceptions." As General Heinz Guderian wrote in an order in late August 1944, "There is no future . . . without National Socialism."[25]

Determined efforts were made by the *Wehrmacht* to influence the *Landsers* through both written propaganda, such as front newspapers, and spoken propaganda, initially from "education officers" and, later, National Socialist Leadership Officers (*National Sozialistische Führungsoffiziere*, or NSFOs); their task, as Wilhelm Prüller indicated in a letter to his wife, was "to support the battle from the philosophical standpoint and to educate the troops along these lines." Front newspapers typically sought to reinforce racial and ideological conceptions, thundering that "we would be insulting the animals if we were to describe . . . [the Jews] as beasts," and referring to the war as an unavoidable struggle "for liberation of the Aryan people from the spiritual and material bondage" of the Jews. Although a constant drumbeat hammered the message that the Jews were "a plague" infecting the German people, an enemy with "Satanic plans," these newspapers also sought to stiffen morale and urge the soldiers on to new exertions by emphasizing the "inner strength" to be derived from National Socialism, "the greatest power of our times." Likewise, the NSFOs' effort to create a reliable National Socialist consciousness among the troops evidently met with some success. In a monthly *Wehrmacht* report from August 1944 which attempted to ascertain the mood of the average *Landser*, the authors pointed to the good comradeship between officers and men and the general acceptance in the ranks of Nazi ideas as evidence of the rootedness of the National Socialist body of thought. To the authors, in fact, faith in Nazism and loyalty to the Führer were taken as "self-evident."[26]

"In our ranks there are certainly those who fight for the sake of the idea of National Socialism," Egon Freytag acknowledged. Some *Landsers*, in fact, saw in Nazism virtually mystical properties. "When we set up our quarters for the night, we set up our wireless set as usual, . . . and we nearly fall flat on our faces when we realize that the Führer is about to speak," cheered Wilhelm Prüller in October 1941. "I've been a soldier for quite a while, a battle soldier, . . . and I really know what our men prefer, if they could choose mail from home . . . or listening to one of the Führer's speeches. No one knows what this beloved voice means to us. . . . What a lift his words give us. . . . Is there a finer reward after a day of battle than to hear the Führer?" Not even the bitter fighting of 1941 and 1942 could shake the ideological faith of many *Landsers*. Trapped in the Stalingrad pocket, Lieutenant P.G. wrote on the first day of February 1943—the last day of German resistance—that "National Socialist Germany has never been taken so seriously as now. . . . We live in a time whose value will be recognized only many years later. Here it is no longer a matter of the individual but of the whole. Only so long as we are conscious of that can victory come." "The Führer made a firm promise to bail us out of here," moaned another Stalingrad soldier in a perverse liturgy of faith. "They read it to us and we believed in it firmly.

Even now I still believe in it, because I have to believe in something. If it is not true, what else could I believe in. . . ? All my life . . . I believed in the Führer." Indeed, claimed Prüller of a Hitler speech in December 1942, "Every word was balm to our souls. . . . With what enthusiasm we shall carry the attack forward to the enemy tomorrow. . . ! Insofar as we went into this war without being National Socialists, . . . now in this war, in these days of battle. . . , even the last man has discarded all foreign things . . . and has shown his colors for Germany, for his people, and thus for the [Nazi] movement too."[27]

By August 1944, with any hope of victory fading rapidly, the *Landser* often looked to his NSFO with enthusiasm. For many, ideological instruction served as a welcome prop in sustaining morale and motivation. One officer reported that the average soldier "manifests an interest in instruction in political and other current issues," showing that "he is more preoccupied with them than one usually thinks." Another claimed that "the soldiers listened to the lectures attentively. In many cases there is an inner response." "Yesterday I was at a lecture given by our division's general and the division's NSFO," related Corporal W.P.C., obviously impressed by the proceedings. "The explanations of both men were appropriate to give us a stiffening for the coming events. The meaning came out in the speeches that our situation is serious, to be sure, but not hopeless. . . . We must not and will not be crushed by this almost overwhelming uncertainty." Reflecting a union of Jünger's impassive warrior and the true Nazi believer, Lieutenant K.N. contended, "War must always remain a calculation of understanding and burning will," insisting that "a propaganda is genuine and good if it clears away obstacles to picturing the defeated enemy quite ice-cold and sober and then brings the spirit of battle and idealism to a boil, so that it gives material strength a heroic flight." Friedrich Grupe, who trained as one of those front fighters who were to serve as "political shock troops" in the German army, noted that the "decisive principle was to be 'reality more than appearance.' " That meant, Grupe explained, that "everything should correspond to the 'social community of deeds.' " In other words, spirit, idealism, and action were to mesh, as German troops were to be inspired less by lectures than by "speaking as one soldier to another."[28]

This notion that ideology should be communicated from one comrade to another was important, for trusted officers and fellow *Landsers* exerted great influence on the beliefs of the men. As the Nazis surely realized, it was not necessary for all or even a majority of troops to be ideologically motivated; a hard core of believers, especially men respected by the others, could motivate and bind the remainder. Guy Sajer provided a glimpse of this dynamic at work in his portrayal of a popular captain brimming with ideological faith:

> "That's why you're fighting," *Hauptmann* Wesreidau, our captain, said to us one day. . . . "So be brave: life is war and war is life."
>
> Captain Wesreidau often helped us to endure the worst. He was always on good terms with his men. . . . He stood beside us during countless gray watches, and came into our bunkers to talk with us, and make us forget the howling storm outside. . . .
>
> "Germany is a great country," he used to tell us. "The system in which we . . . believe is every bit as good as the slogans on the other side. Even if we don't always approve of what we have to do, we must [cling] . . . to these principles in spite of all the hardships. . . .
>
> "We are now embarked on a risky enterprise. . . . We are advancing an idea of unity which is neither rich nor easily digestible, but the vast majority of the German people accept it and adhere to it, forging and forming it in an admirable collective effort. . . . We are trying . . . to change the face of the world. . . ."
>
> Our conversation with Captain Wesreidau made a deep impression on us. His obvious and passionate sincerity affected even the most hesitant, and seemed of another order than the standard appeals to sacrifice. . . . He spent his time with us. . . . We all loved him, and felt we had a true leader, as well as a friend on whom we could count.

Concern, friendship, sincerity, idealism: clearly this was a complex and dynamic relationship, something that could not easily be created by an NSFO alone, yet once developed it could result in a formidable bond. "I couldn't find the words," Sajer later maintained, "to express the intensity of emotion which German idealism created in me."[29]

Many *Landsers*, undoubtedly influenced by Nazi propaganda, thus depicted themselves as conducting an ideological crusade in defense of European civilization and the German community. As their letters and diaries indicated, however, there was more to their ideological motivation than preconditioned racist hatred; the profound disbelief and disgust felt by the *Landser* at the primitive conditions in the Communist heartland, the very brutality of everyday life, produced a sense of waging an apocalyptic struggle against a cruel and backward power. Consequently, events served not merely to sustain ideology but often to create an acceptance of Nazi views among men previously skeptical or untouched by them. The hard fact of the matter was that the reality of the Soviet Union stunned the average *Landser*. To Lieutenant J.H., everything about Russia was backward. "This primitiveness surpasses every conception," he wrote. "There is no yardstick for comparison [with Germany]. For us it is a totally odd feeling. . . . Merely filth and decay; that is the Soviet paradise." "Peasant houses with straw roofs which look more like dog huts," Wilhelm Prüller observed of Russia, "a ragged, dirty, animal-like people. . . . The paradise of the workers [is] nothing but a conglomeration of hunger and misery, murder and mass imprisonments, slavery and torture."[30]

"All those who today still see any kind of salvation in Bolshevism should be led into this 'paradise,' " Karl Fuchs wrote derisively to his wife. "When I get back I will tell you endless horror stories about Russia." "No matter where you look," he concluded in another letter, "you can't find a trace of culture anywhere. We now realize what our great German Fatherland has given its children. There exists only one Germany in the entire world." To his mother, Fuchs exclaimed indignantly, "These people here . . . live like animals. If they could only once see a German living room. That would be paradise for them, a paradise that these communist scoundrels, Jews and criminals have denied them. We have seen the true face of Bolshevism, have gotten to know it and experienced it, and will know how to deal with it in the future." For Fuchs, the German mission was clear: "Our duty has been to fight and to free the world from this communist disease. One day, many years hence, the world will thank the Germans and our beloved Führer for our victories here in Russia."[31]

Nor were these merely the sentiments of middle-class soldiers. *Landsers* from a working-class background who had been reared in the belief that Soviet Russia was the workers' paradise often seemed especially shocked and revolted. Direct experience thus reinforced Nazi propaganda as the men saw for themselves what they regarded as the cruelty and barbarity of Russia. "We are deep in Russia, in the so-called paradise," Private H. wrote disdainfully in July 1941. "Here great misery rules, the people held for over two decades under an oppression that one can hardly imagine. We all would rather die than live through such misery and agony. . . . Often we ask the Russian soldiers why they threw their weapons away, and they answer: 'What should we fight for then, for the years of oppression and the misery that we went through?' " Raged Corporal W.F., "I am fed up with the much praised Soviet Union. The conditions here are antediluvian. Our propaganda has certainly not exaggerated, rather understated." His opinion was seconded by Sergeant H.S., who noted ruefully, "One can almost not imagine how poor and primitive the red paradise is." "Why the men can bear to hold out," echoed another soldier in September 1943, "one can learn here in the east." Commented a working-class soldier disgustedly:

> Our dwelling for the night was a wooden house already occupied by a Russian family. . . . We were bitten all night by vermin. . . . A huge stove served to warm the family and they slept on or near it at night. . . . The inside walls of this hovel were wall-papered with pages from newspapers. . . . The children all had the protruding bellies of long-term malnutrition and this was the Ukraine, the great wheat-growing region of the Soviet Union. . . . The satirical joke I had heard in a Berlin night club years ago but had never really believed had become true. "The first communists were Adam and Eve. They had no clothes to wear, had to steal apples for food, could not escape the place in which they lived and still thought that they were in paradise." The reality of the situation is that in twenty-two years of Communism a salted fish occasionally is for this family . . . the height of luxury. How this country depresses me.[32]

Even the legendary ability of the average Russian to bear hardships seemed to the *Landser* to have something nonhuman about it. "The Russians are poor souls . . . who live a rather wretched existence in their foxholes," observed Harry Mielert, then added, "But the Russian is also more primitive, animalistic, and lives more eagerly and routinely in the ground than we." Observing Russian wounded, the Italian war correspondent Curzio Malaparte remarked wonderingly: "They do not cry out, they do not groan, they do not curse. Undoubtedly there is something mysterious, something inscrutable about their stern, stubborn silence." Similarly, Erich Dwinger noted his awe of the wounded Russians:

> Several of them burnt by flamethrowers had no longer the semblance of a human face. They were blistered shapeless bundles of flesh. A bullet had taken away the lower jaw of one man. . . . Five machine-gun bullets had threshed into pulp the shoulder and arm of

another man, who was without any dressings. His blood seemed to be running out through several pipes. . . . I have five campaigns to my credit, but I have never seen anything to equal this. Not a cry, not a moan escaped the lips of the wounded. . . . Hardly had the distribution of supplies begun than the Russians, even the dying, rose and flung themselves forward. . . . The shapeless burnt bundles advanced as quickly as possible. Some half a dozen of them who were lying down also rose, holding in their entrails with one hand and stretching out the other with a gesture of supplication. . . . Each of them left behind a flow of blood which spread in an ever-increasing stream.[33]

The combustible mixture of astonishment, disgust, and fear with which many *Landsers* viewed Russians caused them to see their enemy as something unreal, the product of a brutish and menacing system that had to be eliminated. "It's not people we're fighting against here," concluded Wilhelm Prüller, "but simply animals." "The war here in Russia is totally different from former [wars] with a state," observed Corporal L.K. And he was in no doubt as to the reason, agreeing with Prüller that the Russians "are no longer people, but wild hordes and beasts, who have been bred by Bolshevism in the last 20 years. One must not allow any sympathy to grow for these people." Indeed, Corporal H.H., observing Russian prisoners, dismissed them as "stupid, animalistic, and ragged." Another soldier asserted that among "this mixture of races the devil would feel at home. It is, I believe, the most depraved and filthiest [people] living on God's earth." Karl Fuchs claimed, "Hardly ever do you see the face of a person who seems rational and intelligent. . . . The wild, half-crazy look in their eyes makes them appear like imbeciles."[34] This combination of ideology, idealism, and firsthand experience was a potent contribution to the extraordinary endurance of the *Landser*, as many, confronted by a culture that seemed alien and barbaric, brutal and threatening, believed that they were fighting for the very existence of the German community.

If the resilient and resolute *Landser* thus went beyond Jüngerian functionalism and embodied to a great extent the Nazi notion of the hard, dynamic soldier in the service of an ideal, what was it he fought for? Certainly the incessant stream of propaganda served to produce in the minds of many soldiers a legitimacy for the Nazi regime, which encouraged willing obedience. The *Landser*, perhaps to a surprising degree, carried ideological beliefs with him into the war, especially in Russia.

The consequence of incessant Nazi indoctrination in the schools, in the Hitler Youth, and in the army seemed to be a body of men with a remarkable cohesion in the face of the tribulations of war. The steady flow of racist and anti-Semitic ideological indoctrination undeniably reinforced a general sense of racial superiority on the part of many *Landsers*. But this negative integration, so thoroughly documented by Omer Bartov, could not by itself have induced the amazing resilience under conditions of extreme disintegration demonstrated by the average German soldier, a point even Bartov seems to have conceded. "When the fighting in the East physically destroyed such socially cohesive groups (primary groups), the sense of responsibility for one's comrades, even if one no longer knew them, remained extremely strong," he admitted in a significant change from his earlier position that savage fighting destroyed such connections irreparably. "At the core of this loyalty to other members of the unit was a sentiment of moral obligation." And what did this sense of obligation entail? "The new sense of existential comradeship extended also far beyond the purely military circle to encompass first the soldier's family and friends in the rear, and ultimately the Reich as a whole, if not, indeed, what the propagandists of the period referred to as 'German culture' and 'European civilization,' " Bartov asserted. "Both the worsening situation at the front and the growing impact of the war on the rear convinced increasing numbers of soldiers that they were in fact fighting for the bare existence of everything they knew and cherished."[35]

As Guy Sajer suggested, the extraordinary resilience of the German soldier demanded the celebration of a positive ideal. But where Bartov referred to home, family, and country as the rather generic ideals for which they fought, with perhaps a vague propagandistic sense of defending German and European culture, many *Landsers* in fact demonstrated a very acute sense of defending another ideal. What many "knew and cherished," what they regarded as essential to save, was precisely that new society—evidently under construction in the 1930s—for which so many had yearned after World War I, a society that would redeem Germany socially, economically, and nationally. The notion of *Volksgemeinschaft*, that seductive idea of a harmonious society which would eliminate class conflict and integrate the individual into the life of the community, holds the key to unlocking the attraction National Socialism asserted for many *Landsers*. Although the importance of the *Volksgemeinschaft* ideal as an agent of social integration within the Third Reich has long been overlooked, denied, or downplayed, it contributed greatly to Nazi success in achieving power and in creating a sense that a new society was in the offing. Especially among the young, the belief in this national community represented a rallying point, an idea that supplied the vital principle around which a new German society was to be organized.

In order to understand the motivational power of *Volksgemeinschaft* for the German soldier in World War II, one must again go back to World War I, at least in its mythical dimension. The outbreak of the Great War illustrated the intoxicating power of the idea of *Volksgemeinschaft*. With the so-called *Burgfrieden* (domestic truce) of 1914, Germany seemed to have overcome class division and internal disunity, as people from every segment of society came together in a profound wave of national enthusiasm. This promise of unity dazzled many Germans for whom the war seemed the birth pangs of, as Thomas Mann put it, a "spiritual revolution" wherein a new world and new society beckoned. Writing to the *Svenska Dagbladet* in May 1915, Mann neatly encapsulated this notion: "Why did Germany recognize and welcome [the war] when it broke upon us? Because she recognized in it the herald of her Third Reich. What is her Third Reich then? It is the synthesis of *might* and *mind*, of might and spirit; it is her dream and her demand, her highest war aim."[36]

In August 1914 many Germans believed that they had achieved just such a synthesis, as an unprecedented wave of unity swept away class divisions in a euphoric millenarian outpouring of emotion. Here, finally, was something to be worshiped. "A god at last," wrote Rainer Maria Rilke in the heady first week of war, later referring to the magical feeling of spiritual unity and idealism as "a new creature invigorated by death." Similarly, Stefan Zweig noted, "Thousands and thousands felt what they should have felt in peacetime, that they belonged together." The war, for many Germans, merged personal duty with communal demands to create a powerful sense of shared destiny. This mood deeply affected Adolf Hitler, the ultimate outsider at this point in his life; he claimed later that World War I made "the greatest of all impressions" by demonstrating that "individual interest ... could be subordinated to the common interest." The trenches of the Great War thus proved a breeding ground for a new idea, the notion that the front experience had forged a community of men in which all social and material distinctions disappeared.[37] The memory of this unity, especially in its mythical dimensions, ensured that the spirit of 1914, when a new society beckoned, would remain a potent political force in Germany.

How disillusioning the postwar period must have been for those Germans imbued with the spirit of 1914, with its political paralysis, social fragmentation, economic dislocation, interest-group squabbling, and national humiliation. What had once been tangible, the great accomplishment of the war, appeared lost, and a mood of crisis was palpable. But perhaps worst of all was the sense of spiritual malaise. The war kindled in Germans a restlessness, a desire for a restored sense of community to replace the lost unity of the war. "It is not freedom [Germans] are out to find," Hugo von Hofmannsthal claimed in 1927, "but communal bonds." The secret of Nazi popularity lay in understanding this and reviving the passions of 1914. National Socialism as an organizing idea owed its existence to the war, to the model of "trench socialism" that Hitler held so dear. As Walter von Brauchitsch, commander-in-chief of the army, noted in 1938, Hitler simply "recast the great lessons of the front-line soldier in the form of National Socialist philosophy. . . . Above and beyond all classes, a new unique fellowship of the nation has been created." The Nazis thus promised a new beginning, a national community that would restore the lost sense of belonging and camaraderie. In this respect, Nazism was idealistic, even if its idealism was based on a sense of crisis. It was a call to the national spirit, a promise of salvation on many levels. It marked a plunge into the future, but the promise of deliverance was beguiling. As Gottfried Benn remarked, "We were not all opportunists."[38]

The basis of this myth of renewal was the community of comrades forged at the front; it would serve as the cell from which a better Germany, one based on national unity and equality, would grow. The purpose, belonging, sacrifice, and meaning found in the war would be restored to a life based on values. Hitler thus proposed to transform the German *Volk* into a group of comrades, equal in status if not in function, under the strong leadership of the new man just back from the front. This National Socialist idea resonated all the more powerfully in that it appealed to many who believed it had already been realized in the trenches of World War I. "The German revolution began in the August days of 1914," exulted Robert Ley, head of the Labor Front in the Third Reich. "The people were reunited in the trenches. . . . The grenades and mines did not ask whether one was high- or low-born, if one was rich or poor, or what religion or social group one belonged to. Rather this was a great, powerful example of the meaning and spirit of community."[39]

Once in power, Hitler did not hesitate to promote both the symbol and, to a lesser extent, the substance of *Volksgemeinschaft*. Although debate rages as to how far he succeeded in recasting German society, less mystery surrounds his efforts to reshape the army.[40] Even before 1933 the *Wehrmacht* was intrigued by the notion of *Volksgemeinschaft*, seeing in it a way to promote a more cohesive and effective military force. Any future war was bound to be a total war that would require the complete mobilization of German society, so military leaders pursued the *Volksgemeinschaft* idea as a means to create an effective national unity. Both Hitler and the army leaders thus shared a vision in which the revered *Frontgemeinschaft* of World War I would be transformed into a permanent state of affairs.

Nor was this mere rhetoric. According to David Schoenbaum, even in the army the Nazis promoted "a quiet social revolution . . . [on the] premise of careers open to talent. . . . The *Wehrmacht* officer corps was en route to becoming the least snobbish in German history . . . [with a] general sympathy for the idea of *Volksgemeinschaft*." Hitler himself welcomed and championed this process. "When you look at the promotion of our younger officers," he said in a speech in September 1942, "the penetration of our National Socialist *Volksgemeinschaft* has already begun here in its full extent. There is no privilege given to a birth certificate, to a previous position in life, there is no conception of wealth, no so-called origins . . . , there is only a sole evaluation: That is the assessment of the brave, courageous, loyal man who is suited to be the leader of our people. An old world is truly being brought to a collapse. Out of this war will emerge a *Volksgemeinschaft* established through blood, much stronger even than we National Socialists through our faith could convey to the nation after the World War."[41] The twin pillars of this new *Volksgemeinschaft* would thus be the party and the army, as the Hitler Youth, Labor Service, and *Wehrmacht* worked to create and reinforce specific values important to the Nazis: camaraderie, sacrifice, loyalty, duty, endurance, courage, obedience.

The "socialist" aspect of National Socialism, in fact, made a significantly greater impact on Germans of the younger generation than is generally acknowledged. What especially gripped the imagination of many *Landsers* was Hitler's apparent ability to fulfill the promise of *Volksgemeinschaft* aborted in the defeat of 1918. Although this notion of community as actually practiced by the Nazis turned out to be chauvinistic and totalitarian, it still retained an explosive appeal because it seemed to affirm a commitment to a new society; and Hitler appeared to many the embodiment of a new force that could complete the dynamic modernization of German life. At the same time, a society based on community offered protection against the tensions and insecurities of that very modernization. The *Volksgemeinschaft* would balance individual achievement with group solidarity, competition with cooperation, as the individual fulfilled and developed his potential within the framework of community. The allure of Nazism, then, lay in its creation of the belief that one was in service to an ideal community which promoted both social commitment and integration.

Despite the coercive nature of society under Hitler, for many *Landsers* the Nazis accomplished just enough in the 1930s—in the restoration of employment, the extension of social benefits, and the promotion of equality of opportunity and social mobility—to sustain their belief that the Führer was sincere about establishing a classless, integrative society. In a study of German prisoners of war, H.L. Ansbacher discovered that large numbers of *Landsers* voiced positive opinions of such Nazi achievements as the provision of economic security and social welfare, the elimination of class distinctions and the creation of communal feelings, concern for every *Volksgenossen* (national comrade), and expanded educational opportunity for poor children. Especially prevalent was the belief that the common people and workers had benefited most from Nazi measures. According to Ansbacher, in fact, labor had more faith in Hitler than virtually all other occupational groups in Germany. To many, Hitler appeared to be "a man of the people"; indeed, a large number of prisoners of war from working-class backgrounds claimed that the Nazi regime had achieved such important socialist goals as increased educational opportunity for the poor, better job opportunities, and social justice. So pervasive was the belief in the benefits of the Nazi revolution that half of Ansbacher's sample of prisoners could find nothing at all wrong with National Socialism. "Hitler's only mistake," claimed Hermann Pfister, a miner, in a postwar interview, "was that we lost the war." And Pfister's was hardly an isolated opinion. Hitler's popularity among German POWs consistently remained above the 60 percent mark, signs of disaffection appearing only in March 1945. Nor was Hitler unaware of this appeal. He ended one of his last messages to the German people, on 24 February 1945, by asserting, "It is our firm will never to cease working for the true people's community, far from any ideology of classes, firmly believing that the eternal values of a nation are its best sons and daughters, who, regardless of birth and rank . . . must be educated and employed." "It was exactly the striving for these goals," Ansbacher concluded, "which represented the essence of the appeal National Socialism had for its followers."[42]

Volksgemeinschaft became a kind of leitmotif for many soldiers. "We stand before the burning door of Europe" exclaimed one in early September 1939, "and only a shower of faith illuminates our path." Proclaimed Hermann Witzemann in June 1941, "I would gladly die for my people and for my German Fatherland," adding almost metaphysically, "Germany was always my primary earthly thought." Siegbert Stehmann yearned for the triumph of a "unitary order, a spiritual cosmos as in the Middle Ages . . . , all-embracing, [with] faith and knowledge indivisibly united." The sense of living in intoxicating times impressed Wolfgang Döring as well, for he regarded "our era as revolutionary." Reinhard Becker-Glauch agreed, sensing in June 1942 that "this epoch appears to be very similar to a threshold."[43]

And what would this revolutionary threshold lead to? "This [battle] is for a new ideology, a new belief, a new life!" exclaimed one *Landser* in a not atypical burst of enthusiasm for "our National Socialist idea." "We know what ideals we fight for," boasted Private K.B. in April 1940, and as if finishing the thought, Hans August Vowinckel insisted in December of the same year, "Our people stands in a great struggle for its existence and for its mission. We must fight for the meaning, for the giving of meaning to this struggle. . . . Where our people fights for its existence, that is for us destiny, simple destiny." Karl Fuchs agreed, arguing in May 1941, "An individual is comparatively insignificant in war and yet, individual sacrifice in the struggle for an ideal is not in vain." And the ideal? In a later letter Fuchs claimed, "We are fighting for the existence of our entire people, of our *Volk*. . . . Our vision must be for the future because we are engaged in a struggle that will assure us of the well-being of our . . . nation." Similarly, Martin Pöppel noted in his diary, "Our joy in living and lust for life are stronger now than they've ever been, but each of us is ready to sacrifice his life for the holy Fatherland. This Fatherland is my faith, and my only hope." Long after the war the intensity of this feeling led Pöppel to reflect: "Now, forty years later, as I sit and look at these notes I wrote then, I can only shake my head in wonder at the way our young people were so inspired."[44]

An anonymous *Landser* insisted in late summer 1944 that although the war had "ripped us out of our childhood and placed us in a struggle for life," he welcomed it, because the "struggle was for our future." And he left little doubt what he meant by the future: "We have recently been frequently debating over the present war and have realized that it is the greatest religious war, for an ideology is the new stamp for the word religion. I draw faith from [Nazi ideology] that the struggle will end in a victory of our . . . beliefs." Following the German conquest of Poland, Wilhelm Prüller exulted, "It is a victory of sacred belief . . . , a victory of National Socialism," adding later, "The others are fighting for a wrong cause. . . . Today we're a different Germany from what we were! A National Socialist Germany." Nor was Prüller in any doubt as to the superiority of this new Germany: "It was the salvation of the Reich that a man arose from its lap and with great effort . . . led the people to find itself again, and provided it with the one *Weltanschauung* (ideology) that could unite the people. . . . A political leadership was established which may be described as ideal: and really one which grew out of the people themselves." Prüller concluded: "When this war ends, I shall return from it a much more fanatical National Socialist than I was before."[45]

"Every German must of course be proud of his homeland and must be happy and thankful to give his life for this country," asserted one soldier. More than mere love of country, this attitude revealed a deep commitment to a national community. "Everything small and base must be remote from us as just now it is in battle and in the face of death," Eberhard Wendebourg exclaimed. "Then the *Volksgemeinschaft*, a true goodness and love among all Germans, will be secured new and better even than in the years before the war." Friedrich Grupe recorded that in a speech given to officer candidates in May 1940 the Führer "emphasized that the German soldier should be . . . ready for any sacrifice for the German people. Always to see in our soldiers national comrades, that is our task; always we should trust the worth and the strength of the German workers. With them he would give our world new meaning, new powers."[46] A world of new content, made of new substances, better even than before the war—this notion of *Volksgemeinschaft* contributed both to the resiliency of the German soldier and to the harshness of the struggle for survival that many *Landsers* felt themselves waging.

"I am giving here much of my best strength, both physical and emotional," Günter von Scheven remarked of the first summer of war in Russia, and later, "The war is becoming a decisive fate for me. . . . What strengthens me is the insight that each individual sacrifice is necessary, because it is connected with the necessity of the whole." And Scheven left no doubt that the necessity of the whole was linked to the *Volksge-*

meinschaft. "One doesn't need to stand in a hail of grenades to experience the change in our era," he claimed. "Your attitude at home has the same consequences as ours at the front . . . because we see in you the necessary foundation for the inner frame of mind that will help determine the future. We are . . . fighting . . . in the belief that the noble and the best must prove their worth anew in the struggle with the ghastly appearance of materialism. I see the whole nation in a recasting process, in a stream of suffering and blood that will enable it to win new heights." Amid the ghastly reality of the Russian war, and perhaps despairing of Germany's ultimate victory, Scheven glimpsed a deeper meaning: "What we see here," he mused in March 1942, is "perhaps the last, unattainable expression of our time." Nor did he doubt that this aspiration was intimately bound up with the *Volksgemeinschaft.* In his last letter, written on the day he died, Scheven reflected: "All our hopes are concentrated on the homeland, the only soil with the authentic people for our creation. It is important that . . . the holy fire is not extinguished. We are internally armed."[47]

Many *Landsers*, in fact, had a clear view of a new creation centered on the homeland. "Can a vision, strong in faith, be born into a new world?" mused an anonymous soldier in a letter to his wife in August 1944. "The social order rooted in National Socialism cannot be delayed for ever." This sense of creating a new society permeated other letters as well. "Despite all its frightfulness," claimed Sebastian Mendelssohn-Bartholdy in October 1944, "the appearances of this war are only of a secondary character. The primary thing, of course, is the necessity of a new social order in the world to overcome the present contrast between acquired and inherited property, between manual and intellectual labor, between followers and leaders who move in the dazzling light." Mendelssohn-Bartholdy could not better have articulated this crucial element in Hitler's vision of a *Volksgemeinschaft* where status would be based on talent and ability, a conception that inspired a good deal of idealism. The "greatness" of the German soldier, claimed Heinz Küchler, lay precisely in going "unbowed [as] a sacrifice to a [new] world order." This was, he argued, "a new struggle for the better future." In November 1944, Mendelssohn-Bartholdy insisted that he was happy "to be one of the nameless in the greater community who takes on every sacrifice for the war in order to serve a future that we don't know and yet in which we still believe." The future was manifest to Klaus-Degenhard Schmidt, who exclaimed in December 1944, "The development of the nation . . .

is for me the goal of this struggle. Only with this premise can every sacrifice be demanded. . . . To me my nation is an earthly law. . . . I believe in its holy purpose and goals, in its reality as divine providence. It fights for its existence against a world. . . . It will undergo its spiritual struggle until the end. We may be allowed to sacrifice and help. At stake is the secret as well as the outward Germany. Every year of distress and war was a school, whose meaning was evident despite all the suffering."[48]

The *Landser* often embraced the notion of *Volksgemeinschaft* with a startling passion, seeing in it the justification for his own sacrifices. "With us soldiers, whoever excludes himself from the comradeship doesn't belong to us and would be disowned and publicly denounced before the entire company, and you [at home] should do it as well," admonished Private W.P. "The entire *Volk* should know such people, so that they recognize who their enemies are." Trapped in Stalingrad, another *Landser* asserted, "I do not begrudge the fate that has placed me here. The harsh difficulty, which could still last for months . . . , is to us merely a requirement of a higher fulfillment of duty, a higher service to the community." "I suddenly feel a great strength," declared Lieutenant H.H., also ensnared in the Stalingrad cauldron. "In times of distress there is only one commandment. What is the individual, when the life of the nation is at stake?" Echoed Lieutenant H.B.: "This war compels us again to make the deepest exertions of all of our powers. . . . But still we want to hold on because we know: it must be done for our own, for our children's, and our people's future. And because we have the belief that our people is not yet exhausted, still has vigorous powers that give it a claim on the future. . . . If we stick it out now, then we have a future. . . . It is terrible that such sacrifices are demanded of us as there in Stalingrad. But the Führer will know why they are necessary."[49]

The cause of *Volksgemeinschaft* led Karl Fuchs to exclaim to his wife, "With loyalty and a sense of duty we must fight for our principles and endure to the end. Our Führer represents our united German Fatherland. . . . What we do for him, we do for all of you; what we sacrifice in foreign lands, we sacrifice for all of you. . . . We believe . . . in the future of our people and our Fatherland. . . . It is our most holy duty and our most beautiful assignment to fight and struggle for this future. It is worthy of every sacrifice we can make." For some, this faith seemed a daily reality. Retreating in the winter of 1943, hungry and bereft of supplies, Guy Sajer nonetheless marveled at "the unity of the *Wehrmacht*. . . . The sense of order which was part of National Socialism was still very much alive among the troops who were fighting for it." In late 1944 Sajer still wondered that he and his comrades "could live only for the cause, . . . and despite all the difficulties and disappointments I had endured, I still felt closely linked to it." "We are advancing an idea of unity," he remembered that his beloved Captain Wesreidau had claimed, "which is neither rich nor easily digestible, but the vast majority of the German people accept it and adhere to it, forging and forming it in an admirable collective effort. . . . We are trying . . . to change the face of the world."[50]

We are trying to change the face of the world; many *Landsers* did indeed see their mission as the creation of a new world. Harry Mielert, in November 1941, spoke of a "fervent seeking after new forms," and a month later Friedebald Kruse emphasized the fierce "desires and require-ments being placed on the new [society]." "We held to this one final idea [of a new society] which would justify our sufferings," Sajer asserted. On another occasion he recalled an officer's injunction: "Think of yourselves as the trailblazers of the European revolution." In June 1942, praising a fellow soldier as "the best comrade," Friedrich Grupe called him "open, without arrogance, and very brave, . . . full of sympathy and understanding for his men. . . . He was . . . a faithful harbinger of a new Germany."[51]

A harbinger of a new Germany: as a soldier put it in September 1943, "We just feel ourselves to be the hearld of our future nation. And that as *Landsers*. There are no individual destinies here." Another *Landser* rejoiced in like fashion in August 1941, "Never has a vision, the soul, an idea. . . , the superiority of a thought . . . so triumphed as today." Claimed yet another, "*We* know what the Führer is fighting for and we don't want to stand in the rear, but rather to be constantly endeavoring to be faithful followers! And should fate also demand sacrifice of blood and property from us, then we will grit our teeth and with determined brow, defiance on our tongue, say: I'll do it. Long live the Führer and his great work!"[52]

Other *Landsers* confirmed this sense of fighting for a new Germany under Hitler. Writing in April 1940, Corporal E.N. declared that "as long as we front soldiers have Adolf Hitler, there will be loyalty, bravery, and justice for his people. I believe that the best days . . . are just coming," because "there will be a day on which the people will have their freedom, peace, and equality returned to them." For many, faith like this meant that no conditions were placed on their loyalty to Hitler. "Now, where the Fatherland has called us," Wilhelm Rubino exclaimed in a letter to his mother, "I belong life and death to the Führer, and you should not despair if the worst should happen to me." "As with me," Grupe later confessed, "all *Landsers* were deeply bound by oath, orders, obedience, and—this still counted for many—by the unshakable belief in Hitler's final victory."[53]

In fact, the July 1944 assassination attempt on Hitler seemed actually to bind many *Landsers* tighter to the Führer and the Nazi regime. "We here in foreign lands really know what a good leader we Germans have" claimed one soldier. Another declared simply, "Now we will be more determined than ever to prove to the others why we German soldiers fight." Private K.K. "greatly welcomed" a Nazification of the army, for an ideological organization "will be better than that previously implemented." Reacting to the assassination attempt, Private B.P. wrote indignantly, "Thank God that Providence allowed our Führer to continue his task of the salvation of Europe, and our holiest duty is now to cling to him even more strongly, in order to make good what the few criminals . . . did without regard for the [welfare of] the entire nation." Lieutenant K.N. thought it "unspeakably tragic that the enemy nations will see symptoms of disunity, where before they perhaps supposed only a unanimous solidity." Corporal C.B. emphasized that unity came from loyalty to Hitler: "I know very well that an unrestrained trust and a strong unshakable belief in our Führer is necessary to overcome this momentarily difficult period," he wrote in August 1944. "Belief gives us the strength to bear all the hard and difficult misfortune. . . . My belief in the Führer and victory is unshakeable. . . . The Führer has always kept his word." To Corporal A.K., Adolf Hitler was "the man who will bring a New Order to Europe and above all also the freedom of all the peoples. How the nation rejoiced . . . that the beloved Führer lived. . . . His death would have been a bad blow to the freedom of the peoples." "These bandits tried to destroy that for which millions are ready to risk their lives," exclaimed Lieutenant H.W.M. indignantly. "It is a good feeling to know that a November 1918 cannot be repeated."[54]

November 1918 represented to many Germans an example of a nation defeated because of internal disunity. Such a happenstance was not likely to recur, according to Reinhard Pagenkopf in his last letter in February 1945, not least because "like all soldiers, I have become something else. Perhaps our belief in many things is also shaken. . . . But the best and greatest, I think, we have nonetheless saved, and that can no longer be taken from us, because it has grown too deeply with us. . . , a certainty that no one can take from us. . . : 'the Reich must yet remain with us!' " "I have found out that culture is only in its smallest part a matter of reason," mused Reinhard Goes in November 1941. "Rather, above all [it is] a matter of the heart, soul, genuine feeling, belief . . . [in] Germany . . . , the homeland toward which I have a great obligation." To the end, this powerful, profound, almost mystical sense of defending not only Germany but a valuable idea remained strong in many soldiers. Reflecting on the world situation in September 1944, Lieutenant K. asserted, "History is today showing a picture that one could term the bankruptcy of the West. What Nietzsche proclaimed a dead world is today hard reality. . . . What is spirit? A function of the material. . . ! What is culture? The realization of the liberal idea. . . ! What the English and Americans win with their blood passes over days later to Bolshevism. . . . In this chaos . . . stands Germany. . . . We are the last bastion, with us stands and falls all that German blood has created over the centuries." As Lieutenant H.H. put it with powerful brevity, "A tangible conception of a country is the only thing that matters. " Indeed, insisted Private F.S., "The German people as the bearer of the creative heritage will not go under!"[55]

Even after the war, unrepentant soldiers such as Hans Werner Woltersdorf clung to the "tried and tested nationalism of the community," taking pride in the "National Socialist idealism [that] redeemed us" after the humiliation of World War I. "My generation was brought up to believe that no sacrifice was too great for the [*Volksgemeinschaft*]," remembered Ulrich Luebke. "The philosophy we were taught was that Germany must live even if we had to die for it." "We believed in a new community, free from class conflict, united in brotherhood under the self-chosen Führer, powerful . . ., national and socialist," agreed Friedrich Grupe, and many people of his generation thought that Hitler, too, believed in this ideal and was doing much to realize it. "The Nazis had set out to impose a new order on the disquieting complexities and social upheavals that the modernization of the twenties had brought with it," suggested Detlev Peukert, and "as they promised, to bring harmony." After the war, Peukert noted, "the mood of *Wirtschaftswunder* [economic miracle] and take-off now profited from the very destruction of tradition and recasting . . . brought about by the Third Reich."[56]

As their letters and diaries illustrated, many *Landsers* indeed wanted a life different from the one they had lived before, a life based on something similar to the sense of community they felt in the army (though without the killing and fear) a life of men bound together in a common endeavor who frankly embraced each other as equals. With modern models and mythic images borrowed from the trenches of the Great War, the Nazis set out to substitute harmony and a feeling of community for the intense upheavals produced by war and economic modernization. "The intention of the movement was to create a new type of human being from whom would spring a new morality, a new social system, and eventually a new international order," Modris Eksteins has noted. "National Socialism was more than a political movement. . . ; it was a desire to create mankind anew." Indeed, Hitler aimed at nothing less than a reorganization of traditional society and the creation of a *Volksgemeinschaft* of social integration where class conflict had vanished. Stripped of its ideological overtones, the Nazi vision of modernization without internal conflict and a political community that provided both security and opportunity seemed not unattractive, for as Peukert observed, "The National Socialists' pervasive intervention in society had meant that it was impossible in 1945 simply to resurrect the conditions of 1932. . . . For most people, the opportunities for integration which in the thirties had been promised but not always delivered, were now realized. *Volkswagen, Volkseigenheim, Volksempfänger*, a car, a home, and a radio (and later a television) set of one's own; these symbols shed the ideological overtones of the Nazi era."[57] To many Germans it was, and remained, so potent a vision of the future that they willingly overlooked its racist and anti-Semitic ideological essence. Nazi efforts to create a new order and new man were real and, as the example of many *Landsers* showed, could inspire a fierce loyalty and devotion. In the quest for the utopian, however, both the ideal and those average soldiers who fought to realize it were perverted by Hitler's racism and sucked into a sea of evil.

9. THE LOST YEARS

Writing in his diary from the eastern front in early May 1942, Helmut Pabst reflected on the personal impact of the war: "The soul . . . becomes still harder and more serious, further removed from petty things. A harsh judgment molds you, which can leave you badly marked." Still, in an attempt to give a positive sense to what otherwise might seem lost years, Pabst insisted:

> But in front of the bleak ground of our existence . . . the beauty of our lost youth appears in a gleaming radiance. . . . All of us have cut ourself off from a carefree life. But that leads not to weariness, not to resignation, for it is . . . a question of asserting yourself. . . . The will to life unfolds powerfully. . . . You live for the moment. . . . Just to live is happiness. But even in the serious moments you feel a life full of content. It is bitter and sweet, all and one, . . . because we have learned to see the essential. . . . In such hours emerges a will to . . . build a second life out of our knowledge. This will rules us with such a power that in this instant the soul cannot be damaged.

Almost exactly a year later Pabst returned to the theme of time lost: "Our life has its age. When the years diminish . . . you can only grit your teeth. It is childish to think that we might be compensated for this. For what possibilities a personal life loses with the peeling away of the years cannot be made up. . . . But perhaps it is also childish to speak of this subject anyway. I tell myself that, because more than in all previous wars our thoughts turn on the sense of events. And I see my attitude in this question neither fully clarified nor free of doubts."[1]

Although Pabst himself, killed in Russia in September 1943, lived neither to confront the meaning of the war nor to discover whether one could recover lost years, his reflections accurately foreshadowed the experiences of many who did survive. At the end of the war, with Germany collapsing and chaos all around, the immediate goal of most *Landsers* was simply to escape the *Kettenhunde*—the guard dogs of the military police—or the roving courts martial of the SS and get home alive. As one put it succinctly, "My first priority was naked survival, not moral regeneration."[2] But as life returned to some semblance of stability, if not normality, they inevitably began to look for meaning in their activities. Most had mixed feelings, realizing as they did the horrors of war yet also perceiving, however reluctantly, something positive in their experiences. For virtually all, the war had been a watershed, impossible either to dismiss or to forget. Branded by its harshness, these men sensed that they remained linked with others who had participated and, equally, that an outsider could not possibly understand the world they had endured—hence their feeling of isolation, as if they were in society but yet detached from it.

Part of the problem in coming to terms with their war experience stemmed from the fact that the ordinary *Landser* saw himself as a decent fellow. As Alfons Heck, a former Hitler Youth leader and soldier, confessed, "I never once during the Hitler years thought of myself as anything but a decent, honorable young German."[3] Precisely because of that self-perception it proved difficult for many to bear when, at the end of the war and later, they were told that the things they had done as young men—hard and distasteful things that had cost the lives of so many of their friends, were not only mistaken but evil. This verdict was especially perplexing to those who in their own eyes had merely sought to do what they had been told was their duty. Now their experiences seemed stripped of any meaning. Some clung to National Socialist values and continued to believe in the old leaders in order to lend their deeds and sacrifices some purpose. Others sank into a sullen apathy or gave way to bitter disillusionment with politics, in either case withdrawing into a private world that few could enter.

For many who had known only faith in Hitler, obedience, and fighting, the end of the war brought a crumbling of their value system, and with their belief in Hitler shattered they found themselves left with only a sense of emptiness and painful disappointment. "The world appears hopeless and bleak to me," wrote Walter D. bitterly in his diary at the end of the war. "The biggest screamers, who were already in the Party when it barely existed, they now were never in the Party. . . . Yeah, I've learned . . . bitter wisdom and have paid with my faith, had to pay with a shattered world of ideals. Within me it is bleak. . . . I was once an idealist; today I am no longer one. What is man except misery? Full of pain, I think of all the young comrades who in all this disastrous confusion never found that they had been wasted. . . . Will they ever find a belief?" A seventeen-year-old soldier declared in despair to the equally young Helmut Altner in the ruins of Berlin at the very end of the war, "Give it up. Life has lost its meaning. . . ! The years in which you have up to now existed are gone forever."[4] If the war really had been senseless, however, equally pointless were the exertions and sacrifices of the men involved, having many former *Landsers*, in their attempt at retrospective assessments, hesitant and uncertain. They could hardly seek justification in National Socialist values, but many also felt an undeniable attachment to what they had perceived as striving after a new social order.

Martin Pöppel reflected this ambivalence in his account of going into captivity at the end of the war. For two hours every day for ten days, Pöppel found himself interrogated by a British Captain, who wanted to know "not about the war as such. . . . Instead, he wanted to see into the heart and soul of a young (and in his opinion still fanatical) officer of Hitler. . . . He tried patiently to show me the evil of the Hitler regime, but failed because of my obstinacy and a kind of blind Nibelungen loyalty which still held me in its grip. I had survived, but I didn't see any reason for me to crawl to these moneybags. . . . In those early days I still couldn't see how the German people had been misused. . . . We men had been educated to stubborn, blind obedience. By the end of the war I had certainly become more critical, but cured, completely cured, I was not." Although he admitted that "in that camp I saw whole worlds collapse," Pöppel's experience illustrates all the complexity of the readjustment process, from his ideologically driven contempt for the British as class-ridden colonialists to his insistence that the average *Landser* had fought to the bitter end primarily because of his fear of harsh Allied retribution associated with the Morgenthau Plan (a proposal made in 1943 by U.S. Treasury Secretary Henry Morgenthau to destroy all industry in postwar Germany). "At the end of the war we were completely demoralized," Pöppel admitted at one point, but then hastened to add, "After some time in captivity . . . the spirit of battle had been reawakened. . . . Perhaps we were just stubborn, not prepared to accept the collapse of our world, the devaluation of all values. In any case, we were drawing new strength from these setbacks."[5]

For all his bravado, however, ambivalence haunted Pöppel. "The vast majority of us were soldiers, often credulous soldiers, but not executioners and not monsters," he insisted. "We had been committed to Germany, but now we had to find new meaning in our lives. Each one of us would have to struggle alone for himself and his family, without being able to stand shoulder-to-shoulder with other soldiers, without the comradeship . . . to support us." Pöppel illustrated both the self-image of the *Landser* as a decent guy and the painful difficulty of finding sense in a shattered world stripped even of basic fellowship. Significantly, he now recognized that, "personal responsibility, which the Führer took away from us, could no longer be avoided." Still, the old identity proved stubborn and hard to discard: "Only in the field is man worth something." Nor could Pöppel easily rid himself of his ideological underpinnings. He betrayed more than a hint of admiration for the unrepentant Nazis in the camp, suggesting that they were "the idealists. Not one bowed head, not one democratic whimper, only discipline and order. . . . For them all explanations were a swindle, the war and its end were the unjust judgment of the world, and the Nazi system remained their ideal. . . . What was especially tragic was that these idealists were often potentially among the best men." Although criticizing their attitude, Pöppel still admitted, "But I could understand them." Indeed, Pöppel counterposed these self-disciplined men of integrity, these unshaken Nazis, with the man he called "our model democrat," who was found guilty of embezzlement from the camp store he managed. "But we all knew about his character," Pöppel wrote contemptuously, "the way he denied his Germanness, and his democratic whimperings."[6]

Among others who found it difficult to adjust to the post-Nazi world was Hans Woltersdorf, who could see no point in discussing the reasons behind the war with his American captor: "His country isn't surrounded by a dozen hostile neighbors; it isn't in danger and hasn't been attacked. He fought . . . for an ideal that was different from our understanding of a nation, a people. . . . He came from an America that hadn't developed organically." Even after the war Woltersdorf spoke positively of "the tried and tested nationalism of the community" and referred contemptuously to de-Nazification and reeducation as "merely the revenge that could be expected" from the victors. In a prisoner-of-war camp Woltersdorf exclaimed to his interrogator, "Until now I was only a soldier, I never bothered with Nazi propaganda or with politics. . . . But here I am, locked up with nothing but Nazis, . . . and I'm beginning to be interested, . . . and I must confess to you that these Nazis are thoroughly decent fellows. . . . If I wasn't a Nazi before, then I'm becoming one now."[7]

This cannot be dismissed as mere bravado, for Woltersdorf highly esteemed the "National Socialist idealism [by which we] redeemed ourselves from an economic grave," as well as the "economic, social, and ethical achievements" of the Nazi regime. To him, the postwar world represented nothing so much as anarchy and chaos. "All our former values of fatherland, comradeship and chivalry, discipline and duty, achievement and order, had been condemned; for they were the roots of those evils from which tyranny, oppression, and crime had grown," he wrote bitterly. "The logical conclusion of the postwar generation was that . . . if former ideals of obedience, discipline, and order were the causes of the chaos, then the opposite must also have the opposite effect. And so they opposed every system of order, while the ever-new ideal of freedom affected primarily the lower instincts and found fulfillment in beat, bed, and hash"[8] (rock music, free love, and drugs).

If Pöppel was stubborn and Woltersdorf remained defiant, many others were simply puzzled as they tried to come to grips with what had happened, and their all-too-human frailties of judgment and foresight. With the end fast approaching, many true believers began to have their doubts. "Many of us have long ago fallen at the front," noted Friedrich Grupe in March 1945, "still in firm belief in our Führer and in the justice of his actions." Yet despite the brave words and the declaration "We will never capitulate," Grupe clearly was troubled. "I am struggling to get a grip on myself," he admitted in late March. "It is clear to me that each death in the final phase of this conflict, every further destruction, is totally irresponsible." Not surprisingly, then, upon hearing of the final surrender, Grupe exclaimed, "Naturally it is clear that in these hours and days, for myself and for millions, a world has foundered, an ideology collapsed, that it has now become a certainty: everything that we did in this war, for which millions upon millions died, was the consequence of power and megalomania!" Even with this realization, though, Grupe shrank from the final recognition: "But with the fatalism of a soldier I now simply push such insights away, for within me there is no room for self-destructive thoughts. The important thing is that the dying has come to an end."[9]

Fifty years after the outbreak of the war, Grupe still refused to acknowledge fully his flash of insight in March 1945, remarking that the war made him a political abstinent, explaining that he and his generation had embraced Hitler because of political inexperience, hunger, and misery, and stressing the idealism of his feelings by eschewing opportunism as a motive. But Grupe betrayed an attachment to his earlier ideals, for although paying obeisance to democracy and a spirit of European community, he nonetheless admitted, "Even with all the thoroughgoing changes in me, and certainly in all the surviving members of the war generation, one thing remains the same: the love for the fatherland, if also free of the once so excessive nationalism." Grupe, indeed, sounded much like Woltersdorf when he lamented, "The misuse of our feelings that were uttered in words like 'comradeship,' 'fatherland,' and 'homeland' led to a total devaluation. In many cases, materialism, egoism, and indifference replaced the onetime youthful exuberance of emotions. Instead of praying to a 'Führer,' it appears as if the successor generation now worships new gods: money and 'status.' The striving after affluence can make one cold and inconsiderate."[10] Despite all the horrors inflicted on Germany and the world because of Nazi-induced and -inflamed passions, Grupe still found it difficult at the end of his reflections to discard the old ideals, nor did he appear to see the incongruity of admonitions about the dangers of materialism coming from a person who had been a willing and enthusiastic supporter of Nazi idealism.

Ensconced in a Russian labor camp and not destined to be freed until 1949, Siegfried Knappe also grappled with the larger meaning of the war and his participation in it. "Losing the war . . . preyed on my mind," he acknowledged. "Being captured had always been a real possibility, . . . but surrendering our country? . . . I felt stunned now, almost as if I were in someone else's bad dream. The war had shattered my life and left only a deep void. . . . It was a feeling of deep desperation." Nor was Knappe able to shake this gloom or the inclination to brood, to seek the sense in what appeared so hopeless, since he now no longer had a nation to return to. "I spent much of those first three weeks [in captivity] going over Germany's experience of the previous six years. Where had we gone so wrong?" he pondered. "I felt that Germany's claim to the Rhineland, the Sudetenland, and the Polish Corridor had been justified. . . . Hitler annexed Austria as a result of a plebiscite by the Austrian people. I felt that our invasion of France had been justified because France had declared war on us." Still, a glimmer of comprehension began to creep into Knappe's reflections:

> It was only now beginning to dawn on me that our treatment of other nations had been arrogant, that the only justification we had felt necessary was our own. . . . I had unquestioningly accepted the brutal philosophy that might makes right; the arrogance of our national behavior had not even occurred to me at the time. . . . What had begun, at least in our minds, as an effort to correct the injustices of the Treaty of Versailles had escalated far beyond anything that any of us could have imagined. In retrospect, I realized that I, and countless others like me, had helped Hitler start and fight a world war of conquest that had left tens of millions of people dead and destroyed our own country. I wondered now whether I would ever have questioned these things if we had won the war. I had to conclude that it was unlikely. This was a lesson taught by defeat, not by victory.[11]

Eventually, however, Knappe, like Grupe, turned away from a full embrace of his understanding. In contemplating the evidence of death camps and the attempt to exterminate a whole people, Knappe could only profess, "We had thought of our participation in the war as noble and honorable. . . . I was sickened by this news. I finally decided that my inability to come to terms with it was going to chip away at my mental and emotional strength . . . so I filed the issue away in a dark corner of my mind. . . . I had to accept the fact that it happened . . . but I did not have to like it or discuss it." For Knappe, as for many of his contemporaries, guilt was seen as objective, not subjective. "I could not escape my share of the guilt, because without us Hitler could not have done the horrible things he had done," he was quick to admit, but then came the all-important qualifier, "but as a human being, I felt no guilt, because I had no part in or knowledge of the things he had done."[12]

Similarly, Alfons Heck puzzled that "a civilized, humane people had allowed ourselves to become indifferent to brutality committed by our own government." Yet in the end his analysis verged on self-pity: "I developed a harsh resentment toward our elders, especially our educators. Not only had they allowed themselves to be deceived, they had delivered us, their children, into the cruel power of a new God." Heck concluded that despite their enthusiastic support for Hitler, his generation filled the role of victim as surely as those cruelly murdered by Nazi aggression: "Tragically, now, we are the other part of the Holocaust, the generation burdened with the enormity of Auschwitz. That is our life sentence, for we became the enthusiastic victims of our Führer." Similarly, though confessing that, "I and with me millions of Germans turned to [Hitler] as the Führer, willingly fought and died honorably for him," Friedrich Grupe still professed shock at the remark of German President Richard von Weizsäcker—himself the son of a diplomat who had served the Nazis—in October 1988 that "the German people were led by criminals and let themselves be led by criminals." "Without a reconciliatory and clarifying word to the onetime soldiers," Grupe complained, "this is a bitter obituary for the millions of German war dead whose death under the swastika was pronounced: 'fallen for *Volk* and Führer.' " Even Claus Hansmann, certainly no apologist for Hitler or the Nazis, at the end of the war fell victim to the "victim" claim: "We are no heroes. . . . Heroes? What are we? Poor, mistreated, mutilated victims of a . . . nightmare."[13]

If some *Landsers* sought but largely failed to discover a larger meaning to the war, many others refused even to consider the greater dimensions of their experiences. For them the war was and remained a personal matter, to be measured in individual gain or loss. Certainly, returning to a devastated homeland that no longer even existed as a nation, viewing the awesome destruction of German cities that had become less places of habitation than piles of rubble, facing the difficulties of readjustment to a civilian society that was not the same as the one they had left, recognizing that they had no careers to return to—all this emphasized for many the solitary nature of their burden. After the war, men found themselves searching everywhere for the lost years, knowing that they could never find them. Those years had been stolen, never to be recovered, and with this realization came either a lingering bitterness or a deep determination not to think of the loss but to work doubly hard to succeed with the remainder of one's life.

Stunned by the extent of the destruction in Germany, many *Landsers* allowed their immediate thoughts to revolve around the notion of luck. Returning home from English captivity in late March 1946, Martin Pöppel was struck that "the mood here was almost . . . completely apathetic. . . . Everywhere there were just women and boys working in patched old uniforms, examining bricks, searching through the ruins for anything that could be used. Then the train journey with its unending procession of shattered towns, villages, factories. . . . The sight made us draw in our breaths . . . , it made us fear for the future." Still, as Pöppel neared his old home in the Munich suburbs, all he could think about was his luck: he was "reporting back after five years of war and one year of captivity in England." Likewise, Siegfried Knappe confessed that he "was finding it difficult to 'justify' my luck during the entire war. I had to accept it as my destiny without feeling guilt . . . that I had lived when so many others had died." Fifty years after the war began, Claus Hansmann referred bitterly to "the careless assessments of those 'graced by a late birth,' " although he admitted that "the only thing that remains with me [from the war] is the most pleasant puzzle of my life: my survival in the field."[14]

Many *Landsers* were convinced that one had to have had luck to survive. They viewed it as something mystical yet almost tangible, a presence that had accompanied the fortunate ones, a quality or property that they came to see as almost a moral lesson of history, as if one had been anointed by "chance" or "fate" for survival. With an emphatic staunchness, Ernst-Peter Kilian appraised his survival as the result of an inscrutable force that had protected him when by all rights he should have been killed. "I have always stressed that I had an improbable luck as a soldier," he admitted, then repeated his statement as if he himself almost didn't believe it: "On the whole I must say that I had completely unlikely good fortunes of war." In like fashion, Hans-Hermann Riedel puzzled afterward that during the war "I was always dodging death." Riedel not only spoke of having luck but sought somehow to make it into a tangible force that had accompanied him. Thus he "escaped by the skin of my teeth," "survived [an air attack] out in the open," "came out of it yet again," and—recalling another bombing raid that killed many of his comrades—"I had been there ever so shortly before." Perhaps troubled by his good fortune, Riedel could explain it only as the result of a force outside himself that favored him for whatever reason. Others, such as Otto Richter and Hugo Nagel, referred as well to an "improbable luck" but transformed the concept into a religious one, both men using such words as "fate," "destiny," "providence," "chance," and "miracle."[15] Hoping to find some sense in their survival but gnawed by the suspicion that it was undeserved, they sought solace in religious explanations of their good fortune. Many former *Landsers* almost had to turn to mystical explanations, so improbable did their survival amid the enormous slaughter seem to them. They could only conclude that fate, in a magical and personal sort of way, had been kind to them.

Despite feeling fortunate to have returned from the war alive, many *Landsers* nonetheless retained a simmering personal resentment at what they saw as stolen years. Even during the war, in fact, some had glimpsed an unsalvageable future. "The last few days were again so gruesome, the nights so tormenting, that they were like what is recounted about olden times, when the people saw gloom in each and every night," despaired Harald Henry. "Here in the snowy fields of Russia our best powers are being murdered, not only in these years that we have lost here but also for the coming ones; even if we return, we are still cheated of the future, enfeebled, beaten down, and numb. An all-consuming hate, a really total void, is gathering in our breast."[16] Henry did not have to face this bleak future; he was killed less than three weeks after writing this letter.

Both Uwe Pries and Emil Dahlke, however, retained their bitterness about the stolen years long after the war ended. "I mean," Pries tried to explain, "in any case they already took many years from us. You can say that our generation is still being swindled. . . . You can say that from '39 really to '49, almost ten years they took from us as well." Dahlke, more than Pries, emphasized the sense of having been the victim of a fraud: "I think that my generation . . . has been swindled twice in our lives, if you take into consideration that we had nothing at all of our youth. Then came the war when we were in a position to marry . . . and what was there? Again, everything was gone. The postwar period, these years—well, you still had nothing."[17] Clearly, both former soldiers believed strongly that the war had cheated them of the normal patterns of life, of the possibility of marrying, starting a family, pursuing a career.

For many, this sense of loss never went away. Arthur Pieper, as an elderly man still yearning wistfully for the six and a half years of his life taken by the war, concluded painfully that "the best years were lost to us." What this notion meant was perhaps best illustrated by Heinz Rieckmann, who was born in 1922, drafted into the army in 1940, and not released from Russian captivity until 1950. "Therefore I did not marry until 1958," he recalled. "I first made up my bachelor period, because I had lost my youth. . . . And in the few years that I was still a bachelor I let off a bit of steam. Then I married." Rieckmann's account illustrates the personal nature of the lost years, for by the time he returned to civilian life and "let off steam," he clearly faced severely limited possibilities in life. Little wonder, then, that many former *Landsers* nursed a sense of grievance. "When I look back I am filled with a total rage at the stolen years that have been very decisive in our whole development," Gerd S. fumed, then added significantly, "and perhaps also over the fact that at that time we were also not more courageous in rejecting the whole thing."[18]

Most men, of course, simply wanted as quickly as possible to return to civilian life and begin the process of building a new existence, but here too they felt themselves victims of a swindle. They could not just return to a career, since most had not had the opportunity to begin one. "Yeah, it was also lost time," answered Ewald Döring when asked his impression of the war years. "Today the people—well, they can go into their occupation, and those are the years that we missed. . . . [And] on that day [of capitulation] . . . [jobs] were no longer there."[19]

Others too remembered the war primarily as an interruption in their occupational pursuits. Walter Nowak, born in 1926, also emphasized the theme of lost years, which seemed especially acute to him since he was on the verge of beginning a career. "They stole ten years of my life," he argued. "For Führer, *Volk*, and Fatherland. For you see, I began an apprenticeship in '41, finished the apprenticeship in '43 after a successful journeyman's examination, and then two months later I was drafted into the army. . . . Ten years of my life, yeah the best, they stole from me."[20] Taken prisoner by the French in 1945, Nowak signed up with the French foreign legion for five years to escape the poor conditions in the POW camp, so his estimate of ten years lost to *Wehrmacht* service is not accurate. Nevertheless, Nowak believed that the war had systematically hindered the pursuit of his career and thereby unnaturally restricted his possibilities in future life. Both Döring and Nowak, like many other *Landsers*, felt that they had lost the ability to determine their own lives, that they had fallen behind in the normal progression of training, job, marriage, career and had never quite caught up.

Some men failed to readjust to civilian life at all. Michael Hörbach, himself a war veteran, chronicled in his postwar novel *Die verratenen Söhne* (Betrayed Sons) the disillusionment, the problems of readjustment, the difficulty in shaking off the imprint of war. Through the characters of Walter Richards and Hugo Fischer, men seeking unsuccessfully to find a stable existence after the war, Hörbach created a powerful sense of loss, of the hole left by the war which remained unfilled even seven years after the capitulation.

"We have lost everything in the war," Richards said. "They have taken everything from us. We look for it, but we can no longer find it. . . . All the young men search after something that no longer exists. . . ."

"How come they can't just forget it?" asked Fischer.

"Can you really forget those years?" asked Richards. "The years that we lost? That made out of you what you are? The great hole. . . ? I was seventeen when they took me. I was twenty-one when they spit me back. And then the miserable period afterward. I look for the lost years everywhere, but I know that I will never find them."

Later, thinking back on the conversation, Fischer wondered:

"What has overcome us. . . ?" He didn't know the answer. . . . His conversation with Richards came back to him, and he thought of the lost years. . . . He had run after the lost years, but had never been able to catch up. . . .

Even without the war perhaps everything would have turned out badly, he told himself. But owing to the war I certainly did so. . . . It had destroyed him. . . . He was not the only one, but that didn't help him. There were millions of others, . . . but the decisive thing was that he was one of the millions.[21]

For the fictional Fischer and those he represented, the war was ever present. No matter how fast they ran they could neither escape the memories of their experiences nor make good the years they had lost. For the "great hole" was not so much the physical loss of these years as the personal sense of despair, disillusionment, and melancholy that accompanied their later lives. As Richards tried to explain to one who had not experienced these years:

At the beginning of 1946 I came back to Frankfurt. I wanted a new life. . . . I told myself . . . you must forget the pain. . . . That allowed me to live for a little while. . . . In the first months after the war you had too much to do to get a roof over your head and a stomach full of food. But the more everything got back to normal, the more time you had left to think. . . . From then on I knew that I was living a life without a purpose or a goal. . . .

It is not so much that it happened, but rather how it happened. . . . They died a senseless death. . . . A life thrown away.

There were millions in this war who perished senselessly . . . and that is the important thing.[22]

For the character Richards—and perhaps for the author Hörbach as well, who committed suicide in 1988—the only lesson of the war was its senselessness: people killed to no purpose at the time, others living a hollow life afterward.

Much of the war literature published in Germany in the first postwar decade was a literature of the "little man," of the corporals and privates who saw the conflict from the perspective of the foxhole. One-time *Landsers* writing from their own personal experiences—novelists such as Michael Hörbach, Heinrich Gerlach, Hans Hellmut Kirst, Wolfgang Ott, and Willi Heinrich—sought to portray the essence of the war "from below," perhaps in the hope thereby of breaking out of their own war-imposed isolation, of making the complexity and ambiguity of their experiences more accessible to others. Critics of this approach, themselves former soldiers such as Heinrich Böll and Alfred Andersch, refused to accept the "normality" of an everyday life in war, especially one fought for National Socialist purposes, and instead sought to illustrate how the war had destroyed the lives and sense of identity of those caught in its midst.[23] Between these two poles of thought lay the problem of interpretation: Should the war experience be shown in its personal aspects, which ran the risk of ignoring or normalizing Nazi crimes, or should it stress the larger issues of Nazi and German guilt, thereby distancing itself from the sufferings and perspective of the "little man"?

At the level of the bookstore, the debate was resolved in favor of neither of these approaches. Although many of the earlier "common soldier" novels have been reissued, and Böll—as the first German author to win the Nobel Prize for literature since Thomas Mann (1929)—looms large on the literary scene, both have been overshadowed in the popular imagination by the pulp fiction of the so-called *Landser-Hefte*, inexpensive serial novels that appear regularly on German newsstands. Ostensibly published as a warning never again to go to war, these novels in fact blur the complexity of the *Landser* experience, reducing the war to an idyllic adventure full of camaraderie and courage, with the hero taking part in exciting, romantic exploits.[24] Since these novels purport to depict historical events, and the majority of their readers are under the age of twenty-five, they run the risk of recreating in the Federal Republic the siege of war novels that belabored Weimar by glorifying the supposed liberating qualities of combat.

For those *Landsers* whose letters and diaries been published post-humously, or who later wrote memoirs of their experiences, the popularity of the *Landser-Hefte* mocks the authenticity of their everyday experiences. Amid a perplexing array of daily challenges, emotions, and perceptions, the average German soldier sought primarily to stay alive and to do what he had been told was his duty. Only after the war did most come to a realization that they had been not just victims but perpetrators of Nazi crimes, an insight that merely made the meaning of the war and their activities more problematic. "The war is now over. The Moloch has spewed me out again," Willy Schröder reflected just after the capitulation. "I'm left, not by my own wish, not through my own merit . . . intoxicated by the will to destruction, made happy by a liberated, carefree life purified by suffering, everything profound and complete. Like a delirium it is behind me. I now feel myself empty and burnt out. Yet somewhere deep inside something remains that still needs a long time to mature."[25] Certainly it is easy after the fact to proclaim that collaboration in evil deeds destroys the collaborator; at the time, however, it seemed perplexing that such youthful idealism could result in such vast destruction. It is difficult at any time to avoid either idealizing or trivializing the "little man," and the attempt to come to grips with the everyday life of the *Landser* is made even more troublesome by the question of their relationship to Nazism and the often broad support among them for Hitler and National Socialist goals. To those who saw themselves as victimized by the Nazi regime, the millions of people killed as a result of Nazi aggression—of which they were the sharp end—stand as a silent reproach.

10. A BITTER TRUTH

The gnawing sense of waste—of lives squandered, youth lost, days and years never to be recovered—that tormented most *Landsers* in the immediate aftermath of the war heightened the difficulty for many in coming to terms with the past. So too did their ambivalent feelings about the nature of war. Most, of course, were simply happy to have survived; only later, as they began to detect the influence of their war experiences on their lives and characters, did the ambiguity, the complexity of emotion, emerge. Most of these men, confronted with the overwhelming devastation and unprecedented atrocities committed in this war of which they had formed an integral part, understood at one level that, as Karl Piotrowski put it, "the worst of all things is war. . . . It is worse than living in bondage."[1] Especially in their attempts to assess its lessons decades after the fact, one finds almost a litany of responses: "War is a swindle," "War is the worst thing of all," "The worst times were during wartime," and "I have nothing more to do with politics." And of course these statements were made and meant sincerely.

The problem, though, was that almost despite themselves, most of these men betrayed contrary emotions, discovered in themselves at least a small part that saw positive aspects to the war experience. Piotrowski, for example, despite his disgust with war, still found it difficult not to express pride in the skill, the technical and tactical expertise, of the German *Landsers*, "the best soldiers of all," who would have triumphed but for the material superiority of the enemy. Likewise, Karl Vogt, although he acknowledged "so much suffering, you wanted not to see it any longer" and spoke of being so hungry that he ate birch bark and grass and "would have gnawed on a person," even Vogt admitted, "I also have good memories of the war. . . . [I] saw wonderful buildings, wonderful monuments. Churches and icons . . . totally fantastic; I would never have gotten to see them, if not for the war."[2] Vogt, trained as a baker's apprentice, imparted a kind of "touristic" quality to the war not uncommon for many average men who, admittedly in harsh and destructive circumstances, traveled to places and saw sights that otherwise would have been inaccessible to them. Although cognizant of the horror, Vogt clearly believed that he had in some strange way been broadened in his outlook, molded and matured by the war. It was almost as if the war, for him, had served the same function as reading the *Bildungsromane* (novels of personal growth) of Goethe or Mann.

Few *Landsers* regarded war as anything but evil, yet in that almost mystical way that outsiders can never understand, most also would have concurred with one of their number who, writing in May 1940, called war "the greatest means of teaching and learning." War formed the man, it was "the great test," a "hard but valuable school . . . that strengthened the soul [and] . . . steeled the will," a school that also taught "the true worth of people." War was, as virtually all who experienced it would attest, "an indelible experience that allowed us to encounter in a totally original sense the deepest laws of our being."[3]

Virtually all soldiers everywhere harbor the feeling that they matured as a result of their war experiences. Another apparently universal sentiment typical of many *Landsers* was the belief that war produced a unique form of friendship, a comradeship so profound that Guy Sajer could refer to it as "my only incentive for life in the midst of despair."[4] Sajer readily admitted that war was vile, but still he expressed the feeling of many that they would not have missed it, given the comradeship, the knowledge gained, the sense of adventure.

Other memories that tied the *Landser* to the universal experiences of soldiers everywhere were the bleak experience of watching a friend die or stirrings of guilt at having oneself survived; anger at the petty injustices of the army; the inner turmoil at being told to kill; constant fear like a living part of one's being; the odor of death emanating from the battlefield, which the years can't eradicate; the indescribable exhaustion that seized every combat soldier and refused to relinquish its grip; the personal rage as well as the exhilaration felt in combat; the sense of isolation and unreality on the front lines; and, not least, the reluctance to consider the consequences of one's actions, that other human beings were being killed. In his very confusion, in his anxiety to preserve his own life while struggling with taking that of others, in his sense of belonging to a world with its own rules and behavior, isolated from normal society, in his recognition that the war branded him and changed his life, the *Landser* reflected many of the universal aspects of war. "Were not we, the enemies on the battlefield, his real comrades," Hans Woltersdorf speculated while surveying a shot-up Russian tank, "the companions in misfortune who in the arena of history had to play a dice game of fortune and misfortune, life and death?" As Guy Sajer concluded, "Others might someday understand that men can love the same virtues on both sides of a conflict, and that pain is international."[5]

Still, some aspects of the *Landser* experience differentiated them from other soldiers such as the American GI. Comradeship, for example, though certainly not unique to the *Landser*, nonetheless represented a more persistent and pervasive theme in his everyday military life. *Wehrmacht* leaders, in fact, raised the concept of camaraderie almost to the level of strategic doctrine, seeing in tight-knit, cohesive groups of comrades the spiritual means by which to overcome, at least partially, the material superiority of the enemy. As an organization the German army went to great lengths to instill and nurture a sense of family; recruitment, training, and replacement policies, as well as relations between officers and men, aimed at creating and maintaining in the *Landser* the sense of belonging to a purposeful and powerful community of men who were enduring the same hardships and sharing the same fate. Whereas the training and especially the replacement policies of the U.S. Army left many GI's complaining of disorientation and an utter ignorance of their purpose, the *Wehrmacht*'s emphasis on group cohesiveness imparted a greater resolve and sense of mission to its troops. As a result of this emphasis on *Gemeinschaft*, the German soldier had an enormous faith and confidence in his noncoms and junior officers, a confidence that contributed to his fierce resilience even under the most severe strain.

Training played a role as well: many *Landsers* firmly believed that more was expected of them than of their American counterparts—indeed, that they should do more than was expected of them. Moreover, as a consequence of the German doctrine of *Auftragstaktik* (mission-oriented tactics), which left considerable tactical control at the lowest possible levels, the *Wehrmacht* seemed to possess a bottomless reservoir of courageous, capable, and quick-thinking soldiers willing to seize the initiative at any moment. Contrary to the stereotypical image of German soldiers as plodding automatons who merely followed orders (a portrait, in reality, more nearly corresponding to British or Soviet troops, who—unlike American GI's—often demonstrated an uncommon inflexibility and inability to learn from experience), the *Landser* displayed a remarkable adaptability. Not only has it been calculated that German soldiers, man for man, "inflicted casualties at about a 50 percent higher rate than they incurred from the opposing British and American troops,"[6] but the German army was saved time and again in the latter stages of the war by the ability of commanders to take surviving *Landsers* from shattered units and throw them together into hastily improvised battle units that proved astonishingly cohesive and effective in action. Success in the latter instance may have been its own reward, as the typical German soldier maintained to the end a firm confidence—approaching hubris—in his own superiority, resolutely believing that only the material preponderance of the enemy could account for Germany's downfall. And this individual superiority, he thought, resulted from his superior training, greater toughness, more resilient morale, and better leadership—all products of the *Wehrmacht*'s stress on camaraderie and *Gemeinschaft*.

This motif of family or community encompassed an important ideological dimension as well and in its various ramifications also set the *Landser* apart from the GI. The *Wehrmacht* not only stressed the notion of comradeship but did so in a consciously ideological manner: the *Frontgemeinschaft* was to be the kernel from which would grow the *Volksgemeinschaft*, the much vaunted national community of unity, belonging, and purpose promised by the Nazis. Because this promise of a new society proved attractive to many Germans, the *Landser* was more self-consciously ideological than has normally been supposed. From their letters and diaries, in fact, one gets the feeling that many German soldiers carried into battle a sense of building a new society, a world of new content and new form corresponding to the Nazi vision of national community. The seemingly innocuous notion of loyalty to one's comrades and country thus disguised a hard ideological core. The *Landser* generally had a clearer sense of his own purpose, of what the war was about, than did the GI, who at times seemed deliberately to deny that there was any point other than to survive and go home. Paul Fussell, in fact, has claimed that the typical American or British soldier operated in an "ideological vacuum" and had little if any idea of what the war was about or what purpose he played in the whole sordid affair.[7] Although

Fussell overstated his argument—by failing to recognize the extent to which American soldiers, after the disillusionment of World War I, consciously played down any notion of idealism for fear of looking naive; or that when the GI said he was fighting merely to get home he was ascribing an inherently positive value, one that he considered self-evident, to his democratic way of life—it is nonetheless true that the *Landser* was markedly more ideological than his American or British counterpart.

In important ways, however, theirs was a perverted idealism, one that aimed at creating a new world yet seethed with revenge against the old, one that sought a conflict-free internal community but held Germany's alleged enemies guilty of a vast conspiracy to destroy that community. The result, especially on the eastern front, was a vicious and brutal racial war. As Manfred Messerschmidt has pointed out, the destruction of the Jews (and, one might add, other so-called racial enemies of Germany) existed as the ultimate goal of the ideological war against Russia, an aim largely shared by the *Wehrmacht* authorities themselves.[8] As letters and diaries indicate, however, it was not only the officer corps that carried Nazi beliefs into combat but the rank and file as well. In part, this resulted from Nazi manipulation and exploitation of pre-existing beliefs. A large proportion of *Landsers*, after all, had grown to adulthood surrounded by the myths of World War I: with Germany seemingly threatened by an implacable ring of enemies as in 1914, the struggle against this encirclement was seen by many as vital to the nation's survival, especially given the memories of the Allied blockade that had strangled Germany and led to so many civilian deaths. Added to this brew was the lingering notion of social Darwinism that communities, like individuals, were engaged in a constant struggle for survival, as well as a simmering resentment that resource-poor Germany had been cheated not only by nature but in the race for colonies. As a result, National Socialist ideas such as *Lebensraum* (living space) resonated among average soldiers who believed that Germany needed new territory to secure its future in a world full of predatory nations. After all, similar notions, such as the *Mitteleuropa* concept popularized by respectable intellectuals in the years prior to World War I, had been floating around for years.

Not surprisingly, then, the *Landser* generally applauded and embraced the nationalistic language of the Nazis and their promise to redeem the failures of the Great War and to end the humiliations of the hated Versailles system. But loyalty to the Nazi idea went beyond mere jingoism. Equally alluring were National Socialist promises to end the chronic internal fragmentation and class conflict that had plagued the Weimar experiment in democracy, to open education and careers to talent rather than social background. Again, such a view corresponded to the legend of the egalitarian *Frontgemeinschaft* of the trenches, where a bullet knew no classes and where one advanced on merit rather than social connections. The notion of *Volksgemeinschaft* attracted adherents among the *Landsers* because the Nazi regime seemed to be serious about its implementation. However imperfectly, during the 1930s the Nazis achieved enough in creating the outlines of a new society to convince many ordinary soldiers—in particular, young men and those from a working-class background—that the promise of social and economic integration was real.

In creating this often surprisingly intense loyalty to the German national community, the Nazis also laid the foundations for an equally fervent hatred and disdain for those outside the *Volksgemeinschaft*. Here again, National Socialist propaganda was able to manipulate prevailing stereotypes or popular beliefs. The notion of a rising threat from Russia, from the "Asiatic hordes" to the east, had taken hold in the popular mind in the anxious years before the outbreak of the First World War, and the Bolshevik revolution and its attendant cruelties did nothing to diminish the sense of menace. Any reasonably diligent newspaper reader in Germany in the 1920s and early 1930s would have been well informed—certainly more so than one in London or New York—of the various atrocities, especially those of Stalin, visited on the unfortunate population of the Soviet Union by the Bolsheviks. And although most recent studies indicate that Nazi anti-Jewish propaganda fell far short of creating an active hatred of the Jews among average Germans, it nonetheless served to isolate the Jews within German society and, at the very minimum, to make those average Germans largely uninterested in the fate of their fellow citizens.[9] If not actually incited to mass murder by Nazi propaganda, *Landsers* remained indifferent to the fate of the Jews, which allowed those running the destructive machinery to get on with their grisly business free from outside interference.

As a consequence, although the ordinary *Landser* saw himself as a decent fellow, the Nazi vision of a racially determined *Volksgemeinschaft* achieved a certain reality on the eastern front as ideology and experience became mutually reinforcing. In soldiers' letters and diaries one finds hardly any real disagreement with the Nazi view of the enemy as *Untermenschen* (subhumans) who deserved their harsh fate, no protest at the special treatment meted out to the Jews. Since the citizens of the Soviet Union fit Nazi racial stereotypes, the Soviet system was deemed by Hitler a part of the so-called "Jewish-Bolshevik conspiracy," and the country itself seemed so backward, brutal, and threatening to the average German soldier that race, ideology, and personal experience all converged to produce a unique kind of horror. Ideology, the objective condition of daily life in Russia, and the chaos and hardships of the eastern war all combined to produce a mind-set of hatred, so that the *Landser* came to see himself as fighting to protect the German community from "Asiatic-Jewish" influences out to destroy the Reich. The *Wehrmacht* made assiduous efforts to convince the *Landser* that he was sacrificing himself for the highest and most profound purpose, was in fact a crusader on a mission to benefit the German *Volk* and that in such a struggle for existence everything was permissible. In a very real sense, then, especially on the eastern front, the *Landser* "lived" the National Socialist *Weltanschauung* (world view), which gave him an amazing resilience and stubborn determination but also led him in its name to commit barbaric atrocities against an enemy deemed subhuman.

Given the generally deeper ideological intensity displayed by the *Landser*, another factor that set him apart from the GI was the much harsher discipline to which he was subjected. This is a paradox not easy to explain; it cannot simply be dismissed with the facile excuse that the U.S. Army was remarkably lenient and permissive. In part, harsh discipline was the logical result of a political order that demanded unquestioning loyalty and obedience from both military authorities and the rank and file. Omer Bartov has noted that the politicization of discipline went hand in glove with a politicization of the army as a whole, as Nazi ideological and legal concepts, as well as codes of behavior, made their way into the ranks.[10] As a consequence, actions and behaviors that otherwise might have been disregarded or merely reprimanded were deemed political crimes warranting often draconian punishment. Moreover, as Nazi racial ideology seeped into the ranks, a curious and multifaceted process of brutalization ensued. Encouraged by Nazi doctrine (and his senior officers), the *Landser* in Russia was free to engage in virtually any criminal behavior, be it plunder, rape, or murder, as long as it was directed against so-called racial enemies of the German *Volk*; he was not only rarely punished but often praised for his racial and ideological consciousness. It could hardly have come as a surprise, therefore, when Soviet soldiers retaliated with gruesome atrocities of their own. As the fighting on the eastern front reached an intensity unknown elsewhere in World War II, and as increasing numbers of *Landsers* sought to evade the battlefield, the *Wehrmacht* responded with brutal disciplinary measures designed to make the men more fearful of their own authorities than they were of the enemy. Since this was an ideological war on behalf of the *Volksgemeinschaft*, anyone seen as doing less than his duty was considered a traitor to Führer and *Volk* who had to be punished accordingly. Finally, as the Nazi Reich crumbled in the latter part of the war, an iron discipline was seen as the only means by which to avert catastrophe. At the most concrete level, the *Landser* in the foxhole was thus subjected to ideological indoctrination designed to clarify the purpose of the war and create in him a willingness to sacrifice for this higher cause, while simultaneously threatening him with the most brutal disciplinary measures if his efforts on behalf of the *Volk* were deemed insufficient.

Perhaps because of the prevalence of death, which seemed to be a creature lurking all around, the letters and diaries of the German soldiers possess a brooding and reflective quality rarely seen in the far more practical and straightforward accounts of American soldiers. Not only did the *Landser* seem more fatalistic about the likelihood of death; he also projected a view of the world and his place in it that was more inclined to emphasize the role of fate, both as an individual matter and as a "community of fate." Moreover, he tended to imbue war with a romantically nihilistic quality. The *Landser* reflected on the intoxicating nature of war, dwelt on its innermost nature and essence, saw it as a drama of horribly beautiful power. War was of necessity a struggle for survival in which destruction was inevitable; and within this process of destruction men were released, allowed to savor the ultimate freedom from restraint, to enter the promiscuous realm of death where they could vent their most primitive feelings and desires. The notion that one had to destroy in order to live, that one could learn of life only while facing death, that the dangerous life was the most liberating, or that sacrifice fulfilled a higher spiritual purpose would seem out of place in a letter from a GI but not from a *Landser*. In a very real sense, the *Landser* came to think and act like a soldier, while most GIs were and remained civilians in uncomfortable uniforms.

Despite these differences, the *Landser*'s self-image was likely not dissimilar from the GIs. He saw himself as a decent person caught up in a vast, impersonal enterprise that threatened both his physical and spiritual well-being. He worried about his wife or sweetheart and his family back home, especially that his marriage might deteriorate or that his wife or girlfriend might be unfaithful. He was apprehensive that his farm or business would suffer in his absence, or that he would not have a job when he returned. He fretted over his spiritual and psychological well-being and puzzled about how the war, with all its killing and violence, might alter him and the folks at home. He grappled with agonizing inner doubts and wanted to be told that what he was doing was right. He understood that he was expendable and that war from ground level was, as the American E.B. Sledge put it, "brutish, inglorious, and a terrible waste," so he wanted desperately to know what he was fighting for.[11]

As a soldier he fought for many reasons: for survival, for his home and family, for his comrades, from the exhilaration of combat. But as Omer Bartov has pointed out, *Landsers* also fought against "Asiatic barbarism," against the alleged "Jewish-Bolshevik conspiracy," and in defense of German culture and the Nazi-inspired racialist *Volksgemeinschaft*. "In this sense," Bartov concluded, "they fought for Nazism and everything that it stood for." In a situation where many of them were becoming accustomed to war as a normal existence, where war had been transformed into the ordinary, the *Landser* might well have had "little influence and saw hardly any possibility of evading the escalation of violence," as one of their number, the historian Hans Mommsen, has argued.[12] Perhaps many individual *Landsers* did see the reality of war as simply death and destruction, giving little thought to the larger political or moral issues involved.

Nevertheless, the hard fact is that they fought courageously and with great determination in the service of a deplorable regime engaged in unprecedented atrocities. To the very end of the war, Hitler retained an amazing popularity with German soldiers, who were obviously among his staunchest supporters. As late as November 1944 almost two-thirds of German prisoners of war in American hands professed support for the Führer, and a mid-December report prepared by the German military maintained that among the troops "there is a firm conviction that the tremendous military efforts of our people will lead us to victory." Even in March 1945, when Nazi Germany was literally falling to pieces, Joseph Goebbels recorded in his diary that the troops had a "mystical faith" in Hitler, that the men had been fighting like "savage fanatics," and that the *Landser* would continue to do his duty. More than is generally accepted, agreement with National Socialist goals had seeped into the consciousness of the rank and file. There were no mutinies by the common soldiers in the *Wehrmacht*; and the attempted assassination of Hitler by a conspiracy of officers was generally regarded by the men at the front as the traitorous action of an unrepresentative aristocratic clique. In a very real sense, the *Landser* had become "Nazified." Field Marshall Wilhelm Keitel acknowledged the importance of the educational process leading from the Hitler Youth to the Labor Service to the army; when Hitler expressed concern about possible army opposition to the introduction of ideological instruction, Keitel replied, "No, my Führer, that is not to be expected. . . . We have already gone too far with their education."[13] In a cruel paradox, these men, often brimming with idealism to create a new and better Germany, in truth became the all-too-successful instruments of Hitler's will. This is indeed a bitter truth, one that the years cannot erase.

NOTES

Sources have been shortened in the notes.
For full information, see the Bibliography.

Chapter 1. The View from Below

1. Letters of Günter von Scheven (14 Feb. and 6 March 1942), in Bähr and Bähr, *Kriegsbriefe,* pp. 113, 115; Sajer, *Forgotten Soldier*, pp. 215–16.

2. Letter of Alois Dwenger (1 May 1942), in Bähr and Bähr, *Kriegsbriefe*, pp. 123–24.

3. Hansmann, *Vorüber—nicht vorbei,* pp. 50–51; diary entry of Ewald H. (Nov. 1942), in Breloer, *Mein Tagebuch,* p. 102. The expression *Schütze Arsch* could be translated politely as "simple private" but is more accurately akin in meaning to the American "grunt," evoking a sardonic image of a man doing the dirty work and suffering the hardships while gaining little recognition.

4. Fox, "Fatal Attraction," p. 15; letter of Kurt Vogeler (Dec. 1941), in Bähr and Bähr, *Kriegsbriefe*, p. 109; Wavell quoted in Holmes, *Firing Line*, p. 7.

5. Keegan, *Face of Battle,* pp. 77–78; Wette, "Militärgeschichte von unten," pp. 13–14, 24; diary entries of Ewald H. (New Year's Eve 1941, 29 Jan. 1942), in Breloer, *Mein Tagebuch*, p. 100. For the Nazi emphasis on the redemptive qualities of death, see Baird, *To Die For Germany,* pp. 202–42.

6. Letters of anonymous soldiers (19 Aug. and 6 June 1941), in Dollwet, "Menschen im Krieg," pp. 317, 298.

7. Hansmann, *Vorüber—nicht vorbei,* pp. 71–73.

8. Browning, *Ordinary Men,* pp. xix-xx; Michael Howard, Introduction to Frederic Manning, *The Middle Parts of Fortune* (London: Buchan & Enright, 1986), pp. v–vi; diary entry of Ewald H. (27 Sept. 1941), in Breloer, *Mein Tagebuch,* p. 99; Sajer, *Forgotten Soldier*, p. ix.

9. Sajer, *Forgotten Soldier*, p. 223.

10. Knoch, "Kriegsalltag," pp. 222–23; Peukert and Reulecke, *Die Reihen fast geschlossen,* p. 15; Borscheid, "Plädoyer für eine Geschichte des Alltäglichen," p. 96.

11. Knoch, "Kriegsalltag," p. 223; Wette, "Militärgeschichte von unten," pp. 19–23; Holmes, *Firing Line,* pp. 8–11; van Creveld, *Fighting Power,* pp. 42–61.

12. Letter of anonymous soldier (27 March 1943), in Dollwet, "Menschen im Krieg," p. 289; see also, pp. 281–82.

13. Buchbender and Sterz, *Andere Gesicht,* pp. 13–14, 24; Dollwet, "Menschen im Krieg," pp. 281–82.

14. Fox, "Fatal Attraction," p. 20.

Chapter 2. Sweat Saves Blood

1. Sajer, *Forgotten Soldier,* p. 19.
2. Ibid., pp. 1–2; Knappe and Brusaw, *Soldat,* p. 79; letter of anonymous soldier (28 Dec. 1942), in Dollwet, "Menschen im Krieg," p. 291.
3. Van Creveld, *Fighting Power,* pp. 65–68.
4. Pöppel, *Heaven and Hell,* p. 11; interview with Alfred Wessel, in Schröder, *Kasernenzeit,* pp. 83–84.
5. Diary entry of Rudolf Halbey (14 Nov. 1942), in Bähr and Bähr, *Kriegsbriefe,* p. 273.
6. Holmes, *Firing Line,* pp. 36–42, 79–81. See also van Creveld, *Fighting Power,* pp. 72–73.
7. Pöppel, *Heaven and Hell,* p. 9; Heck, *Child of Hitler,* esp. pp. 20–35.
8. Grupe, *Jahrgang 1916,* pp. 47, 58, 66–67.
9. Letter of Karl Fuchs (11 April 1937), in Richardson, *Sieg Heil!* p. 24.
10. Grupe, *Jahrgang 1916,* pp. 67–69.
11. Knappe and Brusaw, *Soldat,* p. 92.
12. Pöppel, *Heaven and Hell,* pp. 9–10, 17.
13. Letter of Karl Fuchs (Fall 1939), in Richardson, *Sieg Heil!,* p. 42; Sajer, *Forgotten Soldier,* pp. 2–3.
14. Sajer, *Forgotten Soldier,* pp. 4–6, 19.
15. Grupe, *Jahrgang 1916,* pp. 74–75.
16. Holmes, *Firing Line,* pp. 44–49; letter of Karl Fuchs (27 Feb. 1941), in Richardson, *Sieg Heil!,* p. 90; Woltersdorf, *Gods of War,* p. 99.
17. Holmes, *Firing Line,* p. 47; Knappe and Brusaw, *Soldat,* p. 170.
18. Woltersdorf, *Gods of War,* pp. 25–26.
19. Ibid., pp. 26, 104.
20. Pöppel, *Heaven and Hell,* pp. 174, 176.
21. Sajer, *Forgotten Soldier,* p. 160.
22. Ibid., pp. 161–62.
23. Ibid., *Forgotten Soldier,* pp. 163–64.
24. Kennett, *G.I.,* p. 51.
25. Sajer, *Forgotten Soldier,* pp. 165–68.
26. Interviews with Fritz-Erich Diemke and Gustav Knickrehm, in Schröder, *Kasernenzeit,* pp. 134, 136–37; Knappe and Brusaw, *Soldat,* pp. 105, 136.
27. Dupuy, *A Genius for War,* pp. 234–35.
28. Van Creveld, *Fighting Power,* pp. 6, 11–15.
29. Fussell, *Wartime,* p. 80.
30. Woltersdorf, *Gods of War,* p. 206. See also Van Creveld, *Fighting Power,* pp. 121–46.
31. Interviews with Johann Eisfeld, Erich Albertsen, and Max Landowski, in Schröder, "Man kam sich da vor wie ein Stück Dreck," pp. 186–92; interview with Fritz-Erich Diemke, in Schröder, *Kasernenzeit,* pp. 209–10.
32. Interview with Fritz Harenberg, in Niethammer, "Heimat und Front," p. 168; interview with Heinz Rieckmann, in Schröder, *Kasernenzeit,* p. 129.

33. Interviews with Hermann Blohm, Georg Timm, Werner Karstens, Franz Ehlers, and Albert Gädtke, in Schröder, *Kasernenzeit*, pp. 127–28, 115, 101–4, 143–45.

34. Schröder, "Man kam sich da vor wie ein Stück Dreck," pp. 194–96; Schröder, *Kasernenzeit*, pp. 186–237; Sajer, *Forgotten Soldier*, pp. 79–80.

35. Knappe and Brusaw, *Soldat*, p. 95; Dettmann quoted in Schröder, "Man kam sich da vor wie ein Stück Dreck," p. 195.

36. Interview with Werner Karstens, in Schröder, *Kasernenzeit*, pp. 186–87.

37. Ibid., pp. 189–91.

38. Woltersdorf, *Gods of War*, pp. 110–11.

39. Sajer, *Forgotten Soldier*, p. 167.

40. Letters of anonymous soldiers (22 Sept. 1944, 2 July 1941), in Dollwet, "Menschen im Krieg," pp. 297, 304; Sajer, *Forgotten Soldier*, p. 57.

Chapter 3. Living on Borrowed Time

1. Letter of Harry Mielert (12 April 1943), in Mielert-Pflugradt, *Russische Erde*, p. 70; Holmes, *Firing Line*, pp. 74–75; Ellis, *On the Front Lines*, p. 8.

2. Keegan, *Face of Battle*, pp. 47, 53.

3. Grupe, *Jahrgang 1916*, pp. 148–51.

4. Knappe and Brusaw, *Soldat*, p. 144; diary entry (1 Sept. 1939), in Prüller, *Diary*, p. 12; letters of Wolfgang Döring (7 Dec. 1940) and Helmut Pabst (1 Feb. 1942), in Bähr and Bähr, *Kriegsbriefe*, pp. 18, 247; Opitz, "Die Stimmung," p. 236.

5. Diary entry of Ewald H. (17 Nov. 1943), in Breloer, *Mein Tagebuch*, p.105; letter of Harry Mielert (1 July 1941), in Mielert Pflugradt, *Russische Erde*, p. 12; letters of Ernst Kleist (14 and 28 May 1940), Kurt Reuber (4/5 Jan. 1943), Meinhart Freiherr von Guttenberg (mid-Sept. 1939) and diary entry of Rudolf Halbey (14 Nov. 1942), in Bähr and Bähr, *Kriegsbriefe*, pp. 24–27, 204, 13, 273; letter of anonymous soldier (15 Nov. 1942), in Dollwet, "Menschen im Krieg," p. 304; letter of Hans-Friedrich Stäcker (21 July 1940), in Bähr and Bähr, *Kriegsbriefe*, p. 32.

6. Letters of Harald Henry (30 June and 4 July 1941), in Bähr and Bähr, *Kriegsbriefe*, pp. 69, 71; Knappe and Brusaw, *Soldat*, pp. 148–49.

7. Letters of anonymous soldiers (26 June and 29 July 1941; 1 and 15 Nov. 1942), in Dollwet, "Menschen im Krieg," pp. 298–99, 304; Grupe, *Jahrgang 1916*, p. 159; Sajer, *Forgotten Soldier*, p. 68.

8. Knappe and Brusaw, *Soldat*, p. 151; Sajer, *Forgotten Soldier*, pp. 330, 184, 189.

9. Letters of Harry Mielert (24 Feb. and 14 May 1943), in Mielert-Pflugradt, *Russische Erde*, pp. 54, 80; diary entry (17 Sept. 1939), in Prüller, *Diary*, p. 29.

10. Letter of anonymous soldier quoted in Schneider and Gullans, *Last Letters*, p. 104; letter of Corporal F.B. (24 Jan. 1943), in Buchbender and Sterz, *Andere Gesicht*, p. 151, no. 304; letters of Harry Mielert (27 Nov. 1942, and 3 Feb. 1943), in Mielert-Pflugradt, *Russische Erde*, pp. 39, 49; Sajer, *Forgotten Soldier*, p. 250.

11. Letters of Leopold von Thadden-Trieglaff (16 March 1943), Friedrich Andreas von Koch (16 April 1943), Meinhart Freiherr von Guttenberg (mid-Sept. 1939) and Ernst Kleist (14 May 1940), in Bähr and Bähr, *Kriegsbriefe*, pp. 220, 244, 12, 24; letter of Harry Mielert (7 July 1941), in Mielert-Pflugradt, *Russische Erde*, p. 13.

12. Letters of Harald Henry (17, 18, 20, and 7 Oct. 1941), in Bähr and Bähr *Kriegsbriefe*, pp. 81, 82–83, 78.

13. Letters of Helmut von Harnack (6 Jan. 1942) and Rembrand Elert (9 March 1944), in Bähr and Bähr, *Kriegsbriefe*, pp. 93, 349; letter of anonymous soldier (11 July 1941), in Dollwet, "Menschen im Krieg," p. 314; diary entry (17 Sept. 1939), in Prüller, *Diary*, p. 29, letter of Walther Weber (3 March 1942), in Bähr and Bähr, *Kriegsbriefe*, pp. 140.

14. Letter of Harry Mielert (27 Nov. 1942), in Mielert-Pflugradt, *Russische Erde*, p. 39; letter of Kurt Reuber (29 Dec. 1942), in Bähr and Bähr, *Kriegsbriefe*, p. 202; Grupe, *Jahrgang 1916*, p. 248.

15. Letters of Harry Mielert (1 Oct. and 1 Dec. 1943), in Mielert-Pflugradt, *Russische Erde*, pp. 99–100, 111.

16. Ibid. (8 Nov. and 24 Nov., 12 Oct., and 24 Nov. 1943), pp. 108, 110, 101, 110.

17. Hansmann, *Vorüber—nicht vorbei*, p. 135.

18. Ibid., pp. 135–136.

19. Letter of Leopold von Thadden-Trieglaff (16 March 1943), in Bähr and Bähr, *Kriegsbriefe*, pp. 218–222.

20. Ibid., pp. 222–23.

21. Interview with anonymous *Landser* in Lucas, *War on the Eastern Front*, pp. 159–60.

22. Sajer, *Forgotten Soldier*, pp. 207–08; Hansmann, *Vorüber—nicht vorbei*, p. 115.

23. Diary entries (7 July, 2 Nov., and 22 Dec. 1941), in Prüller, *Diary*, pp. 77, 121, 131.

24. Letter of Bernhard Beckering (2 Jan. 1945), in Bähr and Bähr, *Kriegsbriefe*, p. 431; interview with Werner Paulsen, in Niethammer, "Heimat und Front," p. 191.

25. Woltersdorf, *Gods of War*, pp. 35–41.

26. Ibid., pp. 193–195.

27. Diary entry of Lieutenant Weiner, in Clark, *Barbarossa*, p. 238.

28. Letter of Hans-Heinrich Ludwig (19/20 Nov. 1941), in Bähr and Bähr, *Kriegsbriefe*, p. 68.

29. Letters of Friedrich Leonhard Martius (23 Sept. 1944) and Max Aretin-Eggert (6 Aug. 1943), in Bähr and Bähr, *Kriegsbriefe*, pp. 369, 359.

30. Diary entry (17 Dec. 1941), in Prüller, *Diary*, pp. 127–28.

31. Sajer, *Forgotten Soldier*, pp. 174, 176–78.

32. Ibid., p. 183.

33. Ibid., pp. 184–85, 190–91.

34. Ibid., pp. 192–94; letter of Heinz Küchler (11 July 1941), in Bähr and Bähr, *Kriegsbriefe*, p. 160.

35. Diary entry (1 July 1941), in Prüller, *Diary*, p. 69; Woltersdorf, *Gods of War*, p. 73.

36. Grupe, *Jahrgang 1916*, pp. 176, 208, 223, 249.

37. Letter of Harry Mielert (29 March 1943), in Mielert-Pflugradt, *Russische Erde*, pp. 66–67.

38. Letters of Günter von Scheven (14 Feb. 1942) and Werner Pott (19 Dec. 1941), in Bähr and Bähr, *Kriegsbriefe*, pp. 113, 223–24.

39. Letters of Helmut Pabst (18/19 Aug. 1942, 2 March 1943 and 10 Sept. 1943),

in Bähr and Bähr, *Kriegsbriefe*, pp. 251, 255–56, 260–61; letter of anonymous soldier (4 March 1943), in Dollwet, "Menschen im Krieg," p. 312.

40. Browning, *Ordinary Men*, p. xix; letter of Private H.M. (17 Nov. 1943), in Buchbender and Sterz, *Andere Gesicht*, p. 152, no. 308.

41. Hansmann, *Vorüber—nicht vorbei*, pp. 81–82.

42. Ibid., pp. 83, 76.

43. Letter of Lieutenant A.B. (19 Oct. 1942), in Buchbender and Sterz, *Andre Gesicht*, pp. 150–51 no. 302.

44. Letters of Kurt Vogeler (Dec. 1941); Heinz Küchler (11 July 1941); and Johannes Huebner (14 April 1942), in Bähr and Bähr, *Kriegsbriefe*, pp. 109–10, 159–60, 180; letter of Harry Mielert (14 Nov. 1942), in Mielert-Pflugradt, *Russische Erde*, pp. 36–37; letter of Private L.B. (Aug. 1944), in Buchbender and Sterz, *Andere Gesicht*, p. 157 no. 321.

45. Sajer, *Forgotten Soldier*, pp. 103–5.

46. Ibid., pp. 299, 186–89.

47. Browning, *Ordinary Men*, p. 11; Keitel's decree of 13 May 1941 in Hans-Adolf Jacobsen, "Kommissarbefehl und Massenexekutionen sowjetischer Kriegsgefangener," in *Anatomie des SS-Staates*, Hans Buchheim, Martin Broszat, Helmut Krausnick, and Hans-Adolf Jacobsen, 2:216–18; *Nacht und Nebel* decree of 12 Dec. 1941 in Poliakov and Wulf, pp. 495–98.

48. Bartov, "The Missing Years" pp. 54, 57–58; Steinert, *Hitler's War*, pp. 264–302; Gurfein and Janowitz, "Wehrmacht Morale," pp. 200–208.

49. Sajer, *Forgotten Soldier*, pp. 118–19; interview with Max Landowski, in Schröder, "Erfahrungen deutscher Mannschaftssoldaten," p. 318; letter of Private H. (16 July 1941), in Buchbender and Sterz, *Andere Gesicht*, p. 74 no. 105.

50. Letters of Captain F.M. (15 Aug. 1941) and Private A.V. (16 Sept. 1941), in Buchbender and Sterz, *Andere Gesicht*, pp. 78 no. 115, 80 no. 123; Sajer, *Forgotten Soldier*, pp. 32–33.

51. Letters of Railroad-Inspector K.S. (8 Oct. 1941), Private H.T. (28 Nov. 1941), Sergeant A.R. (23 Oct. 1941) and Corporal H.G. (24 Sept. 1941), in Buchbender and Sterz, *Andere Gesicht*, pp. 170 no. 346, 88 no. 147, 84–85 no. 137, 82 no. 128.

52. Interview with Max Landowski, in Schröder, "Erfahrungen deutscher Mannschaftssoldaten," pp. 317–18.

53. Grupe, *Jahrgang 1916*, p. 154.

54. Interview with Matthias Jung, in Tekampe, *Kriegerzählungen*, pp. 116–17; interview with Fritz Harenberg, in Niethammer, "Heimat und Front," p. 170.

55. Herbert Selle and anonymous soldier quoted in Klee, Dressen, and Riess, *Good Old Days*, pp. 108–11.

56. Anonymous soldier quoted in ibid., pp. 117–18.

57. Anonymous soldiers quoted in ibid., pp. 38–44.

58. Letter of Harry Mielert (12 April 1943), in Mielert-Pflugradt, *Russische Erde*, p. 70; letter of Corporal L.K. (29 Oct. 1941), in Buchbender and Sterz, *Andere Gesicht*, p. 85 no. 139. For more on the ideological aspects of the war and the German dehumanization of Soviet soldiers, see below Chapter 8. See also Bartov, *Eastern Front*, pp. 77–81; Bartov, *Hitler's Army*, pp. 106–78.

59. Letter of Helmut von Harnack (6 Jan. 1942), in Bähr and Bähr, *Kriegsbriefe,* p. 93; letters of Private M.S. (11 Aug. 1941), Private R.L. (1 Aug. 1941), and anonymous private (19 Nov. 1941), in Buchbender and Sterz, *Andere Gesicht,* pp. 76 no. 108, 78 no. 114, 87 no. 144.

60. Anonymous soldiers quoted in Lucas, *War on the Eastern Front,* pp. 33, 193.

61. Hickmann, anonymous soldier, and Hohenstein quoted in Hastings, *Overlord,* p. 183; Pöppel, *Heaven and Hell,* pp. 123, 162.

62. Pöppel, *Heaven and Hell,* pp. 176, 206, 210–13, 238.

63. Letter of Harry Mielert (14 July 1941), in Mielert-Pflugradt, *Russische Erde,* p. 14.

64. Letters of Corporal W.F. (22 Aug. 1941) and Corporal M.H. (2 Sept. 1941), in Buchbender and Sterz, *Andere Gesicht,* pp. 79 no. 118, 79–80 no. 121; letters of Dieter Georgii (April 1944) and Helmut Wagner (27 Nov. 1943), in Bähr and Bähr, *Kriegsbriefe,* pp. 344, 292.

65. Sajer, *Forgotten Soldier,* pp. 327–28.

66. Report of Second Panzer Division in Hastings, *Overlord,* pp. 181–82.

67. Knappe and Brusaw, *Soldat,* pp. 156, 206–7, 162; Woltersdorf, *Gods of War,* p. 105; Pöppel, *Heaven and Hell,* pp. 87–88.

68. Knappe and Brusaw, *Soldat,* pp. 207–8; Woltersdorf, *Gods of War,* p. 116; interview with Josef Paul, in Niethammer, "Heimat und Front," p. 197.

69. Hansmann, *Vorüber—nicht vorbei,* pp. 146–48.

70. Ibid., 150–55.

71. Ibid., 156–57.

72. Ibid., 157–59.

73. Letter of Siegbert Stehmann (15 June 1940), in Bähr and Bähr, *Kriegsbriefe,* p. 413; Sajer, *Forgotten Soldier,* pp. 174, 220.

74. Sajer, *Forgotten Soldier,* p. 166; letters of anonymous soldier in Schneider and Gullans, *Last Letters,* pp. 60, 71, 34.

Chapter 4. Withstanding the Strain

1. Letter of Harry Mielert (20 Sept. 1943), in Mielert-Pflugradt, *Russische Erde,* p. 99; van Creveld, *Fighting Power,* p. 172; Sajer, *Forgotten Soldier,* p. 99; letter of Helmut Pabst (29 March 1942), in Bähr and Bähr, *Kriegsbriefe,* p. 249.

2. Hansmann, *Vorüber—nicht vorbei,* p. 47.

3. Sajer, *Forgotten Soldier,* pp. 199–201.

4. Ibid., pp. 245, 257.

5. Hastings, *Overlord,* p. 182; letter of Harry Mielert (12 Nov. 1941), in Mielert-Pflugradt, *Russische Erde,* p. 28; Sajer, *Forgotten Soldier,* p. 71.

6. Letter of Harry Mielert (25 Dec. 1942), in Mielert-Pflugradt, *Russische Erde,* pp. 43–44.

7. Grupe, *Jahrgang 1916,* pp. 274–75.

8. Grupe, *Jahrgang 1916,* pp. 128, 163; letter of Harry Mielert (20 Sept. 1943), in Mielert-Pflugradt, *Russische Erde,* p. 99; letter of Prosper Schücking (30 Sept. 1943), in Bähr and Bähr, *Kriegsbriefe,* p. 266; Sajer, *Forgotten Soldier,* pp. 75, 367.

9. Grupe, *Jahrgang 1916*, p. 250. Grupe claimed that the so-called "Gustav-Lied" (pp. 250–51) was sung everywhere in his area:

Schön ist die Nacht, die Flak ist erwacht,
die Scheinwerfer suchen, Landser sie fluchen:
"Alarm, Alarm, Alarm!"
Es sind nicht viele, nur Eine Mühle,
die pünktlich wie immer bei Mondscheingeflimmer
uns sucht—uns allein!

Hörst du den Motor? Jetzt setzt er aus!
Nun hat er was vor—
Bomben, die schmeißt er dem Landser vors Haus . . .
Ohne zu lauschen, hörst du sie rauschen,
splittern und krachen, Lärm sehr viel machend
schlägt's ein—oh, wie gemein!

Hast du ihn gehört—Jetzt macht er kehrt!
Gustav fliegt nach Haus
und auch die Flak, die setze jetzt wieder aus—
im Lande der Maüse, Wanzen und Läuse
herrscht wieder stille—jedermanns Wille
ist Ruh', bald ruhst auch du . . . !

The night is beautiful, the flak is alert,
the searchlights hunt, Landsers they curse:
"Alarm, Alarm, Alarm!"
There aren't very many, only a crate,
that punctual as ever by the moonlight's glimmer
seeks us—us alone!

Do you hear the motor? Now he's turned it off!
He now has something outside—
Bombs, that he throws at the Landsers in front of the house . . .
Without really listening, you hear them swishing,
shattering and crashing, making such a racket
one strikes—oh how awful!

Did you hear him—now he's turning around!
Gustav's flying back to his house
and now again the flak has stopped—
in the land of the mice, bugs, and lice
again all is quiet—quiet is
everyone's wish, soon rest comes even to you . . . !

10. Munzel, *Gekämpft*, p. 244.

11. Ibid., pp. 244–45.

12. Ibid., pp. 244, 242. The German rhyme reads as follows:

> Wie das wohl ist, wenn Samt und Seide
> der Damenwelt uns wieder rauschen,
> und nicht mehr in die Nacht wir lauschen,
> dem dunklen Spuk in Wald und Heide;
> wenn alle Stoppeln endlich fallen,
> die jetzt noch wuchern wild und bärtig
> und bis aufs Hemd gesellschaftsfertig,
> den Schlips wir statt des Koppels schnallen?

13. Grupe, *Jahrgang 1916*, pp. 145, 188, 209–10; diary entry (27 July 1941), in Prüller, *Diary,* pp. 85–86; letter of anonymous soldier (Aug. 1944), in Hastings, *Overlord,* p. 219.

14. Diary entries of (12 Aug. and 11 Sept. 1941), in Prüller, *Diary,* pp. 92–93, 104.

15. Letter of Martin Lindner (31 July 1942), in Bähr and Bähr, *Kriegsbriefe,* p. 169; letter of anonymous soldier, in Schneider and Gullans, *Last Letters,* pp. 26–27.

16. Hansmann, *Vorüber—nicht vorbei*, pp. 111–12.

17. Sajer, *Forgotten Soldier*, pp. 123, 127, 219, 354.

18. Hansmann, *Vorüber—nicht vorbei*, pp. 64–65.

19. Letter of anonymous soldier (31 Jan. 1943), in Knoch, "Kriegsalltag," p. 246 n 9.

20. Sajer, *Forgotten Soldier*, pp. 354, 141, 143, 150.

21. Grupe, *Jahrgang 1916*, pp. 129, 145, 147.

22. Letter of Karl Fuchs (5 Nov. 1941), in Richardson, *Sieg Heil!* pp. 152–53.

23. Letter of anonymous soldier (April 1940), in Latzel, "Zumutungen des Krieges," pp. 212–13; letter of anonymous soldier, Schneider and Gullans, in *Last Letters*, p. 82.

24. Letters of Harry Mielert (14 and 17 March 1943), in Mielert-Pflugradt, *Russische Erde*, pp. 59–60, 62.

25. Letters of Harry Mielert (20 March and 11 Sept. 1943), in Mielert-Pflugradt, *Russische Erde*, pp. 62–63, 98.

26. Opitz, "Die Stimmung," pp. 233–34; diary entry (21 June 1941), in Prüller, *Diary*, p. 62; Grupe, *Jahrgang 1916*, p. 145; letter of Lieutenant H.H. (20 May 1941), in Buchbender and Sterz, *Andere Gesicht,* p. 67 no. 88.

27. Diary entries (30 Jan., 26 Feb. and 23 March 1942), in Prüller, *Diary*, pp. 141, 144, 149; letter of Corporal R.M. (Feb. 1942), in Buchbender and Sterz, *Andere Gesicht*, p. 93 no. 157; letter of Martin Lindner (22 July 1942), in Bähr and Bähr, *Kriegsbriefe*, p. 167.

28. Sajer, *Forgotten Soldier*, p. 311. On the importance of camaraderie, see also Chapter 7; van Creveld, *Fighting Power*, and Shils and Janowitz, "Cohesion and Disintegration."

29. Prüller, *Diary*, p. 97; letter of Franz Rainer Hocke (26 July 1944), in Bähr and Bähr, *Kriegsbriefe*, p. 377; letters of anonymous soldiers (19 July 1940, 2 Oct. 1941 and 14 Aug. 1943), in Dollwet, "Menschen im Krieg," pp. 295, 310, 287; Parth, *Vorwärts Kameraden*, p. 399.

30. Letters of Harry Mielert (21 Jan. and 2 Dec. 1943), in Mielert-Pflugradt, *Russische Erde*, pp. 46, 112; letter of Private H.M. (18 Dec. 1941), in Buchbender and Sterz, *Andere Gesicht*, p. 91 no. 152.

31. Letter of Harry Mielert (24 Feb. 1943), in Mielert-Pflugradt, *Russische Erde*, p. 54; Grupe, *Jahrgang 1916*, pp. 227, 253, 244; Pöppel, *Heaven and Hell,* pp. 100, 154, 211.

32. Pöppel, *Heaven and Hell*, p. 233.

33. Letter of Prosper Schücking (25 Nov. 1943) and diary entry of Martin Lindner (20 Nov. 1942), in Bähr and Bähr, *Kriegsbriefe*, pp. 268, 171.

34. Letters of Max Aretin-Eggert (6 Aug. 1943) and Jürgen Mogk (7 Sept. 1942), in Bähr and Bähr, *Kriegsbriefe*, pp. 360, 314.

35. Letters of Sergeant K. (3 May 1943), Corporal E.G. (4 July 1943) and Sergeant H.K. (8 Sept. 1943), in Buchbender and Sterz, *Andere Gesicht*, p. 121 no. 224, 124 no. 231, 126 no. 236.

36. Letter of Harry Mielert (20 Nov. 1941), in Mielert-Pflugradt, *Russische Erde*, p. 32; Buchbender and Sterz, *Andere Gesicht*, pp. 26–27.

37. Letter of anonymous soldier, in Schneider and Gullens, *Last Letters*, p. 46; Sajer, *Forgotten Soldier*, p. 324; letter of Harry Mielert (24 Nov. 1943), in Mielert-Pflugradt, *Russische Erde*, p. 110; letter of Lieutenant W.T. (1 Jan. 1944), in Buchbender and Sterz, *Andere Gesicht*, p. 153 no. 309.

38. Letter of anonymous soldier, in Schneider and Gullans, *Last Letters*, p. 103; letters of Corporal H.M. (18 Dec. 1941), Sergeant W.H. (30 Jan. 1942), and Sergeant K.H. (3 Feb. 1942), in Buchbender and Sterz, *Andere Gesicht*, pp. 91 no. 152, 92 no. 155, 92–93 no. 156; letter of Harry Mielert (20 March 1943), in Mielert-Pflugradt, *Russische Erde*, p. 63.

39. Sajer, *Forgotten Soldier*, p. 423; Hansmann, *Vorüber—nicht vorbei*, p. 43; letters of Harry Mielert (14 May, 10 July, and 3 Nov. 1943), in Mielert-Pflugradt, *Russische Erde*, pp. 80, 87, 107; diary entry of Klaus Löscher (22 March 1944), in Bähr and Bähr, *Kriegsbriefe*, p. 327.

40. Diary entry of Ewald H. (17 Nov. 1943), in Breloer, *Mein Tagebuch,* p. 105; letter of Max Aretin-Eggert (13 Aug. 1944), in Bähr and Bähr, *Kriegsbriefe*, pp. 364–65.

41. Anonymous soldiers quoted in Schneider and Gullans, *Last Letters*, pp. 111–12, 121.

42. Sajer, *Forgotten Soldier*, pp. 194–95, 261.

43. Holmes, *Firing Line*, pp. 332–36; Kitterman, "Wehrmacht Legal System," p. 457; Messerschmidt, "German Military Law," pp. 323–24; Messerschmidt and Wüllner, *Wehrmachtjustiz,* p. 63.

44. Kitterman, "Wehrmacht Legal System," pp. 454–58; Bartov, *Hitler's Army,* pp. 59–60; Messerschmidt, "German Military Law," pp. 323–24; Messerschmidt, "The Wehrmacht and the Volksgemeinschaft," pp. 719–44; Messerschmidt, "Der 'Zersetzer' und sein Denunziant, pp. 255–78; Messerschmidt and Wüllner, *Wehrmachtjustiz,* p. 87 (see also pp. 63–89, 90–168). Exact figures on the number of German soldiers executed in World War II are hard to determine. Earlier authors estimated that 16,000 were sentenced to death, with 10,000–12,000 actually executed; Messerschmidt and Wüllner (*Wehrmachtjustiz*, pp. 29, 73–87, 90–91, 132–38) put the number sentenced to death at 28,000–32,000, with 20,000–22,000 executed; by contrast, between 8 Dec. 1941 and 15

March 1946, the U.S. Army sentenced 763 soldiers to death, of whom 146 were executed, but only one for desertion.

45. Plievier, *Stalingrad*, pp. 1–2; Sajer, *Forgotten Soldier*, p. 166.

46. Letter of anonymous soldier (1 June 1944), in Dollwet, "Menschen im Krieg," pp. 300–301; Sajer, *Forgotten Soldier*, pp. 110–11.

47. Sajer, *Forgotten Soldier*, pp. 451, 219.

48. Ibid., pp. 274–76.

49. Bartov, "Conduct of War," p. S36; Sajer, *Forgotten Soldier*, pp. 388–89. It was, in fact, incumbent on *Wehrmacht* authorities to create "flying courts martial": a memorandum of 15 March 1945 made it mandatory for army officers down to the level of collection officers at roads and bridges not only to establish such instruments of summary justice but to use them in the harshest fashion. See Messerschmidt and Wüllner, *Wehrmachtjustiz*, doc. 13 and pp. 132–168.

50. Sajer, *Forgotten Soldier*, pp. 390, 352–53.

51. Interview with Max Landowski, in Schröder, " 'Ich hänge hier,' " pp. 281–82; interviews with Erwin Lösch and Hans-Rudolf Vilter, in Steinhoff, Pechel, and Showalter, *Deutsche im Zweiten Weltkrieg,* pp. 550, 627.

52. Landowski quoted in Schröder, "Ich Hänge hier," pp. 283–85; Aicher, *Innenseiten des Kriegs,* p. 215; Grebe, *Militärmusik,* pp. 203–5.

53. Schröder, "Ich hänge hier," pp. 286–87, 290; Bartov, *Hitler's Army*, p. 100; Altner, *Totentanz Berlin,* p. 117.

54. Letters of Friedrich Andreas von Koch (3 Oct. and 10 Dec. 1942), in Bähr and Bähr, *Kriegsbriefe*, pp. 238–40.

55. Letters of Corporal J.S. (Nov. 1939 [?]) and Lieutenant Colonel H.Z. (20 Aug. 1944) [original emphasis], in Buchbender and Sterz, *Andere Gesicht*, pp. 46 no. 34, 156 no. 318.

56. Bartov, *Hitler's Army*, pp. 97, 101.

57. Letter of Corporal B., in Buchbender and Sterz, *Andere Gesicht*, p. 157 no. 320.

58. Letter of Private H.K. (27 June 1940), in Buchbender and Sterz, *Andere Gesicht*, p. 62 no. 77; Messerschmidt and Wüllner, *Wehrmachtjustiz*, pp. 218–21.

59. Knappe and Brusaw, *Soldat,* p. 200; Sajer, *Forgotten Soldier*, pp. 266–67; letter of Harald Henry (9 Nov. 1941), in Bähr and Bähr, *Kriegsbriefe*, p. 86; letter of First Lieutenant Taulien (8 Sept. 1943), in Munzel, *Gekämpft*, pp. 221–22; letter of Corporal O.S. (13 Nov. 1942), in Buchbender and Sterz, *Andere Gesicht*, p. 151 no. 303.

60. Letters of Wilhelm Rubino (12 July 1941), Bernhard Beckering (11 April 1942), and Gottfried Gruner (18 Nov. 1942), in Bähr and Bähr, *Kriegsbriefe*, pp. 60, 429, 280; letter of Harry Mielert (26 April 1943), in Mielert-Pflugradt, *Russische Erde*, p. 74.

61. Letters of Heinz Küchler (6 Sept. 1941) and Hans Pietzcker (22 Dec. 1942), in Bähr and Bähr, *Kriegsbriefe*, pp. 161, 215; Knappe and Brusaw, *Soldat*, p. 192; letter of Lieutenant K. (3 Sept. 1944), in Buchbender and Sterz, *Andere Gesicht*, p. 158 no. 323; letter of Helmut Vethake (27 May 1943), in Bähr and Bähr, *Kriegsbriefe*, pp. 236–37.

62. Letters of Hans-Heinrich Ludwig (18/21 Oct. 1941), Heinz Küchler (3 Sept. 1939), Siegbert Stehmann (13 Sept. 1944), and Willi Huber (2 Jan. 1944), in Bähr and Bähr, *Kriegsbriefe*, pp. 67, 156–57, 421–22, 340; letters of Lieutenant H.H. (28 Jan.

1943) and Captain H. (Jan. 1943), in Buchbender and Sterz, *Andere Gesicht*, pp. 104 no. 179, 102 no. 174; Baird, *To Die For Germany,* pp. 213, 208.

63. Letters of Harald Henry (13 Dec. 1941) and Helmut Pabst (29 March 1942), in Bähr and Bähr, *Kriegsbriefe*, pp. 89–90, 248.

64. Letters of Helmut Pabst (8 March 1943) and Bernhard Beckering (16 Jan. 1945), in Bähr and Bähr, *Kriegsbriefe*, pp. 257, 432; letters of Harry Mielert (20 Sept. 1943 and 7 Nov. 1941) in Mielert-Pflugradt *Russische Erde*, pp. 99, 26; letter of Günter von Scheven (6 March 1942) in Bähr and Bähr, *Kriegsbriefe*, p. 115.

65. Letters of Horstmar Seitz (11 July 1943), Gottfried Gruner (22 Sept. 1942), and Siegbert Stehmann (3 Aug. 1941), in Bähr and Bähr, *Kriegsbriefe*, pp. 286, 279, 414–15.

66. Letter of Siegbert Stehmann (13 Sept. 1944), in Bähr and Bähr, *Kriegsbriefe*, pp. 423–24.

67. Letter of Rolf Hoffmann (4 Feb. 1945), in Bähr and Bähr, *Kriegsbriefe*, p. 444.

68. Letters of Wilhelm Heidtmann (8 Sept. 1944) and Walter Wenzl (March 1945), in Bähr and Bähr, *Kriegsbriefe*, pp. 446, 451.

69. Letters of Siegbert Stehmann (13 Sept. 1944), Helmut Pabst (5 May 1942), and Bernhard Beckering (11 April 1942 and 3 Jan. 1945), in Bähr and Bähr, *Kriegsbriefe*, pp. 422, 250, 430.

70. Letter of Wilhelm Spaleck (3 Jan. 1945), in Bähr and Bähr, *Kriegsbriefe*, p. 428; letter of Harry Mielert (31 March 1943), in Mielert-Pflugradt, *Russische Erde*, p. 67.

71. Letter of Harry Mielert (27 Nov. 1942), in Mielert-Pflugradt, *Russische Erde*, p. 39; Sajer, *Forgotten Soldier*, pp. 222, 398.

Chapter 5. The Seasons of War

1. Holmes, *Firing Line,* pp. 132–33; letters of Harry Mielert (19 Dec. 1942, 22 and 25 Sept. 1941), in Mielert-Pflugradt, *Russische Erde,* pp. 42–43, 16.

2. Diary entries (8, 11, and 27 July 1941), in Prüller, *Diary*, pp. 80–81, 85; Grupe, *Jahrgang 1916,* p. 247.

3. Letter of Harry Mielert (18 July 1941), in Mielert-Pflugradt, *Russische Erde*, p. 15; letters of Corporal W.E. (4 Aug. 1941) and Corporal H.T. (31 Aug. 1942), in Buchbender and Sterz, *Andere Gesicht,* pp. 76 no. 109, 97 no. 162.

4. Letters of Helmut Pabst (19 Oct. 1942) and Walther Happich (22 Nov. 1944), in Bähr and Bähr, *Kriegsbriefe,* pp. 252–53, 453; Barbusse quoted in Holmes, *Firing Line,* p. 131.

5. Knappe and Brusaw, *Soldat,* p. 198; letters of Heinrich Witt (24 Oct. 1941), Hans-Heinrich Ludwig (18/20 Sept. 1941), Ernst Kleist (28 May 1940), and Helmut Wagner (29 Oct. 1943), in Bähr and Bähr, *Kriegsbriefe*, pp. 64, 27, 65, 292.

6. Letters of Klaus Löscher (11 April 1944) and Rembrand Elert, in Bähr and Bähr, *Kriegsbriefe*, pp. 329, 348.

7. Diary entry (25 Oct. 1941), in Prüller, *Diary*, pp. 116–17; Munzel, *Gekämpft,* p. 244.

8. Knappe and Brusaw, *Soldat,* p. 187; letters of Günter von Scheven (18 Aug. 1941), Harald Henry (4 July 1941), and Ludwig Laumen (19 July 1942), in Bähr and Bähr, *Kriegsbriefe*, pp. 111, 71, 137.

9. Letters of Martin Penck (7 Sept. 1942) and Rembrand Elert (30 March 1944), in Bähr and Bähr, *Kriegsbriefe*, pp. 154, 354; Hansmann, *Vorüber—nicht vorbei*, p. 119; diary entry (6 July 1941), in Prüller, *Diary*, p. 76.

10. Anonymous soldier quoted in Clark, *Barbarossa*, p. 160; letters of Private L.B. (n.d., probably Aug. 1941), Private H.S. (14 Sept. 1941), and Sergeant H.S., in Buchbender and Sterz, *Andere Gesicht*, pp. 77–78 no. 113, 80 no. 122, 80–81 no. 125;

11. Kreutz quoted in Clark, *Barbarossa*, pp. 369–70.

12. Diary entries (28 Sept., 3, 6, and 7 Oct. 1941), in Prüller, *Diary*, pp. 108–11; letter of Lieutenant H.H. (7 Dec. 1941), in Buchbender and Sterz, *Andere Gesicht*, p. 90 no. 149.

13. Knappe and Brusaw, *Soldat*, pp. 202, 204–5.

14. Sajer, *Forgotten Soldier*, pp. 28–30; Hansmann, *Vorüber—nicht vorbei*, p. 15.

15. Hansmann, *Vorüber—nicht vorbei*, pp. 100–101.

16. Letters of Harry Mielert (5 March and 13 Feb. 1943), in Mielert-Pflugradt, *Russische Erde*, pp. 58, 53; letter of Günter von Scheven (21 March 1942), in Bähr and Bähr, *Kriegsbriefe*, p. 116.

17. Letters of Harald Henry (9 Nov. and 18 Oct. 1941) and Helmut Pabst (5 Feb. 1942), in Bähr and Bähr, *Kriegsbriefe*, pp. 85, 81–82, 247; letter of Sergeant K.H. (3 Feb. 1942), in Buchbender and Sterz, *Andere Gesicht*, pp. 92–93 no. 156.

18. Sajer, *Forgotten Soldier*, pp. 345, 61, 317.

19. Pöppel, *Heaven and Hell*, p. 72; Sajer, *Forgotten Soldier*, pp. 75, 333, 30; Knappe and Brusaw, *Soldat*, p. 202.

20. Letters of Harry Mielert (19 Oct. 1941 and 6 Dec. 1943), in Mielert-Pflugradt, *Russische Erde*, pp. 21, 113.

21. Holmes, *Firing Line*, p. 131; anonymous soldiers quoted in Clark, *Barbarossa*, pp. 181, 160; diary entry (13 Oct. 1941), in Prüller, *Diary*, p. 114.

22. Hansmann, *Vorüber—nicht vorbei*, pp. 103, 138–39.

23. Sajer, *Forgotten Soldier*, p. 39.

24. Ibid., pp. 376–77, 384–86.

25. Woltersdorf, *Gods of War*, pp. 125–26. Instances of cannibalism almost certainly occurred at Stalingrad and in the chaos at the end of the war, when wounded men in unheated cattle cars were often forgotten and left on railroad sidings, where some of them froze to death.

26. Letter of Harry Mielert (31 Aug. 1943), in Mielert-Pflugradt, *Russische Erde*, p. 94; letter of Prosper Schücking (25 Nov. 1943), in Bähr and Bähr, *Kriegsbriefe*, p. 268; Sajer, *Forgotten Soldier*, pp. 344, 404, 441; Ryback, "Stalingrad," p. 66.

27. Anonymous soldier quoted in Lucas, *War on the Eastern Front*, p. 87; Sajer, *Forgotten Soldier*, pp. 333–34; Guderian quoted in Clark, *Barbarossa*, p. 181.

28. Letter of Harry Mielert (6 Feb. 1943), in Mielert-Pflugradt, *Russische Erde*, p. 51; Knappe and Brusaw, *Soldat*, pp. 190–91, 203.

29. Woltersdorf, *Gods of War*, p. 57; Sajer, *Forgotten Soldier*, p. 279; letters of Prosper Schücking (3 Dec. 1943) and Kurt Reuber (3 Dec. 1942), in Bähr and Bähr, *Kriegsbriefe*, pp. 269, 190. Some enterprising *Landser* even composed the "Ballad of the Louse," sung to the tune of Lilli Marlene (quoted in Munzel, *Gekämpft*, pp. 243–44):

Once in the Kaserne things were nice and neat,
But in Russia's vastness there's no such thing as peace!
Never can you take your clothing off,
So daily the "eggs of the devil" itch all over us
the small, sweet louse.

I know your step, your nice soft walk.
Whether I'm awake or snoozing, along my legs you dart.
Soon you'll suffer a misfortune,
For things can't go on like that,
Your constant dashing about.

In a Panje hut in the middle of the night,
They began their rounds, sent a scouting party out.
In each little Panje hut,
There they breathed their last.
The small, sweet louse.

30. Letters of Ernst Jünger (Nov. 1944), Theodor Kinzelbach (29 June 1941), Martin Penck (29 July 1942) and Walther Weber (25 July 1942), in Bähr and Bähr, *Kriegsbriefe*, pp. 397, 53, 152–53, 141.

31. Knappe and Brusaw, *Soldat*, p. 187; letters of Bernhard Buhl (18 July 1942), Siegbert Stehmann (30 June 1944), Werner Pott (19 Dec. 1941) and Harald Henry (1 and 3 Dec. 1941), in Bähr and Bähr, *Kriegsbriefe*, pp. 143, 420, 223, 88.

32. Hansmann, *Vorüber—nicht vorbei*, pp. 119, 113.

33. Letters of Harald Henry (23 and 30 June 1941), Martin Penck (10 Aug. 1942), and Rembrand Elert (21 and 22 March 1944), in Bähr and Bähr, *Kriegsbriefe*, pp. 69–70, 153, 353.

34. Letter of Harry Mielert (26 April 1943), in Mielert-Pflugradt, *Russische Erde*, p. 74; letters of Helmut Pabst (18/19 Aug. 1942 and 8 March 1943) and Ernst Kleist (27 and 28 May 1940), in Bähr and Bähr, *Kriegsbriefe*, pp. 251, 257, 26–27; Woltersdorf, *Gods of War*, p. 25.

35. Diary entries (1, 19, and 26 Dec. 1941), in Prüller, *Diary*, pp. 125, 129, 136.

36. Letter of Harry Mielert (19 Dec. 1942), in Mielert-Pflugradt, *Russische Erde*, p. 42.

37. Sajer, *Forgotten Soldier*, pp. 51–52, 259, 254, 327, 404, 381–82.

38. Letter of Lieutenant H.G. (31 Jan. 1942), in Buchbender and Sterz, *Andere Gesicht*, p. 150 no. 300.

39. Letter of Harry Mielert (27 Feb. 1943), in Mielert-Pflugradt, *Russische Erde*, p. 55.

40. Sienkiewicz quoted in *Smithsonian* 23 (Dec. 1992): 63; Sajer, *Forgotten Soldier*, p. 245; Hansmann, *Vorüber—nicht vorbei*, p. 113; letter of Günter von Scheven (4 March 1942), in Bähr and Bähr, *Kriegsbriefe*, p. 114.

41. Letters of Harry Mielert (29, 20, and 22 Oct. 1941, 30 Dec. 1942, 14 May 1943, 24 Oct. 1941, 24 Feb. 1943, and 18 Nov. 1943), in Mielert-Pflugradt, *Russische Erde*, pp. 25, 22, 23, 46, 81, 24, 54–55, 109.

42. Letters of Wolfgang Kluge (13 Sept. 1943) and Bernhard Ritter (14 Aug. 1941), in Bähr and Bähr, *Kriegsbriefe*, pp. 286, 49–50.

43. Letter of Harry Mielert (7 July 1941), in Mielert-Pflugradt, *Russische Erde*, p. 13; letters of Siegbert Stehmann (5 Jan. 1942), Kurt Reuber (5 Dec. 1942), Günter von Scheven (2 Sept. 1941), and Ludwig Laumen (4 June 1942), in Bähr and Bähr, *Kriegsbriefe*, pp. 417, 190, 112, 134–35.

44. Soldier quoted in Liddell Hart, *History of the Second World War,* p. 162; Knappe and Brusaw, *Soldat*, pp. 194–95; letter of Harry Mielert (7 July 1941), in Mielert-Pflugradt, *Russische Erde*, p. 13; Sajer, *Forgotten Soldier*, pp. 53, 71, 305.

45. Heinrich, *Cross of Iron*, pp. 26, 47, 67.

46. Letters of Harry Mielert (1 and 15 July 1941), in Mielert-Pflugradt, *Russische Erde*, pp. 12–13, 15; Lucas, *War on the Eastern Front*, p. 74.

47. Grupe, *Jahrgang 1916*, p. 247; letter of Siegbert Stehmann (5 Jan. 1942), in Bähr and Bähr, *Kriegsbriefe*, p. 417.

48. Letters of Hans Schmitz (23 Feb. and Spring 1941), Friedrich Gädeke, and Hans Pietzcker (24 Dec. 1941), in Bähr and Bähr, *Kriegsbriefe*, pp. 36–37, 374, 213.

49. Letter of Fritz Trautwein (28 July 1941), in Bähr and Bähr, *Kriegsbriefe*, p. 225.

50. Letters of Walther Weber (25 July 1942), Hans Schmitz (23 Feb. 1941), Theodor Kinzelbach (29 June 1941), and Wilhelm Heupel (1 June 1941), in Bähr and Bähr, *Kriegsbriefe*, pp. 53, 36, 229–230, 141.

51. Letters of Ludwig Laumen (19 July 1942), Alois Dwenger (25 Nov. 1941), and Anselm Radbruch (2 Oct. 1942), in Bähr and Bähr, *Kriegsbriefe*, pp. 138, 122, 174.

52. Letters of Harry Mielert (3 June and 1 Oct. 1941, 2 May 1943), in Mielert-Pflugradt, *Russische Erde*, pp. 11, 17–18, 76; Curzio Malaparte, *Volga Rises in Europe,* p. 102.

53. Letters of Hans Nicol (26 April 1944), Will Thomas (21 Aug. and 16 Oct. 1941), and Günter von Scheven (6 March 1942), in Bähr and Bähr, *Kriegsbriefe*, pp. 338, 96, 114.

54. Letter of Walther Weber (9 Jan. 1942), in Bähr and Bähr, *Kriegsbriefe*, p. 140; Sajer, *Forgotten Soldier*, p. 27; letters of Harry Mielert (16 Dec. 1942, 28 Jan. and 3 Feb. 1943), in Mielert-Pflugradt, *Russische Erde*, pp. 41, 47, 50–51; letter of Prosper Schücking, in Bähr and Bähr, *Kriegsbrief*, p. 265; letter of anonymous soldier, in Schneider and Gullans, *Last Letters,* p. 93.

55. Letters of Harry Mielert (28 Jan. and 8 March 1943), in Mielert-Pflugradt, *Russische Erde*, pp. 47, 59.

56. Letter of Harry Mielert (18 May 1943), in Mielert-Pflugradt, *Russische Erde*, p. 81; Sajer, *Forgotten Soldier*, p. 307.

57. Hansmann, *Vorüber—nicht vorbei*, p. 27.

58. Letter of Harry Mielert (5 Feb. 1943), in Mielert-Pflugradt, *Russische Erde*, p. 51; Grupe, *Jahrgang 1916*, pp. 159, 161.

59. Hansmann, *Vorüber—nicht vorbei*, pp. 86–87.

60. Letter of Harry Mielert (28 Jan. 1943), in Mielert-Pflugradt, *Russische Erde*, p. 47.

61. Letter of Harry Mielert (8 July 1943), in Mielert-Pflugradt, *Russische Erde*, p. 85; letters of Helmut Vethake (5 June 1943), Wolfgang Döring (8 Oct.

1939) and Horstmar Seitz (26 April 1942), in Bähr and Bähr, *Kriegsbriefe*, pp. 237, 16, 281–82.

62. Letter of Günter von Scheven (2 Sept. 1941), in Bähr and Bähr, *Kriegsbriefe*, p. 112.

Chapter 6. The Many Faces of War

1. Letters of Günter von Scheven (6 March 1942) and Siegfried Roemer (4 Dec. 1941), in Bähr and Bähr, *Kriegsbriefe*, p. 114, 332.

2. Holmes, *Firing Line*, p. 142; Sajer, *Forgotten Soldier* p. 316; letters of Hermann Stracke (22 June 1941), Kurt Reuber (7 Jan. 1943) and Helmut Gädeke (10 March 1939), in Bähr and Bähr, *Kriegsbriefe*, pp. 52, 206, 370; letters of Karl Fuchs (9 Feb. 1940 and 24 May 1941), in Richardson, *Sieg Heil!* pp. 50, 104–5.

3. Letter of Captain F.M. (June 1940) in Buchbender and Sterz, *Andere Gesicht*, pp. 59 no. 69, 67 no. 87; letter of Harry Mielert (19 Oct. 1941), in Gerda Mielert-Pflugradt, ed. *Russische Erde. Kriegsbriefe aus Rußland*. (Stuttgart: Reclam-Verlag, 1950), p. 22.

4. Sajer, *Forgotten Soldier*, p. 11; Hansmann, *Vorüber—nicht vorbei*, p. 11; letters of Ernst Kleist (14 May 1940) and Walther Happich (22 Nov. 1944) and diary entry of Klaus Wilms (Oct. 1941), in Bähr and Bähr, *Kriegsbriefe*, pp. 24, 454, 62; Grupe, *Jahrgang 1916*, p. 178; letter of Private H.S. (4 May 1941), in Buchbender and Sterz, *Andere Gesicht*, p. 67 no. 87.

5. Letters of Harry Mielert (1 Dec. and 9 Dec. 1943), in Mielert-Pflugradt, *Russische Erde*, pp. 111, 114; letters of Eberhard Wendebourg (5 Oct. 1941) and Günter von Scheven (6 March 1942), in Bähr and Bähr, *Kriegsbriefe*, pp. 106, 114; letter of Sergeant W.H. (30 Jan. 1942), in Buchbender and Sterz, *Andere Gesicht* no. 155, p. 92.

6. Letters of Kurt Reuber (3 Dec. 1942), Gerhard Meyer (23 July 1941) and Horstmar Seitz (1 Aug. 1942), in Bähr and Bähr, *Kriegsbriefe*, pp. 189–91, 210, 283; letters of Harry Mielert (7 July 1941, 7 March 1943, and 7 Nov. 1941), in Mielert-Pflugradt, *Russische Erde*, pp. 14, 58, 26.

7. Letter of Private K.P. (14 Dec. 1942), in Buchbender and Sterz, *Andere Gesicht*, p. 99 no. 168; Schneider and Gullans, *Last Letters*, p. 111; letters of Helmut Pabst (8 March 1943), Ansgar Bollweg (Nov. 1943), Siegbert Stehmann (13 Sept. 1944), and Siegfried Roemer (9 Dec. 1943), in Bähr and Bähr, *Kriegsbriefe*, pp. 257, 303, 422–23, 334; Buchbender and Sterz, *Andere Gesicht*, p. 17.

8. Letters of Meinhart Freiherr von Guttenberg (mid-Sept. 1939) and Will Thomas (2 Jan. 1942), in Bähr and Bähr, *Kriegsbriefe*, pp. 12, 99; letter of Harry Mielert (31 Jan. 1943), in Mielert-Pflugradt, *Russische Erde*, p. 48; letters of Kurt Reuber (18 Dec. 1942) and Harald Fliegauf (11 April 1942), in Bähr and Bähr, *Kriegsbriefe*, pp. 192, 270.

9. Letters of Siegfried Roemer (4 Nov. 1941), Harald Henry (21 Oct. 1941), and Max Aretin-Eggert (13 Aug. 1944), in Bähr and Bähr, *Kriegsbriefe*, pp. 331, 85, 364; letter of Harry Mielert (21 Jan. 1943), in Mielert-Pflugradt, *Russische Erde*, p. 47; letter of Wolfgang Döring (7 Dec. 1940), in Bähr and Bähr, *Kriegsbriefe*, p. 18; Willi Heinrich, *Cross of Iron*, p. 214; letter of Harald Henry (18 Oct. 1941), in Bähr and Bähr, *Kriegsbriefe*, p. 82.

10. Sajer, *Forgotten Soldier*, p. 446; letter of anonymous soldier (Aug. 1944), quoted in Kretschmer and Vogel, "Feldpostbriefe," p. 106; letter of Klaus Löscher (27–28 March 1944), in Bähr and Bähr, *Kriegsbriefe*, pp. 328–29.

11. Letter of Harry Mielert (18 April 1943), in Mielert-Pflugradt, *Russische Erde*, pp. 70–71; Heinrich, *Cross of Iron*, p. 177.

12. Sajer, *Forgotten Soldier*, pp. 363–64.

13. Sajer, *Forgotten Soldier*, pp. 174, 324, 239; letter of Harry Mielert (23 March 1943), in Mielert-Pflugradt, *Russische Erde*, pp. 64–65.

14. Sajer, *Forgotten Soldier*, p. 173; Grupe, *Jahrgang 1916*, pp. 200–201.

15. Letters of Harry Mielert (14 Dec., 30 and 27 Nov. 1942), in Mielert-Pflugradt, *Russische Erde*, pp. 40, 39; Grupe, *Jahrgang 1916*, p. 185; Sajer, *Forgotten Soldier*, p. 229; Prüller, *Diary*, p. 70; Pöppel, *Heaven and Hell*, p. 182; letter of Martin Lindner (26 July 1942), in Bähr and Bähr, *Kriegsbriefe*, p. 168. One particular terror of the Russian winter nights was, of course, was their sheer length: in many areas, darkness might well last from 3:00 P.M. to 9:00 A.M.

16. Letter of Corporal A.K. (17 May 1944), in Buchbender and Sterz, *Andere Gesicht*, p. 131 no. 251; letter of Harry Mielert (26 April 1943), in Mielert-Pflugradt, *Russische Erde*, pp. 74–75.

17. Letters of Harald Henry (1 and 3 Dec. 1941), in Bähr and Bähr, *Kriegsbriefe*, p. 87; Knappe and Brusaw, *Soldat*, p. 206.

18. Holmes, *Firing Line*, p. 197; Woltersdorf, *Gods of War,* p. 73; letters of Hans-Friedrich Stäcker (21 July 1940) and Günter von Scheven (9 March 1942), in Bähr and Bähr, *Kriegsbriefe*, pp. 32, 115–16.

19. Grupe, *Jahrgang 1916*, p. 173; letters of Harry Mielert (14 Dec. 1942, 31 March 1943, and 1 Dec. 1943), in Mielert-Pflugradt, *Russische Erde*, pp. 40–41, 67, 111; letter of Friedrich Böhringer (1 March 1944), in Bähr and Bähr, *Kriegsbriefe*, p. 320.

20. Heinrich, *Cross of Iron*, p. 15; Grupe, *Jahrgang 1916*, p. 98; Sajer, *Forgotten Soldier*, p. 245.

21. Letter of Frau L.S. (27 Feb. 1942), in Buchbender and Sterz, *Andere Gesicht*, p. 150 no. 301; letter of Harry Mielert (14 May 1943), in Mielert-Pflugradt, *Russische Erde*, p. 80; Grupe, *Jahrgang 1916*, pp. 248–49; letter of anonymous soldier (25 March 1942), in Dollwet, "Menschen im Krieg," p. 313; letters of Bernhard Beckering (5 and 11 April 1942), in Bähr and Bähr, *Kriegsbriefe*, p. 429.

22. Heinrich, *Cross of Iron*, p. 282; letters of Günter von Scheven (Jan. 1942) and Reinhard Becker-Glauch (Feb. 1943), in Bähr and Bähr, *Kriegsbriefe*, pp. 120, 399; Hansmann, *Vorüber—nicht vorbei*, pp. 55–56.

23. Letter of Gerhard Meyer (5 Aug. 1941), in Bähr and Bähr, *Kriegsbriefe*, p. 211.

24. Letters of Friedrich Andreas von Koch (16 April 1943), Klaus Löscher (16 and 18 Jan. 1944), and Prosper Schücking (5 Oct. 1943), in Bähr and Bähr, *Kriegsbriefe*, pp. 244–45, 325, 267.

25. Letter of Harry Mielert (25 Feb. 1943), in Mielert-Pflugradt, *Russische Erde*, p. 55; Knappe and Brusaw, *Soldat*, p. 192.

26. Letters of Franz Rainer Hocke (26 July and 26 Aug. 1944) and Konrad Wilhelm Henckell (10 Sept. 1943), in Bähr and Bähr, *Kriegsbriefe*, pp. 377, 272; letter of Harry Mielert (5 July 1943), in Mielert-Pflugradt, *Russische Erde*, p. 84.

27. Letter of Helmut Pabst (8 April 1942), in Bähr and Bähr, *Kriegsbriefe*, p. 249; letter of Harry Mielert (7 Dec. 1941) and diary entry of Harry Mielert (10 June 1941), in Mielert-Pflugradt, *Russische Erde*, pp. 35, 9–10; Sajer, *Forgotten Soldier*, p. 141.

28. Letter of Wolfgang Döring (7 Dec. 1940), in Bähr and Bähr, *Kriegsbriefe*, pp. 18–19.

29. Letters of Harald Henry (18 Aug. 1941), Günter von Scheven (2 Sept. 1941), Heinz Küchler (22 Sept. 1941), Rudolf Bader (19 Dec. 1943) and Rudolf Halbey (4 Jan. 1943), in Bähr and Bähr, *Kriegsbriefe*, pp. 74, 111, 162, 356, 275; Sajer, *Forgotten Soldier*, p. 288.

30. Letters of Wolfdietrich Schröter (30 May 1940), Wolfgang Döring (7 Dec. 1940), Horstmar Seitz (2 Sept. 1942), and Helmut Pabst (5 May 1942), in Bähr and Bähr, *Kriegsbriefe*, pp. 30, 19, 285, 250; letter of Harry Mielert (28/29 Dec. 1942), in Mielert-Pflugradt, *Russische Erde*, pp. 44–45; letters of Wolfgang Kluge (5 Oct. 1943) and Martin Lindner (31 July 1942), in Bähr and Bähr, *Kriegsbriefe*, pp. 288, 168–9.

31. Letters of Reinhard Becker-Glauch (27 Sept. 1944), Rolf Schroth, (Spring 1942), Eberhard Wendebourg (5 Oct. 1941), and Hans Pietzcker (26 Dec. 1941, 22 Dec. 1942), in Bähr and Bähr, *Kriegsbriefe*, pp. 403, 165, 106, 214–16.

32. Letters of Helmut Pabst (2 March 1943, 10 Sept. 1943), Reinhard Goes (23 July 1944), Hans-Friedrich Stäcker (21 July 1940) and Hans Schmitz (Spring 1941), in Bähr and Bähr, *Kriegsbriefe*, pp. 256, 260, 455, 32, 37. Many young Germans had read and been influenced by Ernst Jünger's works, especially *In Stahlgewittern: Aus dem Tagebuch eines Stosstruppführers* (*The Storm of Steel: The Diary of a German Storm-trooper*), a general account of his experiences in World War I, and *Der Kampf als inneres Erlebnis* (*War as Inner Experience*), which emphasized the collective experience and camaraderie of the war.

33. Letter of Wolfgang Döring (28 May 1940), in Bähr and Bähr, *Kriegsbriefe*, p. 17; Sajer, *Forgotten Soldier*, pp. 85, 178, 183, 234.

34. Letter of Hans August Vowinckel (29 June 1941), in Bähr and Bähr, *Kriegsbriefe*, p. 256; soldier quoted in Lucas, *War on the Eastern Front*, pp. 170–71.

35. Letters of Helmut Pabst (2 March 1943, 10 Sept. 1943), in Bähr and Bähr, *Kriegsbriefe*, pp. 256, 259–60.

36. Letter of Harry Mielert (20 Sept. 1943), in Mielert-Pflugradt, *Russische Erde*, pp. 98–99.

37. Knappe and Brusaw, *Soldat*, pp. 199–200; letters of Günter von Scheven (4 March 1942), Hans-Heinrich Ludwig (1 Dec. 1941), Leopold von Thadden-Trieglaff (16 March 1943), Hans Nicol (26 April 1944), Kurt Reuber (5 Dec. 1942), and Rudolf Halbey (4 Jan. 1943), in Bähr and Bähr, *Kriegsbriefe*, pp. 114, 68, 221, 337, 191, 273; letter of Harry Mielert (6 Dec. 1943), in Mielert-Pflugradt, *Russische Erde*, p. 113.

38. Sajer, *Forgotten Soldier*, pp. 261, 185, 206; letter of anonymous soldier (25 June 1944), in Dollwet, "Menschen im Krieg," p. 290; diary entry of Rudolf Halbey (4 Jan. 1943), in Bähr and Bähr, *Kriegsbriefe*, p. 274.

39. Grupe, *Jahrgang 1916*, p. 172; letter of Walther Happich (27 Feb. 1945), in Bähr and Bähr, *Kriegsbriefe*, pp. 454–55.

40. Grupe, *Jahrgang 1916*, pp. 74, 99, 100–101, 144–48, 172, 165–66.

41. Letter of Harald Henry (4 July 1941), in Bähr and Bähr, *Kriegsbriefe*, p. 71; anonymous soldier quoted in Holmes, *Firing Line*, p. 178; Grupe, *Jahrgang 1916*, p. 187; Knappe and Brusaw, *Soldat*, pp. 148, 197.

42. Malaparte, *Kaputt*, pp. 39–41; letters of Siegbert Stehmann (5 Aug. 1941), Wolfgang Kluge (3 Oct. 1943), and Johannes Huebner (Sept. 1939), in Bähr and Bähr, *Kriegsbriefe*, pp. 414, 288, 177; Sajer, *Forgotten Soldier*, p. 83.

43. Letters of Harald Henry (12 Oct. 1941) and Friedrich Reinhold Haag (12 July 1942), in Bähr and Bähr, *Kriegsbriefe*, pp. 79, 212.

44. Letters of Helmut Neelsen (May 1940) and Hans-Heinrich Ludwig (18/20 Sept. 1941), in Bähr and Bähr, *Kriegsbriefe*, pp. 23, 65; letter of Private H.B. (24 May 1940), in Buchbender and Sterz, *Andere Gesicht*, p. 55 no. 57; letter of Alois Dwenger (24 June 1942), in Bähr and Bähr, *Kriegsbriefe*, p. 125.

45. Letters of Private A.M. (May 1940), Captain F.M. (June 1940), Corporal E.B. (26 May 1940), and Private L.B. (11 Nov. 1941), in Buchbender and Sterz, *Andere Gesicht*, pp. 55 no. 58, 58–59 no. 69, 56 no. 60, 86 no. 142.

46. Sajer, *Forgotten Soldier*, p. 68; letters of Hans Pietzcker (26 Dec. 1941) and Kurt Reuber (Advent 1943), in Bähr and Bähr, *Kriegsbriefe*, pp. 214–15, 208–9.

Chapter 7. The Bonds of Comradeship

1. Letters of Gerhard Meyer (23 July and 5 Aug. 1941), in Bähr and Bähr, *Kriegsbriefe,* p. 210.

2. Heinrich, *Cross of Iron*, pp. 127–28.

3. Letter of Karl Fuchs (27 Feb. 1941), in Richardson, *Sieg Heil!* p. 90; van Creveld, *Fighting Power,* p. 45.

4. Van Creveld, *Fighting Power*, esp. pp. 74–76, 33–37; letter of Karl Fuchs (3 Aug. 1940), in Richardson, *Sieg Heil!* pp. 72–73. On the emotional importance of the *Ersatzbataillone*, see Grupe, *Jahrgang 1916,* pp. 106–15.

5. Grupe, *Jahrgang 1916*, pp. 74–75; letter of Harry Mielert (27 Dec. 1942) in Mielert-Pflugradt, *Russische Erde*, p. 44; Grupe, *Jahrgang 1916*, pp. 113-14.

6. Woltersdorf, *Gods of War*, p. 206; van Creveld, *Fighting Power*, esp. pp. 74–76, 33–37; Bartov, *Hitler's Army*, pp. 30–31; Struve, *Elites against Democracy,* pp. 446–48; Kroener, "Auf dem Weg," pp. 651–82. On the German tradition, see Gordon A. Craig, *The Politics of the Prussian Army, 1940–1945* (New York: Oxford University Press, 1956); Karl Demeter, *The German Officer Corps in Society and State, 1650–1945* (London, 1965); Martin Kitchen, *A Military History of Germany: From the Eighteenth Century to the Present* (Bloomington: Indiana University Press, 1975).

7. Shils and Janowitz, "Cohesion and Disintegration," p. 368; van Creveld, *Fighting Power*, pp. 163–64. On the question of primary group loyalty, see also Gurfein and Janowitz, "Wehrmacht Morale," pp. 200–208; Chodoff, "Ideology and Primary Groups," pp. 569–93; Madej, "Effectiveness and Cohesion" pp. 233–48; Weidenreich, "Why He Fights," pp. 43–45.

8. Hitler's 1933 speech quoted in Rempel, *Hitler's Children*, pp. 1–2; Hitler's speeches at Nuremberg and Reichenberg quoted in Noakes and Pridham, *Nazism*, pp. 416–17.

9. Hitler Youth leader quoted in Noakes and Pridham, *Nazism*, pp. 427–28;

interview with Gustav Köppke in Niethammer, "Heimat und Front," p. 210. On worker support for Hitler and National Socialism within the *Wehrmacht*, see Bartov, "The Missing Years," pp. 46–65; Steinert, *Hitler's War*, pp. 196–302.

10. Grupe, *Jahrgang 1916*, pp. 40, 47,87, 60–61, 65. On the cult of death in Nazi Germany, see Baird, *To Die For Germany*.

11. Grupe, *Jahrgang 1916*, pp. 62–63, 67–69, 72.

12. Grupe, *Jahrgang 1916*, p. 110:

> Die dunkle Nacht ist nun vorbei
> und herrlich beginnt es zu tagen!
> Kamerad, pack an, die Arbeit macht frei—
> frischauf, wir wollen es wagen!
> Grau wie die Erde ist unser Kleid—
> graue Soldaten in sturmschwerer Zeit!

13. Buchner, *Handbuch der Deutschen Infanterie*, p. 15; Holmes, *Firing Line*, pp. 294–95; Woltersdorf, *Gods of War*, p. 99.

14. Pöppel, *Heaven and Hell*, p. 47; Grupe, *Jahrgang 1916*, pp. 89–90, 165, 279; letters of Helmut Vethake (18 April 1943) and Wolfgang Döring (16 June 1941), in Bähr and Bähr, *Kriegsbriefe*, pp. 236, 19–20.

15. Sajer, *Forgotten Soldier*, pp. 40, 83–84, 121.

16. Heinrich, *Cross of Iron*, pp. 173–74; Pöppel, *Heaven and Hell*, pp. 46–47; letter of Karl Friedrich Oertel (22 Jan. 1945, in Bähr and Bähr, *Kriegsbriefe*, p. 439.

17. Letters of Rolf Schroth (Autumn 1942), Helmut Vethake (18 April 1943), and Wolfgang Döring (16 June 1941), in Bähr and Bähr, *Kriegsbriefe*, pp. 166, 236, 19–20.

18. Letter of Helmut Pabst (6 Oct. 1942), in Bähr and Bähr, *Kriegsbriefe*, p. 252.

19. Letter of anonymous soldier (18 May 1941), in Dollwet, "Menschen im Krieg," p. 306; letter of Harry Mielert (27 Nov. 1942), in Mielert-Pflugradt, *Russische Erde*, p. 39.

20. Letters of Harry Mielert (6 Dec. 1943 and 27 Nov. 1942), in Mielert-Pflugradt, *Russische Erde*, pp. 113–14, 39.

21. Letter of Harry Mielert (17 May 1941), in Mielert-Pflugradt, *Russische Erde*, p. 7; Pöppel, *Heaven and Hell*, p. 168.

22. Letters of Harry Mielert (20 Nov. 1942, 3 May 1943), in Mielert-Pflugradt, *Russische Erde*, pp. 37, 76.

23. Pöppel, *Heaven and Hell*, pp. 71–72.

24. Letter of Siegfried Roemer (27 March 1943), in Bähr and Bähr, *Kriegsbriefe*, p. 333; letter of anonymous soldier (24 Nov. 1943), in Dollwet, "Menschen im Krieg," p. 293; Sajer, *Forgotten Soldier*, p. 249.

25. Letter of Will Thomas (19 Jan. 1942), in Bähr and Bähr, *Kriegsbriefe*, p. 100.

26. Letters of Kurt Reuber (3 and 25 Dec. 1942) and "After Christmas," in Bähr and Bähr, *Kriegsbriefe*, pp. 191, 194, 196; Sajer, *Forgotten Soldier*, pp. 311, 113, 461, 118.

27. Letter of Harry Mielert (22 March 1943), in Mielert-Pflugradt, *Russische Erde*, p. 64.

28. Grupe, *Jahrgang 1916*, pp. 215–16:

> Wenn einer von uns müde wird,
> der andre für uns wacht;
> wenn einer von uns zweifeln sollt',
> der andre gläubig lacht.
> Wenn einer von uns fallen sollt',
> der andre steht für zwei,
> denn jedem Kämpfer gab ein Gott
> den Kameraden bei!

29. Sajer, *Forgotten Soldier*, pp. 267, 342.

30. Ibid., pp. 246–47.

31. Pöppel, *Heaven and Hell*, pp. 56, 65.

32. Ibid., pp. 90, 170; diary entry of Bernhard Ernst Buhl (18 July 1942), in Bähr and Bähr, *Kriegsbriefe*, p. 142.

33. Letter of Harry Mielert (8 July 1943), in Mielert-Pflugradt, *Russische Erde*, p. 85.

34. Sajer, *Forgotten Soldier*, pp. 399–400, 410–11.

35. Holmes, *Firing Line*, pp. 311–13; letters of Helmut von Harnack (21 Oct. 1941) and Klaus Löscher (11, 16, and 18 Jan. 1944), in Bähr and Bähr, *Kriegsbriefe*, pp. 91, 324–25.

36. Pöppel, *Heaven and Hell*, p. 88; letter of anonymous soldier (11 July 1941), in Dollwet, "Menschen im Krieg," p. 314; letter of anonymous soldier (Aug. 1944), in Hastings, *Overlord*, p. 219; letter of Siegfried Roemer (7 March 1944), in Bähr and Bähr, *Kriegsbriefe*, p. 334.

37. Letter of Rembrand Elert (21 and 22 March 1944), in Bähr and Bähr, *Kriegsbriefe*, pp. 352–53.

38. Letters of Helmut Vethake (13 June 1943) and Siegbert Stehmann (18 Oct. 1943), in Bähr and Bähr, *Kriegsbriefe*, pp. 237–38, 420; letter of anonymous soldier (7 June 1943), in Dollwet, "Menschen im Krieg," p. 292.

39. Letter of anonymous soldier (15 Sept. 1942), in Dollwet, "Menschen im Krieg," p. 305; letter of Bernhard Ritter (19 Aug. 1941), in Bähr and Bähr, *Kriegsbriefe*, p. 50.

40. Hansmann, *Vorüber—nicht vorbei*, pp. 13, 75; letter of anonymous soldier (19 Aug. 1941), in Dollwet, "Menschen im Krieg," p. 306; Sajer, *Forgotten Soldier*, p. 328.

41. Sajer, *Forgotten Soldier*, pp. 93–96.

42. Letter of Harry Mielert (16 Oct. 1943), in Mielert-Pflugradt, *Russische Erde*, p. 102; Sajer, *Forgotten Soldier*, pp. 375–76.

43. Letter of Hans Martin Stählin (4 Nov. 1941), in Bähr and Bähr, *Kriegsbriefe*, p. 121; letter of Harry Mielert (7 July 1943), in Mielert-Pflugradt, *Russische Erde*, p. 85.

44. Diary entry of Ernst Friedrich Schauer (22 Feb. 1942), in Bähr and Bähr, *Kriegsbriefe*, pp. 290–91.

45. Letter of anonymous soldier (13 June 1943), in Dollwet, "Menschen im Krieg," p. 302.

46. Letter of Private K.B. (2 Oct. 1939), in Buchbender and Sterz, *Andere Gesicht,*

p. 45 no. 29; letters of Helmut von Harnack (23 Sept. 1941) and Bernhard Ernst Buhl (2 Aug. 1942), in Bähr and Bähr, *Kriegsbriefe*, pp. 90–91, 143–44.

47. Letter of Harry Mielert (5 May 1943), in Mielert-Pflugradt, *Russische Erde*, p. 77; letter of anonymous soldier (27 Oct. 1942), in Dollwet, "Menschen im Krieg," p. 311.

48. Letters of Hans Pietzcker (20 Oct. 1942) and Reinhard Goes (24 Nov. 1943), in Bähr and Bähr, *Kriegsbriefe*, pp. 215, 458.

49. Pöppel, *Heaven and Hell*, pp. 222–23; letters of Klaus Löscher (Oct. 1942–April 1944), in Bähr and Bähr, *Kriegsbriefe*, pp. 321–30, include the Hausmann poem:

> Wer des Lichts begehrt, muß ins Dunkel gehn;
> Was das Grauen mehrt, läßt das Heil entstehn.
> Wo kein Sinn mehr mißt, waltet erst der Sinn;
> Wo kein Weg mehr ist, ist des Wegs Beginn.

50. Holmes, *Firing Line*, pp. 74–79; letter of Harry Mielert (5 May 1943), in Mielert-Pflugradt, *Russische Erde*, p. 77.

51. Pöppel, *Heaven and Hell*, pp. 202, 218.

52. Letter of Gottfried Gruner (13 June 1943), in Bähr and Bähr, *Kriegsbriefe*, p. 280; Woltersdorf, *Gods of War*, p. 98.

53. Letter of Helmut Kniepkamp (12/13 Feb. 1944), in Bähr and Bähr, *Kriegsbriefe*, pp. 300–301.

54. Letters of anonymous soldier (22 Aug. and 31 Oct. 1941), in Dollwet, "Menschen im Krieg," p. 307; letter of Lieutenant W.T. (1 Feb. 1943), in Buchbender and Sterz, *Andere Gesicht*, p. 112 no. 200.

55. Letter of Helmut Vethake (13 June 1943), in Bähr and Bähr, *Kriegsbriefe*, p. 238; letter of Karl Fuchs (26 Oct. 1941), in Richardson, *Sieg Heil!*, pp. 147–148.

56. Letter of anonymous soldier (29 Sept. 1943), in Dollwet, "Menschen im Krieg," p. 303; Grupe, *Jahrgang 1916*, p. 266.

57. Letters of Paul Kaysel (23 Feb. 1940), Eberhard Wendebourg (5 Oct. 1941) and Bernhard Beckering (10 Dec. 1944), in Bähr and Bähr, *Kriegsbriefe*, pp. 131–32, 106, 430; Pöppel, *Heaven and Hell*, p. 157; Berghahn, "Meinungsforschung im 'Dritten Reich,' " pp. 83–119.

58. Rempel, *Hitler's Children*, p. 249; Maschmann, *Account Rendered*, pp. 168–69; Grupe, *Jahrgang 1916*, p. 340; Sajer, *Forgotten Soldier*, p. 113.

59. Hansmann, *Vorüber—nicht vorbei*, pp. 140–41.

60. Ibid., pp. 143–44.

60. Sajer, *Forgotten Soldier*, pp. 461–63.

Chapter 8. Trying to Change the World

1. Harsch quoted in Horne, *To Lose a Battle*, p. 126; Watt, *How War Came*, p. 535; Shirer, *Berlin Diary*, pp. 198–201.

2. Baird, *To Die for Germany*, p. xii; Eksteins, *Rites of Spring*, pp. 211, 223, 325; Hüppauf, "Langemarck," pp. 84–96; Herf, *Reactionary Modernism*, pp. 2, 30; Mann, *Diaries*, pp. 23, 25, 47–48, 129–30, 137, 148, 169.

3. Ernst Jünger, "Die Geburt des Nationalismus aus dem Krieg," *Deutsches Volkstum* 11 (1929): 478; Jünger, *Der Kampf,* pp. 22, 33, 38, 89; Herf, *Reactionary Modernism,* pp. 70–76, 92; letter of Horstmar Seitz (31 Oct. 1942), in Bähr and Bähr, *Kriegsbriefe,* p. 285.

4. Jünger, "Totale Mobilmachung," pp. 126-30; Jünger, *Der Kampf,* pp. 24-25; Jünger, *Das Wäldchen,* pp. 54-55; Struve, *Elites against Democracy,* pp. 392, 407; Herf, *Reactionary Modernism,* pp. 93, 104–5, 107; Hüppauf, "Langemarck," pp. 84–85, 89–90, 93, 96; letter of Sebastian Mendelssohn-Bartholdy (27 Nov. 1944), in Bähr and Bähr, *Kriegsbriefe,* pp. 394.

5. Jünger, *Der Arbeiter,* p. 119; Struve, *Elites against Democracy,* pp. 392, 407; Herf, *Reactionary Modernism,* pp. 93, 104–5, 107; Hüppauf, "Langemarck," pp. 84–85, 89–90, 93, 96; letters of Harry Mielert (7 March and 6 Dec. 1943), in Mielert-Pflugradt, *Russische Erde,* pp. 58, 114; letter of Ansgar Bollweg (Nov. 1943), in Bähr and Bähr, *Kriegsbriefe,* p. 302; letter of Karl Fuchs (28 June 1941), in Richardson, *Sieg Heil!* p. 116.

6. Ernst Jünger, "Über die Gefahr," *Widerstand* 3 (1931): 67; Jünger, *Der Arbeiter,* p. 147; Herf, *Reactionary Modernism,* pp. 91, 98, 105; letter of Corporal H.B. (27 Dec. 1942), in Buchbender and Sterz, *Andere Gesicht,* p. 100 no. 170; letter of Sebastian Mendelssohn-Bartholdy (Oct. 1944), in Bähr and Bähr, *Kriegsbriefe,* p. 391. Writing from Poland (7 April 1941, in Bähr and Bähr, *Kriegsbrief,* p. 39) Ital Gelzer confessed that his "most admired model in our times is Ernst Jünger."

7. Jünger, "Totale Mobilmachung," p. 120; Jünger, *Der Arbeiter,* p. 81; Herf, *Reactionary Modernism,* pp. 94, 103; letter of Reinhard Goes (23 Nov. 1941), in Bähr and Bähr, *Kriegsbriefe,* p. 457; Ernst Jünger, "Die Grundlagen des Nationalismus," in *Stahlhelm Jahrbuch 1927,* ed. Franz Schauwecker (Magdeburg, 1927), p. 77; letter of Heinz Küchler (3 Sept. 1939) in Bähr and Bähr, *Kriegsbriefe,* p. 157; Ernst Jünger, "Die Abruster," *Arminius* 8 (1927): 6; Herf, *Reactionary Modernism,* p. 97.

8. Letter of Gerhard Meyer (23 July 1941), in Bähr and Bähr, *Kriegsbriefe,* pp. 209–10; letters of Corporal E.K. (19 Sept. 1941) and Corporal E.K. (no relation); (21 Nov. 1941), in Buchbender and Sterz, *Andere Gesicht,* pp. 80 no. 124, 87 no. 145; diary entries of anonymous soldier (Dec. 1941) and of chaplain of Eighteenth Panzer Division, quoted in Bartov, *The Eastern Front,* pp. 33, 20.

9. Letter of Sergeant W. H. (30 Jan. 1942), in Buchbender and Sterz, *Andere Gesicht,* p. 92 no. 155; chaplain's letter quoted in Bartov, *Hitler's Army,* p. 46; letters of Martin Lindner (15 Sept. and 28 Nov. 1942), in Bähr and Bähr, *Kriegsbriefe,* pp. 170, 172.

10. Letter of Friedrich Reinhold Haag (12 July 1942), in Bähr and Bähr, *Kriegsbriefe,* p. 211; Prüller, *Diary,* p. 143.

11. Letters of Horstmar Seitz (19 July 1942) and Helmut Pabst (29 March 1942), in Bähr and Bähr, *Kriegsbriefe,* pp. 283, 248; letter of Corporal F.B. (24 Jan. 1943), in Buchbender and Sterz, *Andere Gesicht,* p. 151 no. 304; letter of Harry Mielert (1 Dec. 1943), in Mielert-Pflugradt, *Russische Erde,* p. 111.

12. Letters of Siegfried Roemer (27/28 March 1944), Hans Pietzcker (24 Dec. 1941), Will Thomas (19 Jan. 1942), Horstmar Seitz (9 Sept. 1942), and Helmut Pabst (20 Jan. 1943), in Bähr and Bähr, *Kriegsbriefe,* pp. 328, 213, 100, 284, 255.

13. Letters of Harald Henry (18 Aug. and 21 Oct. 1941), in Bähr and Bähr, *Kriegsbriefe*, pp. 74, 83–84.

14. Letter of Hans-Heinrich Ludwig (18/21 Oct. 1941), in Bähr and Bähr, *Kriegsbriefe*, p. 67; letters of Harry Mielert (7 Feb. and 19 Sept. 1943), in Mielert-Pflugradt, *Russische Erde*, pp. 52, 98; letters of Harald Henry (10 Sept. 1941) and Hans-Friedrich Stäcker (21 July 1940), in Bähr and Bähr, *Kriegsbriefe*, pp. 76, 32. Jünger wrote that World War I was "the father of all things . . . [and] our father as well. It hammered, chiseled, and hardened us into what we are." Jünger, *Der Kampf*, p. 13. He also acknowledged: "I have never had so carefree a life as at the front." Jünger, *Das Wäldchen*, p. 6.

15. Letters of Wolfgang Kluge (3 and 5 Oct. 1943), Siegfried Roemer (9 Dec. 1943), Siegbert Stehmann (16 Nov. 1941) and Heinz Küchler (3 June 1940, 11 July 1941), in Bähr and Bähr, *Kriegsbriefe*, pp. 288, 333, 416, 157, 159–60.

16. *Signal* magazine quoted in Laffin, *Jackboot*, p. 142. For further explication of the Nazi fascination with the new man as a product of World War I, the myth of sacrifice, and the redemptive power of youth, see Baird, *To Die for Germany*.

17. Grupe, *Jahrgang 1916*, p. 246; Woltersdorf, *Gods of War*, p. 170.

18. Letters of Corporal A.N. (23 June 1941), Private H.K. (n.d., probably Sept. 1941), and Corporal K.G. (18 July 1942), in Buchbender and Sterz, *Andere Gesicht*, pp. 71–72 no. 98, 81 no. 127, 171 no. 351.

19. Letter of Private F. (3 July 1941), in Buchbender and Sterz, *Andere Gesicht*, pp. 72–73 no. 101; letter of anonymous soldier, quoted in Dollwet, "Menschen im Krieg," p. 298.

20. Letters of anonymous corporal (10 July 1941), Private M.M. (20 Aug. 1941), and Corporal W.F. (17 Nov. 1941), in Buchbender and Sterz, *Andere Gesicht*, pp. 74 no. 104, 78 no. 116, 86–87 no. 143; letters of Karl Fuchs (4 Aug. and 12 Nov. 1941), in Richardson, *Sieg Heil!*, pp. 124, 157.

21. Fallnbigl quoted in Bartov, *Hitler's Army*, pp. 155–56; letters of anonymous soldiers, in Dollwet, "Menschen im Krieg," p. 286; letters of Captain E.P. (15 Feb. 1943), Corporal H.H. (12 June 1943) and Corporal H.G. (24 Sept. 1941), in Buchbender and Sterz, *Andere Gesicht*, pp. 113–14 no. 203, 117–18 no. 216, 82 no. 128.

22. Diary entry (Sept. 1943), in Prüller, *Diary*, p. 166; Paul Lenz, Reinhold Mahnke, Heinrich Sachs, and Hans Kondruss quoted in Bartov, *Hitler's Army*, pp. 160–61.

23. Letter of anonymous soldier (24 Sept. 1939), in Dollwet, "Menschen im Krieg," p. 309; letters of Lieutenant H.C. (7 July 1944) and Corporal F.K. (14 Aug. 1942), in Buchbender and Sterz, *Andere Gesicht*, pp. 173 no. 355, 172 no. 353.

24. Letter of Corporal H.K. (22 July 1942), in Buchbender and Sterz, *Andere Gesicht*, p. 172 no. 352. It is interesting to note that during the war Hitler constantly, and mistakenly, referred to his famous prophecy as having been made on 1 Sept. 1939 and not, as was the actual case, on 30 Jan. 1939. It was on 1 Sept., of course, that the German attack on Poland inaugurated World War II, but in Hitler's mind—as well as in the letter quoted—that date also seemed to mark a declaration of war against the Jews of Europe.

25. Hitler quoted in Keegan, *Second World War*, p. 186; Reichenau and Manstein orders in Klee and Dressen, *Gott mit Uns!* pp. 39–42; Bartov, *Hitler's Army*, pp. 128–31; Guderian quoted in Poliakov and Wolf, *Dritte Reich*, pp. 450-58.

26. Letter (16 Jan. 1945), in Prüller, *Diary*, p. 177; Poliakov and Wolf, *Dritte Reich*, pp. 398–416; Bartov, *Eastern Front*, p. 83 (see generally pp. 68–105); Bartov, *Hitler's Army*, pp. 132–37; Messerschmidt, *Die Wehrmacht im NS-Staat*, pp. 441-80; monthly report of Feldpostprüfstelle, Pz.AOK.3 (2 Sept. 1944), in Buchbender and Sterz, *Andere Geischt*, p. 22.

27. Letter of Egon Freytag (28 Aug. 1941), in Bähr and Bähr, *Kriegsbriefe*, p. 150; diary entry (3 Oct. 1941), in Prüller, *Diary*, p. 110; letter of Lieutenant P.G. (1 Feb. 1943), in Buchbender and Sterz, *Andere Gesicht*, p. 105 no. 181; Schneider and Gullans, *Last Letters*, pp. 50–51; article (Dec. 1942), in Prüller, *Diary*, pp. 160–62.

28. Bartov, *Hitler's Army*, p. 133; letters of Corporal W.P.C. (4 Aug. 1944) and Lieutenant K.N. (31 Aug. 1944), in Buchbender and Sterz, *Andere Gesicht*, pp. 154–55 no. 314, 157–58 no. 322; Grupe, *Jahrgang 1916*, pp. 280, 281, 284.

29. Sajer, *Forgotten Soldier*, pp. 216–18, 291.

30. Letter of Lieutenant J.H. 25 Oct. 1941), in Buchbender and Sterz, *Andere Gesicht*, p. 85 no. 138; Diary entry (21 July 1941), in Prüller, *Diary*, pp. 84–85.

31. Letters of Karl Fuchs (17 July, 15 Aug., and 20 and 15 Oct. 1941), in Richardson, *Sieg Heil!* pp. 119, 125–26, 146–47, 144.

32. Letters of Private H. (9 July 1941), Corporal W.F. (22 Aug. 1941), and Sergeant H.S. (21 Sept. 1941), in Buchbender and Sterz, *Andere Gesicht*, pp. 73 no. 103, 79 no. 118, 80–81 no. 125; letter of anonymous soldier (29 Sept. 1943), in Dollwet, "Menschen im Krieg," p. 303; anonymous soldier quoted in Lucas, *War on the Eastern Front*, pp. 34–35.

33. Letter of Harry Mielert (30 Nov. 1942), in Mielert-Pflugradt, *Russische Erde*, p. 40; Malaparte, *Volga Rises in Europe*, p. 119; Erich Dwinger quoted in Clark, *Barbarossa*, p. 146.

34. Diary entry (4 July 1941), in Prüller, *Diary*, p. 75; letters of Corporal L.K. (29 Oct. 1941) and Corporal H.H. (15 Oct. 1941), in Buchbender and Sterz, *Andere Gesicht*, pp. 85 no. 139, 84 no. 135; anonymous soldier quoted in Bartov, *Hitler's Army*, p. 158; letter of Karl Fuchs (3 Aug. 1941), in Richardson, *Sieg Heil!* p. 122.

35. Bartov, "Conduct of War," pp. S36-S37. In his earlier works, Bartov downplayed the whole notion of primary group loyalty and comradeship as an explanation for the resilience of the German soldier, asserting that the enormous losses suffered on the eastern front must have destroyed any such cohesion. He emphasized instead the role of Nazi propaganda, indoctrination, and ideology in creating a formidable fighting force. See, e.g., Bartov, *Eastern Front*; Bartov, "Extremfälle der Normalität"; Bartov, "Daily Life and Motivation in War," pp. 200–14; Bartov, "Von unten betrachtet," pp. 326–44; Bartov, "Soldiers, Nazis, and War," pp. 44–60; Bartov, *Hitler's Army*. Without disputing the role of ideology (indeed, I agree with its importance), I believe that Bartov overlooked or minimized the impact of more positive ideals such as that of *Volksgemeinschaft* in motivating German troops, an oversight perhaps partially addressed in his article "The Conduct of War," esp. pp. S36–S37.

36. Martin Broszat, "National Socialism," pp. 136–40; Eksteins, *Rites of Spring*, pp. 90, 93–94, 118; Vansittart, *Voices from the Great War*, pp. 21, 67. See also Mosse, *Fallen Soldiers*.

37. Rilke quoted in Eksteins, *Rites of Spring*, p. 193; Zweig and Hitler quoted in Vansittart, *Voices from the Great War*, pp. 27, 261; Bartov, "The Missing Years," p. 51.

38. Eksteins, *Rites of Spring*, p. 257; Stern, "National Socialism as Temptation," pp. 147–57; J. O'Neill, *German Army*, pp. 67–68; Eksteins, *Rites of Spring*, pp. 297, 303, 309, 324.

39. Ley quoted in Mosse, *Fallen Soldiers*, p. 167; on the myth of the new man generally, see pp. 64–65, 78–80, 166–69, 182–85, 208–11. See also Hüppauf, "Langemarck," p. 78; Herf, *Reactionary Modernism*, pp. 37, 38 n. 57; Lane, "Nazi Ideology," p. 23.

40. On the issues of the Nazi social revolution and the debate over whether Nazism promoted a modernization of Germany, see Schoenbaum, *Hitler's Social Revolution;* Dahrendorf, *Society and Democracy in Germany;* Peukert, *Inside Nazi Germany;* Zitelmann, *Hitler,* Prinz, *Vom neuen Mittelstand;* Prinz and Zitelmann, *Nationalsozialismus und Modernisierung;* Harlander and Fehl, *Hitlers sozialer Wohnungsbau;* Smelser, *Robert Ley;* Smelser, "How 'Modern' were the Nazis?" pp. 285–302; Gispen, "National Socialism and the Technological Culture," pp. 387–406; Mason, *Sozialpolitik im Dritten Reich,* Mason, *Social Policy in the Third Reich;* Stephenson, "Modernization, Emancipation, Mobilization"; Childers and Caplan, *Re-Evaluating the Third Reich;* Alber, "Nationalsozialismus und Modernisierung"; Turner, "Fascism and Modernization"; Aly and Heim, *Vordenker der Vernichtung;* Aly and Heim, "Die Ökonomie der 'Endlösung'"; Browning, "German Technocrats, Jewish Labor, and the Final Solution"; Burleigh and Wippermann, *The Racial State.*

41. Schoenbaum, *Hitler's Social Revolution*, pp. 247–49; Hitler speech of 30 Sept. 1942 in Domarus, *Hitler*, p. 1922. See also Zitelmann, *Hitler*, pp. 122–45. On the modernizing aspects of the National Socialist revolution on the army, see Müller, "The Army and the Third Reich: An Essay in Historical Interpretation," in his *Army, Politics, and Society,* pp. 16–53; O'Neill, *German Army*, esp. chap. 5, "The Army and Party Ideology," pp. 62–83.

42. Ansbacher, "Attitudes of German Prisoners of War," pp. 15, 21–38; Niethammer, "Heimat und Front," p. 175; Steinert, *Hitler's War*, pp. 196–302; Berghahn, "Meinungsforschung im 'Dritten Reich' "; Kershaw, *The "Hitler Myth,"* p. 209; Bartov, "The Missing Years," pp. 52–65. On the Nazi revolution, see Schoenbaum, *Hitler's Social Revolution*; Dahrendorf, *Society and Democracy in Germany*; Peukert, *Inside Nazi Germany*; Zitelmann, *Hitler*; Prinz, *Vom neuen Mittelstand*; Prinz and Zitelmann, *Nationalsozialismus und Modernisierung*; Harlander and Fehl, *Hitlers sozialer Wohnungsbau*; Smelser, *Robert Ley*; Smelser, "How 'Modern' Were the Nazis?"; Gispen, "National Socialism and the Technological Culture."

43. Letters of Oskar Prinz von Preussen (Sept. 1939), Hermann Witzemann (21 June 1941), Siegbert Stehmann (16 Nov. 1941), Wolfgang Döring (16 June 1941), and Reinhard Becker-Glauch (23 June 1942), in Bähr and Bähr, *Kriegsbriefe*, pp. 13, 34, 415, 19, 399.

44. Letter of Private von Kaull, in Bartov, *Hitler's War*, p. 166; letter of Private K.B. (15 April 1940), in Buchbender and Sterz, *Andere Gesicht*, p. 48 no. 42; letter of Hans Aug. Vowinckel (18 Dec. 1940) in Bähr and Bähr, *Kriegsbriefe*, p. 41; letters of Karl Fuchs (27 May and 3 June 1941), in Richardson, *Sieg Heil!* pp. 106, 109; Pöppel, *Heaven and Hell,* p. 99.

45. Letter of anonymous soldier, in Dollwet, "Menschen im Krieg," p. 294; diary

entries (8 Oct. and Nov. 1939, Sept. 1943, Dec. 1942), in Prüller, *Diary*, pp. 46, 49, 164, 161.

46. Letter of anonymous soldier (8 Aug. 1940), in Dollwet, "Menschen im Krieg," p. 296; letter of Eberhard Wendebourg (5 Oct. 1941), in Bähr and Bähr, *Kriegsbriefe*, p. 107; Grupe, *Jahrgang 1916*, pp. 113–14.

47. Letters of Günter von Scheven (18 Aug. 1941 and 2. Advent 1941, 9 and 21 March 1942), in Bähr and Bähr, *Kriegsbriefe*, pp. 110–11, 113, 116.

48. Anonymous soldier quoted in Hastings, *Overlord,* p. 219; letters of Sebastian Mendelssohn-Bartholdy (Oct. 1944 and 27 Nov. 1944), Heinz Küchler (3 Sept. 1939), and Klaus-Degenhard Schmidt (11 Dec. 1944), in Bähr and Bähr, *Kriegsbriefe*, pp. 391, 394, 157, 410.

49. Letters of Private W.P. (22 March 1942), Sonderführer H. (1 Jan. 1943), Lieutenant H.H. (28 Jan. 1943) and Lieutenant H.B. (29 Jan. 1943), in Buchbender and Sterz, *Andere Gesicht*, pp. 110 no. 192, 100 no. 171, 104–5 no. 179, 112 no. 199.

50. Letter of Karl Fuchs (9 Nov. 1940), in Richardson, *Sieg Heil!*, p. 80; Sajer, *Forgotten Soldier*, pp. 342, 399, 217.

51. Letter of Harry Mielert (27 Nov. 1941), in Mielert-Pflugradt, *Russische Erde*, p. 34; letter of Friedebald Kruse (31 Dec. 1941), in Bähr and Bähr, *Kriegsbriefe*, p. 316; Sajer, *Forgotten Soldier*, pp. 388, 400; Grupe, *Jahrgang 1916*, p. 252.

52. Letters of anonymous soldiers (29 Sept. 1943, 19 Aug. 1941, 26 Sept. 1942), in Dollwet, "Menschen im Krieg," pp. 303, 317, 319.

53. Letter of Corporal E.N. (15 April 1940), in Buchbender and Sterz, *Andere Gesicht*, p. 51 no. 48; letter of Wilhelm Rubino (12 July 1941), in Bähr and Bähr, *Kriegsbriefe*, p. 60; Grupe, *Jahrgang 1916*, p. 230.

54. Letters of anonymous soldiers (2 Aug. and 23 July 1944), in Dollwet, "Menschen im Krieg," pp. 310, 313; letters of Private K.K. (July 1944), Private B.P. (8 Aug. 1944), Lieutenant K.N. (late July 1944), Corporal C.B. (1 Aug. 1944), Corporal A.K. (late July 1944), and Lieutenant H.W.M. (28 July 1944), in Buchbender and Sterz, *Andere Gesicht*, pp. 144 no. 285, 147 no. 294, 142 no. 280, 154 no. 313, 143 no. 281, 146 no. 289.

55. Letters of Reinhard Pagenkopf (25 Feb. 1945) and Reinhard Goes (23 Nov. 1941), in Bähr and Bähr, *Kriegsbriefe*, pp. 443, 457; letters of Lieutenant K. (3 Sept. 1944), Lieutenant H.H. (17 Sept. 1944), and Private F.S. (30 March 1945), in Buchbender and Sterz, *Andere Gesicht*, pp. 158–59 no. 323, 139 no. 273, 167 no. 344.

56. Woltersdorf, *Gods of War*, pp. 141, 170; Ulrich Luebke quoted in Lucas, *Experiences of War,* p. 188; Grupe, *Jahrgang 1916*, pp. 60–61; Peukert, *Inside Nazi Germany*, pp. 241–42.

57. Eksteins, *Rites of Spring*, p. 303; Peukert, *Inside Nazi Germany*, p. 242.

Chapter 9. The Lost Years

1. Diary entries (early May 1942, 24 April 1943), in Pabst, *Der Ruf der äußersten Grenze*, pp. 93–94, 201–202.

2. Heck, *Child of Hitler*, p. 197.

3. Ibid., p. 206.

4. Diary entry of Walter D. (30 May 1945), in Breloer, *Mein Tagebuch.*, p. 339; Diary entry (28 April 1945), in Altner, *Totentanz Berlin,* p. 160.

5. Pöppel, *Heaven and Hell*, pp. 239–44.

6. Ibid., pp. 244–48.

7. Woltersdorf, *Gods of War*, pp. 136, 149, 186.

8. Ibid., pp. 170, 213.

9. Grupe, *Jahrgang 1916*, pp. 327, 330–31, 340.

10. Ibid., pp. 364–66, 360.

11. Knappe and Brusaw, *Soldat*, pp. 297–98.

12. Ibid., pp. 331–333.

13. Heck, *Child of Hitler*, pp. 206–7; Grupe, *Jahrgang 1916*, p. 364; Hansmann, *Vorüber—nicht vorbei*, p. 160.

14. Pöppel, *Heaven and Hell*, pp. 251, 256; Knappe and Brusaw, *Soldat*, p. 307; Hansmann, *Vorüber—nicht vorbei*, pp. 163, 172.

15. Interviews with Ernst-Peter Kilian, Hans-Hermann Riedel, Otto Richter, and Hugo Nagel, in Schröder, *Die gestohlenen Jahre*, pp. 884, 885–86, 886–87, 888–89.

16. Letter of Harald Henry (1/3 Dec. 1941), in Bähr and Bähr, *Kriegsbriefe*, p. 86.

17. Interviews with Uwe Pries and Emil Dahlke, in Schröder, *Die gestohlenen Jahre*, pp. 897–98, 898–99.

18. Interviews with Arthur Pieper and Heinz Rieckmann, in Schröder, *Die gestohlenen Jahre*, pp. 900, 903; Gerd S. quoted in Focke and Reimer, *Alltag unterm Hakenkreuz*, p. 61.

19. Interview with Ewald Döring, in Schröder, *Die gestohlenen Jahre*, p. 900.

20. Interview with Walter Nowak, in Schröder, *Die gestohlenen Jahre*, p. 901.

21. Hörbach, *Die verratenen Söhne*, pp. 124, 128–129.

22. Ibid., pp. 245–46.

23. Hörbach, *Die verratenen Söhne*; Gerlach, *Die verratene Armee;* Kirst, *08/15;* Ott, *Haie und kleine Fische;* Heinrich, *Das geduldige Fleisch;* Böll, *Der Zug war pünktlich;* Böll, *Wo warst du, Adam?* Andersch, *Die Kirschen der Freiheit.* For more on war literature in postwar Germany, see Baron and Müller, "Die 'Perspektive des kleinen Mannes' in der Kriegsliteratur der Nachkriegszeiten"; Nutz, "Krieg als Abenteuer"; Wagener, "Soldaten zwischen Gehorsam und Gewissen"; Schneider, "Geschichte durch die Hintertür"; Pfeifer, *Der deutsche Kriegsroman.*

24. See Nutz, "Krieg als Abenteuer," p. 277.

25. W. Schröder, *Nur ein Kriegstagebuch*, pp. 189–90.

Chapter 10. A Bitter Truth

1. Interview with Karl Piotrowski, in Schröder, *Die gestohlenen Jahre*, p. 910 (see generally pp. 907–13).

2. Interviews with Karl Piotrowski and Karl Vogt, in Schröder, *Die gestohlenen Jahre*, pp. 909–10, 912.

3. Letter of G. Beug (27 May 1940), in Knoch, "Gewalt wird zur Routine," p. 319; diary entry of Klaus Löscher (1940), letters of Eberhard Wendebourg (5 Oct. 1941) and Wolfgang Döring (7 Dec. 1940), in Bähr and Bähr, *Kriegsbriefe*, pp. 321, 106, 19.

4. Sajer, *Forgotten Soldier*, pp. 118.

5. Woltersdorf, *Gods of War*, p. 74; Sajer, *Forgotten Soldier*, p. 465.

6. Dupuy, *A Genius for War*, pp. 253–54. For an excellent comparative analysis of the German and American armies, see van Creveld, *Fighting Power.* See also Hastings,

Overlord; Holmes, _Firing Line;_ Kennett, _G.I.;_ Perret, _There's a War to be Won;_ Shils and Janowitz, "Cohesion and Disintegration"; Madej, "Effectiveness and Cohesion"; Marshall, _Men against Fire;_ Stouffer, et al., _The American Soldier._

7. Fussell, _Wartime,_ pp. 129–43.

8. Messerschmidt, _Die Wehrmacht im NS-Staat,_ p. 356.

9. See, e.g., Steinert, _Hitler's War;_ William Sheridan Allen, "Die deutsche Öffentlichkeit und die 'Reichskristallnacht:' Konflikte zwischen Werthierarchie und Propaganda im Dritten Reich," in Detlev Peukert and Jürgen Reulecke, eds., _Die Reihen fast geschlossen: Beiträge zur Geschichte des Alltags unterm Nationalsozialismus_ (Wuppertal, 1981), pp. 397–411; Kele, _Nazis and Workers;_ Hamilton, _Who Voted for Hitler?;_ Childers, _The Nazi Voter;_ Kershaw, _Popular Opinion and Political Dissent in the Third Reich;_ Kershaw, "Antisemitismus und Volksmeinung"; Kershaw, "The Persecution of the Jews and German Popular Opinion," Gordon, _Hitler, Germans, and the "Jewish Question";_ Kolka, "'Public Opinion' in Nazi Germany," Marrus, "The Theory and Practice of Anti-Semitism"; Streit, _Keine Kameraden;_ Streit, "The German Army and the Politics of Genocide"; Bartov, _Eastern Front._

10. Bartov, _Hitler's Army,_ p. 60 (see generally chap. 3, "The Perversion of Discipline," pp. 59–105).

11. Sledge, _With the Old Breed,_ p. 315.

12. Bartov, _Hitler's Army,_ p. 182; Mommsen, "Kriegserfahrungen," p. 13.

13. Steinert, _Hitler's War,_ pp. 282–83, 289; Trevor-Roper, _The Goebbels Diaries,_ pp. 95, 21, 113; Keitel quoted in Messerschmidt, _Die Wehrmacht im NS-Staat,_ p. 451. See also Bartov, "The Missing Years," pp. 46–65.

BIBLIOGRAPHY

Letters, Diaries, Contemporary Accounts, Oral Histories, and Everyday Histories

Adam, Wilhelm. *Der schwere Entschuß: Autobiographie.* Berlin, 1974.

Aicher, Otl. *Innenseiten des Kriegs.* Frankfurt, 1985.

Altner, Helmut. *Totentanz Berlin. Tagebuchblätter eines Achtzehnjährige.* Offenbach am Main, 1947.

Alvensleven, Udo von. *Lauter Abschiede: Tagebuch im Kriege.* Frankfurt, Berlin, and Vienna, 1971.

Arnold, Heinz Ludwig, and Stephan Reinhardt, eds. *Dokumentarliteratur.* Munich, 1973.

Arnold, Sabine Rosemarie, and Manfred Hettling. "Briefe aus Stalingrad in sowjetischen Archiven." In *Stalingrad: Mythos und Wirklichkeit einer Schlacht,* ed. Wolfram Wette and Gerd R. Ueberschär, pp. 82-89. Frankfurt, 1992.

Bähr, Hans. *Die Stimmen des Menschen: Briefe und Aufzeichnungen aus der ganzen Welt, 1939–1945.* Munich, 1961.

Bähr, Walter, and Hans W. Bähr, eds. *Kriegsbriefe Gefallener Studenten, 1939–1945.* Tübingen and Stuttgart, 1952.

Bamm, Peter. *Die unsichtbare Flagge: Ein Bericht.* Frankfurt, 1958.

Baron, Ulrich, and Hans-Harald Müller. "Die 'Perspektive des kleinen Mannes' in der Kriegsliteratur der Nachkriegszeiten." In *Der Krieg des Kleinen Mannes: Eine Militärgeschichte von unten,* ed. Wolfram Wette, pp. 344-60. Munich, 1992.

Bauer, Josef Martin. *Die Kraniche der Nogaia: Tagebuchblätter aus dem Feldzug im Osten.* Munich, 1942.

Bayer, Ingeborg, ed. *Ehe Alles Legende wird: Das Dritte Reich in Erzählungen, Dokumenten, Berichten.* Baden-Baden, 1982.

Bayerlein, Fritz. "Battle of Normandy, Operation of Panzer Lehr Division: Notes of Interview with General Bayerlein, August 5th, 1950 (taken down by Chester Wilmot)." Liddell Hart Centre for Military Archives, London. 1950.

———. "Panzer Lehr Division (Jan.–28 July 1944)." In *World War II German Military Studies,* ed. Donald Detwiler, Charles Burdick, and Jürgen Rohwer, vol. 3. New York, 1979.

Beck, Johannes, ed. *Terror und Hoffnung in Deutschland, 1933–1945: Leben im Faschismus.* Reinbek bei Hamburg, 1980.

Benz, Wolfgang, ed. *Die Vertreibung der Deutschen aus dem Osten: Ursachen, Ereignisse, Folgen.* Frankfurt, 1985.

Benz, Wolfgang, and Angelika Schardt, eds. *Kriegsgefangenschaft: Berichte über das Leben in Gefangenenlagern der Allierten von Otto Engelbert, Kurt Glaser, Hans Jonitz, und Heinz Pust.* Munich, 1991.

Berger, Thomas. *Lebenssituationen unter der Herrschaft des Nationalsozialismus.* Frankfurt, 1981.

Beyer, Wilhelm Raimund. *Stalingrad: Unten, wo das Leben konkret war.* Frankfurt, 1987.

————. "Stalingrad—unten, wo das Leben konkret war." In *Der Krieg des Kleinen Mannes: Eine Militärgeschichte von unten,* ed. Wolfram Wette, pp. 240–54. Munich, 1992.

Blumentritt, Günther. "Warum hat der deutsche Soldat in aussichtsloser Lage bis zum Schluß des Krieges 1939–1945 gekämpft?" In *Foreign Military Study B-338,* ed. U.S. Army Historical Division, Europe. Allendorf, 1947.

Borscheid, Peter. "Plädoyer für eine Geschichte des Alltäglichen." In *Alltagsgeschichte: Modetorheit oder neues Tor zur Vergangenheit?* ed. Peter Borscheid, pp. 78-99. Göttingen, 1987.

Borsdorf, Ulrich, and Mathilde Jamin, eds. *Über Leben im Krieg: Kriegserfahrungen in einer Industrieregion, 1939–1945.* Reinbek bei Hamburg, 1989.

Breloer, Heinrich, ed. *Mein Tagebuch: Geschichten vom Überleben, 1939–1947.* Cologne, 1984.

Brockdorff, Dieter. *Einer vom Jahrgang 18: Das Schicksal des Hitlerjungen Günther Fries.* Rastatt, 1963.

Buchbender, Ortwin, and Reinhold Sterz, eds. *Das andere Gesicht des Krieges: Deutsche Feldpostbriefe, 1939–1945.* Munich, 1982.

Bundesministerium für Vertriebene, ed. *Die Vertreibung der deutschen Bevolkerung aus den Gebieten östlich der Oder-Neiße.* 3 vols. Munich, 1984.

Bundeszentrale für politische Bildung, ed. *Leben im Dritten Reich.* Bonn, 1986.

Charman, Terry. *The German Home Front, 1939–1945.* New York, 1989.

Dollinger, Hans, ed. *Kain, wo ist dein Bruder? Was der Mensch im Zweiten Weltkrieg erleiden mußte. Dokumentiert in Tagebüchern und Briefen.* Frankfurt, 1987.

Dollwet, Joachim. "Menschen im Krieg: Bejahung—und Widerstand? Eindrücke und Auszüge aus der Sammlung von Feldpostbriefen des Zweitenweltkrieges in Landeshauptarchiv Koblenz." *Jahrbuch für Westdeutsche Landesgeschichte* 13 (1987): 279–322.

Durian, W. *Infanterieregiment Grossdeutschland Greift An.* Berlin, 1942.

Eckart, Wolfgang. "Von der Agonie einer mißbrauchten Armee: Anmerkungen zur Verwundeten-und Krankenversorgung im Kessel von Stalingrad." In *Stalingrad: Mythos und Wirklichkeit einer Schlacht,* ed. Wolfram Wette and Gerd R. Ueberschär, pp. 108–30. Frankfurt, 1992.

Englemann, Bernt. *In Hitler's Germany: Everyday Life in the Third Reich.* Trans. Krishna Winston. New York, 1986.

Focke, Harald, and Uwe Reimer. *Alltag unterm Hakenkreuz: Wie die Nazis das Leben der Deutschen veränderten.* Reinbek bei Hamburg, 1980.

Franzke, Jürgen. *"All diese Jahre . . . ": Lebensgeschichte des Metallfacharbeiters Ernst Meinking.* Cologne, 1982.

Fröhlich, Roswitha. *Ich konnte einfach nichts sagen: Tagebuch einer Kriegsgefangenen.* Reinbek bei Hamburg, 1981.

Fuchs, Helmut. *Wer spricht von Siegen. Der Bericht über unfreiwillige Jahre in Rußland.* Munich, 1987.

Gericke, B. "Die Deutsche Feldpost im Zweiten Weltkrieg: Eine Dokumentation über Einrichtung, Aufbau, Einsatz, und Dienste." *Archiv für Deutsche Postgeschichte* 1 (1971).

Geyr von Schweppenburg, Leo. "Panzer Tactics in Normandy." In *World War II German Military Studies.* ed. Donald Detwiler, Charles Burdick, and Jürgen Rohwer, vol. 2. New York, 1979.

Golovchanski, Anatoly, et al. *"Ich will raus aus diesem Wahnsinn":Deutsche Briefe von der Ostfront, 1941–1945, aus sowjetischen Archiven.* Wuppertal, 1991.

Gosztony, Peter, ed. *Der Kampf um Berlin 1945 in Augenzeugenberichten.* Munich, 1985.

Granzow, Klaus. *Tagebuch eines Hitlerjungen, 1943–1945.* Bremen, 1965.

Granzow, Klaus, ed. *Letzte Tage in Pommern: Tagebücher, Erinnerungen, und Dokumente der Vertreibung.* Munich, 1984.

Grebe, Karl. *Militärmusik.* Munich, 1958.

Grunert, Hansheinrich. *Der zerrissene Soldat.* Berlin, 1962.

Grupe, Friedrich. *Jahrgang 1916: Die Fahne war mehr als der Tod.* Munich, 1989.

Guderian, Heinz. "Employment of Panzer Forces on the Western Front." In *World War II German Military Studies,* ed. Donald Detwiler, Charles Burdick, and Jürgen Rohwer, vol. 3. New York, 1979.

———. "Panzer Tactics in Normandy." In *World War II German Military Studies,* ed. Donald Detwiler, Charles Burdick, and Jürgen Rohwer, vol. 3. New York, 1979.

Hansmann, Claus. *Vorüber—nicht vorbei: Russische Impressionen, 1941–1943.* Frankfurt and Berlin, 1989.

Hartlaub, Felix. *Im Sperrkreis: Aufzeichnungen aus dem Zweiten Weltkrieg.* Frankfurt, 1984.

Hartung, Hugo. *Schlesien 1944/45: Aufzeichnungen und Tagebücher.* Munich, 1956.

Heck, Alfons. *A Child of Hitler: Germany in the Days When God Wore a Swastika.* Frederick, Colo., 1985.

Heer, Hannes. "Das Fischerhuder Totenbuch: Lebensläufe aus einem deutschen Dorf." In *Terror und Hoffnung in Deutschland, 1933–1945: Leben im Faschismus,* ed. Johannes Beck, pp. 79-110. Reinbek bei Hamburg, 1980.

Henke, Josef. "Exodus aus Ostpreußen und Schlesien: Vier Erlebnisberichte." In *Die Vertreibung der Deutschen aus dem Osten: Ursachen, Ereignisse, Folgen,* ed. Wolfgang Benz, pp. 91-104. Frankfurt, 1985.

Herbert, Ulrich. " 'Die guten und die schlechten Zeiten': Überlegungen zur diachronen Analyse Lebensgeschichtlicher Interviews." In *"Die Jahre weiß man nicht, wo man*

die heute hinsetzen soll": Faschismuserfahrungen im Ruhrgebiet, ed. Lutz Niethammer. Berlin and Bonn, 1983.

Hoehne, Gustav. "In Snow and Mud: 31 Days of Attack under Seydlitz during Early
Spring of 1942." In *World War II German Military Studies,* ed. Donald Detwiler,
Charles Burdick, and Jürgen Rohwer, vol. 19. New York, 1979.

Hohoff, Curt. *Woina, Woina: Russisches Tagebuch.* Düsseldorf, 1951.

Holzapfel, Ingo. "Kriegserfahrung." In *Kriegskinder,* ed. Hellmut Lessing, pp. 37–38.
Frankfurt, 1984.

Hübner, Paul. *Lappland Tagebuch 1941.* Kandern, 1985.

Humburg, Martin. "Die Bedeutung der Feldpost für die Soldaten in Stalingrad." In
Stalingrad: Mythos und Wirklichkeit einer Schlacht, ed. Wolfram Wette and Gerd R.
Ueberschär, pp. 68–79. Frankfurt, 1992.

Institut für Zeitgeschichte. *Alltagsgeschichte der NS-Zeit: Neue Perspektive oder Trivi-
alisierung?* Munich, 1984.

Jünger, Ernst. *Der Arbeiter: Herrschaft und Gestalt.* Berlin, 1932.

———. *Copse 125: A Chronicle from the Trench Warfare of 1918.* Trans. Basil
Creighton. London, 1930.

———. *In Stahlgewittern: Aus dem Tagebuch eines Stosstruppführers.* 13th ed. Berlin,
1931.

———. *Der Kampf als inneres Erlebnis.* 1922; rpt. Stuttgart, 1960.

———. *The Storm of Steel: The Diary of a German Storm-Trooper.* New York, 1975.

———. *Strahlungen.* Linz, Regensburg, and Vienna, 1950.

———. "Die totale Mobilmachung." In *Werke,* vol. 5: *Essays I.* Stuttgart, 1960-1965.

———. *das Wäldchen 125: Eine Chronik aus den Grabenkämpfen 1918.* Berlin, 1925.

Kammler, Jörg. *Ich habe die Metzelei satt und laufe über . . . Kasseler Soldaten zwischen
Verweigerung und Widerstand (1939–1945): Eine Dokumentation.* Fuldabrück,
1985.

Kesselring, Albert. "Rapido River Crossing." In *World War II German Military Studies,*
ed. Donald Detwiler, Charles Burdick, and Jürgen Rohwer, vol. 3. New York, 1979.

Kiersch, Gerhard, ed. *Berliner Alltag im Dritten Reich.* Düsseldorf, 1981.

Klee, Ernst, and Willi Dressen, eds. *"Gott mit uns": Der deutsche Vernichtungskrieg im
Osten, 1939–1945.* Frankfurt, 1989.

Klee, Ernst; Willi Dressen; and Volker Riess, eds. *"The Good Old Days": The Holocaust as
Seen by Its Perpetrators and Bystanders.* Trans. Deborah Burnstone. New York, 1991.

Knappe, Siegfried and Ted Brusaw. *Soldat: Reflections of a German Soldier, 1936–1949.*
New York, 1992.

Knoch, Peter. "Das Bild des Russischen Feindes." In *Stalingrad: Mythos und Wirklichkeit
einer Schlacht.* ed. Wolfram Wette and Gerd R. Ueberschär, pp. 160–167. Frankfurt,
1992.

———. "Feldpost—eine unentdeckte historische Quellengattung." *Geschichtsdidaktik*
11, no. 2 (1986): 154–71.

———. "Gewalt wird zur Routine: Zwei Weltkriege in der Erfahrung einfacher

Soldaten." In *Der Krieg des Kleinen Mannes: Eine Militärgeschichte von unten,* ed. Wolfram Wette, pp. 313–23. Munich, 1992.

———. "Kriegsalltag." In *Kriegsalltag: Die Rekonstruktion des Kriegsalltags als Aufgabe der historischen Forschung und der Friedenserziehung,* ed. Peter Knoch, pp. 222–51. Stuttgart, 1989.

———, ed. *Kriegsalltag: Die Rekonstruktion des Kriegsalltags als Aufgabe der historischen Forschung und der Friedenserziehung.* Stuttgart, 1989.

Kolbe, Georg. *Der Bildhauer Günther von Scheven.* Dessau, 1944.

Kraus, Roland. "Die Arbeit am Verdorbenen." In *Kriegskinder,* ed. Hellmut Lessing, pp. 95–100. Frankfurt, 1984.

Kretschmer, Volker, and Detlef Vogel. "Feldpostbriefe im Zweiten Weltkrieg: Propagandainstrument und Spiegelbild von Kriegsauswirkungen." *Sozialwissenschaftliche Informationen* 2 (1990): 103–10.

Krüger, Horst. *A Crack in the Wall: Growing Up under Hitler.* Trans. Ruth Hein. New York, 1986.

———. *Das zerbrochene Haus: Eine Jugend in Deutschland.* Frankfurt, 1982.

Kuby, Erich. *Mein Krieg: Aufzeichnungen aus 2129 Tagen.* Munich, 1975.

———. *Nur noch rauchende Trümmer: Das Ende der Festung Brest, Tagebuch des Soldaten Erich Kuby.* Hamburg, 1959.

Küchler, Heinz. *Pater, Mater, Heinz.* Heidelberg, 1947.

Kühner, Otto Heinrich. *Nikolskoje: Kriegstagebuch auß Rußland.* Frankfurt and Berlin, 1982.

Lange, Horst. *Tagebücher aus dem Zweiten Weltkrieg.* Mainz, 1979.

Latzel, Klaus. "Die Zumutungen des Krieges und der Liebe—zwei Annäherungen an Feldpostbriefen." In *Kriegsalltag: Die Rekonstruktion des Kriegsalltags als Aufgabe der historischen Forschung und der Friedenserziehung,* ed. Peter Knoch, pp. 204–21. Stuttgart, 1989.

Lessing, Hellmut, ed. *Kriegskinder.* Frankfurt, 1984.

Loest, Erich. *Pistole mit Sechszehn: Erzählungen.* Hamburg, 1979.

Looks, Hans, and Hans Fischer, eds. *Arbeitsmänner zwischen Bug und Wolga: Erlebnisberichte und Bilder vom Einsatz des jüngsten Jahrganges an der Ostfront.* Berlin, 1943.

Lucas, James. *Experiences of War: The Third Reich.* London, 1990.

———. *War on the Eastern Front, 1941–1945: The German Soldier in Russia.* New York, 1982.

Luck, Hans von. *Panzer Commander: The Memoirs of Colonel Hans von Luck.* New York, 1989.

Maaβ, Winfried. *Die Funfzigjährigen: Porträt einer verratenen Generation.* Hamburg, 1980.

Malaparte, Curzio. *The Volga Rises in Europe.* London, 1957.

Mann, Thomas. *Diaries, 1918–1933.* Trans. Richard and Clara Winston. London, 1984.

Maschmann, Melita. *Account Rendered: A Dossier on My Former Self.* Trans. Geoffrey Strachan. London, 1964.

Matthies, Kurt. *Ich hörte die Lerchen singen: Ein Tagebuch aus dem Osten, 1941/45.* Munich, 1956.

Mielert-Pflugradt, Gerda, ed. *Russische Erde. Kriegsbriefe aus Rußland.* Stuttgart, 1950.

Mohrmann, Wolf-Dieter. *Der Krieg ist hart und grausam! Feldpostbriefe an den Osnabrücker Regierungspräsidenten, 1941–44.* Osnabrück, 1984.

————. "Die Sammlung von Feldpostbriefen im Niedersächsischen Staatsarchiv in Osnabrück: Gedanken zu Genese, Quellenwert, und Struktur." In *Kriegsalltag: Die Rekonstruktion des Kriegsalltags als Aufgabe der historischen Forschung und der Friedenserziehung.* ed. Peter Knoch, pp. 25–39. Stuttgart, 1989.

Mommsen, Hans. "Kriegserfahrungen." In *Über Leben im Krieg: Kriegserfahrungen in einer Industrieregion, 1939–45.* ed. Ulrich Borsdorf and Mathilde Jamin, pp. 7–14. Reinbek bei Hamburg, 1989.

Mosse, George L. *Der nationalsozialistische Alltag: So lebte man unter Hitler.* Königstein/Taunus, 1979.

Müller, Rolf-Dieter. " 'Was wir an Hunger ausstehen müssen, könnt Ihr Euch gar nicht denken': Eine Armee verhungert." In *Stalingrad: Mythos und Wirklichkeit einer Schlacht,* ed. Wolfram Wette and Gerd R. Ueberschär, pp. 131–145. Frankfurt, 1992.

Müller, Rolf-Dieter, Gerd Ueberschär, and Wolfram Wette. *Wer zurückweicht wird erschossen! Kriegsalltag und Kriegsende in Südwestdeutschland 1944/45.* Freiburg im Breisgau, 1985.

Nebel, Gerhard. *Unter Partisanen und Kreuzfahrern.* Stuttgart, 1950.

Niethammer, Lutz. "Heimat und Front. Versuch, zehn Kriegserinnerungen aus der Arbeiterklasse des Ruhrgebietes zu verstehen." In *"Die Jahre weiss man nicht, wo man die heute hinsetzen soll": Faschismuserfahrungen im Ruhrgebiet, Lebensgeschichte und Sozialkultur im Ruhrgebiet 1930–1960,* ed. Lutz Niethammer, 1:163–232. Berlin and Bonn, 1983.

————, ed. *"Die Jahre weiss man nicht, wo man die heute hinsetzen soll": Faschismuserfahrungen im Ruhrgebiet, Lebensgeschichte und Sozialkultur im Ruhrgebiet 1930–1960.* vol. 1. Berlin and Bonn, 1983.

Noakes, Jeremy, and Geoffrey Pridham, eds. *Nazism: A History in Documents and Eyewitness Accounts, 1919–1945,* Vol. 1, *The Nazi Party, State, and Society, 1919–1939.* New York, 1983.

Oberkommando des Heeres, ed. *Taschenbuch für den Winterkrieg.* Berlin, 1942.

Opitz, Alfred. "Die Stimmung in der Truppe am Vorabend des überfalls auf die Sowjetunion." In *Der Krieg des Kleinen Mannes: Eine Militärgeschichte von unten,* ed. Wolfram Wette, pp. 230–39. Munich, 1992.

Pabel, Reinhold. *Feinde sind auch Menschen.* Oldenburg and Hamburg, 1957.

Pabst, Helmut. *Der Ruf der äußersten Grenze: Tagebuch eines Frontsoldaten.* Tübingen, 1953.

Papadopoulous-Killius, Rosemarie. "Die Verarbeitung von Todesahnungen." In *Stalingrad: Mythos und Wirklichkeit einer Schlacht,* ed. Wolfram Wette and Gerd R. Ueberschär, pp. 146–159. Frankfurt, 1992.

Peukert, Detlev, and Jürgen Reulecke, eds. *Die Reihen fast geschlossen: Beiträge zur Geschichte des Alltags unterm Nationalsozialismus.* Wuppertal, 1981.

Pleyer, Kleo. *Volk im Feld.* Hamburg, 1943.

Podewils, Clemens. *Don und Wolga: Aufzeichnungen aus dem Jahre 1942.* Munich, 1952.

Poliakov, Leon, and Josef Wulf, eds. *Das Dritte Reich und Seine Diener: Dokumente.* Berlin, 1956.

Pöppel, Martin. *Heaven and Hell: The War Diary of a German Paratrooper.* Trans. Louise Willmot. Tunbridge Wells, U.K., 1988.

Praun, Albert. *Soldat in der Telegraphen- und Nachrichtentruppe.* Würzburg, 1965.

Prüller, Wilhelm. *Diary of a German Soldier.* Ed. and trans. H.C. Robbins Landon and Sebastian Leitner. New York, 1963.

Queckbörner, Ludwig. *Die Schutzenkompanie: Ein Handbuch für den Dienstunterricht.* Berlin, 1939.

Rendulic, L. "The Fighting Qualities of the Russian Soldier." In *World War II German Military Studies,* ed. Donald Detwiler, Charles Burdick and Jürgen Rohwer, vol. 19. New York, 1979.

Richardson, Horst Fuchs, ed. and trans. *Sieg Heil! War Letters of Tank Gunner Karl Fuchs, 1937–1941.* Hamden, Conn., 1987.

Ruhl, Klaus-Jörg, ed. *Deutschland 1945: Alltag zwischen Krieg und Frieden in Berichten, Dokumenten und Bildern.* Darmstadt, 1984.

Ryback, Timothy. "Stalingrad: Letters from the Dead." *New Yorker,* Feb. 1, 1993. pp. 58–71.

Sajer, Guy. *The Forgotten Soldier.* 1967; rpt. Washington, D.C., 1990.

Schäfer, Hans Dieter. *Berlin im Zweiten Weltkrieg. Der Untergang der Reichshauptstadt in Augenzeugenberichten.* Munich, 1985.

Schneider, Franz, and Charles Gullans, eds. and trans. *Last Letters from Stalingrad.* Westport, Conn., 1974.

Schoenberner, Gerhard, ed. *Wir haben es gesehen: Augenzeugenberichte über Terror und Judenverfolgung im Dritten Reich.* Hamburg, 1962.

Schröder, Hans Joachim. "Alltag der Katastrophen: Der Kampf um Stalingrad im Erinnerungsinterview." In *Stalingrad: Mythos und Wirklichkeit einer Schlacht,* ed. Wolfram Wette und Gerd R. Ueberschär, pp. 168–77. Frankfurt, 1992.

———. "Erfahrungen deutscher Mannschaftssoldaten während der ersten Phase des Rußlandkrieges." In *Zwei Wege nach Moscow: Vom Hitler-Stalin-Pakt bis zum "Unternehmen Barbarossa,"* ed. Bernd Wegner, pp. 309–25. Munich, 1991.

———. *Die gestohlenen Jahre. Erzählungsgeschichten und Geschichtungserzählung im Interview: Der Zweiten Weltkrieg aus der Sicht ehemaliger Mannschaftssoldaten.* Tübingen, 1992.

———. " 'Ich hänge hier, weil ich getürmt bin': Terror und Verfall im deutschen Militär bei Kriegsende 1945." In *Der Krieg des Kleinen Mannes: Eine Militärgeschichte von unten,* ed. Wolfram Wette, pp. 279–94. Munich, 1992.

————. *Kasernenzeit: Arbeiter erzählen von der Militarausbildung im Dritten Reich.* Frankfurt and New York, 1985.

————. " 'Man kam sich da vor wie ein Stück Dreck': Schikane in der Militärausbildung des Dritten Reichs." In *Der Krieg des Kleinen Mannes. Eine Militärgeschichte von unten,* ed. Wolfram Wette, pp. 183–98. Munich, 1992.

Schröder, Willy. *Nur ein Kriegstagebuch: Rein menschliche Reflektionen.* Baden-Baden, 1982.

Schuler, Emil, and Hans-Werner Sitrius. *Infanterie im Kampf: Erfahrungen und Lehren aus Gefechtsberichten.* Darmstadt, 1963.

Schumann, Willy. *Being Present: Growing Up in Hitler's Germany.* Kent, Ohio, 1991.

Schwerin, Graf von. "116 Panzer Division from the Seine to Aachen." In *World War II German Military Studies,* ed. Donald Detwiler, Charles Burdick, and Jürgen Rohwer, vol. 2. New York, 1979.

Shirer, William L. *Berlin Diary: The Journal of a Foreign Correspondent, 1934–1941.* New York, 1941.

Simon, Max. "Experience Gained in Combat with Russian Infantry." In *World War II German Military Studies,* ed. Donald Detwiler, Charles Burdick, and Jürgen Rohwer, vol. 19. New York, 1979.

Simonow, Konstantin. *Kriegstagebücher,* vol. 1 *1941*; vol. 2; *1942–1945.* Munich, 1979.

Sledge, E.B. *With the Old Breed.* Novato, Calif., 1981.

Stahlberg, Alexander. *Bounden Duty: The Memoirs of a German Officer.* Trans. Patricia Crampton. London, 1990.

Steinbach, Lothar. *Ein Volk, Ein Reich, Ein Glaube? Ehemalige Nationalsozialisten und Zeitzeugen berichten über ihr Leben im Dritten Reich.* Berlin, 1983.

Steinhoff, Johannes, Peter Pechel, and Dennis Showalter, eds. *Deutsche im Zweiten Weltkrieg: Zeitzeugen Sprechen.* Munich, 1989.

Sterz, Reinhold. "Vom Aufbau einer Briefsammlung aus dem Zweiten Weltkrieg." In *Kriegsalltag: Die Rekonstruktion des Kriegsalltags als Aufgabe der historischen Forschung und der Friedenserziehung,* ed. Peter Knoch, pp. 20–24. Stuttgart, 1989.

Tapert, Annette, ed. *Lines of Battle: Letters from American Servicemen, 1941–1945.* New York,1987.

Tekampe, Ludger. *Kriegserzählungen: Eine Studie zur erzählerischen Vergegenwärtigung des Zweiten Weltkrieges.* Mainz, 1989.

Thamer, Hans-Ulrich. *Verführung und Gewalt. Deutschland, 1933–1945.* Berlin, 1986.

Tost, Fritz. *Der Unverbesserliche.* Munich, 1978.

Trevor-Roper, H.R., ed. *The Goebbels Diaries: The Last Days.* London, 1979.

U.S. Department of the Army. "Combat in Russian Forests and Swamps." In *World War II German Military Studies,* ed. Donald Detwiler, Charles Burdick, and Jürgen Rohwer, vol. 17. New York, 1979.

————. "Effects of Climate on Combat in European Russia." In *World War II German Military Studies,* ed. Donald Detwiler, Charles Burdick, and Jürgen Rohwer, vol. 17. New York, 1979.

————. "Military Improvisations during the Russian Campaign." In *World War II*

German Military Studies, ed. Donald Detwiler, Charles Burdick, and Jürgen Rohwer, vol. 17. New York, 1979.

———. "Operations of Encircled Forces: German Experiences in Russia." In *World War II German Military Studies,* ed. Donald Detwiler, Charles Burdick, and Jürgen Rohwer, vol. 17. New York, 1979.

———. "Small Unit Actions during the German Campaign in Russia." In *World War II German Military Studies,* ed. Donald Detwiler, Charles Burdick, and Jürgen Rohwer, New York, 1979.

———. "Terrain Factors in the Russian Campaign." In *World War II German Military Studies,* eds. Donald Detwiler, Charles Burdick, and Jürgen Rohwer, vol. 17. New York, 1979.

Vansittart, Peter. *Voices from the Great War.* New York, 1984.

Vogel, Detlef. "Der Kriegsalltag im Spiegel von Feldpostbriefen (1939–1945)." In *Der Krieg des Kleinen Mannes: Eine Militärgeschichtge von unten,* ed. Wolfram Wette, pp. 199–12. Munich, 1992.

Volksbund Deutsche Kriegsgräberfürsorge E.V., ed. *Den Gefallenen: Ein Buch des Gedenkens und des Trostes.* Munich and Salzburg, 1952.

Warlimont, Walter. "From the Invasion to the Siegfried Line." In *World War II German Military Studies,* ed. Donald Detwiler, Charles Burdick, and Jürgen Rohwer, vol. 2. New York, 1979.

Weidenreich, Peter H. "Why He Fights." *Infantry Journal* 56, no.2 (1945): 43–45.

Weinberg, Gerhard. "Dokumentation: Adolf Hitler und der NS-Führungsoffizier (NSFO)." *Vierteljahrshefte für Zeitgeschichte* 12 (1964): 443–56.

Weinert, Erich. *Memento Stalingrad: Ein Frontnotizbuch.* Berlin, 1953.

Wette, Wolfram. " 'Es roch nach Ungeheuerlichem': Zeitzeugenbericht eines Panzer-schützen über die Stimmung in einer Einheit des deutschen Ostheeres am Vorabend des überfalls auf die Sowjetunion 1941." *1999: Zeitschrift für Sozialgeschichte des 20. und 21. Jahrhunderts* 4, no. 4 (1989): 62–73.

———. "Militärgeschichte von unten." In *Der Krieg des Kleinen Mannes: Eine Militär-geschichte von unten,* ed. Wolfram Wette, pp. 9–47. Munich, 1992.

———. "Sowjetische Erinnerungen an den deutschen Vernichtungskrieg." In *"Ich wundere mich, daß ich noch lebe": Sowjetische Augenzeugen berichten,* ed. Paul Kohl, pp. 295–315. Gutersloh, 1990.

———. " 'Unsere Stimmung ist auf dem Nullpunkt angekommen': Berichte von Feldpostprüfstellen über die 'Kessel-Post.' " In *Stalingrad. Mythos und Wirk-lichkeit einer Schlacht.* eds. Wolfram Wette and Gerd R. Ueberschär, pp. 90–101. Frankfurt, 1992.

———, ed. *Der Krieg des Kleinen Mannes: Eine Militärgeschichte von unten.* Munich, 1992.

Wieder, Joachim. *Die Tragödie von Stalingrad: Erinnerungen eines Überlebenden.* Deggendorf, 1955.

Wiesen, W. *Es grüßt Euch Alle, Berthold: Die Feldpostbriefe von Bertold Paulus aus Kastel.* Nonnweiler-Otzenhausen, 1991.

Woltersdorf, Hans Werner. *Gods of War: Memoir of a German Soldier.* Trans. Nancy Benvenga. Novato, Calif., 1990.

Zentner, Christian, ed. *Lexikon des Zweiten Weltkriegs mit einer Chronik der Ereignisse von 1939–1945 und Ausgewählten Dokumenten.* Herrsching, 1977.

Ziesel, Kurt, ed. *Krieg und Dichtung. Soldaten werden Dichter—Dichter werden Soldaten, Ein Volksbuch.* Vienna, 1943.

Zwerenz, Gerhard. *"Soldaten sind Mörder": Die Deutschen und der Krieg.* Munich, 1988.

Novels, Short Stories, and Essays

Andersch, Alfred. *Die Kirschen der Freiheit: Ein Bericht.* Zurich, 1968.

———. *Winterspelt.* Zurich, 1977.

Bender, Hans, ed. *Geschichten aus dem Zweiten Weltkrieg.* Munich and Zurich, 1983.

Berthold, Will. *Das letzte Gefecht.* Munich, 1987.

Bienek, Horst. *Erde und Feuer.* Munich, 1985.

Böll, Heinrich. *Absent without Leave: Two Novellas by Heinrich Böll.* Trans. Leila Vennewitz. New York, 1975.

———. *Adam and The Train: Two Novels by Heinrich Böll.* Trans. Leila Vennewitz. New York, 1970.

———. *Als der Krieg ausbrach, als der Krieg zu Ende war.* Frankfurt, 1962.

———. *The Casualty.* Trans. Leila Vennewitz. New York, 1989.

———. *Die Verwundung.* Bornheim, 1983.

———. *Wo warst du, Adam?* Cologne, 1951.

———. *Der Zug war pünktlich.* Cologne, 1949.

Bosper, Albert. *Der Hiwi Borchowitsch.* Stuttgart, 1958.

Boyd, Mitchell. *The Gentle Infantryman.* Los Angeles, 1985.

Döbler, Hansferdinand. *Kein Alibi: Ein deutscher Roman, 1919–1945.* Berlin, Frankfurt, and Vienna, 1980.

Gerlach, Heinrich. *Die verratene Armee: Ein Stalingrad-Roman.* Munich, 1959.

Goodman, Mitchell. *The End of It.* 1961; rpt. New York, 1989.

Gregor, Manfred. *Die Brücke.* 1958; rpt. Munich, 1983.

Hasemann, Richard. *Gejagt.* Stuttgart, 1953.

Heinrich, Willi. *The Cross of Iron.* Trans. Richard and Clara Winston. 12th ed. New York, 1977.

———. *Das geduldige Fleisch.* Munich, 1955.

Heym, Stefan. *Der bittere Lorbeer.* 1948; rpt. Munich, 1983.

Hofmann, Gert. *Unsere Vergeßlichkeit.* Darmstadt, 1987.

Horbach, Michael. *Die verratenen Söhne.* 1957; rpt. Herrsching, 1989.

Ihlenfeld, Kurt. *Wintergewitter.* Berlin, 1953.

Kiesel, Otto Erich. *Die unverzagte Stadt: Roman in drei Büchern.* Goslar, 1949.

Kirst, Hans Hellmut. *08/15: Trilogie.* 1954; rpt. Klagenfurt, 1977.

Kluge, Alexander. *Schlachtbeschreibung: Der organisatorische Aufbau eines Unglücks.* 1964; rpt. Munich, 1978.

Kolbenhoff, Walter. *Von unserm Fleisch und Blut.* 1947; rpt. Frankfurt, 1983.

Konsalik, Heinz G. *Der Arzt von Stalingrad.* 1956; rpt. Munich, 1984.

Landgrebe, Erich. *Von Dimitrowsk nach Dimitrowsk.* Linz, 1948.

Lange, Horst. *Die Leuchtkugeln: Vier Erzählungen.* 1939–46; rpt. Cologne, 1982.

Ledig, Gert. *Die Stalinorgel.* Hamburg, 1955.

———. *The Tortured Earth: A Novel of the Russian Front.* Chicago, 1956.

Lenz, Hermann. *Neue Zeit.* Frankfurt, 1982.

Lenz, Siegfried. *Ein Kriegsende.* Hamburg, 1984.

———. *The Selected Stories of Siegfried Lenz.* Trans. Breon Mitchell. New York, 1989.

Loest, Erich. *Jungen, die übrig bleiben.* 1950; rpt. Frankfurt, 1985.

Malaparte, Curzio. *Kaputt.* Trans. Cesare Foligno. 1946; rpt. Marlboro, Vt., 1982.

Nekrassow, Viktor. *In den Schützengraben von Stalingrad.* Berlin, 1948.

Noll, Dieter. *Die Abenteuer des Werner Holt: Roman einer Jugend.* 1960; rpt. Cologne, 1982.

Nutz, Walter. "Der Krieg als Abenteuer und Idylle: Landser-Hefte und triviale Kriegsromane." In *Gegenwartsliteratur und Drittes Reich: Deutsche Autoren in der Auseinandersetzung mit der Vergangenheit,* ed. Hans Wagner, pp. 265–283. Stuttgart, 1977.

Ott, Wolfgang. *Haie und kleine Fische.* 1956; rpt. Munich, 1983.

Parth, Wolfgang W. *Vorwärts Kameraden, Wir Müssen Züruck.* 1963; rpt. Klagenfurt, 1963.

Pfeifer, Jochen. *Der deutsche Kriegsroman, 1945–1960: Ein Versuch zur Vermittlung von Literatur und Sozialgeschichte.* Königstein/Taunus, 1981.

Plievier, Theodore. *Stalingrad.* Trans. Richard and Clara Winston. 1948; rpt. New York, 1984.

Pump, Hans. *Vor dem großen Schnee.* Hamburg, 1956.

Richter, Hans Werner. *Die Geschlagenen.* Munich, 1949.

Schneider, Gerhard. "Geschichte durch die Hintertür: Triviale und populärwissenschaftliche Literatur über den Nationalsozialismus und den Zweiten Weltkrieg." *Aus Politik und Zeitgeschichte* 6 (1979): 3–25.

Simon, Claude. *Die Straße in Flandern.* 1960; rpt. Munich, 1985.

Simonow, Konstantin. *Die Lebenden und die Toten.* 1972; rpt. Berlin, 1981.

Stachow, Hasso G. *Der kleine Quast.* Munich and Zurich, 1979.

Wagener, Hans. "Soldaten zwischen Gehorsam und Gewissen: Kriegsroman und -tagebücher." In *Deutsche Autoren in der Auseinandersetzung mit der Vergangenheit,* ed. Hans Wagener, pp. 241–64. Stuttgart, 1977.

Wöss, Fritz. *Hunde, wollt ihr ewig leben?* 1958; rpt. Frankfurt and Berlin, 1983.

Zand, Herbert. *Letzte Ausfahrt: Roman der Eingekesselten.* 1953; rpt. Vienna, 1971.

National Socialism and World War II

Alber, Jens. "Nationalsozialismus und Modernisierung." *Kölner Zeitschrift für Soziologie und Sozialpsychologie* 41 (1989): 346–365.

Aly, Götz, and Susanne Heim.. "Die Ökonomie der 'Endlösung': Menschenvernichtung und wirtschaftliche Neuordnung." In *Beiträge zur Nationalsozialistischen Gesundheits- und Sozialpolitik,* vol. 5, *Sozialpolitik und Judenvernichtung: Gibt es eine Ökonomie der Endlösung?* ed. Götz Aly and Susanne Heim. Berlin, 1987.

———. *Vordenker der Vernichtung: Auschwitz und die deutsche Pläne für eine neue europäische Ordnung.* Hamburg, 1991.

Ambrose, Stephen. *Band of Brothers: E Company, 506th Regiment, 101st Airborne from Normandy to Hitler's Eagle's Nest.* New York, 1992.

Ansbacher, H.L. "Attitudes of German Prisoners of War: A Study of the Dynamics of National-Socialistic Followership." *Psychological Monographs: General and Applied* 62, no. 1 (1948): 1–42.

———. "German Military Psychology." *Psychological Bulletin* 38 (1941): 370–92.

Baird, Jay W. *To Die for Germany: Heroes in the Nazi Pantheon.* Bloomington, Ind., 1990.

Bartov, Omer. "The Conduct of War: Soldiers and the Barbarization of Warfare." *Journal of Modern History* 64, supp. (Dec. 1992): S32–S45.

———. "Daily Life and Motivation in War: The Wehrmacht in the Soviet Union." *Journal of Strategic Studies* 12 (1989): 200–14.

———. *The Eastern Front, 1941–45: German Troops and the Barbarisation of Warfare.* New York, 1986.

———. "Extremfälle der Normalität und die Normalität des Aussergewühnlichen: Deutsche Soldaten an der Ostfront." In *Über Leben im Krieg: Kriegserfahrungen in einer Industrieregion, 1939–1945,* ed. Ulrich Borsdorf and Mathilde Jamin. Reinbek bei Hamburg, 1989.

———. *Hitler's Army: Soldiers, Nazis, and War in the Third Reich.* New York, 1991.

———. "The Missing Years: German Workers, German Soldiers." *German History* 8 (1990): 46–65.

———. "Soldiers, Nazis, and War in the Third Reich." *Journal of Modern History* 63, no. 1 (March 1991): 44–60.

———. "Von Unten betrachtet: Überleben, Zusammenhalt, und Brutalität an der Ostfront." In *Zwei Wege nach Moscow: Vom Hitler-Stalin-Pakt bis zum "Unternehmen Barbarossa,"* ed. Bernd Wegner, pp. 326–44. Munich 1991.

Baynes, John. *Morale: A Study of Men and Courage.* New York, 1967.

Berghahn, Volker. "Meinungsforschung im 'Dritten Reich': Die Mundpropaganda-Aktion der Wehrmacht im letzten Kriegshalbjahr." *Militärgeschichtliche Mitteilungen* 1 (1967): 83–119.

———. "NSDAP und 'Geistige Führung' der Wehrmacht." *Vierteljahrshefte für Zeitgeschichte* 17 (1969): 17–71.

Breithaupt, Hans. *Die Geschichte der 30. Infanterie-Division.* Bad Nauheim, 1955.

Broszat, Martin. *Nationalsozialistische Polenpolitik 1939–1945.* Stuttgart, 1961.

———. "National Socialism: Its Social Basis and Psychological Impact." In *Upheaval and Continuity: A Century of German History,* ed. E.J. Feuchtwanger, pp. 134-51. Pittsburgh, 1974.

Browning, Christopher. "German Technocrats, Jewish Labor, and the Final Solution: A Reply to Götz Aly and Susanne Heim." In *The Path to Genocide: Essays on Launching the Final Solution,* ed. Christopher Browning, pp. 59–76. New York, 1992.

————. *Ordinary Men: Reserve Police Battalion 101 and the Final Solution in Poland.* New York, 1992.

Buchner, Alex. *Das Handbuch der Deutschen Infanterie, 1939–1945.* Friedberg/Hesse, 1989.

————. *Ostfront 1944: The German Defensive Battles on the Russian Front, 1944.* Trans. David Johnston. West Chester, Pa., 1991.

Burleigh, Michael, and Wolfgang Wippermann. *The Racial State: Germany 1933–1945.* Cambridge, Eng., 1991.

Carell, Paul. *Invasion—They're Coming!* Trans. Ewald Osers. New York, 1962.

————. *Scorched Earth: The Russian-German War, 1943–1944.* Trans. Ewald Osers. Boston, 1970.

Childers, Thomas. *The Nazi Voter: The Social Foundations of Fascism in Germany, 1919–1933.* Chapel Hill, N.C., 1983.

Childers, Thomas, and Jane Caplan, eds. *Re-Evaluating the Third Reich.* New York, 1993.

Chodoff, E.P. "Ideology and Primary Groups." *Armed Forces and Society* 9, no. 4 (1983): 569–93.

Clark, Alan. *Barbarossa: The Russian-German Conflict, 1941–1945.* 1965; rpt. New York, 1985.

Cooper, Matthew. *The German Army, 1933–1945.* London, 1978.

Dahrendorf, Ralf. *Society and Democracy in Germany.* New York, 1967.

Dallin, Alexander. *German Rule in Russia, 1941–1945: A Study of Occupation Policies.* London, 1957.

de Zayas, Alfred Maurice. "The Wehrmacht Bureau on War Crimes." *Historical Journal* 35, no. 2 (1992): 383–99.

————. *The Wehrmacht War Crimes Bureau, 1939–1945.* Lincoln, Neb., 1990.

Dicks, Henry V. "German Personality Traits and National Socialist Ideology: A War-Time Study of German Prisoners of War." In *Propaganda in War and Crisis,* ed. Daniel Lerner, pp. 100–161. New York, 1972.

Diehl, James. *The Thanks of the Fatherland: German Veterans after the Second World War.* Chapel Hill, N.C., 1993.

DiNardo, R.L. *Mechanized Juggernaut or Military Anachronism? Horses and the German Army of World War II.* Westport, Conn., 1991.

Dinter, Elmar. *Held oder Feigling: Die körperlichen und seelichen Belastungen des Soldaten im Krieg.* Herford, 1982.

Domarus, Max, ed. *Hitler: Reden und Proklamationen, 1932–1945.* Wiesbaden, 1973.

Dülffer, Jost. "Vom Bündnispartner zum Erfüllungsgehilfen im totalen Krieg. Militär und Gesellschaft in Deutschland, 1933–1945." In *Der Zweite Weltkrieg: Analysen, Grundzüge, Forschunsgbilanz,* ed. Wolfgang Michalka. Munich, 1989.

Dupuy, Trevor N. *A Genius for War: The German Army and the General Staff, 1807–1945.* Englewood Cliffs, N.J., 1977.

Eksteins, Modris. *Rites of Spring: The Great War and the Birth of the Modern Age.* New York, 1989.

Ellis, John. *On the Front Lines: The Experience of War through the eyes of the Allied Soldiers in World War II.* New York, 1990.

Evans, Arthur R., Jr. "Assignment to Armadeddon: Ernst Jünger and Curzio Malaparte on the Russian Front, 1941–43." *Central European History* 14, no. 4 (1981): 295–321.

Fleischhauer, Ingeborg. *Das Dritte Reich und die Deutschen in der Sowjetunion.* Stuttgart, 1983.

Förster, Jürgen. "The Dynamics of Volksgemeinschaft: The Effectiveness of the German Military Establishment in the Second World War." *Military Effectiveness,* vol. 3, *The Second World War,* ed. Allan R. Millett and Williamson Murray, pp. 180–220. Boston, 1988.

―――. "The German Army and the Ideological War against the Soviet Union." In *The Policies of Genocide: Jews and Soviet Prisoners of War in Nazi Germany,* ed. Gerhard Hirschfeld. London, 1986.

―――. "Der historische Ort des Unternehmens Barbarossa." In *Der Zweite Weltkrieg: Analysen, Grundzüge, Forschungsbilanz,* ed. Wolfgang Michalka, pp. 626–40. Munich, 1989.

―――. "New Wine in Old Skins? The Wehrmacht and the War of 'Weltanschauungen,' 1941." In *The German Military in the Age of Total War,* ed. Wilhelm Deist, pp. 304–22. Leamington Spa, 1985.

―――. "Das Unternehmen Barbarossa als Eroberungs- und Vernichtungskrieg." In *Das Deutsche Reich und der Zweite Weltkrieg,* vol. 4, *Der Angriff auf die Sowjetunion,* pp. 440–47. Stuttgart, 1983.

―――. "The Wehrmacht and the War of Extermination against the Soviet Union." *Yad Vashem Studies* 14 (1981): 413–17.

Fox, Robin. "Fatal Attraction: War and Human Nature." *The National Interest* (Winter 1992–1993): 11–20.

Frei, Norbert, ed. *Der nationalsozialististische Krieg.* Frankfurt, 1990.

Fussell, Paul. *Wartime: Understanding and Behavior in the Second World War.* New York, 1989.

Grams, Rolf. *Die 14. Panzer-Division, 1940–1945.* Bad Nauheim, 1957.

Gerns, Ditte. *Hitlers Wehrmacht in der Sowjetunion: Legenden—Wahrheit—Tradition—Dokumente.* Frankfurt, 1985.

Gispen, Kees. "National Socialism and the Technological Culture of the Weimar Republic." *Central European History* 25, no. 4 (1992): 387–406.

Gordon, Sarah. *Hitler, Germans, and the "Jewish Question."* Princeton, N.J., 1984.

Großmann, Horst. *Geschichte der rheinisch-westfälischen 6. Infanterie-Division, 1939–1945.* Bad Nauheim, 1958.

Gurfein, M.I., and Morris Janowitz. "Trends in Wehrmacht Morale." In *Propaganda in War and Crisis,* ed. Daniel Lerner, pp. 200–208. New York, 1972.

Hamilton, Richard. *Who Voted for Hitler?* Princeton, N.J., 1982.

Harlander, Tilman, and Gerhard Fehl. *Hitlers sozialer Wohnungsbau, 1940–1945.* Hamburg, 1986.

Hastings, Max. *Overlord: D-Day and the Battle for Normandy.* New York, 1984.

Heinrich, Graf von Einsiedel. *The Onslaught. The German Drive to Stalingrad.* Trans. Arnold J. Pomerans; foreword by Max Hastings. New York, 1985.

Herf, Jeffrey. *Reactionary Modernism: Technology, Culture, and Politics in Weimar and the Third Reich.* Cambridge, Eng., 1984.

Hillgruber, Andreas. "Der Ostkrieg und die Judenvernichtung." In *"Unternehmen Barbarossa": Der deutsche überfall auf die Sowjetunion 1941,* ed. Gerd Ueberschär and Wolfram Wette, pp. 219–36. Paderborn, 1984.

———. "Das Rußland-Bild der führenden deutschen Militärs vor Beginn des Angriffs auf die Sowjetunion." In *Zwei Wege nach Moscow: Vom Hitler-Stalin-Pakt bis zum "Unternehmen Barbarossa,"* ed. Bernd Wegner, pp. 167–184. Munich, 1991.

Hoey, Albert van. "Todesmarsch und Befreiung." In *Verschleppt zur Sklavenarbeit. Kriegsgefangene und Zwangsarbeiter in Schleswig Holstein,* ed. Gerhard Hoch and Rolf Schwarz, pp. 7–12. Alveslohe, 1985.

Hoffmann, Joachim. *Die Ostlegionen, 1941–1943.* Freiburg, 1974.

Holmes, Richard. *Firing Line.* London, 1985.

Horne, Alistair. *To Lose a Battle: France 1940.* Harmondsworth, Eng., 1969.

Hossbach, Friedrich. *Infanterie im Ostfeldzug 1941/42.* Osterode, 1951.

Howell, Edgar M. "The Soviet Partisan Movement." In *World War II German Military Studies,* ed. Donald Detwiler, Charles Burdick, and Jürgen Rohwer, vol. 18. New York, 1979.

Hüppauf, Bernd. "Langemarck, Verdun, and the Myth of a New Man in Germany after the First World War." *War and Society* 6, no. 2 (1988): 70–103.

Jacobsen, Hans-Adolf. "Kommissarbefehl und Massenexekutionen sowjetischer Kriegsgefangener." In *Anatomie des SS-Staates,* ed. Hans Buchheim, Martin Broszat, Helmut Krausnick, and Hans-Adolf Jacobsen. Freiburg, 1965.

Kamaradschaftsbund 16. Panzer-und Infanterie Division, ed. *Bildband der 16. Panzer-Division.* Bad Nauheim, 1956.

Keegan, John. *The Face of Battle.* New York, 1976.

———. *The Second World War.* New York, 1989.

———. *Six Armies in Normandy: From D-Day to the Liberation of Paris, June 6th-August 25th, 1944.* New York, 1982.

Kehrig, Manfred. *Stalingrad: Analyse und Dokumentation einer Schlacht.* Stuttgart, 1974.

Kele, Max H. *Nazis and Workers: National Socialist Appeals to German Labor, 1919–1933.* Chapel Hill, N.C., 1983.

Kellet, Anthony. *Combat Motivation: The Behavior of Soldiers in Battle.* Boston, 1982.

Kennett, Lee. *G.I.: The American Soldier in World War II.* New York, 1987.

Kershaw, Ian. "Antisemitismus und Volksmeinung: Reaktion auf die Judenverfolgung." In *Bayern in der NS-Zeit*, by Martin Broszat et al., 2:281–300. Munich, 1979.

———. *The 'Hitler Myth': Image and Reality in the Third Reich.* Oxford, 1987.

———. "The Persecution of the Jews and German Popular Opinion in the Third Reich." *Leo Baeck Institute Year Book* 26 (1981): 261–89

———. *Popular Opinion and Political Dissent in the Third Reich: Bavaria 1933–1945.* New York, 1983.

Kitterman, David H. "The Justice of the Wehrmacht Legal System: Servant or Opponent of National Socialism?" *Central European History* 24, no. 4 (1991): 450–62.

Klatt, Paul. *Die 3. Gebirgs-Division, 1939–1945.* Bad Nauheim, 1958.

Klose, Werner. *Generation im Gleichschritt.* Oldenburg and Hamburg, 1964.

Knopp, Guido. *Der verdammte Krieg: Das Unternehmen Barbarossa.* Munich, 1991.

Kolka, Otto Dov. " 'Public Opinion' in Nazi Germany and the 'Jewish Question.' " *Jerusalem Quarterly* 25 (1982): 121–44.

Kroener, Bernhard. "Auf dem Weg zu einer 'Nationalsozialistischen Volksarmee': Die soziale Öffnung des Heeresoffizierkorps im Zweiten Weltkrieg." In *Von Stalingrad zur Währungsreform: Zur Sozialgeschichte des Umbruchs in Deutschland*, ed. Martin Broszat, Klaus-Dietmar Henke, and Hans Woller, pp. 651–82. Munich, 1988. •

Kuby, Erich. *Als Polen deutsch war, 1939–1945.* Ismaning bei Munich, 1986.

———. *Das Ende des Schreckens: Januar bis Mai 1945.* Hamburg, 1984.

Kurowski, Franz. *Die Heeresgruppe Mitte, 1942–1943.* Friedberg, 1989.

Kviz, Frederick J. "Survival in Combat as a Collective Exchange Process." *Journal of Political and Military Sociology* 6 (Fall 1978): 219–32.

Laffin, John. *Jackboot: The Story of the German Soldier.* Newton Abbot, U.K., 1989.

Lakowski, Richard. "Zwischen Professionalismus und Nazismus: Die Wehrmacht des Dritten Reiches vor dem überfall auf der UdSSR." In *Zwei Wege nach Moscow: Vom Hitler-Stalin-Pakt bis zum "Unternehmen Barbarossa,"* ed. Bernd Wegner, pp. 149–66. Munich, 1991.

Lane, Barbara Miller. "Nazi Ideology: Some Unfinished Business." *Central European History* 7, no. 1 (1974).

Lewis, S.J. *Forgotten Legions: German Army Infantry Policy, 1914–1941.* New York, 1985.

Liddell Hart, B.H. *History of the Second World War.* New York, 1979.

Lucas, James, and J. Barker. *The Killing Ground.* London, 1978.

Lukas, Richard. *The Forgotten Holocaust: The Poles under German Occupation, 1939–1944.* Lexington, Ky., 1986.

Madej, Victor. "Effectiveness and Cohesion of the German Ground Forces in World War II." *Journal of Political and Military Sociology* 6 (Fall 1978): 233–48.

Marrus, Michael. "The Theory and Practice of Anti-Semitism." *Commentary*, Aug. 1982: 38–42.

Marshall, S.L.A. *Men against Fire.* Washington, D.C., 1947.

Mason, Timothy. *Social Policy in the Third Reich: The Working Class and the "National Community," 1918–1939.* Oxford, 1993.

————. *Sozialpolitik im Dritten Reich*. Opladen, 1977.

Merritt, Anna, and Richard Merritt. *Public Opinion in Occupied Germany: The OMGUS Surveys, 1945–1949*. Urbana, Ill., 1970.

Messerschmidt, Manfred. "German Military Law in the Second World War." In *The German Military in the Age of Total War*, ed. Wilhelm Deist, pp. 323-35. Leamington Spa, UK., 1985.

————. "Völkerrecht und 'Kriegsnotwendigkeit' in der deutschen militärischen Tradition seit den Einigungskriegen." *German Studies Review* 6, no. 2 (1983): 237–70.

————. "The Wehrmacht and the Volksgemeinschaft." *Journal of Contemporary History* 18 (1983): 719–44.

————. *Die Wehrmacht im NS-Staat: Zeit der Indoktrination*. Hamburg, 1969.

————. "Wehrmacht, Ostfeldzug und Tradition." In *Der Zweite Weltkrieg: Analyzen, Grundzüge, Forschungsbilanz*, ed. Wolfgang Michalka, pp. 314–28. Munich, 1989.

————. "Der 'Zersetzer' und sein Denunziant. In *Der Krieg des Kleinen Mannes: Eine Militärgeschichte von unten*, ed. Wolfram Wette, pp. 255–78. Munich, 1992.

Messerschmidt, Manfred, and Fritz Wüllner. *Die Wehrmachtjustiz im Dienste des Nationalsozialismus: Zerstörung einer Legende*. Baden-Baden, 1987.

Meyer-Detring, Wilhelm. *Die 137. Infanteriedivision im Mittelabschnitt der Ostfront*. Nördlingen, 1962.

Mosse, George E. *Fallen Soldiers: Reshaping the Memory of the World Wars*. New York, 1990.

Mühlberger, Detlef. *Hitler's Followers: Studies in the Sociology of the Nazi Movement*. London, 1991.

Müller, Klaus-Jürgen. *The Army, Politics, and Society in Germany, 1933–1945: Studies in the Army's Relation to Nazism*. Manchester, U.K., 1987.

Müller, Rolf-Dieter. "Die Konsequenzen der 'Volksgemeinschaft': Ernährung, Ausbeutung, und Vernichtung." In *Der Zweite Weltkrieg: Analysen, Grundzüge, Forschungsbilanz*, ed. Wolfgang Michalka, pp. 240–48. Munich, 1989.

Munzel, Oskar. *Gekämpft—Gesiegt—Verloren. Geschichte des Panzerregiments 6, 1740–1980*. Herford, 1980.

Murawski, Erich. *Der deutsche Wehrmachtbericht*. Boppard am Rhein, 1962.

O'Neill, Robert J. "Doctrine and Training in the German Army, 1919–1939." In *The Theory and Practice of War*, ed. Michael Howard, pp. 143–65. London, 1965.

————. *The German Army and the Nazi Party, 1933–1939*. New York, 1966.

Padover, Saul K. "A Folio of German Types." In *Propaganda in War and Crisis*, ed. Daniel Lerner, pp. 162–99. New York, 1972.

Perret, Geoffrey. *There's a War to Be Won: The United States Army in World War II*. New York, 1991.

Peukert, Detlev. "The Genesis of 'the Final Solution' from the Spirit of Science." In *Reevaluating the Third Reich*, ed. Thomas Childers and Jane Caplan, pp. 234–52. New York, 1993.

————. *Inside Nazi Germany: Conformity, Opposition, and Racism in Everyday Life*. Trans. Richard Deveson. New Haven, Conn., 1987.

Piekalkiewicz, Janusz. *Der Wüstenkrieg in Afrika, 1940–1943.* Munich, 1985.

Podzun, Hans-Henning. *Weg und Schicksal der 21. Infanterie-Division.* Bad Nauheim, 1951.

Prinz, Michael. *Vom neuen Mittelstand zum Volksgenossen: Die Entwicklung des sozialen Status der Angestellten von der Weimarer Republik bis zum Ende der NS-Zeit.* Munich, 1986.

Prinz, Michael, and Rainer Zitelmann, eds. *Nationalsozialismus und Modernisierung.* Darmstadt, 1990.

Quarrie, Bruce. *Panzer-Grenadier Division "Grossdeutschland".* London, 1977.

Reinhardt, Klaus. *Die Wende vor Moskau: Das Scheitern der Strategie Hitlers im Winter 1941/42.* Stuttgart, 1972.

Rempel, Gerhard. *Hitler's Children: The Hitler Youth and the SS.* Chapel Hill, N.C., 1989.

Rose, Arnold. "The Social Psychology of Desertion from Combat." *American Sociological Review* 16 (Oct. 1951): 614–29.

Schäfer, Hans Dieter. *Das gespaltene Bewußtsein: Über deutsche Kultur und Lebenswirklichkeit, 1933–1945.* Munich and Vienna, 1981.

Scheibert, Horst. *Nach Stalingrad—48 Kilometer! Der Entsatzvorstoß der 6. Panzerdivision Dezember 1942.* Heidelberg, 1956.

———. *Zwischen Don und Donez: Winter 1942/43.* Neckargemünd, 1961.

Schoenbaum, David. *Hitler's Social Revolution: Class and Status in Nazi Germany, 1933–1939.* New York, 1966.

Schulte, Theo. *The German Army and Nazi Policies in Occupied Russia.* Oxford, New York, and Munich, 1989.

Seaton, Albert. *The Battle for Moscow, 1941–1943.* New York, 1971.

———. *The Fall of Fortress Europe, 1943–1945.* London, 1981.

———. *The German Army, 1933–1945.* London, 1982.

———. *The Russo-German War, 1941–1945.* London, 1971.

Selz, Barbara. *Das Grüne Regiment: Der Weg der 256. Infanterie-Division aus der Sicht des Regiments 481.* Freiburg, 1970.

Shils, Edward, and Morris Janowitz. "Cohesion and Disintegration in the Wehrmacht." In *Propaganda in War and Crisis,* ed. Daniel Lerner. pp. 367–415. New York, 1972. Rpt. from *Public Opinion Quarterly* 12 (1948): 280–315.

Siedler, Franz. *Deutscher Volkssturm: Das letzte Aufgebot, 1944–1945.* Munich, 1989.

Smelser, Ronald. "How 'Modern' Were the Nazis? DAF Social Planning and the Modernization Question." *German Studies Review,* 13, no. 2 (1990): 285–302.

———. *Robert Ley: Hitler's Labor Front Leader.* New York, 1988.

Spaeter, H. and W. Ritter von Schramm. *Die Geschichte des Panzerkorps Grossdeutschland.* 3 vols. Bielefeld, 1958.

Steiger, Rudolf. *Armour Tactics in the Second World War: Panzer Army Campaigns in German War Diaries.* Oxford, 1991.

Steinert, Marlis. *Hitler's War and the Germans: Public Mood and Attitude during the Second World War.* Trans. Thomas E.J. deWitt. Athens, Ohio, 1977.

Stephenson, Jill. " 'Emancipation' and Its Problems: War and Society in Württemberg, 1939–1945." *European History Quarterly* 17 (1987): 345–65.

———. "Modernization, Emancipation, Mobilization: Nazi Society Reconsidered." In *Elections, Mass Politics, and Social Change in Modern Germany,* ed. Larry E. Jones and James Retallack. New York, 1992.

Stern, Fritz. "Germany 1933: Fifty Years Later." In *Dreams and Delusions: National Socialism in the Drama of the German Past,* ed. Fritz Stern, pp. 119–46. New York, 1987.

———. "National Socialism as Temptation." *Dreams and Delusions. National Socialism in the Drama of the German Past,* ed. Fritz Stern, pp. 147–91. New York, 1987.

Stouffer, Samuel, et al. *The American Soldier.* 2 vols. Princeton, N.J., 1949.

Stoves, Rolf. *1. Panzer-Division, 1935–1945: Chronik einer der drei Stamm-Divisionen der deutschen Panzerwaffe.* Bad Nauheim, 1961.

Streim, Alfred. *Die Behandlung sowjetischer Kriegsgefangenen im "Fall Barbarossa."* Heidelberg and Karlsruhe, 1981.

———. *Sowjetische Kriegsgefangene in Hitlers Vernichtungskrieg: Berichte und Dokumente, 1941–1945.* Heidelberg, 1982.

Streit, Christian. "Die Behandlung der sowjetischen Kriegsgefangenen und völkerrechtliche Probleme des Krieges gegen die Sowjetunion." In *"Unternehmen Barbarossa": Der deutsche überfall auf die Sowjetunion 1941,* ed. Gerd Ueberschär and Wolfram Wette, pp. 197–218. Paderborn, 1984.

———. "The German Army and the Politics of Genocide." In *The Policies of Genocide: Jews and Soviet Prisoners of War in Nazi Germany,* ed. Gerhard Hirschfeld, pp. 1–14. London, 1986.

———. *Keine Kameraden: Die Wehrmacht und die sowjetischen Kriegsgefangenen, 1941–1945.* Stuttgart, 1978.

———. "Sowjetische Kriegsgefangene—Massendeportation—Zwangsarbeiter." In *Der Zweite Weltkrieg: Analysen, Grundzüge, Forschungsbilanz,* ed. Wolfgang Michalka, pp. 747–60. Munich, 1989.

Struve, Walter. *Elites against Democracy: Leadership Ideals in Bourgeois Political Thought in Germany, 1890–1933.* Princeton, N.J., 1973.

Turner, Henry A. "Fascism and Modernization." In *Reappraisals of Fascism,* ed. Henry A. Turner, pp. 117–39. New York, 1975.

Ueberschär, Gerd R., and Wolfram Wette, eds. *"Unternehmen Barbarossa": Der deutsche überfall auf die Sowjetunion, 1941.* Paderborn, 1984.

U.S. Strategic Bombing Survey, Morale Division. "Social and Psychological Factors Affecting Morale." In *Propaganda in War and Crisis,* ed. Daniel Lerner, pp. 355–366. New York, 1972.

U.S. War Department. *Handbook on German Military Forces.* Intro. Stephen E. Ambrose. Baton Rouge, La., 1990.

van Creveld, Martin. *Fighting Power: German and U.S. Army Performance, 1939–1945.* Westport, Conn., 1982.

Van Doorn, Jacques. "Ideology and the Military." In *On Military Ideology,* ed. Morris Janowitz and Jacques Van Doorn, pp. xv-xxix. Rotterdam, 1971.

Watt, Donald Cameron. *How War Came: The Immediate Origins of the Second World War, 1938–1939.* New York, 1989.

Wegner, Bernd, ed. *Zwei Wege nach Moscow: Von Hitler-Stalin-Pakt bis zum "Unternehmen Barbarossa."* Munich, 1991.

Welcker, I., and F.F. Zelinka. *Qualifikation zum Offizier? Eine Inhaltsanalyse der Einstellungsvoraussetzungen für Offiziere vom Kaiserheer zur Bundeswehr.* Frankfurt, 1982.

Werthen, Wolfgang. *Geschichte der 16. Panzer-Division, 1939–1945.* Bad Nauheim, 1958.

Wette, Wolfram. "Difficult Persuasion. The Psychological Mobilization of the German Population for World War II." *UNESCO Yearbook on Peace and Conflict Studies,* 1985: 49–71.

Wette, Wolfram, and Gerd R. Ueberschär, eds. *Stalingrad: Mythos und Wirklichkeit einer Schlacht.* Frankfurt, 1992.

Zitelmann, Rainer. *Hitler: Selbstverständnis eines Revolutionärs.* Stuttgart, 1987.

Zydowitz, Kurt von. *Die Geschichte der 58. Infanterie-Division, 1939–1945.* Kiel, 1952.

INDEX